I0675267

ROTH FAMILY FOUNDATION

Imprint in Music

Michael P. Roth

and Sukey Garcetti

have endowed this

imprint to honor the

memory of their parents,

Julia and Harry Roth,

whose deep love of music

they wish to share

with others.

The publisher and the University of California Press Foundation gratefully acknowledge the generous support of the Roth Family Foundation Imprint in Music, established by a major gift from Sukey and Gil Garcetti and Michael P. Roth.

The Doctor Faustus *Dossier*

CALIFORNIA STUDIES IN 20TH-CENTURY MUSIC

Richard Taruskin, General Editor

The *Doctor Faustus* Dossier

Arnold Schoenberg, Thomas Mann,
and Their Contemporaries, 1930–1951

Edited by

E. RANDOL SCHOENBERG

With an Introduction by Adrian Daub

Translated by Adrian Feuchtwanger and
Barbara Zeisl Schoenberg

University of California Press

University of California Press, one of the most distinguished university presses in the United States, enriches lives around the world by advancing scholarship in the humanities, social sciences, and natural sciences. Its activities are supported by the UC Press Foundation and by philanthropic contributions from individuals and institutions. For more information, visit www.ucpress.edu.

University of California Press
Oakland, California

© 2018 by E. Randol Schoenberg

Library of Congress Cataloging-in-Publication Data

Names: Schoenberg, E. Randol, 1966– editor. | Daub, Adrian, writer of introduction. | Feuchtwanger, Adrian, translator. | Schoenberg, Barbara Zeisl, translator. | Container of (expression): Schoenberg, Arnold, 1874–1951. Correspondence. English (Doctor Faustus Dossier) Selections. | Container of (expression): Mann, Thomas, 1875–1955. Works. English (Doctor Faustus Dossier) Selections.
Title: The Doctor Faustus dossier : Arnold Schoenberg, Thomas Mann, and their contemporaries, 1930–1951 / edited by E. Randol Schoenberg ; with an introduction by Adrian Daub ; translated by Adrian Feuchtwanger and Barbara Zeisl Schoenberg.
Other titles: Apropos Doktor Faustus. English
Description: Oakland, California : University of California Press, [2018] | Series: California studies in 20th-century music ; 22 | Previously published in German as: Apropos Doktor Faustus. | Includes bibliographical references and index. |
Identifiers: LCCN 2017058335 (print) | LCCN 2017061106 (ebook) | ISBN 9780520969155 (ebook) | ISBN 9780520296824 (cloth : alk. paper) | ISBN 9780520296831 (pbk. : alk. paper)
Subjects: LCSH: Schoenberg, Arnold, 1874–1951—Correspondence. | Mann, Thomas, 1875–1955—Correspondence. | Mann, Thomas, 1875–1955—Diaries. | Mann, Thomas, 1875–1955. Doktor Faustus.
Classification: LCC ML410.S283 (ebook) | LCC ML410.S283 A4 2018 (print) | DDC 780.92—dc23
LC record available at https://lccn.loc.gov/2017058335

27 26 25 24 23 22 21 20 19 18
10 9 8 7 6 5 4 3 2 1

Contents

Foreword by E. Randol Schoenberg   xi

Acknowledgments   xvii

Introduction: California Haunting: Mann,
Schoenberg, Faustus   1
by Adrian Daub

SECTION I. LETTERS, DIARIES, ETC. (1930–1948)

Schoenberg to Mann, November 1, 1930	31
Mann to Schoenberg, November 4, 1930	33
Schoenberg to Mann, November 8, 1930	35
Mann to Schoenberg, November 26, 1930	37
Mann's Diary	38
Schoenberg to Mann, December 28, 1938	42
Mann to Schoenberg, January 9, 1939	44
Schoenberg to Mann, January 15, 1939	46
Mann's Diary	49
Mann to Schoenberg, July 30, 1943	61
Mann's Diary	62
Mann to Schoenberg, September 14, 1943	65
Mann to Schoenberg, September 14, 1943	66
Schoenberg to Mann, September 19, 1943	67
Mann's Diary	69
Mann to Agnes Meyer, September 28, 1944	77
Mann's Diary	78
Schoenberg to Mann, October 3, 1944	79

Schoenberg to Mann, October 11, 1944   80

Gottfried Bermann-Fischer to Schoenberg,
November 6, 1944   81

Mann's Diary   82

Schoenberg to Gottfried Bermann-Fischer,
January 16, 1945   83

Mann's Diary   84

Mann to Bruno Walter, March 1, 1945   85

Mann's Diary   87

Schoenberg to Mann, June 6, 1945   89

Mann's Diary   90

Mann to Theodor Wiesengrund-Adorno,
December 30, 1945   91

Schoenberg to Mann, April 24, 1946   95

Mann's Diary   96

SECTION II. LETTERS, DIARIES, ETC. (1948–1951)

Mann to Schoenberg, January 15, 1948   105

Mann to Michael Mann, January 31, 1948   107

Mann to Otto Basler, February 14, 1948   108

Mann's Diary   109

Schoenberg to Mann, February 1948   110

Hugo Triebsamen, 1948   111

Mann's Diary   113

Mann to Schoenberg, February 17, 1948   114

Mann's Diary   116

Mann to Schoenberg, February 24, 1948   118

Mann's Diary   119

Schoenberg to Mann, February 25, 1948   120

Mann's Diary   122

Aline Valangin in *Unsere Meinung*, March 1948   123

Mann to Rudolf Jakob Humm, May 19, 1948   124

Aline Valangin in *Die Auslese*, April 1948   125

Mann's Diary   131

Schoenberg to Josef Rufer, September 30, 1948   132

Schoenberg to Gottfried Bermann-Fischer,
October 7, 1948   133

Mann's Diary   134

Mann to Schoenberg, October 13, 1948 — 135

Gottfried Bermann-Fischer to Schoenberg,
October 14, 1948 — 137

Schoenberg to Mann, October 15, 1948 — 138

Mann's Diary — 140

Gertrud Schoenberg to Alma Mahler-Werfel,
October 19, 1948 — 141

Schoenberg to Josef Rufer et al., October 20, 1948 — 143

Mann to Erika Mann, November 6, 1948 — 145

Gertrud Schoenberg to Alma Mahler-Werfel,
November 10, 1948 — 146

Schoenberg to the *Saturday Review of Literature*,
November 13, 1948 — 147

Mann's Diary — 150

Mann to the *Saturday Review of Literature*,
December 10, 1948 — 151

Mann to Theodor Wiesengrund-Adorno,
December 11, 1948 — 154

Mann's Diary — 155

Theodor Wiesengrund-Adorno to Eduard
Steuermann, December 22, 1948 — 156

Mann's Diary — 158

Schoenberg's Note, January 6, 1949 — 159

Mann's Diary — 161

Manfred Bukofzer to Mann, January 20, 1949 — 163

Mann to Manfred Bukofzer, January 25, 1949 — 167

Schoenberg to Josef Rufer, February 8, 1949 — 169

Mann's Diary — 170

Willi Schuh in *Neue Zürcher Zeitung*,
February 12, 1949 — 172

Mann's Diary — 178

Der Monat, March 1949 — 179

H.H. Stuckenschmidt's Biography of
Arnold Schoenberg — 181

Schoenberg Undated Notes — 182

    Leverkühn's Twelve-Tone Goulash — 182

    Schoenberg's Fragment on Mann's "Author's
    Note" from the Year 1949 — 182

    Schoenberg's Note (unpublished) — 183

Mann's Diary 184

Schoenberg in *Music Survey* (Fall 1949) 186

Schoenberg to H. H. Stuckenschmidt,
December 5, 1949 192

Schoenberg to Josef Rufer, December 5, 1949 194

Schoenberg to Kurt List, December 10, 1949 196

Mann's Diary 198

Mann to Schoenberg, December 19, 1949 199

Schoenberg to Mann (undated and not sent) 201

Mann's Diary 202

Schoenberg to Mann, January 2 and 9, 1950 203

Mann to Theodor Wiesengrund-Adorno,
January 9, 1950 204

Mann to Schoenberg, January 12, 1950 205

Mann's Diary 206

Schoenberg on Wiesengrund, 1950 207

Mann to Schoenberg, April 17, 1951 212

Schoenberg to Mann, April 20, 1951 213

Mann's Diary 214

Mann to H. H. Stuckenschmidt, October 19, 1951 215

SECTION III. ADDITIONAL READING

The Story of *The Story of a Novel* 219
Richard Hoffmann

"Schoenberg Will End Our Friendship":
Concerning the *Doctor Faustus* Controversy
between Arnold Schoenberg and Thomas Mann 228
Bernhold Schmid

SECTION IV. APPENDICES

Appendix I. Arnold Schoenberg, "A Four-Point
Program for Jewry" (October 1938) 251

Appendix II. Thomas Mann Radio Address,
"Listen, Germans!" (1942) 268

Appendix III. Thomas Mann, "The Fall of
the European Jews" (1943) 271

Appendix IV. Arnold Schoenberg, "Composition
with Twelve Tones" (1941)   275

Appendix V. Theodor W. Adorno, from *Philosophy
of New Music* (1949)   306

Appendix VI. Thomas Mann, Chapter 22 of
Doctor Faustus (1947)   319

Selected Bibliography   329

Works   335

Index   337

Foreword

Sunset Boulevard curves its way from downtown Los Angeles twenty-two miles westward along the southern side of the hills of Hollywood, Bel Air, Beverly Hills, Brentwood, and Pacific Palisades, where, facing the red, late-afternoon sun, it empties into the Pacific Ocean. During World War II, the leading figures of the European emigré community found refuge in the sunny hills above Sunset Boulevard, and it was along the westernmost portions of that renowned thoroughfare that Arnold Schoenberg and Thomas Mann lived as neighbors for nearly ten years.

When Thomas Mann first moved to Los Angeles in the summer of 1940, he lived a few blocks up the street from Arnold Schoenberg in Brentwood, which was then a distant and unpopulated suburb some forty-five minutes by car from downtown Los Angeles. Later, Mann built a home less than one mile to the west, on the other side of Mandeville Canyon, in Pacific Palisades. In their immediate vicinity lived the writers Lion Feuchtwanger, Bertolt Brecht, Aldous Huxley, Heinrich Mann, and Salka Viertel; the composers Hanns Eisler and Ernst Toch; the cellist Gregor Piatigorsky; and Mann's consultant on modern musical matters, the philosopher and one-time music composition pupil of Alban Berg, Theodor Wiesengrund-Adorno. A little farther away lived the conductors Otto Klemperer and Bruno Walter; the musicians Arthur Rubinstein, Vladimir Horowitz, and Jascha Heifetz; the composers Igor Stravinsky, Mario Castelnuovo-Tedesco, Erich Korngold, and Eric Zeisl; the director Max Reinhardt; and the writer Franz Werfel and his wife, and intermediary in the Mann-Schoenberg dispute, Alma Mahler-Werfel.

Although they were close neighbors geographically, Arnold Schoenberg and Thomas Mann were not close friends. They met only occasionally, mostly at the salons of Alma Mahler-Werfel and Salka Viertel, who each had close ties to literary and musical circles. Alma Mahler-Werfel, the widow of Gustav Mahler and (after his death in 1945) Franz Werfel, and ex-wife of the Bauhaus architect Walter Gropius, was Schoenberg's oldest and perhaps closest friend in Los Angeles. Salka Viertel, wife of the author Berthold Viertel, was a successful screenwriter and close friend and confidante of Greta Garbo. Her brother, Eduard Steuermann, was a renowned pianist and former pupil of Schoenberg. Accomplished intellectuals in their own right, Alma and Salka also provided the social glue that made the exiles into a community and relieved the isolation from which all the uprooted artists and intellectuals suffered so greatly. The Manns and Schoenbergs also played host at social gatherings. Mann visited Schoenberg at his home several times, and his diary mentions Gertrud Schoenberg's excellent coffee. But outside their brief social contacts, Mann and Schoenberg had very little to do with one another.

Thomas Mann, the second of two literary brothers from a well-off Hanseatic family from Lübeck, won the Nobel Prize for Literature in 1929 in recognition of the success of his many short stories and novels, including *Buddenbrooks* and *Magic Mountain*. Arnold Schoenberg, by contrast, came from a poor Viennese-Jewish family, but by 1926 he had attained what his biographer H. H. Stuckenschmidt called "the highest grade in the hierarchy of music teaching" with his appointment to teach the master class in composition at the Prussian Academy of the Arts in Berlin. In December of 1928 the Berlin Philharmonic premiered his Variations for Orchestra, op. 31, under the direction of Wilhelm Furtwängler. By 1930, Schoenberg and Mann were indisputably the leading exponents of German culture. Their initial correspondence, an exchange concerning the architect Adolf Loos, is what one might expect from two such cultural luminaries.

The fall of the Weimar Republic altered this situation dramatically. Thomas Mann's books were burned, and Arnold Schoenberg's music was banned. On February 11, 1933, Mann left Germany. On March 17, 1933, he resigned from the Prussian Academy of the Arts. After the confiscation of his home and the issuance of a warrant for his arrest if he were to return to Germany, Mann moved to Switzerland in September 1933. In 1938 he came to the United States, where he remained until 1952. Similarly, Schoenberg resigned from the Prussian Academy of Arts on March 20, 1933. He was forced to abandon his teaching position and fled from Berlin to Paris on May 16–17, 1933. Five months later, he found refuge in the United States, where he remained until his death in 1951.

During his flight into exile, Arnold Schoenberg wrote numerous essays on the perilous situation of the Jews in Europe, which in 1938 he compiled into one large article entitled "A Four-Point Program for Jewry." Unable to find a publisher, Schoenberg turned to Thomas Mann, then living in Princeton, New Jersey, for help and advice. "A Four-Point Program for Jewry" begins with the premise—at that time not widely accepted—that all the Jews in Europe were in grave and immediate danger. "Is there room in the world for almost 7,000,000 people?" Schoenberg asks. "Are they condemned to doom? Will they become extinct? Famished? Butchered?" Schoenberg argues that the most important task facing the leaders of the Jewish people must be not the futile effort of opposing anti-Semitism but rather the creation of a united Jewish party with the sole aim of erecting a Jewish state using whatever means necessary. Mann's reply was not what Schoenberg had hoped for. Although already in 1937 he had spoken of the problem of anti-Semitism, Mann objected to Schoenberg's tactics, labeling them fascist and terroristic, while at the same time admitting the importance of Schoenberg's message. Unlike Schoenberg, Mann could not imagine what lay ahead, but he had the ear of President Roosevelt, and later, during the war, he broadcast speeches on Free German Radio from the BBC. Schoenberg understood that in the face of Nazi aggression only extraordinary measures would save the lives of Europe's Jews, but he was unable to publish the article, and his warnings went unheeded.

The controversy that ensued several years later between Arnold Schoenberg and Thomas Mann over the novel *Doctor Faustus* was based not so much on any superficial similarity between Mann's antihero, Adrian Leverkühn, and Arnold Schoenberg (for example, their names, first and last, have the same number of letters, using the original German spelling of *Schönberg*) but rather on the manner in which Mann misunderstood and mishandled Schoenberg's artistic and intellectual creation. The twelve-tone method described in chapter 22 of the novel was not solely a device or system, as Mann referred to it in his author's note; rather, it was a method that encompassed Schoenberg's entire musical and moral philosophy. Its sources can be found in Schoenberg's *Theory of Harmony* of 1911, from which Mann freely appropriated ideas for the early chapters of his novel, as well as in the text of *Jacob's Ladder*, which Mann had denigrated as fermented religious poetry in his *The Story of a Novel*. The opening lines of *Jacob's Ladder*—

> Whether right or left, forwards or backwards, upward or downward—
> one has to go on, without asking what lies ahead or behind

—represent Schoenberg's theosophical motto. It is no accident that these lines also describe the elemental focus of the twelve-tone method, with its use of retrogrades and inversions, and its emphasis on the relativistic relationship of every note to the fundamental row or series.

Arnold Schoenberg believed that the twelve-tone method gave his music a divine unity that corresponded to the religious subject matter of his late works *(Moses and Aron, A Survivor from Warsaw, Israel Exists Again,* and the *Modern Psalms).* It is no wonder that Schoenberg was deeply offended by the attribution of his fundamental creation to a syphilitic madman's unholy pact with the devil. Thomas Mann's incredible claim that the character of Leverkühn had "no point of contact" with Schoenberg only deepened the rift by implying that the creator of the twelve-tone method was separable from his creation. For Schoenberg, the twelve-tone method was not a discovery, like a scientific equation or a chemical formula that could have been found by anyone. It was, as with all his works, the unique expression of his own inimitable personality.

Mann's public defense during the dispute was very effective. He outwardly pretended that he could not understand why Schoenberg was upset, and most of his acolytes, then and now, have accepted his claims of innocence at face value. Privately, however, Mann's diaries and letters reveal a somewhat different story. Even before the publication of the novel, he had confided to his friend Agnes Meyer that he feared Schoenberg would end their friendship. When Schoenberg made a veiled threat of a lawsuit, Mann imagined himself ruined. The unguarded and private Mann recognized he had done something wrong.

Schoenberg, for his part, sometimes comes off as a person who imagined an insult, and in a sense this is true. Unable because of his failing eyesight to read the novel, he had to rely on reviews and excerpts read to him and from gossip from his friends. A book is published by his eminent neighbor and fellow emigré, with whom he has been on friendly terms, and it turns out that he is the last to learn that his most personal creation figures prominently—and not in the most positive light. Everyone else seems to have been in on the big secret. He senses that something is very wrong but cannot put his finger on it, so he lashes out, often at unintended slights. Had he been able to read the entire novel, he might have discovered an even greater affront, which goes almost unmentioned during the controversy. In the contemporary setting of the novel, the fictional characters discuss most of the leading musicians, artists, and intellectuals of the day, including Mann himself, but Schoenberg is absent. Mann had invented a world without Schoenberg at precisely the moment in history when the hell-bound armies of the Third Reich had set out to accomplish the same thing.

In a copy of *Doctor Faustus* given to one of his other Los Angeles neighbors, the composer Ernst Toch, Mann inscribed the following dedication: "Ernst Toch, who doesn't need the devil, neighborly dedicated." In comparison, the dedication to Arnold Schoenberg, "the real one," seems not quite so neighborly. This unprecedented collection of letters and writings provides a new perspective on the conflict that erupted between Thomas Mann and Arnold Schoenberg, when fate and forced exile brought them so close together on the shores of the Pacific Ocean.

The book is organized to help the reader access the available sources for the Schoenberg-Mann controversy. It begins with an essay by Adrian Daub, which provides the necessary context for the two protagonists (Schoenberg and Mann), as well as the leading supporting figure (Adorno). In the main body of the book, the letters, diaries, and other materials are broken up into two chronological sections, before and after Mann's delivery of a copy of *Doctor Faustus* to Schoenberg in January of 1948. These sections also include letters and articles written by and to several related figures connected with the main characters, such as the two letters from Gertrud Schoenberg to Alma Mahler-Werfel. The extensive footnotes are intended to provide further background materials to round out the story without slowing it down or introducing threads too soon. Be sure to read the ones concerning the history behind Adorno's role in the controversy (notes 78–80 in sec. 1; note 91 in sec. 2). After the letters and diaries, the reader will find a firsthand account by Schoenberg's assistant Richard Hoffmann and an analytical essay by Bernhold Schmid, as well as an appendix of original essays and writings by Schoenberg, Mann, and Adorno that are referenced in the letters and diaries. The volume should provide the reader with the ability to understand this famous episode in our cultural history, when these luminaries of twentieth-century music, literature, and philosophy collided in the sunny hills of West Los Angeles.

E. Randol Schoenberg
Los Angeles, 2017

Acknowledgments

Although this is the first English-language publication of the complete Thomas Mann–Arnold Schoenberg correspondence, there are many predecessors to acknowledge. A great portion of this book consists of items that have been published elsewhere but are collected and assembled here together for the first time to give the reader a complete overview of the source materials related to the famous dispute between Mann and Schoenberg regarding Mann's novel *Doctor Faustus*.

Many of the letters, both originals from Mann and carbon copies of Schoenberg's letters, from the Schoenberg correspondence archives at the Library of Congress, Washington, DC (Music Division), were first transcribed by Ivan Voytech, who did not publish them. In 1991 I obtained copies of the letters and drafts in the Mann archive from Prof. Hans Wysling, director of the Thomas Mann Archive of the Swiss Federal Institute of Technology in Zurich, Switzerland. In 1993 the resulting complete set of letters with my foreword and a previously published essay by Dr. Berthold Schmid were published in an Italian translation by Rosalino Archinto in Milan. That book was later published in French, with a revised version of Schmid's article, by La Bibliothèque des Arts in Lausanne, Switzerland, in 2002. A proposed 2006 publication of the letters in the *Thomas Mann Jahrbuch* by Christine Albert was put aside in favor of the present, more comprehensive, volume, which was first published entirely in German by Czernin Verlag in Vienna in 2009.

Besides the letters themselves, we have included in this book extensive quotations from Thomas Mann's diaries, from the compilations edited by Peter de Mendelssohn and Inge Jens. Many of the footnotes, especially those identifying persons mentioned in Mann's diaries, are taken directly from the work of those editors. Equally important have been the various editions of letters, especially *Theodor W. Adorno–Thomas Mann Briefwechsel, 1943–1955* (2002), edited by Dr. Christoph Gödde and Dr. Thomas Sprecher.

Many very fine essays have been written about the Mann-Schoenberg controversy, and we have profited from all of them. The selected bibliography at the end of the book will give some idea of the number of scholars who have approached the subject. Adrian Daub provides a new scholarly contribution with his introductory essay contrasting the lives and artistic approaches of the three principals: Mann, Schoenberg, and Adorno. Schmid's essay, translated here into English, provides a comprehensive review of the correspondence, also with a focus on Adorno's role. Finally, we decided that Prof. Richard Hoffmann's eyewitness account must be included, as much for its value as source material as for the insights he provides.

We could have included many other essays, including very fine analyses by Prof. Erhard Bahr in his book *Weimar on the Pacific* (2007) and Prof. James Schmidt in *The Cambridge Companion to Adorno* (2004). Prof. Bahr was kind enough to review the manuscript of the German edition of this book and provide helpful comments and corrections.

We have also included essays and writings by Mann and Schoenberg to provide context for the letters and diary entries. These include Schoenberg's prescient "A Four-Point Program for Jewry," which was sent to Mann at the end of 1938. By way of comparison we have included a few of Mann's speeches and essays on the same subject.

Although we presume that the reader will have read, or will go on to read, Mann's novel, we have included chapter 22 of *Doctor Faustus*, where the twelve-tone method is described in detail. By way of comparison, we also provide the text of Schoenberg's essay "Composition with Twelve Tones," published in 1950 after a lecture given at the University of California, Los Angeles, in 1941.

Many people have assisted in creating this book. My aunt Nuria Schoenberg-Nono supported this project from the beginning, and she included some of the Mann-Schoenberg correspondence in her book *Arnold Schoenberg, 1874–1951: Lebensgeschichte in Begegnungen* (1992). From the Thomas Mann Archiv in Zurich, under the direction of Dr. Thomas Sprecher, we have received many useful items that appear in this volume, especially from the librarian Rolf Bolt. Similarly, from the Arnold Schönberg Center in Vienna, under the direction of Dr. Christian Meyer and Angelika Möser, we have received extensive assistance from the archivists Dr. Therese Muxeneder and Eike Fess, who also compiled the bibliography. Eike Rathgeber and Anna Maria Morazzoni assisted with Schoenberg's essays. My assistant Aditya Rao helped with scanning and transcribing and tracking down missing items. D. Michael Puccinelli attended to the painstaking work of putting together the various pieces that made up the English translation and assisted with permissions and many other tasks, without which this book could not have been completed.

Myron Kolatch, executive editor of the *New Leader,* provided archival copies of hard-to-find articles that were used by Mann in preparing an important speech on the extermination of the Jews. For the essay of Aline Valangin we thank Francine Rosenbaum, Simon Cornaro, and Peter Kamber. For the essay by Willi Schuh we thank Eleonore Briner.

Permissions for use of Mann family materials, as well as other comments and advice, has been generously provided by Dagmar Schreiber and Roland Spahr of S. Fischer Verlag, and their United States representative, Markus Hoffmann, of Regal Hoffmann and Associates. Allison Jakobovic of Penguin Random House granted permission to use excerpts from the English version of *Doctor Faustus* translated by H.T. Lowe-Porter. Gisela Fischer-Braun kindly permitted publication of her father's letters.

With regard to Theodor Wiesengrund-Adorno, I have been assisted by Dr. Christoph Goedde of the Adorno Archive at the Institute for Social Research, Frankfurt am Main, as well as his colleague Michael Schwarz at the Walter Benjamin Archive at the Academy of Arts, who provided permission to publish several previously unpublished letters. Jeff Moen of the University of Minnesota Press granted permission to use excerpts from Adorno's *Philosophy of New Music,* translated by Robert Hullot-Kentor. Research for letters from Wiesengrund-Adorno in the Rudolf Kolisch collection at the Houghton Library at Harvard University was conducted for me by David Trippett, a student of Prof. Anne Shreffler. Permission to publish portions of Wiesengrund-Adorno's published writings came from Dr. Petra Christina Hardt at Suhrkamp Verlag.

Tamara Hovey Gold and David Lebrun provided permission to make stills of the film footage taken by Tamara and her brother, Serge Hovey, of Mann and Schoenberg in Malibu, California. The original film is located in the Sonya Levien collection at the Huntington Library in San Marino, California. We are grateful to Gayle Richardson of the Huntington Library for assisting in obtaining stills from the film. The digital transfer was done by IVC Digital Film, with special thanks to Dick Millais and Joe Van Essen.

For the German edition, the lion's share of translating from English into German many of the letters, texts, and my footnotes was undertaken by my colleague Susanne Müller, who served as a second editor for the project.

For the English edition, many original translations were created by Adrian Feuchtwanger and my mother, Barbara Zeisl Schoenberg. For texts that have been previously published in English, we relied primarily on those prior translations. Under my direction we have undertaken to make the book readable by silently correcting many obvious typographical errors, standardizing the format (for example, changing underlinings to italics), and expanding abbreviations—all the while presenting the content as faithfully as possible. There are many difficulties in such an undertaking—for example, where the authors completed two somewhat different versions of the same text (one in German and one in English) and we were required to combine the two. We hope that we have achieved our goal. This book does not pretend to be a scholarly edition or dissertation. Anyone wishing to check the originals can find them at the Library of Congress or the Thomas Mann Archiv, or even online from the Arnold Schönberg Center at www.schoenberg.at. We have tried to include citations of the numerous books and articles used by us to compile this volume so that interested readers can refer to them and obtain more information. As with any project of this magnitude, we anticipate that there will be errors and omissions, for which we are responsible but for which we hope to be forgiven.

As always, I have tried to keep my grandfather's example in mind as I worked to complete this project. With regard to translations, I am instructed by what he wrote to Lee Glasser of the Philosophical Library on July 25, 1944, concerning the translation of his essays for the book *Style and Idea:* "I think I must leave the responsibility for the translation to the publisher. I follow in this regard the suggestion of Thomas Mann who told me that he feels it is out of his power to check the translations of his works, and he leaves it to the translator. I am ready to ask a few friends of mine—if you wish it—to read the manuscript, and I will answer problematic cases as well as I can. But I think the book would never be finished if I insist upon controlling everything."

Arnold Schoenberg from home movies of Tamara and Serge Hovey (1938).

Thomas Mann from home movies of Tamara and Serge Hovey (1938).

Introduction

California Haunting: Mann, Schoenberg, Faustus

Adrian Daub

Thomas Mann arrives in Los Angeles in 1940, eventually settling at 1550 San Remo Drive. By May of 1943 he begins to outline *Doctor Faustus,* writing to Bruno Walter about a novel "about pathological-illegitimate inspiration" and asking how to research composition training and music history. By May 8 his main character has the name "Leverkühn" and by May 17 the first name "Adrian." Mann begins writing his first chapter on May 23, 1943, the same date as the novel's narrator, Serenus Zeitblohm, begins to tell Leverkühn's story.

Mann meets Theodor Wiesengrund Adorno in July 1943 at a dinner party hosted by Adorno's erstwhile colleague at the Frankfurt Institute for Social Research, Max Horkheimer. By October he has asked Adorno to supply him with "musical intimacy and characteristic detail"[1] for the *Faustus* project; over the next few years, Adorno writes fictional critical texts, descriptions of Mann's protagonist's fictional music, and descriptions of composition technique for Mann. Mann finishes the book on January 29, 1947, and celebrates final edits in February 1947, "with a champagne dinner to celebrate the completion of *Faustus,* and a reading of the Echo-chapter" to a "visibly seized" audience.[2]

The German edition appears with Fischer Verlag in 1947. In January of 1948 Mann sends a copy to Schoenberg with the inscription: "For Arnold Schoenberg, the *real one* [dem *Eigentlichen*], with best wishes" (see image on page 105 of this volume). Schoenberg never reads the entire novel because of his failing eyesight.[3] Nevertheless, in February he responds with a literary parody imagining a third-millennium historian, "Hugo Triebsamen," writing about a now-forgotten musician named Arnold Schoenberg and his "battle with the well-known German writer Thomas Mann, who was clearly the inventor of the method of composing with twelve tones." Mann replies immediately that his portrait constituted "no diminution of your place in history." Mann agrees to append a note acknowledging Schoenberg's role and his fictionalization of it to the US translation by Helen Lowe-Porter.

By March of 1948 the controversy spills out into the press—somewhat ironically precisely because of Mann's note and his personal dedication. Schoenberg and his camp think the note insufficient and the dedication's reference to "the real one" an indicator that Schoenberg is the model for the novel's syphilitic stand-in for Nazi Germany, which Schoenberg considers "an insult," one for which he "might have to draw consequences." Aline Valangin publishes an attack on *Faustus* in the Swiss periodical *Unsere Meinung*. And in a November 1948 letter to the *Saturday Review of Literature*, Schoenberg reaffirms his sense that "in his novel *Dr. Faustus*, Thomas Mann has taken advantage of my literary property," and he fingers Adorno as "the informer" who has helped in Mann's theft. At this point Mann has already completed *The Story of a Novel*, his own account of the writing of *Doctor Faustus*. This document, an attempt to set the record straight in a number of respects, becomes the subject of a tug-of-war between Adorno, who would like his contributions recognized, and Katia and Erika Mann, who can't stand Adorno and wants the same contributions minimized.

This introductory essay is not intended to provide a definitive version of events nor to offer a conclusive interpretation of them. There are already many impressive attempts to do that.[4] The essay intends instead to guide readers through the thicket of acquaintances, old grudges and new anxieties, problems of politics and aesthetics that resonate—sometimes faintly, sometimes clearly—between the lines in the essays and exchanges gathered here. These are, after all, one reason scholars, students, and lay readers have returned to the *Faustus* controversy time and time again. The other is that rarely has a literary controversy spoken so directly to a unique place and time: *Faustus* could not have been written, and *Faustus* could not have generated the controversy that it did, outside of the highly peculiar setting of Southern California during the Second World War.

The *Faustus* affair pitted a writer whose dominant stature in German letters had translated smoothly into his new American environs against a composer who feared he had lost his relevance in the transition. The controversy surrounded a book that created a fictional portrait of a composer corrupted by fascism, at a time when the Nazis were parading vicious caricatures of "degenerate" composers before German audiences. Caught in the middle stood then-unknown Theodor Adorno, captivated by both men but with a desire to please, to make a name for himself, and to have the great writer channel his ideas, which only added fuel to the fire. Southern California may be the invisible fourth party in their dispute. That world, the positions Mann, Schoenberg, and Adorno occupied in it, and the different paths that took them there, will be my topic in what follows.

THREE ROADS INTO EXILE

The main story laid out by the letters, diary entries, lectures, and articles collected in this volume begins in 1933. On January 30 of that year Adolf Hitler became Reich Chancellor. After the burning of the Reichstag on February 27, the "Enabling Laws" of March 1933 dissolved parliament and gave Hitler dictatorial powers. The reprisals against unions and left-wing organizations, as well as the boycotts of Jewish businesses, commenced almost immediately. Even before the "Law for the Restoration of the Professional Civil Service" and other laws enabled, and later mandated, the firing of Jewish employees, many cultural institutions, working, as Ian Kershaw put it, "towards the *Führer*,"[5] purged their "non-Aryan" members.

By the summer, many of Germany's Jews and anti-Nazi intellectuals who could afford it were considering emigration. Almost five hundred thousand German citizens would take the opportunity while it lasted. Many of them were writers, artists, critics, and intellectuals, and among them were Thomas Mann (1875–1955), Arnold Schoenberg (1874–1951), and Theodor Wiesengrund Adorno (1903–69). Hitler's rise to power caught each of these three men at different stages of their lives and careers, and each reacted differently to it. And even though their biographies would coincide in broad outlines over the next decade and a half—opposition to Nazism, flight from Germany, exile in Los Angeles—their first few months under Hitler's "Third Reich" suggest just how differently they responded to similar circumstances.

Schoenberg, after a few months' hesitation, left his post at the Prussian Academy in May 1933, in what was initially supposed to be a leave of absence. The letter in which the new president of the Academy, Max von Schillings, granted that leave left little doubt that Schoenberg would soon be fired.[6] Schoenberg left first for Paris, later for Arcachon in southwestern France, but by the summer he had taken decisive steps toward a new life. He formally returned to his Jewish faith in July; he decided to help found a United Jewish Party; and in September he declared his intention to emigrate to the United States. Compared to Adorno, his break with Germany was thorough and complete. Schoenberg arrived in New York in October of 1933 but soon found himself deeply disappointed by opportunities there. In

September of 1934 he moved his family to Pasadena, then to Hollywood. In 1936 he would settle in Brentwood Park. Before long, the two other protagonists of the *Faustus* affair would settle nearby.

Thomas Mann was at the height of his fame when the Nazis came to power. He had received the Nobel Prize for Literature in 1929; he lived in patrician splendor in Munich; and, after abandoning long-held conservative views, had become an outspoken defender of the moribund Weimar Republic. As such, he was caught almost immediately in the new regime's crosshairs, and his children, above all Erika and Klaus Mann, made sure he never made any overture to Germany's new government. He had declared the Nazis a "massive wave of eccentric barbarism" as early as 1930. When Hitler became chancellor, Mann gave one last scheduled lecture (on Richard Wagner, appropriately enough) and then left Germany for a lecture tour. He would not return until 1949.

After settling in Switzerland, Mann traveled to the United States for lecture tours in 1934 and 1935. The National Socialists had stripped him of his German citizenship, but so great was the interest in his person in the United States that he was allowed in even without a passport—during a period in which many "stateless" persons were desperately trying to make it to America. In 1938 he relocated permanently, settling in Princeton, New Jersey. Lecture tours, honorary doctorates, and radio and newspaper interviews kept him busy, and his novels sold well. Once war broke out, Mann lent his voice to the BBC program *Deutsche Hörer!* From his Pacific Palisades home he recorded appeals, eventually broadcast from London, to the German civilian population. When Mann arrived in Southern California in 1941, he was at the zenith of his influence.

When Theodor Wiesengrund Adorno arrived, it was for him the latest in a series of setbacks that had—for a time, at least—cut short a promising academic career. Adorno was twenty-nine years old when the Nazis came to power. Both a musical and intellectual prodigy, he had completed his dissertation at twenty-one years of age, then moved to Vienna to study composition with Alban Berg. Although he became a constant companion to Berg, even during this musical apprenticeship his main interest was clearly aesthetics. In 1927 he made a first attempt to receive the *venia legendi* (license to teach), but his "habilitation" was rejected. He eventually received his license in early 1931 with a book on Kierkegaard[7] and seemed on the cusp of a burgeoning scholarly career. Then came Hitler.

Adorno's book on Kierkegaard appeared in print one day before the Enabling Laws granted Hitler dictatorial powers. He was denied teaching privileges that spring, and his license to teach was officially revoked on his thirtieth birthday, September 11, 1933. During this period Adorno tried desperately to find a way to survive in German academia (applying to the Reich Chamber of Literature, which unsurprisingly was unreceptive) and, most notably, changing his last name from Wiesengrund to his mother's name, Adorno. Hannah Arendt, no fan of Adorno's ("no way he's coming into my home"[8]), was sure that he had changed his name as a "vain attempt to get out of [Nazi persecution] with the name of his mother who was of Italian origin."[9] Schoenberg never went quite so far, but the fact that he kept calling Adorno "Wiesengrund" throughout the altercation seems less than accidental.[10]

His biographers all insist that this "shaving off" (as the poet Christian Morgenstern caustically referred to it) of "Wiesengrund" was being misinterpreted. But Adorno, younger and unknown, certainly had fewer international prospects than either Schoenberg or Mann: leaving the German-speaking world meant starting over. Adorno was able to secure a position at Merton College Oxford, where he attempted to undertake research for a PhD—surely a bitter pill to swallow for a man who had been a university professor before he was thirty. In 1938 Adorno and his wife, Gretel, moved to New York, where his friend and former colleague Max Horkheimer had refounded the Frankfurt Institute for Social Research under the auspices of Columbia University. When Horkheimer moved to Pacific Palisades in 1940, the Adornos, who were largely dependent on Horkheimer's money, quickly followed, settling at 316 Kenter Avenue in Brentwood.[11]

Adorno came to California still a young man denied the recognition he believed he deserved. Thomas Mann arrived as a literary elder statesman, displaced and melancholy but convinced of his role and his mission. As the critic Ludwig Marcuse put it, Mann was the "emperor among the German émigrés."[12] Schoenberg was a little bit of both—convinced of his importance and anxious at the relative lack of recognition afforded him in his new home. He complained at length about his reception, but he was also pleased by what recognition he did receive. Recent studies by Sabine Feisst and Kenneth H. Marcus suggest that the image of a profoundly alienated Schoenberg misses the mark.[13] Nevertheless, he settled into his new environs only with a certain unease, and his sensitivity to slights and neglect increased. *Faustus* would trigger both.

The *Faustus* affair brought together three men whose very different experience of the same events brought them into perhaps inevitable conflict. All three men were wrapped up in deeply incongruous self-conceptions, and each nevertheless insisted on arrogating expertise in each other's fields. Mann was quite comfortable weighing in on music, a field where his taste was out of step with his time; Adorno insisted on feeding Mann a philosophical vocabulary that Mann spilled half-digested onto the page; and Schoenberg didn't seem interested in parsing out the ways in which the terminology with which Adorno operated in embedding Schoenberg's compositions into a story of modernity would differ from the terminology he used when teaching his students.

Yet the individual misunderstandings and grievances that gave rise to l'affaire Faustus nevertheless shed light on broader political and aesthetic questions: for one thing, the category of modernism circulates uneasily among the three men, without ever being invoked directly. Mann's stature in the United States rested to some extent on the fact that his more modest, gentler modernism was palatable to larger swaths of the public than were Schoenberg's twelve-tone compositions. His portrait of the composer Adrian Leverkühn—who pushes his art by means of a devil's pact toward ever more rarefied, but ever less hospitable, aesthetic spheres—constitutes to some extent late romanticism's judgment of the aesthetic of modernism. Adorno's whisperings, by contrast, were at times critical of Schoenberg but came from a place that was thoroughly and emphatically modernist, advocating what he would later call a music that was not just "distressed" but also "distressing."[14]

Doctor Faustus is a novel about a kind of modernism characterized by formal innovation and experimental rigor, one that the novel itself pointedly avoids.[15] Mann's modernism turns on the way categories like self, authenticity, and expression become subtly problematic in his novels without ever being abandoned. His desire to look as though he was saying something about music, and his concomitant desire to actually say something about music, was what made him turn to Adorno and what roused Schoenberg's ire. This led to the paradoxical situation that, once Schoenberg objected to Mann's ways of absorbing it all into his massive novel, Mann withdrew into a skin-deep defense of a "montage technique"—the ultimately conventional storyteller pleading modernism to the inventor of twelve-tone composition.

Mann viewed form in a way that spoke to Adorno's own aesthetic position: distended by the pressure of subjective expression yet left standing, a way of doing inevitable, necessary, and yet deeply troubling violence to the material. Schoenberg tended to view expression through form fairly unproblematically—which is why the violence that Doctor Faustus imputes to the twelve-tone method must have rankled him and his students. Above it all hovered the question of fascism: the notion that the violence with which form wrestled content into shape might have something to do with real-world violence became one of Adorno's overriding ideas, and it is likely that it shaped his contributions to Mann's portrait of Leverkühn.

WEIMAR BY THE PACIFIC

For the refugees from Nazi Germany, the United States was rarely the first stop, but as the Nazis expanded their reign of terror, it became one of the last safe havens. While some emigrants ended up in the United Kingdom, Argentina, Brazil, Mexico, or Russia, more and more opted for the United States. Many who wanted to come didn't make it or were overtaken by the Nazi onslaught in Europe. The novelist Ernst Weiss watched the German troops march down the Champs Elysees from his hotel room, lay down in his bathtub, and slit his wrists. The critic Walter Benjamin took poison when it became clear he would not make it across the French border into Spain.

Most of the scientists, and many of the artists and intellectuals who left Germany, made the US East Coast their new home—Princeton, New Jersey, for instance, or New York City. Those who had trouble making ends meet on the East Coast—writers writing in a language few around them understood, musicians with repertoires that seemed alien on Broadway, philosophers working on questions rarely pondered at American universities—moved on to California. Between ten thousand and twenty thousand émigrés from central Europe would eventually make their home in Los Angeles by 1945, about 70 percent of them Jewish.[16]

They were new arrivals in a city of new arrivals. Between 1920 and 1940 the population of Los Angeles almost tripled. The massive expansion of housing stock and new developments, the comparatively low cost of living, and above all the siren call of the entertainment industry made it a preferred destination for Weimar intellectuals, artists, and writers. Twenty thousand people in a city of 1.5 million did not constitute a massive community, but like most immigrants, the central Europeans tended to cluster: in Santa Monica, Pacific Palisades, Brentwood, Westwood, and Hollywood, often in close proximity to each other.

Some of the credit for this concentration may rest with the realtors of Los Angeles, who seem to have been keen to match like with like. In an interview, Max Horkheimer recalled that on his arrival in 1940, a realtor showed him a house and, as realtors do, launched into praise of the neighborhood. Just recently, the realtor explained, another house had been sold to another gentleman from Germany—"a Mr. Mann." The sheer density of German luminaries could be truly staggering. Among the literati there were the Mann brothers, world-famous Thomas and increasingly luckless Heinrich, Lion Feuchtwanger, Vicki Baum, and Franz Werfel with his wife, Alma Mahler-Werfel. Bertolt Brecht arrived from the Soviet Union in

1941, disposing of his edition of Lenin's collected works somewhere in Los Angeles harbor before making landfall.[17]

Music, too, was well represented: German exiles like Hanns Eisler, Eric Zeisl, and Ernst Toch joined European émigrés like Igor Stravinsky. Transplants, like Erich Wolfgang Korngold and Franz Waxman, shaped the emerging sound of Hollywood. Conductors like Bruno Walter and Otto Klemperer had settled in Southern California. Whereas the German emigrants across the United States represented something of a cross-section of the German professional classes, the group that came to concentrate in Southern California was particular. Scientists and academics were underrepresented; artists and creative types of all stripes were overrepresented. This was partly due to Hollywood—about two thousand members of Germany's burgeoning film industry resettled in California.[18] The cultural stature and the sheer concentration of intellectual heft gave the western enclave its luster. Here, some of the most austere exponents of central European culture lived under palm trees by the beach.

At least some of the mythic stature that this "Weimar on the Pacific" has in the German-speaking world today, it acquired in the immediate post-war period, when a deeply shamed German intelligentsia cast about for an uncorrupted chapter of German cultural history from which to derive legitimacy. When Thomas Mann visited the Frankfurt Institute of Social Research in 1952, Adorno wrote a quick welcome speech for director Max Horkheimer, full of swaying palm trees and Pacific breezes (Horkheimer declined to deliver it). This world, thousands of miles removed from the compromised proponents of "inner emigration," offered an easy point of orientation for postwar Germans—the Germany they liked to remember was gathered here in the same cluster of neighborhoods, a standing reserve of tradition and legitimacy for the new German states.

A sense of amazement at this little colony of arts and learning pervades the writings of the protagonists themselves. Mann marvels in June 1943 at "how many musicians, virtuosi and composers have made their way here. At the moment I'm actively trying to spend time with them, so that I can learn a little."[19] Schoenberg, too, was taken in by his new home. The very place seemed to him almost hyperreal: "It is Switzerland, the Riviera, the Vienna woods, the desert, the Salzkammergut, Spain, Italy—everything in one place."[20] There are statements to similar effect from just about all of the exiles: as Schoenberg does here, the places they list are mostly vacation spots rather than places where they had lived. Not only was California less-than-real; so was being there.

The diaries and letters of the period give the impression of an expatriate community that, though far from insular, was distinct from the city around it. Mann's diaries are full of walks along the shore in Santa Monica and movies in Malibu. He corresponds with editors, journalists, and academics across the United States. But the dinners he hosts and attends seem largely to comprise European exiles—not necessarily famous ones, not necessarily German ones, but recent arrivals like him. The Werfels, Franz and Alma, are a constant presence, and so are the Horkheimers, Marcuses, and Feuchtwangers.

Some of the infrastructure for the German community in which Mann circulated had been created by earlier, more voluntary, transplants: Salka Viertel's soirees are a mainstay in his diaries. Salka was the wife of director Berthold Viertel, an Austrian avant-garde film director who had come to Hollywood in 1928 and found success with Paramount Pictures and Warner Bros.[21] Mann and Schoenberg met at a "musical soiree" at her house in Santa Monica Canyon in September 1940. In his diaries Mann notes that there was a "great crowd"[22] *(großer Kreis)*, and even though he doesn't specify, other diary entries give us an idea of the sheer caliber of cultural luminaries gathered on Mabery Road: Mann, Schoenberg, Brecht, Feuchtwanger, and the Werfels would rub shoulders with Aldous Huxley, Christopher Isherwood, W. H. Auden, Charlie Chaplin, and Igor Stravinsky.[23]

But if some unusual friendships appear to have blossomed under the California sun, other relationships never quite transcend the divisions thrown up in a long-vanished Old World. And it seems to have been perfectly easy to avoid one another even in a community as tight-knit as the German cultural expatriates. Thomas Mann and fellow novelist Alfred Döblin, for instance, had had many disagreements back in Europe. Döblin arrived in Los Angeles in 1940 and left in 1945, and although Mann's tone toward him softens a bit during these five years (tensions would flare once again postwar), the two writers seem to have met exactly once during their time in California: at Heinrich Mann's seventieth birthday party.

But the hagiographic depiction of "Weimar on the Pacific," so common after the war, misses another set of feelings that runs through the letters and diaries of the period. In his 1945 novel *Prater Violet*, the British expat writer Christopher Isherwood erected a literary monument to Berthold Viertel. "You cannot know what it is like to be an exile, a perpetual stranger," the novel's Viertel stand-in, Bergmann, tells the narrator. "I am bitterly ashamed that I am here, in safety."[24] The cognitive dissonance between the idyllic enclaves by the Pacific Ocean and the intensifying horror back home was enormous. The geographic distance kept the war at a remove, but its irruptions into everyday life were constant and surreal. In September of 1940 Mann notes the "sad news about torpedoing of a British ship full of children headed for Canada" at the hands of a German U-boat, only to learn days later that his own daughter was on the ship in question, the SS *City of Benares,* and that his son-in-law had drowned in the sinking.

The émigrés themselves experienced the seemingly marvelous concentration of talent and intellect as less than idyllic. While some of them thrived in their new home, others struggled; bitterness and competition were inevitable. In *The Magic Mountain,* Mann describes the "great petulance" and "nameless impatience" that take hold of the cloistered residents of an alpine sanatorium.[25] A similar irritability, it seemed, circulated along the beaches and hills of Southern California.

In his recent *The Rest Is Noise,* the music critic Alex Ross framed his story of modern music in exile around an incident Marta Feuchtwanger reported. Shopping at the Brentwood Country Mart, she found herself accosted by an irate Arnold Schoenberg, who, she claimed, insisted unbidden that "you have to know, I never had syphilis."[26] It is telling that in Feuchtwanger's recollection Schoenberg never explains that he is referring to *Doctor Faustus,* to Mann's syphilitic protagonist, Leverkühn. Perhaps more remarkably, he never has to. Proximity bred irritation, not just when it came to *Faustus.* "I feel here as if I were in Tahiti," Brecht wrote, "surrounded by palm trees and artists, *it makes me nervous.*"[27] Like so many émigrés, Mann, Schoenberg, and Adorno had experienced their exile as a precipitous drop in prestige and above all audience—the threat of oblivion crept up on each of them differently, but it crept up on them all.

Much of the cultural production of those years is safely part of the literary canon in Germany today but is forgotten in the country where it actually originated. This can obscure the fact that many of the German exiles found considerable success in their adopted country. The composer Erich Wolfgang Korngold, who arrived in 1934 to write film soundtracks for Warner Bros., found immense success, recognition, and wealth. The novelist Lion Feuchtwanger was able to purchase the Villa Aurora in Pacific Palisades from selling the movie rights to his works. Franz Werfel's novel *The Song of Bernadette,* published in German in 1941 and in English in 1942, spent more than a year on the *New York Times* best-seller list and became a hit movie that won four Academy Awards.

Some of this was luck, or willingness to meet the new environment, above all the Hollywood studios, halfway. But some of it was uncomfortably bound up with questions of aesthetics. While a crowd-pleasing director like Fritz Lang, a realist author like Werfel, or a composer with musical theater credibility like Kurt Weill could find immense and immediate success, those whose aesthetics were more clearly avant-garde, or more proximately tied to the specific concerns and traditions of the German-speaking world, often found it hard to gain footing.

Alfred Döblin, fêted author of the massive *Berlin, Alexanderplatz*, labored in relative obscurity as a script doctor. Bertolt Brecht found himself humiliated by having to

> go to the market where lies are bought.
> Hopefully
> I take up my place among the sellers.[28]

And Thomas Mann's own brother, Heinrich, whose work had been adapted into hit movies during the Weimar years, found it impossible to work in the studio system; around the same time as Thomas moved into his final California villa, his brother had to cancel his membership in the Screen Writers' Guild because he could no longer afford the ten-dollar membership fee.[29] In his *Hollywood Elegies* Brecht described the artist's work in this "dreadful idyll" as akin to prostitution:

> Under the green pepper trees
> Musicians walk the streets in pairs
> With writers.[30]

Mann's work wore its modernism extremely lightly. His prolix, ironic, stately prose translated well and seemed ready-made for global relevance. And his US publishers seemed intent on giving his books an even less avant-garde tint. When *Lotte in Weimar* was to appear in English in 1940, the book was to have an advance run of twenty-five thousand copies. Alfred A. Knopf insisted that the book be published with the title *The Beloved Returns*—the proper names were not the problem, but the "phonetic difficulty customers would have in asking for [*Lotte in Weimar*] in a bookshop."[31] Mann thought the title was overly sentimental but was mollified once the German title was kept on as the book's subtitle. Paul Rosenfeld, reviewing the novel for the *Saturday Review of Literature*, praised it as "graceful, scintillant," but lamented its "unfortunate title."[32]

Rosenfeld's reaction speaks to the fraught role aesthetics played even for as widely recognized an artist as Mann. To really succeed in the American market, Mann had to assent to a sentimental, melodramatic version of his title, which a bona fide modernist like Rosenfeld, once a close collaborator of Sherwood Anderson and Randolph Bourne, could not quite get on board with.[33] Whether it was Hollywood or Broadway, the émigrés were often avant-gardists working on less-than-avant-garde fare. "This was movie-work, hack-work," Isherwood has his narrator say in *Prater Violet*. "It was something essentially false, cheap, vulgar. It was beneath me."[34]

The elite of German culture had an intense distrust of what Adorno and Horkheimer in the fourth chapter of *Dialectic of Enlightenment* would call the "culture industry." Now they were living in what was arguably the capital of that industry, and much of their income came from what Brecht dubbed "the market where lies are sold."[35] Being repulsed by lies and illusion was of course more than a matter of preference for the émigrés. Having witnessed the ends to which Joseph Goebbels's Propaganda Ministry had put popular entertainment in Nazi Germany, they were deeply suspicious of what damage ideology could do. Adorno, in particular, spared nary an aspect of American culture of his suspicious gaze: back east he had studied anti-Semitic preachers for the Radio Research Project and the Rockefeller Foundation. In California he searched for the origins of fascism in the astrology columns of the *LA Times* and the "perennial fashion" of big band jazz.

Brecht lamented that "here art is ashamed of its usefulness, but not its exchange value."[36] But Schoenberg, too, inveighed against the materialism he saw dominating his new city, which, he wrote in a fund-raising appeal for the LA Philharmonic, "seems to endanger the whole sphere of spiritual culture."[37] At the same time, they very much partook of the cultural life of their adoptive country. Even the most mandarin among them were not automatic in their rejection of American popular culture. This was particularly true of the musicians. As Kenneth Marcus has written, so thorough was the interpenetration between elite musicians and the Hollywood studio system, that strict borders "between classical and popular music . . . had less of a place in the diversified environment of modern music in the region."[38]

In *Minima Moralia* Adorno wrote: "Repudiation of the present cultural morass presupposes sufficient involvement in it to feel it itching in one's finger-tips."[39] Decades later he would frequently recall how Charlie Chaplin watched him embarrass himself at a party and imitated him[40]—in one of his lectures he would even call it "the greatest honor of my life." Besides, there was plenty of high culture that the émigrés believed they had to reevaluate in light of the rise of fascism—the neoclassicism of Stravinsky and Sibelius reminded Adorno fatally of the pillared monstrosities Albert Speer was erecting in Berlin. Adorno, Mann, Schoenberg, and many others wrestled with the legacy of Wagner and the uses to which he was being put in Nazi Germany.[41]

If California's reaction to the German intellectuals ran a broad gamut, from total neglect to rapturous welcome, the three émigrés who would collide over *Doctor Faustus* found themselves on different points along that spectrum. Mann, the Nobel Prize winner and literary institution, had found the transition fairly easy and spent the war years in a highly publicized effort lobbying for the Allied cause and providing a voice of reason to the denizens of the Nazi Reich. Mann had never lacked for a sense of his own status, but in the 1940s he was undeniably and objectively important: an integral counterweight to the corruption and debasement of German culture under Hitler, a reminder that there was something in the country of Goethe and Luther that was worth saving.

Adorno found himself completely ignored in England, pushed into sociological work ill-suited to his interest on the East Coast of the States, and dependent on his friend Max Horkheimer's patronage and money once he came to Los Angeles. Adorno never forgave either the United Kingdom or the United States that they harbored him but would not pay any attention to him. His "Glosse über Sibelius" was a poison pen letter to the United Kingdom, then undergoing a somewhat baffling love affair with the composer, and *Minima Moralia*, Adorno's "Reflections from Damaged Life," heaps scorn on the commodified society he encountered in California.

Arnold Schoenberg fell somewhere in the middle. Neither as neglected as Adorno nor garnering the sort of recognition he had been used to, his position was a teetering, precarious one. Twelve-tone music put him on the cultural map in America, but it also consigned his influence to certain cultured enclaves. And Los Angeles was less than hospitable to it. Given their continued fame and influence today, the idea that these three men seriously feared that they might one day be forgotten seems strange. But one doesn't do the *Faustus* affair justice if one underestimates how seriously especially Schoenberg took the possibility of being forgotten.

The very landscape seemed to invite amnesia. Adorno would later write that "American consciousness" represented "the nightmare of a humanity without history."[42] California meant safety and comfort, but it was also a place inhospitable to the kind of intellectual immortality on which Schoenberg, Mann, and Adorno had once safely counted. On Horkheimer's terrace at 13524 D'Este Drive, Adorno and Horkheimer penned the famous excursus on Odysseus for the *Dialectic of Enlightenment*. In their interpretation Odysseus emerges as the bourgeois subject par excellence, someone who has learned to make use of his reason to demystify, manipulate, and ultimately control a world of gods and monsters.

In their chapter they dwell on Odysseus's encounter with the Lotus-eaters. The trade offered by the Lotus-eaters, they wrote, is memory in exchange for bliss. It is likely they thought of the beaches and farmers' markets along the Pacific when they did so. Odysseus, of course, extricates his men from the bliss and amnesia the Lotus-eaters offer. There is his home in Ithaca to think of, after all.

"Odysseus is therefore right not to endure life among the Lotus-eaters," Adorno and Horkheimer write. In a sly Californian self-portrait they describe a situation in which two projects, that of cunning Odysseus and that of the blissed-out Lotus-eaters, though equally legitimate, come into conflict. The Lotus-eaters transgress against Odysseus by suggesting that utopia is simply a matter of dropping out, of ingesting some narcotics, but Odysseus knows that utopia has to be realized "through historical work." But he wrongs them in turn, because the only way he knows out of their bliss is by violence and domination.[43]

THE CASTAWAY: ARNOLD SCHOENBERG

Although his stature in his new homeland was far greater than the Marxist scolds of D'Este Drive, Arnold Schoenberg was possessed of similar anxieties. He feared that he was being forgotten, that his mother tongue was atrophying. "Provided my German is still good enough," he half-seriously hedged in one of his letters to Mann. Mann entertained no such worries but instead proclaimed to the *New York Times*, "Where I am, there is Germany. I carry my German culture in me." Mann's self-confidence in such matters was legendary and predated his exile. Schoenberg, by contrast, felt that exile merely exacerbated what had already been a history of misunderstanding and neglecting his achievements. As Dorothy Lamb Crawford writes, "memories of past repudiations and his sense of his own importance made him hypersensitive to any slight, even if imagined."[44]

And like Adorno, Schoenberg worried about not being heard, not being noticed—in fact, his first overture to Thomas Mann constituted an attempt to fix this. Schoenberg's first California letter to Mann in December 1938 concerned an article, "A Four-Point Program for Jewry," that the composer had tried and failed to get published: "In the face of such a complete failure I had begun to doubt whether what I had written was useful. That is really the worst thing that could possibly happen, feeling insecure about one's work. Why: it isn't even possible for me to get an article accepted?"[45]

As his "Four-Point Program" made clear, Schoenberg's anxiety about his reception was compounded by the fact that he had urgent, prescient things to say, and he wanted to say them to as wide an audience as possible. Propelled by the same distaste for bending back the arrow of musical progress as possessed Adorno, he didn't bother meeting the audience halfway when it came to compositional practice. But his topics—the *Kol Nidre*, op. 39, or *A Survivor from Warsaw*, op. 46, for instance—were intended for, and even necessitated, the biggest possible audience. Ehrhard Bahr points to a "complete reversal of his former elitist attitude toward his audience."[46] The catastrophe of the Jewish people playing out half a world away tended to demand a certain maximalism—like fellow exile Kurt Weill, Schoenberg felt his music had to send out a clarion call to a people cast adrift by Nazi terror.[47]

In this situation, not having one's music heard was more than a matter of personal disappointment. Schoenberg's musical aesthetics were always keenly attuned to "what was necessary to be expressed"[48] at a certain point in history, but what if one expressed what was necessary and no one was there to hear it? In an essay about the *Kol Nidre*, Schoenberg writes, "I assume that at the time when these words were spoken for the first time, everybody understood them perfectly."[49] There is an immense desire to be understood in these pieces, a wish to tell and preserve stories.

In other words, Schoenberg's anxieties at the time and the pressures of the historical moment were such that Mann's casual erasure of Schoenberg's story and ascriptions of his achievements to a fictional character were a match to potent tinder. But Mann, from the very beginning of their exile correspondence, seemed taken in by the enthusiasm with which Schoenberg argued his political positions but troubled by the positions themselves. Not only did Schoenberg's appeal for help in publishing the "Four-Point Program" come to naught; Mann's reply suggested, however gently, that the "overall intellectual stance . . . comes across as somewhat fascist." Memories of this reaction likely stoked Schoenberg's ire when he found his "intellectual property" (as he put it) espoused by a fictional character intended to stand in for German fascism.

Schoenberg was anxious that his connection with the culture of his old homeland was fraying and that his new homeland wasn't quick to embrace him. He found himself questioning his productivity: "Composing is something I haven't done for two years," Schoenberg wrote to Jakob Klatzkin in July 1938. "I have had too much other work. And anyway: for whom should I write?"[50] He was concerned that he would only be recognized as "the composer of the *Verklärte Nacht*,"[51] the only piece of his that seemed to find consistent success in America. He worried that his new composition students in Los Angeles were not up to the task of carrying on his legacy. And he found himself confronted with a fictional version of his own music and person—a grotesque caricature—designed as a kind of *damnatio memoriae*.

In May of 1938 the exhibition *Entartete Musik (Degenerate Music)* had its premiere in Düsseldorf. Here the music critic Hans Severus Ziegler had assembled artifacts related to compositions by a veritable who's-who of modern German music.[52] Unlike in the more famous show on "degenerate art," which had premiered in Munich the previous year, degenerate here seemed to largely mean "Jewish." There were few strictly aesthetic characteristics that Ziegler's show seemed to object to, late romantics like Franz Schreker were presented alongside jazz, neoclassicists, and atonal composers of Schoenberg's Second Viennese School. Since the show didn't feature much music, it sought to convince its audience with unflattering photographs and autographs by the composers in question.

Most of the show's unwitting protagonists, insofar as they were still alive, made their homes in the United States by May 1938. Before long, almost all of them (Ernst Krenek, Hanns Eisler, Ernst Toch, Igor Stravinsky, and of course Arnold Schoenberg) would become West Coast transplants. The awareness of the cultural politics of the Third Reich was naturally limited among the exiles, but they were aware of the bizarre counternarratives being spun about their music in their erstwhile homeland. The question for Schoenberg, unlike for Mann, was not just whether he'd be forgotten. It was whether a mendacious, fictional version of himself, of the kind Ziegler offered to audiences in the "Reich," would replace the actual person Arnold Schoenberg. It is not hard to see why Schoenberg might see Doctor Faustus as doing exactly that.

There was something about exile that made the German émigrés take the extremely long view. In the remarks Adorno drafted for Horkheimer's welcome to the Frankfurt Institute in 1952, he points to how distant the return felt that was, in terms of mere years, actually so near: "If someone had told us during those years when we lived as neighbors in Pacific Palisades by the Silent Ocean, that we would meet again in Germany and in an official capacity, we both would have smiled in disbelief."[53] People thought about their legacies in decades, centuries. When the Italian fascist composer Alfredo Casella (1883–1947) wrote an article proclaiming victory over German chromaticism, especially in its "extreme consequence" of atonality, Schoenberg's response dripped with sarcasm: "What a glorious victory! But this victory, does it not bring to mind other such victories? For example, the victory over Bach, which made his work fall thus perfectly into desuetude, so that his greatest works were unknown by the musical public already fifty years after his death."[54]

At the same time, the Nazi denunciations of "degenerate" music were uncomfortably echoed in Mann's own take on modern music. They had grown in the same late romantic soil and perhaps sprang from a similar dilettantism. This was of course where the connection ended. But as Walter

Levin has pointed out, Schoenberg clearly sensed a commonality.[55] And on some less-than-conscious level there may well have been something to his suspicion: in his diaries Mann notes after one soiree in May 1943 that "according to Schoenberg, modern music—including twelve-tone music—has been permitted in Germany again since about 1940 and even to some extent encouraged despite 'degenerate art.'"

It is not clear what Mann or Schoenberg were referring to. They were aware that few, isolated modernist composers—Paul von Klenau or Winfried Zillig—had found some acceptance in spite of Nazi hostility. But as the example of Schoenberg's (non-Jewish and fairly Nazi-friendly)[56] student Anton Webern makes clear, the Nazis ordinarily did not soften their stance on music once deemed "degenerate." What is clear is the lesson Mann takes away from Schoenberg's supposed remark—a permission to associate modern music with the very people who wouldn't let it be heard: "Must bear that in mind. State may have contradictory attitude towards Leverkühn."

THE CLIMBER: THEODOR W. ADORNO

As much for reasons of convenience as for reasons of substance, Adorno would emerge as Schoenberg's *bête noire* in the *Doctor Faustus* affair: Mann and Schoenberg made peace soon enough, but Schoenberg's hatred for Adorno remained implacable. This in spite of the fact that Adorno was, and remained, an admirer of Schoenberg. Adorno's early mentions of Schoenberg, above all in his letters to his composition-mentor Alban Berg, who had in turn been Schoenberg's student, are thoroughly positive. Adorno composed music throughout the 1920s and 1930s, and in the late 1920s even wrote a series of songs he described to Berg as "the strictest twelve-tone music."[57] Schoenberg would later mock Adorno's music, and his immense slowness in producing it, suggesting that "he knows everything about twelve-tone music, but has no idea of the creative process involved."[58]

In exile Adorno undertook a project that was to center on a critique of Schoenberg's music. *Philosophy of New Music* was not intended as an attack on Schoenberg but instead as an immanent critique of certain tendencies in Schoenberg's compositional practice in light of the broader cultural critique Adorno would undertake in *In Search of Wagner* and *Dialectic of Enlightenment*. Nevertheless, Adorno sensed that it contained enough "formulations" that would lead the chapter's subject to understand it as an attack. "I intend to subject the whole thing to self-censorship one more time if it does get published," Adorno writes to the violinist Rudolf Kolisch

(Schoenberg's brother-in-law) in June of 1942—and he reacts in complete panic when Kolisch passes a copy on to Schoenberg's son-in-law.[59]

When *Philosophy of New Music* did appear in print in 1949, many of these formulations were indeed removed, and the Schoenberg chapter was paired with what was truly an all-out assault on Igor Stravinsky— Schoenberg was clearly not, or no longer, a target of the book. Given all of Adorno's panicked information-management, it is somewhat surprising that Adorno took the seemingly risky step of giving his text to Thomas Mann. Mann received a draft on July 21, 1943, and finished reading it by July 27. He immediately recognized that it would be important to the *Faustus* project, and Adorno seems to have known that this was why Mann was interested.

Why hand a manuscript he sought to keep from Schoenberg to a world-famous author not known for keeping the private private? Adorno's motivation to part with the copy likely had the same source as his reticence to let it out of his orbit otherwise: Adorno was at this point in his life keenly aware of status. He arrived in Los Angeles as a nobody, and the precariousness of his new life seemed to heighten a certain sycophantic bend. His exchanges with his composition-teacher Berg drip with supplication ("Dear Master and Teacher"), and his early overtures to Mann border on the obsequious. Adorno had seen Mann once during a vacation on the island of Sylt but had been too timid to speak to him. Now he was clearly somewhat star struck and at once keen to ingratiate himself and to think of himself and Mann as on the same level. Although his financial situation was anything but rosy, he seems to have rejected any notion of being paid for his services.

He seems to have tried with Schoenberg as well, but Schoenberg would have none of it. "I could never really stand him," he confessed in 1950, adding a portrait of deranged fandom: "He engulfed me with his piercing eyes, advancing on me ever nearer until a wall prevented further escape."[60] Schoenberg thought of Adorno as an epigone, student of his student, desperate to impress. Adorno, for him, was all "oily pathos, bombast, the affected passion of his veneration."[61] He hated Adorno's very mode of expression—a style that Mann frequently lauded, that made it into some of Kretzschmar's lectures and Zeitblom's analyses in *Doctor Faustus*, that as *Adorno Stil* would devastate German academic writing for three decades.

Mann, by contrast, seemed charmed, but perhaps more importantly he sensed that Adorno would be useful. The collaboration between the established author and the young philosopher was from the beginning rather parasitic. Though it was Schoenberg who would later accuse Thomas Mann of plagiarism, there is no other word for what Mann was doing to Adorno—

albeit, one must note, with Adorno's complete compliance. Adorno sent Mann prose "descriptions" of Adrian Leverkühn's fictional works, and Mann incorporated several of them almost unchanged. Significantly, Adorno would later deny (on request by Katia Mann) that he felt plagiarized, emphasizing that he had given "friendly advice," that he had been a "witness to the writing of the book."

This seems to have mattered most to Adorno: he was greatly invested in seeing himself and Mann as communicating at eye-level; he seemed to swat away any suspicions, though he must have entertained them, that he was being treated like the help. Adorno lived long enough to find out that Mann had evidently not thought of it that way at all: when Mann's letters came out in print in the mid-1960s, Adorno learned that Mann had thought he had unduly inflated his role in the creation of the novel.[62] In this Mann manages to be both spectacularly ungrateful and not entirely wrong: Adorno had shown immense devotion to Mann and was in general quite discreet about the aid he had given the writer, but behind his devotion lay a burning desire for recognition.

The work of Adorno's California period was not music criticism, aesthetics, or even traditional Marxism. Although works such as *Dialectic of Enlightenment, In Search of Wagner,* and *Minima Moralia* touched on artwork from Homer via the Marquis de Sade to Igor Stravinsky, their collective aim was a critique of purposive rationality, which, Adorno claimed, was founded on a more basic irrationality.[63] This was what he and Horkheimer would identify as the "dialectic of enlightenment": Western rationality had learned to control nature but had never in the process questioned the nature of that control itself.

It was as part of this work, the critique of absolute rationality, that twelve-tone music became an object of Adorno's critique: it functioned as an analogue to the categories of enlightenment, to the operations of the "identity principle," to the fungibility of the market. This parallelism to some extent forced Adorno's hand: Schoenberg was always annoyed that Adorno mischaracterized his "method" as a "system."[64] And he likely had too little interest in Adorno's philosophy to see why Adorno persisted in using the word, that indeed he was not making a claim about Schoenberg's "creative process" (as Schoenberg suspected) but that he was expressing a worry about a form of expression that seemed to make a fetish of a certain kind of objectivity.[65] For one thing, in their exchange of letters both Adorno and Berg refer to twelve-tone composition as a "technique" or "style," in other words somewhat akin to the way Schoenberg would. But, more importantly, as Adorno makes clear in his later lectures on *Philosophical*

Terminology, our "everyday" understanding of *system* is quite different from the way philosophy uses it.[66]

Adorno worries there about a "moment, which cuts off the freedom of reflection and turns the system dominating and violent."[67] Adorno's *Philosophy of New Music* doesn't propose that twelve-tone composition is uncreative but that it is insufficiently reflective of its own presuppositions. This may still be an inaccurate critique, but it is clearly not the critique Schoenberg thought Adorno was making. Still, Schoenberg was correct insofar as Alban Berg had clearly fostered in Adorno an exaggerated sense of the strictness of Schoenberg's technique. In a letter from August of 1928, Berg claims that there is nothing "stricter than Schoenberg's Quintett [op. 26] in which there isn't a single 'free' note (other than as a printer's error)."[68] Adorno, a student of Neo-Kantians, a serious-minded citizen of prosaic Frankfurt, probably took the universality implicit in twelve-tone technique more seriously than the Viennese Schoenberg. In this respect, too, Schoenberg erred in thinking that Adorno simply didn't like his music. Berg made this comment to caution Adorno, who in fact thought that he'd outdone Schoenberg in sheer stringency in his George-songs: the "systematizing" impulse that he faults Schoenberg for Adorno recognized well in himself.

THE "EMPEROR": THOMAS MANN

But the most serious misunderstanding was likely Mann's. In his *The Story of a Novel (Die Entstehung des Doktor Faustus),* published two years after the novel itself, he defended himself by pointing out that it was only natural for a writer to turn to "benevolent connoisseurs" *(wohlwollenden Kennern)* in planning and writing a novel as complex as *Faustus.*[69] Comments about Adorno's "expertise" and "learning" are sprinkled throughout Mann's correspondence with Adorno. But this entails a massive misunderstanding of what Adorno was offering Mann.

Granted, an essay like "Beethoven's Late Style," which Mann used to write Wendell Kretzschmar's lecture on Beethoven's op. 111 in *Doctor Faustus,* represented a kind of expertise easily incorporated into Mann's undertaking. But *Philosophy of New Music* was not intended as highly competent music criticism but a young scholar's bracing, new, and highly idiosyncratic intervention into the history and theory of postromantic music. Adorno sensed as much, writing to Horkheimer after completing his *Philosophy of New Music* that "this time everyone, except you, will consider me mad."[70] The Marxist premises that so contravened Mann's own aesthetic judgments were only the beginning of the odd fit.[71] Adorno was offering a theory of fascism directly opposed to the one that Mann seemed to suggest in *Faustus*. Mann's Leverkühn surrenders to irrationality, infecting himself deliberately with syphilis. Adorno's Schoenberg has a troubling tendency to occlude the irrationalist origins of his music with the objectivity of his technique.

But it was not just the material he imported that was bound to cause confusion. So was the way in which he imported it. He enthused to Adorno about the way he "montaged" the philosopher's idea into the novel, but the actual manuscript suggests that Mann had perhaps a less-stringent understanding of what montage entailed than the composers. In his very first letter to Adorno he writes: "I am not worried about *montage* in this connection, and never have been. What belongs in the book must go into it, and will be properly absorbed in the process. . . . As in the earlier case of little Hanno's typhoid fever, my 'initiated' ignorance required precise *details [Exaktheiten]* to enhance the literary illusion and structure of the composition."[72]

The case of "little Hanno" is instructive. Mann is referring here to the jarring episode in the eleventh part of his 1901 novel *Buddenbrooks*. There, following a lengthy description of a day in the life of Hanno Buddenbrook, last scion of the declining titular family, Mann's narrator opens his next chapter with a text that could be drawn from a medical textbook: "Typhoid runs the following course."[73] The description remains clinical throughout; the narrator's humanizing touches are absent; the name Hanno is never even uttered. The effect is both jarring and unforgettable.

The example suggests that Mann imported text into his novels, but he deployed and manipulated it to his own overall aims. Real people inspired his characters, but those characters were never portraits. And while the translation as "details" may obscure Mann's meaning a bit, what Mann solicited from Adorno were "exactitudes," not facts; they were intended to create the effect of realism, the effect of learnedness, not to be either of those things. Mann wanted to sprinkle his prose with a dash of "exactitudes"—its very plural form suggests how ironic he is being.

In *Doctor Faustus* Zeitblom himself thinks Leverkühn deploys "quotation as disguise, the parody as pretext." And he suggests that without quoting, "how could the word have been written down that pressed to be written down?"[74] Only in quoting and in appropriating, only by playacting, can Leverkühn say what at this moment has to be said. We can safely presume Leverkühn's creator, anxious to grapple with what had happened to his homeland, sensing deep, troubling connections to the very culture he now represented, felt much the same way. The sheer enormity of what Mann sought to express required him to overreach, to overabsorb, to appropriate.

Schoenberg was predisposed to see matters differently. His compositional technique implied that quotation always meant an adaptation of pre-existing material rather than its wholesale importation. In a letter he sent to the *New York Times* music critic Olin Downes in 1938, Schoenberg addresses the question of how he "quoted" the theme "B-A-C-H" in his Variations for Orchestra, op. 31. What he describes there suggests a very different understanding of what quoting entailed than what we see in Mann: "If I should explain why I used these quotations," he writes, "I saw suddenly the possibility and did it." Comparing his way of proceeding to Beethoven's Diabelli Variations and Mozart's *Don Giovanni*, he allows that "of course my quotation is not as humorous as both of these before mentioned. But again I have an excuse: I believe I have woven it in rather thoroughly."[75] Quotation was not something one could hide behind.

So did Schoenberg simply misunderstand Mann's technique? It isn't as simple as that, for in the very same letter to Adorno, Mann asks Adorno to "intervene and correct such details . . . if they should appear mistaken, misleading, or put in such a way as to provoke the scorn of experts."[76] Here Mann the novelist came into conflict with Mann the public intellectual. The Mann of *Buddenbrooks* had not intended for his description of typhoid to cement his medical credentials; but as his stature grew, he had increasing trouble distinguishing between imbuing his narrators with an aura of expertise and actually being himself an expert in something. Given his own self-presentation, then, the misunderstanding that Zeitblom's account in *Doctor Faustus* represented a verdict (specifically Adorno's verdict) of Schoenberg almost forced itself on the reader.

At the same time, Mann's invocation of the encyclopedia article on typhoid fever suggests a fatal lack of respect for the texts and ideas with which he was grappling in his novel: incorporating an encyclopedia text simply isn't the same thing as incorporating the highly peculiar ideas of a young, energetic scholar eager to make a name for himself, ideas moreover about a particularly recondite school of elite music. Mann liked to call himself a "magician," and he admired Goethe greatly; in dealing with Adorno on twelve-tone technique, he reminds one instead of Goethe's sorcerer's apprentice—overconfidently invoking what will, in the wrong hands, bear uncanny fruit.

When Schoenberg expressed pique about Mann's thoughtless appropriation of his own biography, he joined a rather distinguished crowd: Mann serially included figures modeled after famous contemporaries, or even his family members, into his works, and he seemed genuinely surprised each time when they reacted badly.[77] In some cases he recognized as much. When he populated "The Blood of the Walsungs" with anti-Semitic versions of his in-laws and based the story's incestuous twins on his wife and her twin brother, the family pressured him to withdraw the publication.[78] And in his *Story of a Novel* he expresses regret over using his own grandson Fridolin in creating the character of Nepomuk ("Nepo") Schneidewein, who dies toward the climax of *Doctor Faustus*.

But in other cases—and especially when it came to other artists and thinkers—he seemed to know far less compunction. Even if we grant that Leverkühn was not Schoenberg, one couldn't fault Schoenberg for suspecting that he was: after all, in *Faustus* alone Sixtus Kridwiß is modeled after Mann's Munich friend Emil Preetorius, and Chaim Breisacher is a stand-in for the cultural pessimist Oswald Spengler.[79] Gerhart Hauptmann wasn't exactly thrilled when Mann turned Mynheer Peeperkorn in *The Magic Mountain* into a virtual parody of the writer.[80]

Mann was universally cavalier about these borrowings. Again and again he pleaded unconscious borrowing where those who had watched his writing process saw very intentional parodies.[81] "That is what it is," Mann wrote about the Peeperkorn-Hauptmann connection in a 1925 letter to Herbert Eulenberg: "a product of the imagination which involuntarily and half unconsciously [is] colored by a powerful real experience."[82] By the time he turned Schoenberg into grist for his fiction, then, Mann had decades of practice and a well-honed sense of artistic entitlement to his contemporaries' likenesses and stories. He had lifted bits of text and incorporated them verbatim into his works. He had also witnessed decades of more or less outraged reactions to his aesthetic vampirism.

But Schoenberg's specific outrage points to a broader puzzlement: it appears that the composer picked consistently the wrong points on which to fault *Faustus*. For one thing, as Bojan Bujic has put it, it is curious that Schoenberg focused so much "on the acknowledgment of his authorship."[83] For another, Schoenberg seemed inclined to grant *Faustus* a kind of magical power over historical memory—an ability to rewrite history, to obliterate memory, to reverse chronology—that no novel could possibly hope for or want. In other words, Schoenberg ascribed to *Faustus* things Nazi Germany (and indeed post-Nazi Germany) did or would do. The more glaring problems—Mann's arrogant late-romantic judgments of musical modernism, his blinkered association of modernism with fascism—were never the real target of Schoenberg's ire. Why foreground the question of whether fictional composer Adrian Leverkühn or very real Arnold Schoenberg was the inventor of twelve-tone composing? Was not Mann's philistine judgment of twelve-tone composition as a symptom of Nazi-like national decline far more troubling?

Ironically, though, the reason why Schoenberg's much more ill-founded charge of "plagiarism" stuck probably had to do with developments in the country Schoenberg and Mann had left behind. Accusations of plagiarism had a curious role in the West German intelligentsia's relationship to the returning émigrés and Holocaust survivors. Critics and scholars, most of whom had either participated in Nazi crimes or claimed for themselves the hazy status of "inner emigrants," were curiously predisposed to believe claims of plagiarism when they arose. When Yvan Goll's widow accused the poet Paul Celan of having plagiarized her late husband's poems, the charge, absurd on its face, resounded through the German feuilleton for nearly a decade.[84] Hometown audiences seemed never happier than when these accusations pitted two émigrés—like Goll and Celan, like Mann and Schoenberg—against each other.

But if its resonance was a result of events in Germany, the genesis of the *Faustus* controversy is inseparably bound up with California and with the curious entwinement of proximity and exile that characterized Pacific Palisades. Schoenberg's focus on the authorship question was inevitable, given his anxieties about the possible disappearance of his work, about the funhouse-mirror version of him that stalked through the Nazis' "degenerate music" exhibition. It was galling to have his ideas spread far and wide by someone else after having been unable to spread them when it mattered most. And perhaps he was incensed by the seigneurial manner in which Mann—wealthy, famous, non-Jewish, perhaps less at risk of Nazi barbarism—appropriated and consistently failed to credit the labor of impoverished Jewish artists living around him.

But behind it loomed what Ehrhard Bahr has called the "crisis of modernism." The émigrés came to California anxious to continue the work that had made them famous but sensing that it could not go on as it had in Weimar Germany—that certain aesthetic practices had lost their critical power or had even become deeply suspect after the rise of fascism. The "great petulance" that seemed to lay hold of the émigrés may have ultimately spoken to an artistic and intellectual elite suspicious even of what little security remained for them. "It is part of morality not to be at home in one's home," Adorno wrote in *Minima Moralia*.[85] By that metric, amid the shifting categories and uncertain political terrain, Mann, Schoenberg, and Adorno, precisely when they misunderstood and mistreated each other, were at their most moral.

NOTES

1. Theodor W. Adorno and Thomas Mann, *Correspondence, 1943–1955*, ed. Christoph Gödde and Thomas Sprecher, trans. Nicholas Walker (Malden, MA: Polity, 2006), 3.

2. Thomas Mann, *Tagebücher, 28.5.1946–31.12.1948*, ed. Inge Jens (Frankfurt am Main: S. Fischer, 1989), 95. To conserve space, subsequent citations of this source will use the shortened form *Tagebücher, 1946–1948*.

3. Malcolm McDonald, *Arnold Schoenberg* (Oxford: Oxford University Press, 2008), 85.

4. See James Schmidt, "Mephistopheles in Hollywood: Adorno, Mann and Schoenberg," in *The Cambridge Companion to Adorno*, ed. Tom Huhn (Cambridge: Cambridge University Press, 2004), 148.

5. Ian Kershaw, *Hitler, the Germans, and the Final Solution* (New Haven, CT: Yale University Press, 2008), 29.

6. Bojan Bujic, *Arnold Schoenberg* (London: Phaidon, 2011), 167.

7. Theodor W. Adorno, *Kierkegaard: Konstruktion des Ästhetischen* (Tübingen: Mohr, 1933); see also Stefan Müller-Doohm, *Adorno: A Biography* (Malden, MA: Polity, 2005).

8. Dirk Auer, Lars Rensmann, and Julia Schulze Wessel, eds., *Arendt und Adorno* (Frankfurt am Main: Suhrkamp, 2003), 199–233.

9. Hannah Arendt and Karl Jaspers, *Correspondence, 1926–1969*, ed. Lotte Kohler and Hans Saner, trans. Robert Kimber and Rita Kimber (New York: Harcourt Brace Jovanovich, 1992), letter 399.

10. Dorothy Lamb Crawford, "Schoenberg in Los Angeles," *Musical Quarterly* 86, no. 1 (2002): 6–48, 13.

11. See Cornelius Schauber, *Hollywood Haven: Homes and Haunts of the European Emigres and Exiles in Los Angeles* (Riverside, CA: Ariadne, 1997).

12. Cited in David Wallace, *Exiles in Hollywood* (Pompton Plains, NJ: Limelight, 2006), 97.

13. Sabine Feisst, *Schoenberg's New World: The American Years* (Oxford: Oxford University Press, 2011); Kenneth H. Marcus, *Schoenberg and Hollywood Modernism* (New York: Cambridge University Press, 2016).

14. Theodor W. Adorno, "The Ageing of New Music," in *Essays on Music*, ed. Richard Leppert (Berkeley: University of California Press, 2002), 181.

15. Gerald Izenberg, *Modernism and Masculinity* (Chicago: University of Chicago Press, 2000), 98.

16. Ehrhard Bahr, *Weimar on the Pacific: German Exile Culture in Los Angeles and the Crisis of Modernism* (Berkeley: University of California Press, 2007), 4.

17. Stephen Parker, *Bertolt Brecht: A Literary Life* (London: Bloomsbury, 2014), 431.

18. Helmut G. Asper, *Etwas besseres als den Tod—Filmexil in Hollywood* (Marburg: Schüren, 2002), 20.

19. Mann to Meyer, June 11, 1943, in Thomas Mann and Agnes E. Meyer, *Briefwechsel, 1937–1955*, ed. Hans Rudolf Vaget (Frankfurt am Main: S. Fisher, 1992), 488.

20. Cited in Crawford, "Schoenberg in Los Angeles," 6.

21. Donald Prater, *Thomas Mann: A Life* (New York: Oxford University Press, 1995), 325.

22. Thomas Mann, *Tagebücher, 1940–1943* (Frankfurt: S. Fischer, 1988), 152.

23. Parker, *Bertolt Brecht*.

24. Christopher Isherwood, *Prater Violet* (New York: Methuen, 1946), 76.

25. Thomas Mann, *The Magic Mountain*, trans. John E. Woods (New York: Knopf, 1995), 814.

26. Alex Ross, *The Rest Is Noise* (New York: Picador, 2007), 36.

27. Bertolt Brecht, *Letters, 1913–1956*, ed. Ralph Manheim and John Willett (New York: Methuen, 1990), 336; Schmidt, "Mephistopheles in Hollywood," 149.

28. Bertolt Brecht, "Hollywood" (1942), in *Poems, 1913–1956*, ed. John Willett and Ralph Manheim (New York: Methuen, 1976), 382.

29. Manfred Flügge, *Heinrich Mann: Eine Biographie* (Reinbek: Rowohlt, 2006), 406.

30. From Brecht, "Hollywood Elegies IV," quoted in Albrecht Betz, *Hanns Eisler: Political Musician*, trans. Bill Hopkins (Cambridge: Cambridge University Press, 1982), 189.

31. David Horton, *Thomas Mann in English: A Study in Literary Translation* (London: Bloomsbury, 2012), 143.

32. Paul Rosenfeld, "Mann's Measurement of Genius," review of *The Beloved Returns*, *Saturday Review of Literature*, August 24, 1940, 5.

33. Hugh Potter, "Paul Rosenfeld: Criticism and Prophecy," *American Quarterly* 22, no. 1 (1970): 82–94.

34. Isherwood, *Prater Violet*, 26.

35. Claudia Albert, *"Das Schwierige Handwerk des Hoffens": Hanns Eislers "Hollywooder Liederbuch"* (Stuttgart: Metzler, 1991), 36.

36. Cited in Parker, *Bertolt Brecht*, 433.

37. *Los Angeles Herald Examiner*, April 15, 1936.

38. Marcus, *Schoenberg and Hollywood Modernism*, 58.

39. Theodor W. Adorno, *Minima Moralia: Reflections on a Damaged Life*, trans. E. F. N. Jephcott (London: Verso, 2005), 29.

40. Detlev Clausen, *Theodor W. Adorno: One Last Genius* (Cambridge, MA: Belknap, 2008), 165.

41. Brigitte Hamann, *Winifred Wagner: A Life at the Heart of Hitler's Bayreuth* (London: Granta, 2005), 204.

42. Theodor W. Adorno, *Critical Models: Interventions and Watchwords* (New York: Columbia University Press, 2005), 344.

43. Max Horkheimer and Theodor W. Adorno, *Dialectic of Enlightenment*, ed. Gunzelin Schmid Noerr, trans. Edmund Jephcott (Stanford, CA: Stanford University Press, 2002), 49.

44. Crawford, "Schoenberg in Los Angeles," 7.

45. Schoenberg to Mann, Jan. 15, 1939 (see herein).

46. Bahr, *Weimar on the Pacific*, 273.

47. Melissa Kagen, "'Alle Wege der Welt': Wandering in Jewish German Opera in the Early 20th Century" (PhD diss., Stanford University, 2016).

48. Arnold Schoenberg, *Style and Idea*, ed. Leonard Stein (Berkeley: University of California Press, 1975), 53.

49. Joseph Auner, ed., *A Schoenberg Reader* (New Haven, CT: Yale University Press, 2003), 282.

50. Cited in Bujic, *Arnold Schoenberg*, 184.

51. Schoenberg to Engel, cited in Crawford, "Schoenberg in Los Angeles," 8.

52. See Adrian Daub, *Tristan's Shadow: Sexuality and the Total Work of Art after Wagner* (Chicago: University of Chicago Press, 2013), 57–58.

53. Theodor W. Adorno, *Gesammelte Werke* (Frankfurt am Main: Suhrkamp, 1986), 20:2.467.

54. Auner, *A Schoenberg Reader*, 269.

55. Walter Lewin, "Adorno's 'Zwei Stücke für Streichquartett,' Opus 2 (und Gedanken zum gestörten Verhältnis Schönberg/Adorno," in *Theodor W. Adorno: Der Komponist,* ed. Heinz-Klaus Metzger and Rainer Riehm (Munich: Edition Text & Kritik, 1989), 78.

56. Michael H. Kater, *The Twisted Muse: Musicians and Their Music in the Third Reich* (Oxford: Oxford University Press, 1997), 73–75.

57. Theodor W. Adorno and Alban Berg, *Correspondence, 1925–1935,* ed. Henri Lonitz, trans. Wieland Hoban (Cambridge: Polity, 2005), 184.

58. Cited in Lorenz Jäger, *Adorno: A Political Biography* (New Haven, CT: Yale University Press, 2004), 133.

59. Adorno to Kolisch, June 26, 1942 (see sec. 1, note 79).

60. Cited in Jäger, *Adorno,* 132.

61. Ibid.

62. Hermann Kurzke, *Thomas Mann: Life as a Work of Art* (Princeton, NJ: Princeton University Press, 2002), 473.

63. Myung-Woo Nho, *Die Schönberg-Deutung Adornos und die Dialektik der Aufklärung* (Marburg: Tectum, 2001).

64. Crawford, "Schoenberg in Los Angeles," 13.

65. "Schönberg hat Adorno nie leiden können," *Melos* 41 (1974): 262–64.

66. Theodor W. Adorno, *Philosophische Terminologie: Band 2* (Frankfurt am Main: Suhrkamp, 1974), 618.

67. Ibid., 622.

68. Adorno and Berg, *Briefwechsel,* 187.

69. Thomas Mann, *Die Entstehung des Doktor Faustus* (Frankfurt am Main: S. Fischer 2012), 145.

70. Theodor W. Adorno and Max Horkheimer, *Briefwechsel, Band II, 1938–1944,* ed. Christoph Gödde and Henri Lonitz (Frankfurt am Main: Suhrkamp, 2004), 116.

71. Evelyn Cobley, "Avant-Garde Aesthetics and Fascist Politics," *New German Critique,* no. 86 (Spring-Summer 2002): 43–70, 44.

72. Adorno and Mann, *Correspondence,* 3, 13.

73. Thomas Mann, *Buddenbrooks* (New York: Knopf, 1994), 725.

74. Thomas Mann, *Doctor Faustus* (New York: Knopf, 1992), 147.

75. Arnold Schoenberg, *Letters,* ed. Erwin Stein, trans. Eithne Wilkins and Ernst Kaiser (Berkeley: University of California Press, 1984), 206.

76. Adorno and Mann, *Correspondence,* 13.

77. Todd Kontje, *Thomas Mann's World: Empire, Race, and the Jewish Question* (Ann Arbor: University of Michigan Press, 2011), 58.

78. Hans Vaget, "'Von hoffnungslos anderer Art': Thomas Manns Wälsungenblut im Lichte unserer Erfahrung," *Thomas-Mann-Studien* 30 (2004): 35–58.

79. Barbara Beßlich, *Faszination des Verfalls: Thomas Mann und Oswald Spengler* (Berlin: Akademie Verlag, 2002), 133.

80. T.J. Reed, *Thomas Mann: The Uses of Tradition* (Oxford: Clarendon, 1973), 258.

81. Hermann Kurzke, *Thomas Mann: Epoche, Werk, Wirkung* (Munich: Beck, 2010), 211.

82. Thomas Mann, *Letters of Thomas Mann, 1889–1955* (Berkeley: University of California Press, 1975), 120.

83. Bujic, *Arnold Schoenberg,* 207.

84. Barbara Wiedemann, *Paul Celan. Die Goll-Affäre: Dokumente zu einer "Infamie"* (Frankfurt am Main: Suhrkamp, 2000).

85. Adorno, *Minima Moralia,* 39.

Letters, Diaries, etc. (1930–1948)

SCHOENBERG TO MANN, NOVEMBER 1, 1930

Berlin W 50
Nürnberger-Platz 3
Tel: Bavaria 4466
November 1, 1930
Mr. Thomas Mann

My dear Sir,

I unfortunately do not have the honor of knowing you in person. If in spite of it I approach you with the request that you sign the enclosed appeal,[1] I do so only because I know it to be the most fervent wish of Adolf Loos that six or seven people from among the elite of today lend their support, by way of this appeal, to have his yearning fulfilled: to be permitted to teach.

I would implore you to help in the fulfillment of this wish, if for no other reason than the fact that Loos is so ill that one renders that service perhaps to a dying man.

I can, however, offer a better reason, and if my conviction is correct that people of a certain position innately know who is one of them and who is not, then you will believe me when I say that Loos is truly a great person—as you may know better already than I do.

I'd be very grateful to you if you would send the enclosed sheet, immediately after signing it, to Mrs. Claire Loos, Baden bei Wien, Lakatos Sanatorium, or to me at the above address; for the sixtieth birthday of Loos, which is to be celebrated, is on the tenth of December, and the time is already short.

Meanwhile I remain yours most respectfully and most sincerely,
Arnold Schoenberg

---

1. The influential architect Adolf Loos (1870–1933) had been Schoenberg's close friend and mentor since the turn of the century. When asked by Loos's wife Claire, Schoenberg turned to some of the leading intellectuals (Albert Einstein, Thomas and Heinrich Mann), asking them to join in signing a petition in celebration of Adolf Loos's sixtieth birthday. Schoenberg also wrote to the mayor of Vienna, Dr. Karl Seitz (1869–1950), a Social Democrat, and suggested that Loos design a monument for the city of Vienna. The petition for Loos stated: "Adolf Loos, whom future generations will view as the great benefactor of mankind, liberator from the thrall of superfluous labor, will be 60 years old in December. Those ornamentalists, whose needless designs and harmfulness Loos combated throughout his life, had wanted to get rid of this uncomfortable man who sought to destroy their existence, by hushing up and pretending he did not exist. Their cliques managed to boycott any

publication of Loos' work for decades. They were united in their attempts to prevent any exhibition of Loos' work. Loos, the born teacher, was never granted a teaching position. With private means, quite selflessly, he founded the Loos-School before the war. We know that we could secure the greatest joy for him if we proclaimed and took up his theories again. Admittedly he has been victorious in the battle against ornamentation. But his name has been concealed and there have been books written on the history of doing away with ornamentation that never even mention his name. But as a result of founding the Loos School, we will see to it that the conclusions Loos derived from his theory of freedom from ornamentation, his invention of cubic architecture, will not fall into the wrong hands and be distilled or distorted. We appeal to all who recognize beauty in the dismissal of ornamentation, those who are capable of grasping the grand social plan behind it, to purchase a building block for the future of the Adolf Loos School. Hundreds of young architects the world over are awaiting the opportunity to be able to call themselves Loos' pupils. For those in the know, this is the greatest honor that might be bestowed upon a young architect" (*Prager Tageblatt,* Dec. 4, 1930, 3).

MANN TO SCHOENBERG, NOVEMBER 4, 1930

Dr. Thomas Mann
Munich
Poschingerstrasse 1
November 4, 1930

Dear Mr. Schoenberg:

Many thanks for your impressive letter dated the first of the month. Your entreaties were such that I find it genuinely difficult not to meet your request. However, I hereby appeal to your sense for truthfulness and ask you: what should I do? I have simply never had the good fortune, nor sufficient intellectual prudence, ever to have come into contact with Adolf Loos, his work, his writings or in person. Naturally I am familiar with the name, but it conjures up only very vague associations and I would come across as an insincere hanger-on if, further to your pleas, I were to sign this petition. In light of this confession you are certainly entitled to call me poorly educated; but in what is clearly a very important case my failure can perhaps partly be attributed to the divisive force which a political boundary, namely that between Austria and Germany, still exerts even today. As things stand, I can merely hope you will understand my scruples about signing this petition.[2]

Respectfully yours,
Thomas Mann

---

2. Ultimately the petition in support of Loos was signed by Schoenberg and the writers Karl Kraus (1874–1936), Valéry Larbaud (1881–1957), James Joyce (1882–1941), and Heinrich Mann (1871–1950). On November 10, 1930, Heinrich Mann proposed an amendment: "May I suggest the petition be modified as indicated? Portraying Loos's accomplishments by making various negative points, for example 'liberator from the thrall of labor' and 'sought to destroy their existence,' won't achieve the desired effect. It's important to make positive statements. Once you've made the changes I will gladly sign the petition." On November 12, 1930, Schoenberg replied: "I myself am unhappy with the first sentence, as it's only comprehensible to someone very familiar with Loos' activities and achievements. Nonetheless, I think it's a nice idea: Loos as benefactor of mankind, liberator from the thrall of superfluous labor. It's important to note that Loos doesn't refer to himself as an 'artist,' though I feel he's wrong in that respect when you look at the beauty of his buildings, though perhaps right if you consider his struggle against craftwork. That's the thinking behind the formulation in the first sentence. At any rate, personally I can't agree with the formulation you're proposing. I at least have always found it offensive when people classify me as one of the leaders or initiators or creators of modern music (the creators of the other kind being the better, actual geniuses). The same applies in Loos' case: it is not that he made a contribution to the

architecture of the other kind (or at best calmly allowed himself to be robbed), but rather that he created modern architecture, or if you like the architecture of the coming century. So please don't make your signature dependent on the inclusion of that sentence. If necessary we can quite easily omit the sentence 'sought to destroy their existence' but purely linguistically I do like the relationship between 'hush up' and 'destroy their existence,' though the subordinate clause seems rather weakly tacked on at the end. But I admit the petition does need a positive, easily comprehensible sentence, so by all means add one (as I think I've already mentioned, the petition was not written by me). By the way, here is Claire Loos' address: Baden bei Wien, Sanatorium Lakatos. Many thanks for your prompt and friendly response."

SCHOENBERG TO MANN, NOVEMBER 8, 1930

Herrn Dr. Thomas Mann
München, Poschingerstrasse 1
November 8, 1930

My dear Mr. Mann,

I not only understand your reluctance, I not only anticipated it, but I must confess moreover that, were I in your place, I could not have reacted otherwise.[3] And the difference in our positions toward Loos is neither to my credit nor to your discredit. After all, Loos, who did so much in support of many artists, failed to do what even those most detached from the world do: he neither let anything be exhibited nor photographed, and only now and then something slipped through, on which one could base an opinion. Had I not been friends with him for thirty-five years, I would hardly know more than everyone else.

I consider it a hint of fate that in my attempt yesterday to arrange anew my library after our move here, I came upon a volume by Loos, entitled *Spoken into the Void, 1897–1900*.[4]

I do not want to influence you (I am not presumptuous enough to do that), but I do want to carry out my mission as fully as possible. Hence I am taking the liberty of sending you this volume.

Since it is a presentation copy, I beg you to forgive me for burdening you with the trouble of returning it. I would be happy if you took away from it some impression regarding Loos: of what he already knew before 1900!

I remain most respectful and sincerely yours,
Arnold Schoenberg

---

3. At other times, Schoenberg was less sympathetic to those, such as Albert Einstein, who did not wish to sign the petition, or Heinrich Mann, who set conditions. Thus he wrote to Claire Loos on November 17, 1930: "I include the responses from Einstein and one from Heinrich Mann. I wanted to answer Einstein as follows: '. . . I really do understand something about this; hardly less than the professional newspaperman whom everyone would believe. And I say: Loos has in his profession just as much importance as I do in mine; and perhaps you know that I fancy myself as having paved the way of musical composition for the next one hundred years. As to the other side of the equation: The main purpose of your signature might be to verify that someone of the stature of Adolf Loos at 60 ought not to be unknown to you at this point.' But I am not answering him just as I am not answering [Heinrich] Mann to whom I would have said: 'If I were in Loos' position, I could certainly do without your signature!'" However, Schoenberg wrote to the conductor Fritz

Stiedry (1883–1968) on June 2, 1931: "I received the following letter from the Fr.d.Soz.Monatshefte and send you my reply which I ask you to read and then drop into the mailbox. I hope you value my point of view and understand that it is my ardent desire that this petition be successful. But I am really not at all enthusiastic about these innumerable petitions that always contain the same 30–50 signatures (with Einstein or Thomas or Heinrich Mann at the very top), that are extracted and are hardly read by anyone any more. At the next opportunity, I will show you several petitions that circulated in Berlin that I refused to sign. And you know that I balked at signing the petition for Loos despite my admiration for him, and only did so because he was extremely ill at the time. And so I hope you understand me and I hope very much that with or without a petition you will receive a respected position in Berlin."

4. Loos was the author of numerous articles. Those written from 1897 to 1900 were published in the collection *Ins Leere Gesprochen* (Spoken into the Void). Schoenberg had received a copy in 1923 with a personal dedication as a gift from Loos. The text of the dedication is as follows: "To my like-minded companion along the same path, to my dear, dear friend Arnold Schoenberg in remembrance of a day in Traunkirchen. Adolf Loos."

MANN TO SCHOENBERG, NOVEMBER 26, 1930

Dr. Thomas Mann
Munich 27
Poschingerstrasse 1
November 26, 1930

Dear Maestro,

Many thanks for the literary introduction to Adolf Loos. He is definitely a potent, liberated and important figure. I read many of the essays. Some of what he writes is a little passé (though time has proved him right, and he has certainly helped shape our era), but perhaps only in certain details and externals. Barbarism and patriotic stupidity persist, and for the small group of individuals who want to banish them from the earth, the polemical works of a pioneer will always make a satisfying read.

Yours,
Thomas Mann

MANN'S DIARY

Beverly Hills,[5] Wednesday, April 6, 1938

Slept extremely well. Breakfast with Katia,[6] Erika[7] and young Konrad.[8] Continued writing diary entries. Down to the oceanfront around midday, strolled, lunch on the terrace of the Miramar.[9] Concert organizer Mrs. Frisch[10] came to tea apropos Klaus Pringsheim.[11] Dictated several letters. Unfortunately could not lay hands on London Film Joseph contract.[12]— Cable from Bermann:[13] "Reisiger free."—Very warm around midday. Wore new summer suit at teatime.—Party given by writer Vicki Baum.[14] Nearly all guests German-speaking. The architect Neutra,[15] comedian, musician, actor, Dr. Klemperer,[16] Schoenberg[17] etc. Long conversation before dinner. Buffet dinner. Followed by Bali film[18] with youths in ritual trance.— Beautiful young male Indian dancer.—At home with Colin.[19] Late.

Beverly Hills, Tuesday, April 19, 1938

Very warm. Lunch at the Miramar. Extremely hot in room while taking afternoon rest. To the Dieterles[20] at five in the garden. Iced coffee and cake. Very cold. Film screening: *Pasteur*. Tired, no appetite during Chinese dinner. Conversation afterwards with Schoenberg and Jessner.[21] Good cigar. At home the Franks[22] paid a visit.—Mail, German and Swedish letters of sympathy. Meyer[23] on the Toronto affair. Golo[24] on the mood in Zurich.

---

5. Thomas Mann left Germany in February of 1933 for a reading tour for the fiftieth anniversary of the death of Richard Wagner. He lived in Sanary-sur-Mer for a short period before moving to Switzerland later in 1933. Sanary, on the Côte d'Azur, became home to numerous other German and Austrian writers such as Lion Feuchtwanger (1884–1958), Ludwig Marcuse (1894–1971), Bertolt Brecht (1898–1956), and Franz Werfel (1890–1945). After several years in Switzerland, including numerous lecture tours, Mann moved to the United States in 1938. He visited Los Angeles in March and April of that year; on March 31 he took part in a gala fundraiser for refugees from Nazi Germany, held at the home of film producer Jack Warner, and gave a lecture to six thousand people on the imminent victory of democracy. During the trip he visited various leading cultural figures in the area, including director Max Reinhardt (1873–1943), film producer Walt Disney (1901–66), director Ernst Lubitsch (1892–1947), author Upton Sinclair (1878–1968), architect Richard Neutra (1892–1970), and writer Vicki Baum (1888–1960), many of whom had also fled Nazi Germany. It is clear from Mann's diary entries (April 8, 1938: "Party given by Max Reinhardt. Beautiful, well-situated house"; April 10, 1938: "Party given by Lubitsch. Another beautiful house") that he was impressed by the other refugees' circumstances. He remained in Princeton from the end of 1938 until July 1940 before moving to Los Angeles.

6. Mann's wife, Katia, née Pringsheim (1883–1980). Her father, mathematics professor Alfred Pringsheim (1850–1941), had been an early admirer and correspondent of Wagner's and the first sponsor of the Bayreuth Festival.

7. Mann's eldest daughter, Erika (1905–69), journalist and author, married to English writer W.H. Auden (1907–73).

8. Konrad Kellen (Katzenellenbogen) (1913–2007) was Mann's secretary from 1941 to 1943.

9. Built in 1921, the Miramar Hotel in Santa Monica overlooks Ocean Avenue, Palisades Park (dubbed "the Promenade" by Mann), and the Pacific Ocean.

10. The singer, music pedagogue, and concert organizer Fay Templeton Frisch.

11. Mann's brother-in-law Klaus Pringsheim (1883–1972), a composer and conductor. Pringsheim studied under Gustav Mahler and became musical director at the Deutsches Theater in Prague before emigrating to Japan, where he took a professorship. His signature appears on two postcards sent to Schoenberg from Prague: the first was signed by conductor and critic Karl Horwitz, Gustav Mahler, Alma Mahler, Alban Berg, Otto Klemperer, conductor Arthur Bodansky (whose brother married Schoenberg's cousin Malvine Goldschmied), Ida Bodansky, and Klaus Pringsheim on September 20, 1908; the second was signed by Schoenberg's brother-in-law Alexander Zemlinsky, Ida Zemlinsky, singer Mizzi Pappenheim (librettist for Schoenberg's opera *Erwartung*), Karl Horwitz, Fritzi Handl, Will Handl, Klaus Pringsheim, Mizzi Horwitz, Felix Adler, pianist Etta Werndorff (who performed at the 1920 premiere of Schoenberg's Three Piano Pieces, op. 11), Toni Koehnen, Winkelmann and Keussler, on the occasion of the premiere of the opera *Es war einmal*, by Alexander Zemlinsky. Pringsheim also wrote to Schoenberg from Berlin in November of 1929 about the Society of German Film Music Authors, around the time Schoenberg was working on his Accompaniment to a Film Scene, op. 34.

12. Since 1933 Mann had been in negotiations over the film rights to *Joseph and His Brothers*. Here he is referring to an offer from Sir Alexander Korda's London Film in Great Britain. None of the proposed projects ever saw the light of day. Mann, *Tagebücher, 1937–1939*, 688.

13. Mann's publisher, Gottfried Bermann-Fischer (1897–1995), had been head of his father-in-law Samuel Fischer's publishing house since 1928. Bermann-Fischer left Germany in 1935 and reestablished the publishing house in Vienna. In 1938 he fled again and reestablished the business in Stockholm. In 1941 he fled Sweden for the United States. Thomas Mann, *Tagebücher, 1944–1.4.1946*, ed. Inge Jens (Frankfurt am Main: S. Fischer, 1986), 353–54. To conserve space, subsequent citations of this source will use the shortened form *Tagebücher, 1944–1946*.

14. Austrian writer Vicki Baum (1888–1960) had studied harp in Vienna and married the conductor Richard Lert. Her novel *Grand Hotel* (1929) was filmed in 1932, winning an Oscar in the Best Film category. From 1933 to 1942 she lived at 1461 Amalfi Drive in Pacific Palisades, close to where Thomas Mann built his house. Cornelius Schnauber, *Hollywood Haven* (Riverside, CA: Ariadne, 1992), 107.

15. Austrian architect Richard Neutra (1892–1970) studied under Adolf Loos and worked for a time with Erich Mendelsohn (1887–1953) in Germany. In 1923 he moved to the United States, where he spent a short period working with Frank Lloyd Wright (1867–1959). He then lived and worked with his wife and fellow émigré Austrian Rudolf Schindler. On March 18, 1938, Neutra drove Mann to the beachside homes he had built, which Mann described disparagingly as "Cubist glass box style, awful." Mann, *Tagebücher, 1937–1939*, 210. On January 24, 1936, Schoenberg wrote to architect Heinrich Kulka (a colleague of Loos): "I'll probably be able to build myself a house here, and as you can imagine it's terribly sad that Loos is no longer alive and that I can't have it built by one of his pupils such as yourself. At any rate, I want a modern house and am therefore in contact with two modern architects. One is American, the other is Richard Neutra, who is from Vienna and whom you probably know. Evidently he is also from Loos' circle and

designs very handsome homes, though perhaps a little more doctrinaire than Loos, more deliberate, and to some extent influenced by Bauhaus principles. But, as ever, he has Viennese taste and is familiar with authors' needs." Ultimately Schoenberg did not in fact have a house built, instead buying a Spanish Colonial–style home in Brentwood Park.

16. German conductor Otto Klemperer (1885–1973) helped Mahler premiere his Eighth Symphony and from 1927 to 1931 conducted at the Kroll Opera, including the Berlin premiere of Schoenberg's *Erwartung.*

17. This was the first documented occasion on which Schoenberg and Thomas Mann met. Following the Nazis' book-burning campaign (May 10, 1933), Schoenberg had fled Berlin with his wife, Gertrud (1898–1967), and their daughter Nuria (b. 1932) on May 16–17, 1933, having received a telegram from Gertrud's brother, the violinist Rudolf Kolisch, containing the encrypted message: "Due to asthma urgently recommend change of air." The family stayed several months in France before coming to the United States on October 3, 1933. Schoenberg taught for one winter at the small Malkin Conservatory in Brookline, Massachusetts. In September of 1934, following his sixtieth birthday, he moved to Los Angeles, this time genuinely owing to his asthma. He initially taught at the University of Southern California and then at UCLA until his retirement in 1944.

18. In the late 1930s a number of Balinese films previously censored owing to scenes containing female nudity were released in the United States. They included *Goona Goona* (1930), *The Island of Demons* (1933), and *Legong: Dance of the Virgins* (1935).

19. Rumanian impresario, theater and film agent Samuel C. Colin (1909–67), who had immigrated to the United States in 1935, was trying to produce Mann's *Joseph* novel for the screen. Mann used Colin as the model for the concert agent Saul Fitelberg in *Doktor Faustus.* Thomas Mann, *Tagebücher, 1940–1943,* 783.

20. German actor and director William Dieterle (1893–1972) and his wife, Charlotte, had been working in Hollywood since 1932, where among other things he had directed *The Story of Louis Pasteur* and *The Life of Emile Zola.* The Dieterles were close friends of the Schoenbergs, and in 1936 Charlotte Dieterle approached Schoenberg with her text for a Beethoven film. Schoenberg demurred: "Because of my position in the world of music, I would have to adopt a particular approach, despite not actually feeling that way myself. If, working from my own imagination and sensibility, I were to conjure up an image of Beethoven and use it for a film, the world would have to duly accept that: the entire conception would be a musical one from the outset, and what I then did with Beethoven's music would be not merely an application but a fantasy, a symphonic-dramatic fantasy which in artistic terms would be just as justifiable as if I were to write variations on a Beethoven theme. However, if, in an ancillary fashion, I were to rework Beethoven's music for someone else's text, even a good one (and I'm in no doubt that yours is good), that would not sit well with what's expected of me, namely producing my own material." Schoenberg advised Dieterle to approach Klemperer about the music and for the title role suggested Peter Lorre (1904–64), who had become well-known for his portrait of a serial killer in Fritz Lang's *M* (1931).

21. Expressionist and antinaturalist director Leopold Jessner (1878–1945) had been director of the Staatliches Schauspielhaus in Berlin. In 1933 he emigrated first to Palestine and then to the United States. He was on the committee of the Jewish Club of 1933, Inc., which provided assistance to Jewish refugees arriving in Los Angeles. On one of the club's preprinted contribution forms, on which Jessner had written by hand "To Mr. Schoenberg," Schoenberg wrote: "The Jews haven't yet taken on board that my first name is Arnold. Yet no doubt they're familiar with the

first names Paul [Hindemith], Béla [Bartók], Igor [Stravinsky] and Jan [Sibelius]. The Jewish community probably doesn't see my activities as much of an achievement."

22. The writer and dramatist Bruno Frank (1887–1945), a close friend of Mann's since 1911 and his neighbor in Munich, and his wife, Elisabeth (1903–79), daughter of operetta diva Fritzi Massary. The Franks fled Berlin on the day after the Reichstag fire (March 27, 1933), arriving in Hollywood—where Bruno Frank began working for Metro-Goldwyn-Mayer—in 1937.

23. Political journalist Agnes E. Meyer, née Ernst (1887–1970), wife of American banker, philanthropist, and editor of the *Washington Post* Eugene Meyer (1875–1959). Meyer was a frequent contributor to the *Washington Post*, the *New York Times Book Review, Atlantic Monthly,* and *Reader's Digest.* Mann corresponded with her regularly for nearly twenty years. Thomas Mann and Agnes E. Meyer, *Briefwechsel, 1937–1955,* ed. Hans Rudolf Vaget (Frankfurt am Main: S. Fisher, 1992).

24. Mann's son, the writer Golo Mann (1909–94), left Germany in 1933, emigrating initially to France and then to Switzerland. He visited his parents in Princeton in 1939. Following internment at Les Milles in 1940, he fled on foot across the Pyrenees, accompanied by Heinrich and Nelly Mann and Franz and Alma Mahler-Werfel. After the war he taught history at Claremont College in California.

SCHOENBERG TO MANN, DECEMBER 28, 1938

Dec. 28, 1938

My dear Dr. Mann,

May I ask you for a favor?

Would you read the enclosed article[25] and help me to get it published?

I have tried in vain now for at least four weeks to get it published in one of the larger magazines, and even the "agencies" that handle the placement of articles rejected it. The reasons they gave were 1) enough has already been written on this subject, 2) the article contains, to be sure, very interesting ideas, but "too many" of them and I had better enlarge just "a few" of them, and then it would perhaps be of general interest.

In short, I should prattle, chat, repeat myself a hundred times, as do indeed all the authors hereabouts.

That I cannot and will not do.

So I am now asking you for advice. What can I do? Or can you help me?

I have thought of sending the article to some place or other in Europe, but I have no connections in England, France, or Switzerland. Could you do anything to help or tell me to whom to turn. I do believe that a word of recommendation from you could overcome the superstition that (even when he can think) a musician cannot write about anything but music.

May I ask you to return, along with your answer, the article which you hopefully have read, for I am eager to find you concurring regarding the importance of its subject matter.

I remain with cordial regards and respectfully your,
Arnold Schoenberg

----

25. This letter refers to Appendix I, Arnold Schoenberg's "Four-Point Program for Jewry." In this article, the culmination of five years of writing and discussions over "Jewish Affairs" (as Schoenberg referred to it), Schoenberg focuses on the necessity of a mass emigration of Jews from Europe. Schoenberg himself had fled Berlin shortly after the book burning in May 1933. He arrived in Los Angeles a year later. Nevertheless, by way of newspaper articles and his active correspondence, Schoenberg was well aware of the catastrophic situation in Europe. His "Four-Point Program," in which he foresees the extermination of seven million European Jews, is undoubtedly one of the most precise predictions of the Holocaust. Schoenberg had been aware of the danger that Hitler posed from as early as April 1923, when the first newspaper reports about his anti-Semitic speeches were printed. Schoenberg's letter of May 4, 1923, to the painter Wassily Kandinsky not only mentions Hitler by name but asks, "Where should Anti-Semitism lead to, if not to

acts of violence?" Similarly, in his letter of January 1, 1934, to the composer Anton Webern, Schoenberg declares, "I don't know what your thoughts are on this, but I find it outrageous that a man like [the writer Gerhard] Hauptmann can today agree with a party that not only has a program, but carries it out to the letter. And this program has as its goal nothing more nor less than the extermination of all the Jews!"

MANN TO SCHOENBERG, JANUARY 9, 1939

Thomas Mann
65 Stockton Street
Princeton, N.J.
January 9, 1939

Arnold Schönberg
116 N. Rockingham Avenue
Brentwood Park
Los Angeles, California

Dear Mr. Schoenberg,

You've done me the honor of sending your manuscript and in doing so caused me a period of considerable disquiet. My inner response fluctuated between warm approval and slight dismay over the sometimes powerful allure, not only of your individual polemical statements but also of your overall intellectual stance, which, however, definitely comes across as somewhat fascist. You'll perhaps forgive me for using that term, which naturally is inappropriate from a content standpoint; but what I mean is a certain disposition towards terrorism, which in my view constitutes descending to the level of fascist attitudes. There's something very human about that kind of reaction to brutal pressure and attack; but I do feel we mustn't give in to that temptation, and in particular that taking an unconditional position in power politics ill becomes the Jewish community's special spirituality, which you so rightly describe as fundamentally religious.

It goes without saying that your essay contains important and welcome things. I found the polemic against anti-antisemitism particularly admirable. In reality the appeal to reason and logic has been so fruitless that in real struggles one really can't build on it. Clearly your essay needs to be published, and we need to think carefully about the various options. It deals with the question of the Jews, and belongs in a Jewish journal. But from a human standpoint a Jewish journal understandably might not be falling over itself to publish a piece in which Jewish leadership as a whole is attacked so radically and in such unrestrained terms. I do feel you should tone down the defamatory and very personal element before thinking about offering the article for publication. I'm returning the manuscript with thanks and suggest you take another look at it from a practical journalistic standpoint.

In the meantime I will continue to think about various options for publishing it. An obvious idea would be to consider our Swiss journal *Mass und Wert*.[26] However, so far we've avoided addressing specifically Jewish problems in the journal, and I doubt I could persuade the editorial team to accept an article of that kind. At any rate, there would have to be a German version.

Respectfully yours,
Thomas Mann

---

26. *Mass und Wert* covered "free German culture," with an editorial team consisting of Mann, Konrad Falke (1880–1942), and Ferdinand Lion (1883–1965). Published in Switzerland by Oprecht, it evidently caused Mann considerable headaches: "Big family lunch. Spoke with Erika afterwards about the problems with *Mass und Wert*, the (Russian?) money, Golo, Lion, the question of editorial approach. Major difficulties." Mann, *Tagebücher, 1937–1939*, 347 (January 14, 1939, diary entry).

SCHOENBERG TO MANN, JANUARY 15, 1939

January 15, 1939

Dr. Thomas Mann
65 Stockton Street
Princeton, N.J.

Most esteemed Dr. Mann,

Heartfelt thanks for your letter. It gave me much encouragement. For although I am accustomed to failures, in the face of such a complete failure I had begun to doubt whether what I had written was useful. That is really the worst thing that could possibly happen, feeling insecure about one's work. Why: it isn't even possible for me to get an article accepted?

In a democratic country everyone has the right to state openly his opinion. The right, to be sure, but not necessarily the possibility of doing so: for that is only possible for those in power. And they are the ones who say exactly what others really want to hear.

I do not hesitate in acknowledging that I am not a Leftist, insofar as that I would not grant to everyone the right of giving his opinion, but only to those who truly have opinions worthy of being stated. I also would not call myself a Rightist, because I do not believe in the equalizing value of dulling the mind. Maybe I am just a progressive conservative, who would like to further and develop things that ought to be preserved.

You find my article to be caustic. Is it unduly caustic? I placed no blame on anyone, but I cannot prevent the facts from having the effect of being insulting. "It's not I who am screaming," I once said, when they accused me unfairly. "It's the Truth that is screaming." How ought we to handle leaders whose incompetence has caused unprecedented catastrophes as those of the present? How do we get rid of them? How do we educate people not to believe in that which is near and convenient, but rather to sacrifice themselves for what is necessary.

I doubt that one can talk Jews into uniting merely by way of soft-talking them into submission. I doubt very much that one could urge them into an all-inclusive action without using a strong, all-inclusive remedy. But I am also sure that these eloquent leaders will not have been brought to silence, even after there will no longer be anyone present to listen to them. They have to be gotten rid of.

Pulling teeth and amputation are also deeds of violence. Annihilation by means of unmitigated representations of destructive facts is, by comparison, purely an act of violence on the will.

Please do not misunderstand me. I understand the value of a democracy, although I am just not able to overlook its weakest points: that through the orthodox exaggeration of its principles, it thus includes the possibility of its own destruction. Free speech allows anyone to make propaganda concerning a change of the form of government, and everywhere democracy has proven itself incapable of preventing this consequence. And I do not overlook the evil of Fascism, which cannot help but place its inherent power in the wrong hands.

Certainly until now there has never been a form of government that has been able to make human society happy, except for a few individuals, inasmuch as their happiness would depend upon a certain form of government.

You are certainly right when . . .

I had to interrupt here in order to go to my class[27] and I have only been able to continue today from where I left off.

But since I have to leave again now, and fear that I will not be able to recapture the thread of what I was saying, I would like to close now and put this letter in the mail.

Let me thank you most whole-heartedly once again. I am afraid that I have spent over two weeks working most strenuously on the article for nothing: writing it in English and then working on it with an American[28] in order to make certain it was correct, and also improve it.

Perhaps I will hear from you again in this matter.[29] In any case, should a German version be needed, I could prepare it in a few days, provided my German is still good enough.

With heartfelt respect and genuine devotion. Yours,
Arnold Schoenberg

---

27. Schoenberg taught at the University of California, Los Angeles (UCLA), as well as his home in Brentwood.

28. This refers to the music scholar Noel Heath Taylor, who had written Schoenberg in August of 1938, asking for an interview. Schoenberg hired Taylor, who took dictation and corrected English texts, among them the "Fundamentals of Musical Composition." On January 15, 1939, Schoenberg wrote to Taylor: "I received a very encouraging answer from Thomas Mann yesterday. He was very interested in my ideas, but had doubts that, given the aggressive nature of the text, it might be difficult to publish the article. I still do not know what I can do with it. He is going to try for a possibility in Switzerland." "A Four-Point Program for

Jewry" was only first published in 1979: *Journal of the Arnold Schoenberg Institute* 3, no. 1 (1979): 49–67.

29. Schoenberg's biographer, H.H. Stuckenschmidt, reported: "In 1939 [*sic*] Thomas Mann who had for a year been Professor at Princeton University, moved to Los Angeles, because the climate seemed more beneficial to him than on the East Coast. He soon met with Schoenberg who spoke to the writer about his theories concerning a United Jewish Party. Mann reacted in a respectful, reserved manner." H.H. Stuckenschmidt, *Arnold Schoenberg: His Life, World and Works* (New York: Schirmer, 1977), 436.

MANN'S DIARY

Brentwood,[30] Sunday, September 22, 1940

Did a little work on Zawi-Rê-Kap during the morning.[31] Lunch with the Walters.[32] Coffee in the garden. Optimistic observations about politics. Spain's rejection of the war. Ribbentrop's meetings with Mussolini.— Finished the wonderful *Dämonen.*—Walk after tea (with Liesl Frank). Then wrote to Heinrich[33] in Lisbon. Went with Gumpert[34] and the children to musical evening at Salka Viertel's.[35] Lot of people there. Schoenberg arranged a performance of his old-fashioned-modern *Pierrot Lunaire*[36] with Erika Wagner[37] (Fiore). Dinner party at the Walters.[38] Coffee too strong. Sad news about torpedoing of a British ship[39] full of children headed for Canada.—Greeted Schoenberg. Home in good time.

Pacific Palisades,[40] Sunday, August 17, 1941

Rather emotional this morning upon completion of the retrospective on courage; created structure for a new section covering Joseph's period in office. At 12:30 we were driven by the son of the household to H.'s,[41] at the beach half an hour from here. Numerous people there, the Schoenbergs,[42] the Lewisohns[43] from New York, young people. Walked along the beach with Mrs. Lewisohn while others swam. Buffet lunch in the garden.[44] Arranged a meeting with the Lewisohns for New York. Back home by four, had a rest. Went for a walk with Katia after tea, then dictated letters to Huldschinsky[45] and Oprecht[46] to her.—Amusing evening news item about Hitler's return to Berchtesgaden, evidently sick with anger over the resistance the Russians are putting up to his noble intentions. Stupid fool. Professor Sauerbruch[47] and Swiss psychiatrist.—Savage Russian counterattacks, heavy German losses. Imminent meeting between the three world powers in Moscow. Large loan to Russia.[48]—Book about Kafka by Tauber,[49] sent by Oprecht.

Pacific Palisades, Friday, September 17, 1942

Reworked penultimate passage of Washington speech.[50] Corrected typed version of *Verkündigung.*[51] Went for a short walk, was picked up by car by Katia. Lunch in the restaurant opposite the Chalet, as latter closed. Weather cleared following overcast, cool morning. Read *The Nation*[52] at home. Had a rest. At 6:30 went to a cocktail party at the Leydens;[53] lot of people there, Feuchtwanger,[54] Remarque,[55] agreeable Chinese woman, Bernheimer, the actor T., Swedish aristocrat with among other things Italian background. Read parts of Bismarck's *Erinnerungen* before and after dinner. Resistance on the outskirts of Stalingrad continues. At any rate, capture of the city delayed so long that moral impact all but lost. Essay by Don Sturzo[56] in the *New Leader*[57] about Germany's future following its defeat, which is being taken as a given. Report on the Jewish horror in Europe.[58] Goebbels:[59] The Jews will be eradicated regardless of whether Germany is defeated or victorious.[60]

Pacific Palisades, Saturday, September 26, 1942
   Spent the morning struggling over a new broadcast to Germany about the Jewish horror.[61] . . .—"Nazis losing grip in Stalingrad."

Pacific Palisades, Sunday, September 27, 1942
   In the morning rapidly wrote down the program about the Jewish horror. . . . Stalingrad is holding firm. Extensive coverage in the paper.

Pacific Palisades, Tuesday, September 29, 1942
   . . . At midday drove to NBC, read the message about the Jews, went well.[62]

Pacific Palisades, Monday, May 3, 1943
   Cloudy and cool. Wrote some notes on *Dr. Faust*.[63] Went for a hike in the morning, drove back. Lunch with Fridolin.[64] Journals. Dictation in the afternoon. Dinner with the Werfels and Frank. Conversation about Nietzsche,—the sympathy he evinces—with him, and more general hopelessness. Prospect of meetings[65] with Schoenberg[66] and Stravinsky.[67] . . .

Pacific Palisades, Sunday, May 8, 1943
   In the morning wrote letter to Agnes Meyer in Washington; concealed none of my bitterness. Went to Westwood for a haircut. Long wait, as the shop full of young soldiers, engineers or artillery cadets. Much to Katia's relief the housekeeper, the young Miss Gussy,[68] has returned. After lunch read the *New Leader*, numerous interesting things. Finished the letter to Agnes Meyer after tea. At seven went to Beverly Hills to the Werfels; took a long time to find the house.[69] Evening with the Schoenbergs. Got him to talk at length about music and life as a composer; fortunately he is himself insisting we see more of them. Left later. Read a little of the *Zürcher Weltwoche*. Articles recalcitrantly circuitous and malicious. Cultural matters caused me pangs of homesickness for Europe.—According to Schoenberg, modern music—including twelve-tone music—has been permitted in Germany again since about 1940 and even to some extent

encouraged despite "degenerate art."[70] Must bear that in mind. State may have contradictory attitude towards Leverkühn's music and towards Nietzsche.

Pacific Palisades, Friday, May 14, 1943
. . . More unrest in Europe. Further executions in Holland. Massacre in the Warsaw Ghetto, inmates evidently chose to fight despite lost cause.

Pacific Palisades, Sunday, May 15, 1943
. . . German Leningrad offensive. Prelude to summer offensive. Heavy bombing on the continent. Have been asked by United Jewish Committee, San Francisco to give a speech on the Jewish horror on June 10.

Pacific Palisades, Monday, May 17, 1943
Finished the extracts that define Leverkühn's musical type. First name will be Anselm, Andreas or *Adrian.* . . .[71]

Pacific Palisades, Friday, June 11, 1943
Spent the morning working on third chapter of the novel. "The strange life of Adrian Leverkühn, narrated by a friend."—Went for a brief stroll with Katia. Numerous journals arrived by mail. Dictated the end of the San Francisco speech this afternoon.[72] Then started letter to Agnes Meyer.[73] Schoenbergs and Hardts[74] to dinner . . .

Pacific Palisades, Friday, July 2, 1943
. . . Finished letter to Agnes Meyer, wrote to Arlt[75] about Schoenberg's *Harmonielehre.*[76]

Pacific Palisades, Wednesday, July 21, 1943
Woke late. Under the influence of the slow movement *Dankgebet des Genesenen* in yesterday's Beethoven quartet.—Wrote a little of Chapter VII. Bereaved young Katzenellenbogen paid a visit. Strolled on the Promenade. Rembrandt album from Phaidon Verlag, New York newspapers. In the afternoon wrote to Agnes Meyer.[77] Text from Dr. Adorno[78] entitled *Philosophy of New Music.*[79] Russian general offensive. Orel the new Stalingrad? Enna captured in Sicily. More staunch German resistance.

Pacific Palisades, Monday, July 26, 1943
. . . Finished reading the Adorno text.[80] Moments of conjecture as to how to position Adrian. Difficulties must emerge in their entirety before they

can be overcome. Art's desperate situation a harmonious moment. Must keep sight of main idea of bought inspiration carried away by exhilaration.

Pacific Palisades, Monday, July 30, 1943
   . . . After tea wrote letters to Lubitsch and Schoenberg. Spoke to Bruno Frank on the telephone about the Russia's Free Germany announcement. In the evening listened to Russian atonal music on the radio, Prometheus tone poem.[81] . . .

––––––––––

30. Mann arrived in Los Angeles on July 5, 1940, and immediately moved into a Spanish Colonial–style house at 441 North Rockingham Avenue in Brentwood Park, just a few blocks from Schoenberg's house at 116 North Rockingham. Mann's son Klaus described the house in his diary as "appealingly spacious, with a remarkable view, nice swimming pool. Rather sparsely furnished and messy. Otherwise attractive." Klaus Mann, *Tagebücher, 1940–1943*, ed. Joachim Heimannsberg, Peter Laemmle, and Wilfried F. Schoeller (Spangenberg: Rowohlt, 1991), 46. At that time Brentwood Park had not yet been fully developed, and at various times of year many of the larger lots were used as small flower gardens. The Schoenbergs moved into their twenty-year-old Spanish Colonial–style house in 1935. The Depression, and the considerable distance from downtown Los Angeles at a time when the freeways had not yet been built, meant these homes were still very affordable. The street gradually underwent development, eventually attracting celebrities such as Shirley Temple, Linda Ronstadt, and O. J. Simpson.
   31. Joseph's prison in Egypt, in Mann's *Joseph, der Ernährer.*
   32. The conductor Bruno Walter (1876–1962) was Gustav Mahler's assistant at the Vienna State Opera in 1901 and later conducted the first performances of Mahler's *Lied von der Erde* and Ninth Symphony. Having fled the Nazis, he settled in Beverly Hills (608 Bedford Drive, near the home of Franz and Alma Werfel).
   33. Mann's elder brother, Heinrich (1871–1950) (major works include *Professor Unrat* [1905; filmed as *Der blaue Engel*] and *Der Untertan* [1919]; president of the poetry section of the Prussian Academy of Arts from 1931 to 1933). Heinrich Mann had left Germany in February of 1933 and settled in Sanary. On September 13, 1940, with the help of Varian Fry (1907–67) and US Vice Consul Hiram Bingham IV (1903–88), he fled across the Pyrenees along with his wife, Nelly; his nephew Golo; and the Werfels (Thomas Mann received a telegram about their whereabouts on September 20). After reaching Lisbon, they sailed to New York, arriving on October 13. Alma Mahler-Werfel, *Mein Leben* (Frankfurt am Main: S. Fischer, 1960), 314–21. Once in Los Angeles, Heinrich Mann took a modest-paying job with Warner Bros. studios.
   34. The Berlin doctor and writer Martin Gumpert (1897–1955), who had immigrated to New York in 1936. Erika Mann was a close friend of Gumpert, though evidently not interested in marrying him.
   35. The actress Salka Viertel, née Steuermann (1887–1978). Salka Viertel was the sister of pianist and Schoenberg student Eduard Steuermann (1892–1964) and of actress Rose Gielen (mother of conductor Michael Gielen [b. 1927]), and the mother of screenwriter Peter Viertel (1920–2007). Salka Viertel had married the author Berthold Viertel (1885–1953) and moved to Los Angeles in 1928. After the latter moved to New York, she separated from him and began a relationship with the young director Gottfried Reinhardt (1911–94), son of Max Reinhardt. She

was also a friend of actress Greta Garbo (1905–90) and worked on screenplays for many of her films, including *Queen Christina* and *Anna Karenina*. Salka Viertel's house on Mabery Road in Santa Monica became a kind of salon for many of the European émigrés, Thomas Mann and Schoenberg included. One of the notable episodes from that period was the birthday dinner for Heinrich Mann in May 1941, described in her book *The Kindness of Strangers* (New York: Holt, Rinehart, and Winston, 1970), 250–51 (at which Schoenberg was probably not present). During the dinner the Mann brothers gave seemingly endless speeches of mutual praise and admiration, to the detriment of the roast beef waiting to be served.

36. *Pierrot Lunaire* (1912) (German by Otto Erich Hartleben), for one voice, piano, flute (also piccolo), clarinet (also bass clarinet), violin (also viola), and violoncello, op. 21, is considered one of Schoenberg's most important works. Its free tonality proved tremendously popular and was referred to by Stravinsky as "the solar plexus and spirit of all modern music from the early twentieth century." This performance at Salka Viertel's coincided with recording of the work at CBS studios (September 24–26, 1940) under Schoenberg's conductorship. Along with Stiedry-Wagner, the other performers were Salka Viertel's brother Eduard Steuermann (piano), Schoenberg's brother-in-law Rudolf Kolisch (violin/viola), Stefan Auber (cello), Leonard Posella (flute), and Kalman Bloch (clarinet/bass clarinet). See Avior Byron, "The Test Pressings of Schoenberg Conducting *Pierrot Lunaire: Sprechstimme* Reconsidered," *Music Theory Online* 12, no. 1 (2006): www.mtosmt. org/issues/mto.06.12.1/mto.06.12.1.byron.html.

37. The actress Erika Stiedry-Wagner (1892–1974), wife of conductor Fritz Stiedry (1883–1968), who had been assistant to Mahler in Vienna and conducted at the premiere of Schoenberg's opera *Die glückliche Hand.* Her reputation was partly based on her performances of *Pierrot Lunaire* under Schoenberg's own direction. She had also played Fiore in the December 1919 Vienna premiere of Mann's *Fiorenza.*

38. Salka Viertel recalled: "The two great composers, Stravinsky and Schoenberg, avoided each other ostentatiously, and in fact only shortly before Schoenberg's death did they mutually acknowledge their importance. Later Stravinsky paid great homage to Schoenberg and to his music. During his first years in Los Angeles, Schoenberg was teaching counterpoint at the University of California. His classes were crowded not only by students but also by jazz musicians of whom many also took private lessons from him. Edward used his summer vacations in Santa Monica to rehearse and prepare performances of Schoenberg's compositions, one of which, the *Pierrot Lunaire,* took place in our living room, with Schoenberg conducting and the lovely Erika Wagner (Mrs. Fritz Stiedry in private life) speaking the text. All the literary and musical elite was present, among others three famous conductors: Bruno Walter, Otto Klemperer and Fritz Stiedry. The applause was not unanimous, but it was led by Thomas Mann, clapping his hands heartily while Bruno Walter whispered in his ear, obviously disapproving." Viertel, *The Kindness of Strangers,* 259–60. Klaus Mann wrote in his diaries: "This was followed by a small-scale afternoon party at Salka Viertel's, with the people from the Kolisch Quartet, Gottfried Reinhardt, Arnold Schoenberg etc. (Schoenberg comes across as very urbane and clever, with an ugly wife, himself rather ghastly, but two very cute children)." Klaus Mann, *Tagebücher, 1940–1943,* 47.

39. The SS *City of Benares* was torpedoed on September 18, 1940. On board were Mann's daughter Monika (1910–92) and her husband Jenö Lányi (1902–40), along with ninety children being evacuated from Britain by the Children's Overseas Reception Board. Of the passengers, 248, among them Lányi and seventy-seven of the evacuated children, drowned. After twenty hours in a lifeboat Monika was rescued, having watched her husband drown. Thomas Mann only discovered they had

been on board six days later on September 24. He wrote in his diary: "In the morning a cable arrived from Erika saying Moni and Lányi were on board the torpedoed ship, Lányi is dead and Moni is in hospital in Scotland (in what condition?!). Erika is picking her up from the hospital, so evidently she's able to travel.—Horror and repugnance. Sympathy for poor, fragile child." Thomas Mann, *Tagebücher, 1940–1943*, 153.

40. Following a long trip to the East Coast, during which Mann met with President and Mrs. Roosevelt on April 8, 1941, Mann moved house to 740 Amalfi Drive in Pacific Palisades, just over a mile west of the house on Rockingham. Later Mann commissioned the emigré German architect J. R. Davidson to build a new house at 1550 San Remo Drive in Pacific Palisades, where he lived from 1942 to 1952.

41. Mann possibly means the composer Serge Hovey (1920–89), who had studied with Schoenberg and Hanns Eisler (1898–1962) (Eisler had also emigrated and was living in Malibu). Cf. the editors' comment in Thomas Mann, *Tagebücher, 1940–1943*, 855 ("Not clear who is meant. Probably film producer John Houseman, who lived in Malibu.") Hovey and his sister Tamara, offspring of Carl and Sonya Hovey, shot film footage of Mann and Schoenberg, possibly for different reasons, at their house in Malibu. Filmmaking equipment was provided specifically for this purpose by their screenwriter mother (whose film scripts included *The Hunchback of Notre Dame*). This footage is available on YouTube: www.youtube.com /watch?v=hr_ViW2rNt4. The footage of Mann was shot on April 16, 1938, when Mann was visiting the Hoveys along with Agnes Meyer and Elizabeth Meyer. Mann, *Tagebücher, 1937–1939*, 208–9 ("Moovy-Aufnahmen der Kinder"). Mann's daughter Monika was probably a guest at one of these parties, as on November 5, 1950, she wrote to Schoenberg: "I clearly recall having a nice chat with you years ago in Los Angeles, at a garden party somewhere by the ocean."

42. On March 26, 1941, Schoenberg had given a lecture entitled "Method of Composing with Twelve Tones" at UCLA. Normally Schoenberg did not provide his students with instruction in his twelve-tone method, but he had already given earlier versions of this lecture at Princeton (on March 6, 1934) and at the University of Southern California (in 1935). See Claudio Spies, "Vortrag / 12 T K / Princeton," in *Perspectives of New Music* 13, no. 1 (1974): 58–136. Schoenberg gave the lecture on one further occasion, in Chicago on May 2, 1946. It was published for the first time in 1949, in a French translation by René Leibowitz, and also appeared in English in Schoenberg's *Style and Idea* (New York: Philosophical Library, 1950).

43. The American writer and translator Ludwig Lewisohn (1882–1955)—an early proponent of Thomas Mann—and his wife, Thelma.

44. Monika Mann's American notes written in 1940 probably referred to a similar party: "Garden party at which we sat at Schoenberg's table. There's something slightly athletic about him (we got a sense of the connection with the *Gurrelieder*)." Monika Mann, *Das fahrende Haus: Aus den Leben einer Weltbürgerin* (Reinbek: Rowohlt, 2007), 51. In 1972, in a letter to H. H. Stuckenschmidt, she recalled: "Later in California we found ourselves sitting next to Arthur Rubinstein. Funnily enough I didn't realize it. He only 'revealed' who he was during the course of our conversation—you know how that is. . . . Anyway, it was all very pleasant. Schoenberg, who kept shoveling wonderful titbits onto my plate, resembled a very sly tennis coach (in white)." Ibid., 62. She elaborated on the story in "Ich besitze kein Autogramm": "I was at a garden party in Hollywood, with all sorts of film people, racing drivers and intellectuals, globetrotters, virtuosi, new philosophers, hangers-on and agents. A man came and sat down next to me. He was small, upright, sun-tanned and dressed from head to toe in woolen whites. He looked a well-preserved seventy, no doubt some former professional sportsman, an Olympic skater perhaps. Nice

weather, he said, or something to that effect. Clutching a plate in each hand, he climbed over the back of the bench to join me. The mood at our table was hale and hearty, feudal almost. I always think for two, it keeps me young, he said, putting one of his plates down in front of me. As he had helped himself generously at the Swedish buffet, it was somewhat superfluous that I kept chattering on about the weekend's polo, a bicycle race in Marseille and the Finnish swimmer who had sensationally broken every record: we had our hands full coping with the crispbread and mayonnaise. Around us, exotic-looking slave-girls and slave-boys pranced around with hot vol-au-vents, whisky, and coffee, moving in and out between the giant flowerbeds and the ornate fountains spouting colored water. Coffee should be served in glass—preferably crystal—given the laws of physics, remarked my neighbor. Hastily discarding my assumption he was a former professional sportsman, I lightly raised the topic of nuclear physics, just as a helicopter arrived overhead to shower us with gifts.—Bonbonnières and Moroccan-leather-bound horoscope books, silver ping-pong sets and tiny baskets of strawberries, a baby's pram even, probably made from fluffy white cloud. . . . We managed to catch a party cracker, a big rainbow-colored one. We closed our eyes, held our breath and, tugging at both ends, duly produced a sulfurous puff of smoke which, once it had cleared, revealed a lady seated at a grand piano—a pink porcelain figure advertising Steinway pianos. For me of all people, groaned my neighbor. Are you not fond of music, I asked. Well, that's certainly been said of me, he answered. Though my *Gurrelieder* . . . You're? . . . Schoenberg. Arnold Schoenberg." Ibid., 57–58.

45. Film set and interior designer Paul Huldschinsky (Hulle) created the interior design for Mann's new house on San Remo Drive.

46. Zurich book dealer and publisher Emil Oprecht (1895–1952), editor of *Mass und Wert*.

47. Berlin surgeon and professor Ferdinand Sauerbruch (1875–1951).

48. The Battle of Stalingrad had begun that week.

49. Herbert Tauber, *Franz Kafka: Eine Deutung seiner Werke* (Zurich: Oprecht, 1941).

50. "The Theme of the Joseph Novels." Mann gave the speech on November 17, 1942, at the Library of Congress in Washington and was introduced to Vice President Henry A. Wallace.

51. Thomas Mann, *Joseph and His Brothers. Joseph, the Provider. Part Six: The Holy Game* (New York: Knopf, 2005).

52. The well-known New York–based left-wing political and cultural periodical.

53. The Dutch painter Ernst Leyden (1892–1969) and his wife, Karin.

54. German-Jewish writer Lion Feuchtwanger. Mann and Feuchtwanger were fellow exiles in Sanary after 1933. In 1940 Feuchtwanger found himself in the internment camp in Les Milles, whence—with the help of Varian Fry, US Vice Consul Hiram Bingham IV, and his colleague Miles Standish—he escaped and made his way across the Pyrenees, taking the same route as Heinrich and Golo Mann and the Werfels had taken. See Marta Feuchtwanger, *Nur eine Frau* (Munich: Langen Müller, 1983), 289–301. Feuchtwanger moved to Pacific Palisades in 1941, where he bought the impressive Spanish Colonial–style Villa Aurora—now an artists' residence and historic landmark funded by the German government.

55. German writer Erich Maria Remarque (1898–1970), whose best known work is *All Quiet on the Western Front* (Boston: Little, Brown, 1929).

56. Italian theologian and politician Luigi Don Sturzo (1871–1959), founder of the Partito Populare Italiano (1919) and of the journal of that name, spent the period from 1924 to 1946 in exile, the last six years of which were spent in the United States. His article, which ran in the September 12, 1942, issue of the *New Leader*

and continued in the September 19 issue, was entitled "Free Germany Created Now Could Hold Out Hope for Germans, Aid Post-War Democracy."

57. New York–based liberal periodical founded in 1924.

58. The September 12, 1942, issue of the *New Leader* contained an article by the Russian journalist and director of the Jewish Labor Committee Jacob Pat (1890–1966), with the headline "Nazis Gas 11,000 Jews in the Warsaw Gau, but Resistance in Ghetto Continues." Until 1938 Pat had been general secretary of the Jewish Labor Federation's Central Association of Yiddish Schools in Warsaw. He was on a fund-raising visit to the United States when war broke out and stayed on. His article, which drew on a May 1942 report by the Jewish Socialist Federation in Poland, clearly described the gassings, other executions, and deportations being perpetrated in Europe, but at that time no credence was given to this. "As terrible as these stories of horror and murder are, they pale in significance to the inhuman torture and humiliation to which the Nazis are subjecting Europe's Jewish community, which are beyond the power of any normal person living in a civilized democratic society to imagine." The details of the Jewish Socialist Federation's report were so appalling that many people, even in the Jewish press, did not believe them until they were confirmed later that year. See Haskel Lookstein, *Were We Our Brother's Keepers? The Public Response of American Jews to the Holocaust, 1938–1944* (New York: Hartmore House, 1985), 106–7.

59. Joseph Goebbels (1897–1945), Reich minister of propaganda. On September 3, 1942, the *New York Times* ran an article headlined "Goebbels Demands More Hate" with the subheadline "His warnings to the Germans are an indication they are listening to British radio transmissions." Mann had been sending out messages via the BBC. None of his early speeches mention the Nazi persecution of the Jews, but this changed in 1942, when he briefly mentioned "the thousands of Jews who have perished in the Warsaw ghetto." In June 1942 Mann corrected his earlier report on the Jews in Holland, stating that in fact "nearly 800 people in captivity at that time were taken to Mauthausen, where they were gassed." Obviously this was (inadvertently) a huge underestimate of the unimaginable slaughter going at the time. In June 1942 the BBC had reported that seven hundred thousand Polish Jews had been killed, whereas by that time the figure was already close to two million.

60. Pat's September 12, 1942, article stated: "Just a few weeks ago, in a statement on the radio, Dr. Goebbels warned Europe's Jews: 'It is our goal to annihilate the Jews. We must achieve that objective regardless of whether we are defeated or victorious. If Germany's armies are forced to retreat, they will obliterate the last of the Jews as they do so.' That is quite literally Hitler's policy with regard to the Jews: swift annihilation using the most brutal methods."

61. See Appendix II: "Listen, Germans!" dated September 27, 1942, a radio broadcast in which Mann draws attention to the plight of Europe's Jews. The speech drew extensively on Pat's article.

62. The recording was sent by airmail to New York and played over the telephone to a London recording studio, whence it was broadcast to Germany.

63. The Faust project in fact dated back to 1901, when Mann had jotted down a few brief notes on a piece of paper. He took up the idea again in early 1943 after completing his Joseph tetralogy.

64. Mann's grandson Fridolin Mann (b. 1940), who was three at the time.

65. On May 6, 1943, Mann wrote to Bruno Walter: "I'm now considering something quite different, something rather eerie and theological-demonic, . . . a novel about pathological-illegitimate inspiration, the hero of which will, this time, indeed be a musician (composer). I'm ready to take the risk, but anticipate having to occasionally ask you for more advice and concrete information, e.g. about what sort of

specialized training a creative musician typically undergoes. Presumably it varies a lot and doesn't necessarily involve going to a conservatory? Hugo Wolf seems never to have done so. Nor does Stravinsky, who says he found studying harmony very dull, but really enjoyed counterpoint. His early development took place under Rimsky-Korsakov's supervision. Should I perhaps read a composition textbook? Do you have one? Anyway, I intend to ask Schoenberg for advice." Thomas Mann to Bruno Walter, May 6, 1943, in Mann, *Briefe*, vol. 2 (Frankfurt am Main: S. Fischer, 1979), 311–12; *Blätter der Thomas-Mann-Gesellschaft*, no. 9 (Zurich: Thomas Mann Gesellschaft, 1969), 25.

66. Up to this point Mann evidently had had little interaction with Schoenberg. By contrast Bertolt Brecht, for example, attended one of Schoenberg's lectures at UCLA on July 29, 1942, along with Hanns Eisler. Although Schoenberg's biographer, H.H. Stuckenschmidt, states that Mann also attended the lecture, there is no corresponding entry in Mann's diaries, and it seems unlikely he came. See Stuckenschmidt, *Arnold Schoenberg*, 456; Mann, *Tagebücher, 1940–43*, 300. According to Brecht's journal, Schoenberg taught "modern composition." Bertolt Brecht, *Arbeitsjournal: Erster Band 1938 bis 1942*, ed. Werner Hecht (Frankfurt am Main: Suhrkamp, 1973), 502–3 ("Went with Eisler to a lecture by Arnold Schoenberg at UCLA about modern composition. He is very lively and adopts a polemical stance. Talks about the emancipation of dissonance. He explains the brevity and overemotionality of the first compositions by his school by citing the effort involved with the technique, and the fact that it is as yet underdeveloped. Couldn't understand the musical-technical side, though basically it all seemed very clear. Pity we're not sufficiently educated in music to at least know what we don't know. Went to Schoenberg's house afterwards, a villa on sunset. Surrounded by very young children, he is a slightly bird-like 70-year-old, very charming, agreeably dry and acerbic manner. . . . I really liked the old fellow. He views himself in very historical terms. when someone mentioned that so and so had finished Schubert's unfinished for a contest, he immediately remarked: 'I could do it better, but I wouldn't have the nerve.' "). For a slightly different translation of this journal entry see Bertolt Brecht, *Journals, 1934–1955* (New York: Routledge, 1996), 250–51. Schoenberg basically did not teach his twelve-tone method and only lectured on it occasionally. See Appendix IV for his first lecture (written out in full) on twelve-tone composition.

67. The composer Igor Stravinsky (1882–1971) moved to Los Angeles in 1940. Mann read Stravinsky's *Erinnerungen* (1937) in November of 1942.

68. The Manns' housekeeper.

69. After fleeing from France, the Werfels arrived in Los Angeles on December 30, 1940. They moved into their new house at 610 Bedford Drive, Beverly Hills, in September 1942. See Mahler-Werfel, *Mein Leben*, 331. "I bought the smallest house I could find, as I'm aware that large houses have become unmanageable due to the problems with servants and the expense. . . . I spent a lot of energy making it as cozy as possible, and it is now rather charming."

70. See Angelika Abel, *Musikästhetik der Klassischen Moderne* (München: Wilhelm Fink, 2003), 213–14.

71. It was just nine days after meeting Schoenberg that Mann opted for the name Adrian, with its obvious similarities with the name Arnold. Clearly there was more than mere coincidence involved. Mann began writing the first chapter of *Doktor Faustus* ten days later, on May 27, 1943 (also the date on which Zeitblom begins telling the story of Leverkühn).

72. See Appendix III. Mann gave the speech at a large-scale demonstration by ten thousand people in San Francisco on June 17, 1943. Also on the three-hour program was violinist Isaac Stern. Mann, *Tagebücher, 1940–1944*, April 19, 1943, 589.

73. "... I also dictated the end of a speech to be given in San Francisco on the seventeenth, at a mass meeting against the Nazi atrocities in Europe, particularly the massacres of Jews. I'm not keen on the whole thing, as I'd much rather be thinking about my unusual novel.... I'm finishing this letter late at night; all the guests, among them Arnold Schoenberg, have left. It's amazing how many musicians, virtuosi and composers have made their way here. At the moment I'm actively trying to spend time with them, so that I can learn a little...." Mann to Meyer, June 11, 1943, in Mann and Meyer, *Briefwechsel, 1937–1955*, 488.

74. The German recitalist Ludwig Hardt (1886–1947) and his wife, Giulia. Hardt had met Mann in Munich in 1920, and it was he who first introduced him to the works of Kafka. He left Germany in 1933, arriving in Los Angeles in 1938. T. Mann, *Tagebücher, 1940–1943*, 761–62.

75. Gustave Arlt (1895–1986), professor of German at UCLA and translator of some of Franz Werfel's works.

76. Schoenberg had lent a copy of his *Harmonielehre*, at that time hard to come by, to his UCLA colleague Arlt, the latter having expressed an interest in translating it into English. Schoenberg probably advised Mann to get the copy from Arlt. Ultimately Schoenberg lent Mann another copy (see letter dated September 19, 1943). Mann took considerable time to return it, which led to an argument following the publication of *Doktor Faustus.*

77. "... I'm still on Chapter VII, but that sounds further advanced than it actually is, because there are going to be numerous chapters, and I'm still in the atmospheric preparations and on the hero's youth. The problems are just beginning, the biggest of which will be fictitiously-convincingly placing an important musician (composer) within contemporary music history, as those roles and positions are already occupied, namely by Schoenberg, Bartok, Alban Berg, Stravinsky, Krenek etc.... I'm having to invent a high-profile artist personality, along with his works. That's a ridiculously difficult set of challenges, and there are plenty more to come." Mann and Meyer, *Briefwechsel, 1937–1955*, 498.

78. Philosopher, sociologist, music theorist, and composer Theodore Wiesengrund-Adorno (hereafter, "Adorno") (1903–69), a student of Schoenberg's students Alban Berg and Eduard Steuermann. Adorno, who fled Germany in 1933 and subsequently held positions at Oxford, Princeton, and the University of California, was a key figure in the Frankfurt School, along with Max Horkheimer and Herbert Marcuse. In California he lived at 316 Kenter Avenue in Brentwood, not far from Schoenberg and Mann, and was introduced to Mann by Horkheimer in 1943. He became one of Mann's sources of information on Schoenberg's twelve-tone method (see also Theodor W. Adorno and Thomas Mann, *Correspondence, 1943–1955*, ed. Christoph Gödde and Thomas Sprecher, trans. Nicholas Walker [Cambridge: Polity, 2006]). Though Adorno never studied under Schoenberg, he participated in polemical debates about Schoenberg's music, particularly in his capacity as author and editor of the journal *Musikblätter des Anbruchs.* Hence Schoenberg himself wrote: "Dr. Adorno belongs to my school without actually having been one of my students." (Schoenberg to Frau Geis in November of 1932). Schoenberg praised Adorno for his essay in the 1927 issue of *Pult und Taktstock.* (Schoenberg to Erwin Stein on May 13, 1927: "Wiesengrund [Adorno] then underwent a major improvement. He is now writing quite differently from before. And his analysis is excellent.") On January 25, 1933, Schoenberg wrote the following report on Adorno to the Prussian Academy of Arts: "I will refrain from praising W.A. (You praise him, Meister Vogelsang ... [Wagner, *Die Meistersinger*, act I, scene 3]). Exams should not be given for their own sake, nor to simply create difficulties for the applicant; they should only be given if it is impossible to determine via other methods whether an

applicant has reached instructor level. In this case there is enough material to form an opinion. I don't feel W. is a composer, but he can definitely do what can be taught; and there can be no doubt about his level. As regards the other subjects, I would be interested to know how many composers would pass this exam. Moreover, one should bear in mind that the attached analyses constitute important contributions to music theory."

79. Adorno completed the first draft of *Philosophy of New Music*, which is principally a criticism of Schoenberg, in May of 1941, when he was living in New York. On May 20, 1941, Adorno wrote to Horkheimer: "It's basically centered around Schoenberg and so to speak bids him farewell. He'd never forgive me for the fact that this time everyone, except you, will consider me mad. Please nurture my hope that the hatred I garner from all sides will at least have been earned." Adorno and Horkheimer, *Briefwechsel, Band II, 1938–1944* (Frankfurt am Main: Suhrkamp, 2004), 116. Adorno also gave a copy to his close friend the violinist Rudolf Kolisch (1896–1978), Schoenberg's brother-in-law, insisting that he keep it secret. On January 14, 1942, shortly after arriving in Los Angeles and renewing his acquaintance with Schoenberg, Adorno wrote to Kolisch: "I have not given him [Schoenberg] a copy of this, and I haven't even mentioned it. On the contrary: I have translated it into English and my self-censorship went far beyond the merely linguistic. If I succeed in ensuring Schoenberg does not get wind of the whole business, I can look forward to a pleasant retirement." When Kolisch inadvertently gave Schoenberg's son-in-law and former student Felix Greissle a copy, Adorno was furious: "Your letter came as a horrible shock. Literally, I am not exaggerating. The veto on communicating 'On the Philosophy of New Music' was not in any sense rescinded, and I cannot understand how you reached that conclusion, after I gave you the manuscript on the strict agreement you would be utterly discreet. If, for God knows what reason, some third party had felt the veto had been rescinded, you should at least have consulted me about the situation. My relations with Schoenberg have become very friendly, and I am very happy and grateful for that. It will be disastrous if, through the grapevine, he finds out about certain formulations in the essay, e.g. the ones regarding universal genius, but many others too. He would never forgive me. The planned publication isn't yet a certainty. In the raw English translation I produced six months ago, I erased parts which might be injurious to Schoenberg, and I intend to subject the whole thing to self-censorship one more time if it does get published. I urgently and insistently implore you: do everything possible to make sure nothing bad comes of this. 1) Please discuss the entire contents completely openly with Greissle, and ask him and his wife [Schoenberg's daughter Trudi] to swear on everything they hold sacred to not mention the existence or contents of the essay to AS [Schoenberg] or anyone else, let alone mention the formulations it contains. 2) Do not give the work to [Erich Itor] Kahn or [Paul] Dessau. Explain to them that due to the very different English version I don't want anyone laying hands on the German version. Notwithstanding readers' loyalty, broadening the circle of readership would inevitably cause precisely the kind of disaster I want at any cost to avoid. Don't under any circumstances leave me in the lurch in this matter, and do what you can to make good on the damage that has occurred. This is as serious a matter as it gets without actually involving the immediate destruction or preservation of a life. Angrily yours, . . . Teddie. [Handwritten PS]: It's particularly important that [Artur] Schnabel does not come to hear of the matter via [Paul] Dessau." (Adorno to Kolisch, June 26, 1942). The letters from Adorno to Kolisch are in the Houghton Library at Harvard University, MS Mus 259. Adorno had written in a similar vein to Hanns Eisler on January 8, 1942: "I've translated the music essay [the Schoenberg parts of *Philosophy of New Music*] into pidgin English and so

fundamentally castrated it that Schoenberg can no longer be angry about it. However, he may be angry nonetheless if he does find out about its publication. I've written a foreword completely in line with what you suggested and based on the notion that this is just music—what on earth must the world be like." *Adorno: Eine Bildmonographie* (Frankfurt am Main: Theodore W. Adorno Archive/Suhrkamp, 2003), 179–81.

80. For extracts from Adorno's *Philosophy of New Music* see Appendix V. In *The Story of a Novel* Mann comments that reading Adorno's essay was a key event in the genesis of the novel: "Here indeed was something important. The manuscript dealt with modern music both on an artistic and on a sociological plane. The spirit of it was remarkably forward-looking, subtle and deep, and the whole thing had the strangest affinity to the idea of my book, to the "composition" in which I lived and moved and had my being. The decision was made of itself: this was my man." Thomas Mann, *The Story of a Novel* (New York: Knopf, 1961), 43. Mann liked Adorno's critique of Schoenberg and appropriated it: "The manuscript he gave me at that time was relevant and strikingly suitable to the sphere of my novel. This grabbed my attention. Essentially the subject matter was Schoenberg, his school, and the twelve-tone method. While the author is clearly convinced of Schoenberg's outstanding importance, the text is a penetrating, incisive critique of his system. Its style is very concise, perhaps even excessively sharp, and owes a little to Nietzsche and even more to Karl Kraus. It discusses the destiny that causes (objectively necessary) constructive elucidation of music (on equally objective grounds) to swing back into something dark and mythological, over the artist's head as it were. What better for my world of the 'Magic Square'? I actually discovered in myself—or rediscovered, as something very familiar—a perfectly reasonable willingness to appropriate what I considered my own, or belonging to me and the matter at hand. The portrayal of serialism and the critique thereof rendered in dialogue in Chapter XXII of *Dr. Faustus* is entirely based on Adornian analysis. So are various remarks about the tonal language of late Beethoven found early on in the book, in Kretzschmar's expectorations, in other words about the eerie relationship that death engenders between genius and convenience. In Adorno's manuscript I found these ideas strangely familiar. I have only this to say about the—how should I put it?—sense of calm with which, in various ways, I put these ideas into the mouth of my stammerer: after a long period of acting upon the mind, things one earlier tossed to the wind often return, reshaped by a new hand and placed in different juxtapositions, reminding one of oneself and one's own concerns. Ideas about tone and form, I and the Objective, seem to me—the author of a Venetian novella thirty-five years ago—like recollections per se. They seem to have asserted a position for themselves in the philosophic writings of one's younger self, playing a functional role in my depiction of the soul and the epoch. In the eyes of the artist, an idea per se never has much intrinsic value or value as something owned. Its importance lies in the way it functions in the work's intellectual mechanisms." Mann, *The Story of a Novel*, 706–7.

81. *Prométhée, le poème du feu* (1911), by Alexander Scriabin (1872–1915). Thomas Mann, *Tagebücher, 1940–1943*, 1002.

MANN TO SCHOENBERG, JULY 30, 1943

Thomas Mann
1550 San Remo Drive
Pacific Palisades, California
July 30, 1943

Dear Mr. Schoenberg,

In case you think I've neglected the matter, permit me to report on how strangely things have gone with Professor Arlt and my request for your book.[82] I've written to him twice asking whether he could spare me the book; subject to your approval, I want to pick it up from him. The first letter had the wrong address yet was not returned. The second, sent ten days ago, definitely must have reached him, but I haven't received any answer so far.

As the saying goes, I'm faced with a conundrum. Do you have any explanation for this silence? Have you yourself made any unsatisfactory attempts to get the book back from Arlt? It seems I should abandon hope of laying hands on it.

I do hope we can see one another again soon. Last time there was too little opportunity to talk about "the real thing," namely music and your contribution to its fate. For various very sound reasons, these matters are of great concern to me at present.

Warmest wishes to you and your wife from both of us. Respectfully yours,
Thomas Mann

---

82. Schoenberg's *Harmonielehre.* See footnote 76 above.

MANN'S DIARY

Pacific Palisades, Thursday, August 19, 1943
   Evening at the Werfels, small group for dinner, including the Franks,[83] then other guests arrived. Talked to Werfel and Frank about George,[84] Wagner.[85] Spoke with Frau Joseph[86] and Torberg[87] about Schoenberg. Torberg made a disparaging assessment of *Venedig.*

Pacific Palisades, Friday, August 27, 1943
   Continued writing Chapter VIII (stammering).[88] Walked as far as the old house.[89] Ideal weather. Eva Herrmann to lunch.[90] Read some of Schindler's *Beethoven.*[91] Started a letter to Agnes Meyer. Went to dinner with the Schoenbergs in Brentwood. Very hospitable. Badly behaved children.[92] Excellent Viennese coffee. Long talk with him about music.

Pacific Palisades, Sunday, August 28, 1943
   Finished the letter to Agnes Meyer[93] after receiving phone call in which she offered to translate the lecture. Then continued writing Chapter VIII. Walk on the Promenade at midday. Read *Time* and *Die Weltwoche* after lunch. Bruno Walter with wife and daughter to tea. Talked about the *Matthäus-Passion* with two choirs for four voices with chorale melody over them. Walters lingered a long time. Then went to dinner at the Werfels; Stravinsky, Mr. Sheean[94] and Maria Jeritza[95] were there. Other guests arrived after dinner. Mme. Zernatto.[96] Long conversation with Stravinsky. About Schoenberg. Alma Werfel against Walter's museum-like conservatism; his wife backed her up on this.—Dreadful bombing of Nuremberg.

Pacific Palisades, Monday, September 13, 1943
   Up early. First wrote letter to Agnes Meyer, friendly and restrained, then worked on the lecture. Haircut, shaved, changed, quarter to one. Picked up by the Singers[97] after coffee. Driven to the lecture at the Los Angeles Hadassah Club.[98] Theater with around one thousand people, mostly women. Gave the lecture satisfactorily. Very hot. Meeting and greeting. The violinist Szigeti.[99] Got back at half past four. Mail. Had a nap. Tea at six. Went with Katia to the Schoenbergs at seven; buffet dinner to celebrate his sixty-ninth birthday. Numerous guests. Ate with Arlt, Klemperer, Else Heims[100] and others. Spent a long time with Klemperer and Schoenberg. Talked too much.—Dubious comedy of Mussolini's abduction by the Germans. Heavy fighting in Italy, some of it between Italians and Germans, some between Americans and Nazi troops. Occupation of ports on the eastern coast

(Balkan invasion). "Swift clampdown" by the Germans in Italy has sent clear message to the satellite countries about the dangers of desertion. Gestapo in Milan etc. Party and labor leaders arrested and shipped off to Germany. Dreadful. Means they can now be martyred before the eyes of the kidnapped Mussolini.

---

83. Bruno and Elisabeth Frank lived at 513 Camden Drive, Beverly Hills, a block east of the Werfels and Bruno Walter. Schnauber, *Hollywood Haven*, 85–87.

84. German poet Stefan George (1868–1933). In his early works Schoenberg made frequent use of George's poems: String Quartet No. 2, op. 10; Two Songs, op. 14; and *Fifteen Poems from "The Book of the Hanging Garden,"* op. 15. Although some of George's circle were ardent Nazis, he also influenced members of the resistance, among them Claus Schenk Graf von Stauffenberg, one of the leading figures in the failed plot to assassinate Hitler on July 20, 1944.

85. Richard Wagner (1813–83). Like George, Wagner was admired by both the Nazis and their opponents. In a January 1940 letter Mann brought this phenomenon to the attention of the editor of the journal *Common Sense:* "If two people want the same thing, and one of them is an inferior person, does that make the object of their desire inferior?" Thomas Mann, *Wagner und unsere Zeit* (Frankfurt am Main: S. Fischer, 1963), 154. Mann was also drawn to Nietzsche and his critique of Wagner, and therefore described his own feelings for Wagner as "ambivalent." See Mann to Agnes Meyer, Feb. 18, 1942, in ibid., 161.

86. Possibly the wife of Dr. Albrecht Joseph, film editor and occasional secretary to Mann.

87. Austrian writer Friedrich Torberg (1908–79) immigrated to Los Angeles and worked for a short period for Warner Bros. Schoenberg knew Torberg through the Werfels. On September 9, 1943, Schoenberg sent Torberg a letter (c/o the Werfels) in which he thanked him for his book *Mein ist die Rache* (1943), which describes the horrors of the Nazi concentration camps: "I quickly read the book and was deeply moved by it. Irrespective of its degree of accuracy, the story provides a spot-on characterization of the Nazis and their so-called philosophy. Your Wagenseil figure says and does exactly what they say and do. After reading the book I was depressed for several days, as though I'd myself been present during the atrocities described. I wish every anti-Nazi could read your book, as we wouldn't need to worry about the Germans going unpunished." Torberg recalls Schoenberg warmly in his anecdote collection *Tante Jolesch:* "I met Arnold Schoenberg in Hollywood. And however many important or brilliant contemporaries I may have met—at the time, or prior to that, or subsequently—none of them gave me the feeling as compellingly or upliftingly that I was in the company of genius. . . . Schoenberg's strength lay in his succinct observations, which were usually at the expense of the person involved. These remarks, and the way they were uttered, were like shots fired accurately from a pistol: his chiseled, wonderfully cerebral face would distort itself into a half-caustic, half-winking grimace, which was immediately followed by an emphatic gesture to complete the execution. 'You're going to Bruno Walter this evening?' he asked me, when Walter was conducting the Los Angeles Philharmonic in a very classical concert. 'What does he have on the program?' All I could come up with was Beethoven's First. 'Really?' said Schoenberg pointedly. 'He's got that far, has he?' On another occasion, the conversation turned to Puccini: 'Puccini? Isn't he the one who pre-impersonated Lehár?' " Friedrich Torberg, *Tante Jolesch; or, The Decline of*

the West in Anecdotes, ed. Sonat Birnecker Hart, trans. Maria Poglitsch Bauer (Riverside, CA: Ariadne, 2008), 182.

88. A reference to Wendell Kretschmar in chapter 8 of *Doktor Faustus*. Thomas Mann, *Tagebücher, 1940–1943*, 1007.

89. Mann's house on Amalfi Drive, not far from San Remo Drive.

90. The illustrator Eva Herrmann (1901–78), a close friend of Erika and Klaus Mann. Thomas Mann, *Tagebücher, 1940–1943*, 753.

91. Anton Schindler's Beethoven biography, published in 1909.

92. Schoenberg had three children by his second wife, Gertrud née Kolisch (1898–1967): Nuria (b. 1932), Ronald (b. 1937), and Lawrence (b. 1941). In her memoirs Katia Mann complained: "The Schoenbergs had two boys. They were so badly behaved there was always a danger that, when their parents had guests for dinner, they might come downstairs in their pajamas and demand something to eat. The only way to keep them quiet was to allow them to sleep in their parents' beds, with the very pretty elder sister Nuria—who subsequently married the musician [Luigi] Nono—supervising. Otherwise at dinner there would be no peace at all for the parents and guests.... One of these ill-behaved boys was later the top tennis player at his college and won numerous prizes, of which Schoenberg was naturally very proud." Katia Mann, *Meine ungeschriebenen Memoiren* (Frankfurt am Main: S. Fischer, 1976), 133–34. Having been a highly ranked junior player, Ronald Schoenberg went on to even greater success at the age of fifteen, by which time his father had died (in 1951). Ronald Schoenberg was the number two player at Notre Dame University for four years and on the team that won the national championships in 1958. He later studied law at the University of California at Berkeley and was a Los Angeles municipal court judge for twenty years. The younger of the two boys, Lawrence, graduated from the University of Southern California and for many years taught mathematics at Pacific Palisades High School.

93. "...We were invited to the Schoenbergs, and I discussed music with him for a long time during the course of the evening. It's amazing how much feeling and reverence, even love these modern composers have for the old music, the whole world of harmony and the romantic period. When we discussed Wagner he displayed great warmth, and I found it excellent that he condemned the long drawn-out passages, yet felt that cuts of the kind perpetrated by Weingartner were completely out of the question. But once again, how characteristic that he can't stand *Venedig!*" Mann to Agnes Meyer, August 27, 1943, in Mann and Meyer, *Briefwechsel, 1937–1955*, 510; Mann, *Wagner und unsere Zeit*, 162.

94. American journalist and author Vincent Sheean (1899–1975), well-known for his novel *Sanfelice* (1936), about fascist Italy.

95. Czech opera singer Maria Jeritza (1887–1982).

96. The widow of Austrian politician Guido Zernatto (1903–43), who committed suicide on February 8, 1943, in New York.

97. American portrait painter William Earl Singer (1910–81) and his wife, Elsa.

98. A Zionist women's organization, founded in 1912 by Henrietta Szold (1860–1945).

99. The Hungarian violinist Joseph Szigeti (1892–1973) had come to the United States in 1926. In October of 1942 he published an article in *American Music Lover* entitled "The Phonograph in Thomas Mann's *Der Zauberberg*."

100. The actress Else Heims (1878–1958), first wife of Max Reinhardt. The offspring from this marriage were Wolfgang and Gottfried.

MANN TO SCHOENBERG, SEPTEMBER 14, 1943

Thomas Mann
1550 San Remo Drive
Pacific Palisades, California
September 14, 1943

Dear Mr. Schoenberg,

I'm awfully sorry that, out of ignorance, we arrived empty-handed yesterday.

Herewith, therefore, a book[101] which you probably don't have in your library, at any rate not in this edition, with belated best wishes for your birthday.

I have also enclosed my Zurich Wagner speech,[102] which I recently suggested to you that you read.

Once again, best wishes for your birthday and many thanks for a very enjoyable evening! Respectfully yours,

Thomas Mann

---

101. A copy of *Der Zauberberg.*
102. "Richard Wagner und *Der Ring des Nibelungen*" (November 1937), published in Mann, *Wagner und unsere Zeit,* 127–50.

MANN TO SCHOENBERG, SEPTEMBER 14, 1943

[Fig. 1.1, handwritten dedication to Schönberg in a copy of *Der Zauberberg*]

For Arnold Schoenberg, the Daring Master, on September 13, 1943, from one who is also endeavoring to create music.

Thomas Mann

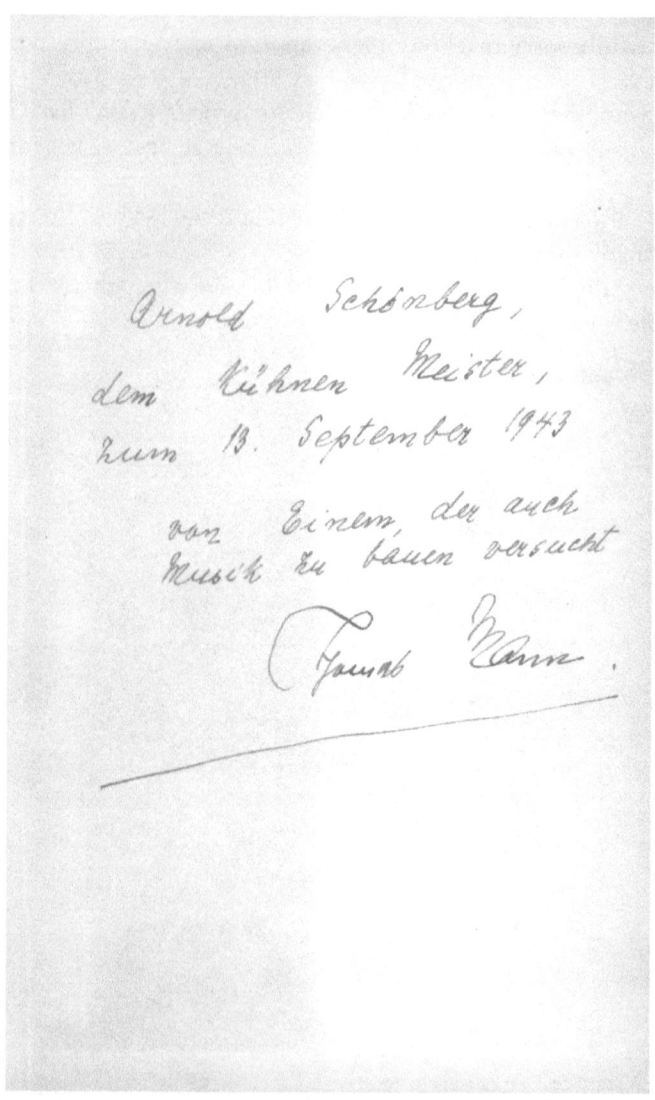

FIGURE 1.1.   Thomas Mann, dedication of *The Magic Mountain* to Arnold Schoenberg (1943).

SCHOENBERG TO MANN, SEPTEMBER 19, 1943

September 19, 1943

Dear Mr. Mann,

I have already read quite far and with increasing excitement into your *Magic Mountain.* I am especially happy that I have thoroughly absorbed the introduction.[103] But I am certain that I would have understood your thoughts even without it. Yes, I believe that because I am a composer it would have to be like that—or you would have written in vain for a reader like me.

For a long time I have wanted to send you my *Jacob's Ladder,*[104] and even more so my *Moses and Aron,*[105] an opera text. I would be very gratified if you were to gather from my literary attempts that my understanding of your thoughts is not in the least superficial.

Thank you for your *Magic Mountain* and for your congratulations. In friendship and respect, your,

Arnold Schoenberg

[P.S.] I am sending you the *Harmonielehre* with this—should you still need it.

---

103. Introduction to *The Magic Mountain* (1939), subsequently written by Mann for his students at Princeton University. In this introduction Mann describes himself as a "musician among the poets," in whose work music always influenced and was an integral part of his style. Thomas Mann, *Gesammelte Werke* (Frankfurt am Main: S. Fischer, 1960–74), 11:611.

104. Composed between 1915 and 1917, before Schoenberg enlisted in the Austrian army. The unfinished oratorio, *Jacob's Ladder* for soloists, choir, and orchestra, was only published and performed after the composer's death. The idea for the text, first published in 1917 without music (Universal Edition 6061), dates back at the very least to the year 1912, when Schoenberg wrote to the poet Richard Dehmel *(Transfigured Night):* "For a long time now, I have wanted to write an oratorio, that would have as its content, how the person of today, who has gone through Materialism, Socialism, Anarchy, who was an Atheist, but who has retained a smattering of the old belief (in the form of superstition), how this modern person would argue with God (see also *Jacob Wrestles,* by [August] Strindberg), until he finally reaches the point of finding God and becoming religious. Learning to pray! Not a plot, no strikes of fate, nor even a love story should effect this change. Or at the very least they ought to be used only as suggestions, as an impetus, but remain in the background. And foremost: it should be in the manner of speaking, in the manner of thinking, in the way of expression of the person of today: it ought to address the problems that oppress us. For in the Bible, those who struggle with God also express themselves as people of their own time, speak of their matters, maintain their social

and intellectual level. That is why they are artistically strong, yet unable to be composed by an artist of today, who is fulfilling his calling." Nuria Schoenberg-Nono, *Arnold Schönberg, 1874–1951: Lebensgeschichte in Begegnungen* (Klagenfurt: Ritter, 1992), 144–45.

105. Begun in 1923, the text to the incomplete opera *Moses and Aron* was finished in 1928. After having completed the first two acts in 1932, Schoenberg was unable to complete the composition because of the emerging political situation in Germany and his having been forced to flee in May 1933. The first two acts were performed for the first time in 1954 and since then have been performed to great success by opera houses worldwide.

MANN'S DIARY

Pacific Palisades, Tuesday, September 21, 1943

Up at 8:30, went for a short walk. After breakfast made corrections and changes to text for speech. Then resumed work on the end of Chapter VIII. Went for a walk at midday and drove down to the Promenade. Swirling mist suddenly came in off the ocean, enveloping everything, conditions remained clear over our part.—After lunch read the paper and the *New Yorker*. Schoenberg's Oratorio *[Jacob's Ladder]*. Religious poetry, not fully developed.—After tea wrote letters to van Leyden and Golo. Went for a brief walk. Strange, hot desert winds blowing down from the hills, initially only in certain areas. Katia went to a tea party at the van Leydens; the Ludwigs[106] and the Feuchtwangers there. Tackled Schoenberg's theology again in the evening. Hot; kept the windows closed and switched on the ventilation. Cooler indoors than out. Listened to Beethoven's *Quartett* op. 132 and old music.

Pacific Palisades, Saturday, December 25, 1943, Christmas Day

Sunny and pleasant. Worked on Chapter IX during the morning. At midday went for a walk and then drove back with Eva Herrmann and Golo, who had been at the beach. They stayed for lunch. Coffee on the terrace. Read more of Schoenberg's *Harmonielehre*.[107] Wrote a letter to Agnes Meyer from 6 to 8:30. Golo went to the Werfels and the Franks. Had a good laugh about Agnes Meyer with him. Troops making heavy use of the railroads. Very evident, deliberate preparations for the European invasion which, under Eisenhower, will be 75 percent carried out by the Americans. Progress towards Rome (Cassino).—Schoenberg's *Theory of Harmony*.

Pacific Palisades, Sunday, December 26, 1943

Worked unsuccessfully on Chapter IX, deleted certain parts. Went for a walk in the desert winds and strong sun. Extraordinary windblown clarity, allowing one to see the snow-capped mountains. Drove home with Golo and Eva Herrmann. Read more of Schoenberg's *Theory of Harmony* . . .

Pacific Palisades, Tuesday, December 28, 1943

Rained. Worked on Chapter IX. Uncertain. Went for a short walk on my own. Myrtle the maid has been back for several days. After lunch read the paper and Schoenberg's *Theory of Harmony*. Schalom Asch[108] and his wife came for tea. . . .

Pacific Palisades, Sunday, January 2, 1944

Up earlier, shortly after eight. Raining. Interim preparations, musical. Didn't write. Short walk with Katia in the rain. Read more of Schoenberg's *Theory of Harmony.* Young people to tea, lieutenant and sergeant with Anglo-Irish background and their wives, admirers. Made further notes on musical matters. In the evening the San Francisco Philharmonic, brilliant, Polish symphony by Chabrier, masterfully conducted by Monteux.[109] Movements from Dvorak's New World [Ninth Symphony]. Work by young French composer. In between came news about successes in the Pacific and in Russia, close to the old Polish border, also not far from the Romanian border. Invasion fever.—More Schoenberg.

Pacific Palisades, Friday, January 7, 1944

Up at eight. Clear, summer-like day. Worked on Chapter IX. Went for a walk towards the ocean and drove back. Cable from Klaus[110] saying he has successfully reached his foreign destination. Read more of *Theory of Harmony. . . .*

Pacific Palisades, Sunday, January 9, 1944

Up at 8:30. Worked on Chapter IX. Wrote. Nice weather, went for a mid-day stroll with Katia in the neighborhood. Sunday lunch, no maid. Read more of *Theory of Harmony* and finished it in the evening. Also, yesterday, finished Stein's book on the Peasants' War.[111] Started reading *Anton Reiser.*[112]—Drove over to the Feuchtwangers in the afternoon, had tea in their new, spacious and very well situated house. I would find the isolation oppressive. He expects the European offensive to begin on March 15th.— Upset stomach since midday. Ate nothing except gruel and baked apple for supper.—Intriguing letter from *Overseas Press,* proposing that I write an article for the *London Evening Standard* on "What to do with Germany." Precarious, responsible—and am I perhaps only somewhat drawn to the idea?[113] Also possible that unforeseen circumstances may in fact relieve me of this responsibility. We face a revolutionized, proletarianized, naked, pale, shattered, ruined populace, turned inside out and stripped of belief. Still conceivable that national bolshevism may be declared, involving union with Russia. At any rate, the country is completely lost to decent liberal democracy.

Pacific Palisades, Sunday, February 20, 1944

. . . Re-read some of Schoenberg's *Theory of Harmony.* Evening concert from San Francisco, conducted by Wallenstein.[114] Tchaikovsky's *Swan*

Lake. Modern American music, jaunty, rhythmic jazz elements.—Germans driven back at Anzio, with much bloodshed. . . .

Pacific Palisades, Wednesday, March 1, 1944
Dark, rainy. Up at 8:30. Continued writing Chapter XII. At midday drove to NBC to do reading of the German radio program. In the afternoon started writing article for "Know Your Bible."[115] Guests in the evening: the Schoenbergs,[116] Frau Arnhold[117] and Dr. Matthias.[118]—Novel by L. Lewisohn with dedication.[119]

Pacific Palisades, Wednesday, April 5, 1944
The day spent traveling yesterday, in unventilated space, shattered my nerves. In the afternoon heavy cold, cough and blocked-up nose, difficult to get to sleep. Up at eight today, eggs and coffee in the dining car. Read the newspaper in the Club car. Warm and sunny. Arrived in Los Angeles around midday, picked up by the Singers, who told us about Chaplin's acquittal in ridiculous legal proceedings.[120] Accompanied them to lunch at the Brown Derby in Beverly Hills. They drove us home. Sat in the garden. Relaxed and settled in. Tea with Katia . . . News—phone call—that Bruno Frank is now seriously ill; blood vessels in his heart, as with so many other people. Schoenberg similarly afflicted. Must consider myself still in good shape. . . .

Pacific Palisades, Sunday, July 9, 1944
Wrote more of Chapter XX. Went for neighborhood stroll. Cloudy and humid. Read the paper after lunch. Positive review of *Joseph*. Wrote to Dr. Flinker[121] in Tangiers in the afternoon. The Adornos came over after supper. He played *Six Little Piano Pieces*[122] by Schoenberg and his own *Songs*— settings of Trakl[123] and George.[124] I gave a reading of various poems earmarked for Adrian.[125]—Fall of Caen and Vilnius. Calamity of the robot bombs. Dreadful rise in the number of massacres of Jews across Europe.

Pacific Palisades, Tuesday, August 15, 1944
Warm summer's day. Walk in the morning. Difficulties with the chapter. Must hold back on certain material that would be too weighty at this point and would come across as too thematic. Idea of having the devil appear in threefold mask: as pimp, music scholar, and naked demon, each time veiled in frigid ice.—Went to Westwood for haircut. A great deal of mail again. Newspapers. After tea spoke on the phone with Robinson[126] about copyright headaches. Handwritten letters (Révy,[127] Herzog,[128] petition for Schoenberg).—New

invasion of France from the south, near Toulon, St. Raphael. Little resistance. Kluge's army in tatters. Ruin must be approaching.

Pacific Palisades, Friday, August 25, 1944

Completed Chap. XXI and prepared dates for next one. . . . Started letter to Mrs. Meyer.[129] Went to the Tochs[130] for dinner. They played the record of his Passover oratorio.[131] Classical language. He made various conflicting remarks about the future of the new music. Difficult to love it. Bartok's[132] refusal. Confusion among young composers, laziness in the new methods of composition, use of atonality to hide weaknesses. Chamber orchestra arrangements of quartets. For Mozart, using the orchestra available to him in those days was always a matter of choice. No trombones in his symphonies.

Pacific Palisades, Friday, September 9, 1944

Hot, but with an ocean breeze. Reluctantly worked on the essay. Went for a walk on the Promenade with Anna Jacobson.[133] Had lunch with her. Letter from Agnes Meyer, who is unwell. Read *Time;* a certain amount about Germany. Morale on the home front allegedly better than among the army. Eisenhower has set a deadline of November for defeating the Germans.—Finished the letter to Heinrich after tea. In the evening listened to Schoenberg's *Transfigured Night.*[134] . . .

Pacific Palisades, Wednesday, September 13, 1944

Letters to Slochower[135] and to Mrs. Meyer.—Strolled on the Promenade. Very cool. Read the papers after lunch. Tea in bedroom. Went to the Schoenbergs bearing flowers, to wish him a happy seventieth birthday. He wasn't home; gave instructions to the housekeeper. He is in poor health. Leonhard Frank[136] came for dinner. Long conversation about Germany. . . .

Pacific Palisades, Thursday, September 14, 1944

Made some improvements to the novel. Started writing Chapter XXII. Went for just a short walk nearby. Went to the newsreel theater in Hollywood with Katia after tea; footage from liberated Paris. In the evening listened to Toch's *Quintett;* the contemplative and dramatic movements the best parts. Then listened to *Parsifal* on the radio. *Parsifal* rather than *Tristan* perhaps the origin of what is really new. Indulged in my fondness of chromatic passing notes on the piano.—Spent a long time reading Nietzsche's dreadful *Ecce homo.* What a choice of title, given the book's insufferable high spirits. He was aware that jubilant despair is, *au fond,* a bloodied face with a crown of thorns. Paralytic affectation; style that consists of easily emulated, stereotyped mannerisms, while he evidently considers it flashingly brilliant, something universally self-hating.—Goebbels has warned the Allies not to make assumptions about the outcome of the war. Aachen and Warsaw about to fall.

Pacific Palisades, Friday, September 22, 1944
Wrote a little of Chapter XXII. Am experiencing a certain hesitancy, caused by indecision over the musical aspects. . . .

Pacific Palisades, Monday, September 25, 1944
Ocean breeze, cooler. Hard work on XXII (twelve-tone music, studies, excerpts). . . . Adorno's treatise on Wagner.[137]

Pacific Palisades, Tuesday, September 26, 1944
Working hard on the form for the musical elements in XXII. . . .

Pacific Palisades, Thursday, September 28, 1944
Worked on XXII, laborious. Changes will be necessary. Went for a walk on Amalfi Drive. Read the papers after lunch. In the afternoon wrote long letter to A. Meyer.[138] In the evening read some of Adorno's essay on Wagner. Stayed up late listening to "Elsa's Dream" [*Lohengrin*], the magical "In Splendid, Shining Armor" [*Lohengrin*], the Rome story [*Tannhauser*], very powerful, then the closing scene of *Rheingold* with the indescribably sentimental and deeply affecting "Tender and true 'tis but in the waters." The triad world of the *Ring* is basically my musical home. And on the piano I can't get enough of the Tristan chord.—Churchill also refusing to deny that the European war may go on for several months of 1945. Perhaps, after all, I won't be able to use German paper to record the end of what started in 1933.

---

106. The writer Emil Ludwig (1881–1948) and his wife, Elga.

107. In *The Story of a Novel* Mann writes: "At this time Schoenberg sent me his book on harmony, the *Harmonielehre*, and the libretto of his oratorio, *Jacob's Ladder*, whose religious poetry I found impure. On the other hand, I was all the more impressed by his extraordinary textbook, whose pedagogic attitude is one of sham conservatism, the strangest mingling of piety toward tradition and revolution" (52).

108. The Polish writer Schalom Asch (1880–1957), author of *The Nazarene* (1939).

109. Evidently *Fête polonaise* by Emanuel Chabrier (1841–94). French conductor Pierre Monteux, conductor of the San Francisco Symphony Orchestra from

1935 to 1952, had conducted at the premieres of Stravinsky's *Petrushka* (1911), *The Rite of Spring* (1913), Debussy's *Jeux* (1913), and Ravel's *Daphnis et Chloé* (1912). In April 1945 Monteux conducted at a performance of Schoenberg's Chamber Symphony No. 2, op. 38, in San Francisco.

110. Mann's son Klaus (1906–49), a fellow writer [*Mephisto* (1936)], was serving as a sergeant in the US Fifth Army. On September 1, 1943, Klaus Mann wrote to Schoenberg asking him for his autograph for a war bonds auction in Kansas City, Missouri. On September 8, 1943, Schoenberg responded with two manuscript pages from his Chamber Symphony No. 2, op. 38, and *Kol Nidre*, op. 39. On October 11, 1943, Klaus Mann reported that the auction had been a great success, as the entire collection of autographs had been auctioned for $1 million. He added: "I wanted to write in person to tell you how delighted I was to discover just how many friends and admirers you have in this country. Your doubts about how attractive your manuscript would be to the general public proved completely unfounded. In actuality we received more offers for your musical fragments than for any other item (including Stravinsky's manuscript of his version of the *Star Spangled Banner*)."

111. Karl Heinrich Stein, *Tilman Riemenschneider im deutschen Bauernkrieg: Geschichte einer geistigen Haltung* (Vienna: Herbert Reichner, 1937).

112. Karl Philipp Moritz, *Anton Reiser* (Berlin: Friedrich Maurer, 1785–90).

113. Mann did not in fact produce an article for the *Overseas Press*, instead airing his views on the topic in the essay "Germany and the Germans" and in his BBC radio broadcast "Listen, Germans!" Mann, *Tagebücher, 1944–1946*, 343.

114. American composer Alfred Wallenstein (1898–1983) was musical director of the Los Angeles Philharmonic from 1943 to 1956. In 1948 Schoenberg complained to the young composer Henry Cowell: "Mr. Wallenstein has been here in Los Angeles for six years and hasn't played a single one of my pieces yet." In 1949 Wallenstein conducted "Song of the Wood Dove" from Schoenberg's *Gurrelieder*.

115. The article appeared in *Good Housekeeping*, August 1944, 17, 141. Mann, *Tagebücher, 1944–1946*, 384.

116. On June 20, 1944, Mann wrote to Erich von Kahler: "At present I'm benefiting from spending time with the musicians, Stravinsky, Schoenberg, Toch, Rubinstein—they're all here."

117. Lise Arnold, wife of the Dresden banker Heinrich Arnold. Mann knew the Arnolds from his early exile years in Zurich. Heinrich Arnold did not leave Germany and died in 1935. Mann, *Tagebücher, 1944–1946*, 341.

118. The sociologist and political scientist Dr. Leo Matthias (1893–1970) immigrated to Mexico in 1933; in 1935 he came to the United States, where he taught at various universities before returning to Europe in 1950.

119. Ludwig Lewisohn, *Breathe Upon These* (1944).

120. The actor Charlie Chaplin (1889–1977) was acquitted of charges under the Mann Act, which banned the transport of women across state lines "for immoral purposes." The charges related to his relationship with actress Joan Barry (1920–96). The latter had brought a paternity suit against Chaplin, ultimately winning the case when a blood test that would have refuted her allegations was ruled inadmissible.

121. The Viennese book dealer, author, and journalist Martin Flinker (1895–1986) emigrated in 1938, was captured on the way to England, and spent the war in internment in Tangiers.

122. Schoenberg, Six Little Piano Pieces, op. 19 (1911).

123. Theodor Wiesengrund-Adorno, *Klage*, op. 5; *6 Lieder nach Texten des österreichischen Lyrikers Georg Trakl* (1887–1914).

124. Adorno, Lieder für Singstimme und Klavier nach Gedichten des deutschen Dichters Stefan George, op. 1 and op. 7.

125. Probably a poem by German romantic poet Clemens von Brentano (1778–1842). Along with Achim von Arnim, Brentano edited the important folk song collection *Des Knaben Wunderhorn*, songs from which were set to music by Mahler, Schoenberg, and numerous other composers. Mann, *Tagebücher, 1944–1946*, 450.

126. American literary agent Armin L. Robinson was involved in a lawsuit concerning his anthology *The Ten Commandments*, for which he had secured the rights to Mann's Moses novella *The Tables of the Law*. Mann, *Tagebücher, 1944–1946*, 451.

127. Mann knew the actor and director Richard Révy (1885–1964) from Munich. The latter was also friendly with Schoenberg in Los Angeles. Mann, *Tagebücher, 1944–1946*, 356.

128. Writer and journalist Wilhelm Herzog (1884–1960), one of Mann's close friends. Mann, *Tagebücher, 1944–1946*, 356.

129. "This evening we were invited over to the composer Ernst Toch, who for some reason wants to play a new work to me, and Ernst Krenek came to visit us recently too. I spoke to him at length about the current position of music, about Schoenberg and about Stravinsky—such an attractive person." Mann to Meyer, August 25, 1944, in Mann and Meyer, *Briefwechsel, 1937–1955*, 581.

130. The Austrian composer Ernst Toch (1887–1964) left Germany in 1933 and from 1936 taught at the University of Southern California. He and his wife, Lilly, were friends of the Schoenbergs. On August 27, 1944, Mann wrote to Jonas Lesser: "I often go to bed late, as there's a lot of socializing in the far superior 'Europe' assembled here on the coast. Music plays more of a role than previously, thanks to its mysterious, magnetic qualities. There's a personal side to that too: Schoenberg, Stravinsky, Toch, Klemperer, Adorno-Wiesengrund—they're all here. Ernst Krenek also paid us a visit recently, and suddenly I find myself in fairly frequent contact with all of them, without actually having been involved in that process. We've also had chamber music played here in our home by first-rate musicians ([Henri] Temianka, [William] Vandenberg), especially while our youngest son, who plays viola in the San Francisco Symphony Orchestra, was staying here with his Swiss wife and two young sons." On October 7, 1944, Mann wrote to Gerhard Albersheim: "I can merely reiterate that I found your lecture ['Contemporary Music in Light of the History of Musical Art' (September 15, 1944)] excellent and highly instructive both as a lecture and as a portrayal of the current situation. What I want is to be instructed and no more, as I'm not nearly enough of a musician to be able to participate in the debate. I wasn't at all surprised by the message of your essay, if one can call it that. In fact I heard Ernst Toch say much the same thing, and in doing so he certainly wasn't setting out to deny his modernism. The counter-movement against Schoenberg, Berg, Krenek, etc. you mention has undoubtedly been necessary from an artistic and social standpoint. Yet the movement itself has definitely been both necessary and utterly serious in terms of analyzing contemporary issues and materials, and I interpret your viewpoint as suggesting it won't have been in vain. I think one has to link the crisis in *all* the arts—is it any different in painting or in the novel?—to the problems and unjustifiable nature of our social circumstances, which force artists either to produce 'goods' or to raise objections, at least intellectually, to everything that has gone before. As for myself, I'm a slack traditionalist compared with Joyce or Picasso. Yet I fully understand the fear of everything used-up, and I have a lot of respect for hatred of the market and critical determination in intellectual and artistic matters."

131. Toch's *Cantata of the Bitter Herbs*, op. 65 (1938) was commissioned by Rabbi Jacob Sonderling (1874–1964), who also commissioned Schoenberg's *Kol Nidre*, op. 39 (1938), Korngold's *Passover Psalm*, op. 30 (1941), and Zeisl's *Requiem Ebraico* (1945).

132. Hungarian composer Béla Bartók (1881–1945).

133. Anna Jacobson (1888–1972), who taught German literature at Hunter College in New York, published numerous articles on Mann. Mann, *Tagebücher, 1944–1946*, 379.

134. *Transfigured Night, Sextet for Two Violins, Two Violas, and Two Violoncellos*, op. 4 (1899), inspired by a poem by Richard Dehmel, was Schoenberg's most successful postromantic work. In 1902 he wrote: "I wrote using Richard Dehmel's poem *Transfigured Night* as inspiration, hoping to reproduce in chamber music the new forms that have appeared in orchestral music based on poetic ideas. The orchestra possesses (so to speak) the epic-dramatic qualities of tone poem composition, while chamber music constitutes the more lyrical-epic. If one argues that the latter's resources are inferior to the orchestra's in terms of tone-poetic powers of expression (that shortcoming is only noticeable in comparisons; however, if it actually is a shortcoming, it constitutes an argument in favor of the symphony over the string quartet with regard to *color*), then what they have in common is the principle of creation of form. This is an ancient principle, with origins among the old masters who used textual repetition (which nowadays seem rather endless) to weave lengthy musical fantasies around a poetic thought until all possible moods and meanings had been teased out—one could almost say until they had analyzed that poetic thought."

135. Literary historian Harry Slochower (1900–1991).

136. The writer Leonhard Frank (1882–1961) fled Germany in 1933; in 1940 he was held in internment in France before emigrating to the United States.

137. Cf. Adorno, *In Search of Wagner* (London: Verso, 2005).

138. See next letter, Mann to Meyer, September 28, 1944.

MANN TO AGNES MEYER, SEPTEMBER 28, 1944

September 28, 1944
1550 San Remo Drive
Pacific Palisades
California

Dear Agnes,

. . .

Work[139] is progressing rather slowly at the moment. It's very difficult to make certain things easy, enjoyable and suitable for dialogue, and to keep them from sounding too much like a treatise. What's involved here is of course various specific aspects of music: how Adrian, of his own devices and without being aware of the Viennese, is able to invent the twelve-tone system and arrange the song *Oh Dear Girl, How Bad You Are!* [Brentano] based on the series h-e-a-e-es [B-E-A-E-E♭] (Hetaera Esmeralda), such that serial music comes across as a work of the devil. Schoenberg will end our friendship! All the very best,

T.M.

---

139. *Doktor Faustus,* chap. 22.

MANN'S DIARY

Pacific Palisades, Friday, September 29, 1944

Worked on XXII. Despite the fact that montage is one of the book's compositional principles, assembling Adorno's musical ideas is in practice proving awkward. Witty and compelling composition will be the only way to justify the effort.[140] ...

Pacific Palisades, Sunday, September 30, 1944

Worked on XXII. (Twelve-tone system). Integrating what I've studied and acquired into the work's atmosphere and context has been a pleasure.[141] ... Notes on technical aspects of music. In the evening finished Adorno's *Wagner.* Enormously intelligent and insightful.

Pacific Palisades, Wednesday, October 4, 1944

Completed Chapter XXII.[142] Have achieved a certain conformity, as each chapter is about twenty pages long. This one has been hard work, but satisfactory as part of the overall composition. ...

---

140. See Mann's letter to Adorno dated December 30, 1945.

141. In a half-deleted passage in *The Story of a Novel,* Mann wrote: "Should I also cite the transfer of the Schoenbergian idea of twelve-tone or serial music to Adrian Leverkühn—to which certain parties have raised objections—as an example of an act of montage of this kind, and as an example of stealing from reality? In fact I will probably have to do so in future: at Schoenberg's request, the book will have to bear a postscript explaining intellectual property rights to the uninitiated. This is somewhat against my wishes. Not because a statement of that kind would constitute a minor breach of my novel's spherical, self-contained world, but because there has been no theft or expropriation, either in earnest or jest. It is true that, in keeping with the book's aforementioned spherical, self-contained nature, neither of the names Schoenberg or Nietzsche is mentioned. However, at no point does the text state that Leverkühn (and *not* Schoenberg) is the inventor of the twelve-tone system. He does not make that allegation, nor is that allegation made about him. During the stroll with the friend who knows nothing of Vienna, Hauer, or Schoenberg, he develops the complex theory of a new "rigorous style," of which there are certain initial traces in his earlier output, though he does not say he invented it. The danger is not that the reader may believe my composer to be the originator of the theory, but that he or she may, quite consistently, believe that I am. I have taken that risk into account for the simple reason that, within the sphere of the book and its coloration, the idea of the twelve-tone system takes on a quality which—am I not right?—it does not actually possess and which to some extent makes it my own property, i.e., the property of the book. Schoenberg's idea and my *ad hoc* version differ so radically that, aside from the issue of improper style, I feel it would be somewhat offensive to mention his name in the text." Mann, *Die Entstehung des Doktor Faustus* (Frankfurt am Main: S. Fischer, 2002), 700; Mann, *Tagebücher, 1944–1946,* 943. See also Abel, *Musikästhetik der Klassischen Moderne,* 228.

142. See Appendix VI: "Thomas Mann, Chapter 22 of *Doctor Faustus.*"

SCHOENBERG TO MANN, OCTOBER 3, 1944

Los Angeles, California[143]
October 3, 1944

Mr. and Mrs. Thomas Mann,

For more than a week I tried composing a letter of thanks to those who congratulated me on the occasion of my seventieth birthday. Still I did not succeed: it is terribly difficult to produce something if one is conceited enough to believe that everybody expects something extraordinary from you at an occasion like this.

But in fact the contrary might be true: at this age, if one is still capable of giving once in a while a sign of life, everybody might consider this already as a satisfactory accomplishment. I have acknowledged this when my piano concerto was premiered and to my great astonishment so many were astonished that I still have something to tell. Or perhaps, that I do not yet stop telling it—or that I still am not wise enough to suppress it— or to learn finally to be silent at all?

Many recommend: "Many happy returns!"

Thank you, but will this help?

Will I really become wiser this way?

I cannot promise it, but let us hope.

Most sincerely with many thanks, yours,

Arnold Schoenberg

---

143. A printed "Thank You" letter, which Schoenberg sent to all those who had sent him congratulations on the occasion of his seventieth birthday on September 13, 1944.

SCHOENBERG TO MANN, OCTOBER 11, 1944

Dear Mr. Mann:[144]

The great delay of this letter is not only due to the embarrassment I mention above, but also to the printer who needed two weeks and to the great number of letters I have to answer. But I want, though "late but not least," to express the great pleasure and surprise when we came home from Riverside and we found your flowers. They were really beautiful[145]—as bad as my English is, it doesn't even begin to match the banality of all these phrases that I can only render with uncertainty. No, but really: it was very gracious of you—even much more than that—that at precisely this point of my life you observed my birthday; that with everything else going on you even took the time to do that! I personally am not so happy about the fact that right now—when I would need to be young—I am already so old! I think there was a mistake in my timing, or I might have easily avoided this.

Well, after all, I should still be able to joke around a little! Or perhaps—now especially?

Again: heartfelt thanks and many greetings, yours truly,

Arnold Schoenberg

---

144. Handwritten letter that was sent together with the official printed "Thank You" letter. Apparently Mann only received the letter of October 3 together with this letter of October 11.

145. At this point Schoenberg switches to German.

GOTTFRIED BERMANN-FISCHER TO SCHOENBERG, NOVEMBER 6, 1944

November 6, 1944
Prof. Arnold Schoenberg
West Los Angeles, Cal.

Dear Professor:

Thomas Mann will be turning seventy on June 6, 1945. Our Publishing House intends to bring out a special edition of his magazine, *Die Neue Rundschau,* which had fallen victim to the Nazis, and thereby call back into life this lost voice of a free thinker.

The special edition will contain a collection of significant contributions by important international personalities—essays written specifically with the intention of honoring Thomas Mann, or literary works dedicated to him, poems, narratives, or essays. It will appear in Stockholm, Sweden, at the end of May 1945, and at the time of its publication will be distributed to all responsive countries. The proceeds from the sales of this publication will be turned over to Thomas Mann to be given to writers in exile who are in need of support.

The publishers are asking you to join those who wish to honor the writer and send your contribution in any form such as those suggested above, approximately 600 words, to 381 Fourth Ave. New York 16, N.Y. Respectfully,

G.B. Fischer
Bermann-Fischer Publishers

MANN'S DIARY

Pacific Palisades, Friday, December 1, 1944

Breakfast in bed, took a bath afterwards. Tired, not much writing. Read some Shakespeare and some of *Lotte in Weimar*. Singer came to tea; must write a report about him for the Guggenheim Foundation. Brought a carton of Pall Mall. Wrote to Hardt in New York. In the evening listened to Schoenberg's *Transfigured Night*.

Pacific Palisades, Wednesday, December 6, 1944

Up at eight. Longer walk in beautiful weather. Worked on the chapter (changes). With Katia on the Promenade. Bench overlooking the ocean. American demonstration against British policy in Greece and Italy, sensational. Tea in bedroom and bathroom. Dinner party at the Schoenbergs. Discussion of music. *Parsifal* harmonics checked for unresolved dissonances. Eisler's odd criticism: "So poorly composed!"—Discussion of archaic forms of variation. Autograph.[146]

---

146. In *The Story of a Novel* Mann recalls one evening at the Schoenbergs: "On the other hand, Hanns Eisler was to be met at Schoenberg's house. I always took the greatest pleasure in Eisler's sparkling conversation, especially when it centered around Wagner and the comical ambivalence of Eisler's relationship to the great demagogue. Eisler would 'catch on to his tricks,' shake his finger in the air, and cry out: 'You old fraud!' It made me shake with laugher. I recall how he and Schoenberg one evening, at my urging incidentally, went through the *Parsifal* harmonic system at the piano, searching for unresolved dissonances. To be precise, there was only one: in the Amfortas part of the last act. They then explained archaic forms of variation about which I had inquired for good reasons of my own, and Schoenberg presented me with a penciled sheet of notes and figures illustrating the matter." Mann, *The Story of a Novel*, 103–4. The whereabouts of the autograph are unknown. Eisler subsequently began work on a *Dr. Faustus* opera, the libretto of which was completed on July 13, 1951, the day of Schoenberg's death. Hanns Eisler, "Notes on *Dr. Faustus*," in *Hanns Eisler: A Miscellany*, ed. David Blake (Luxembourg: Harwood, 1995), 251–56.

SCHOENBERG TO GOTTFRIED BERMANN-FISCHER, JANUARY 16, 1945

Mr. G. B. Fischer
Bermann-Fischer Verlag
381 Fourth Avenue
New York, N.Y.
January 16, 1945

Most esteemed Mr. Fischer:

In a separate mailing I am sending you the original on transparent paper of my contribution of a dedication on the occasion of Thomas Mann's seventieth birthday, and a copy thereof is included in this letter.

As you can see I did not title it as I had originally mentioned in my earlier letter. It has to remain untitled, with the exception of *To Thomas Mann, June 6, 1945*. It would have taken too much time to place the words under the parts and I would not have been able to keep my promised deadline.[147]

I suggest that you have one, or better yet, two photocopies or blueprints made of my original in New York and then send the original back to me, because I would like to give it to Mr. Mann personally. Of course the copy would have to be perfect, if the printer in Stockholm wants to reproduce it as a facsimile. However, my copy ought to be quite sufficient for purposes of engraving.

I assume that my copy can be shrunk enough to fit the format for the pages of the paper *Die Neue Rundschau*. I assume it will be about half the size of my original and still be legible. With all good wishes I remain your loyal,

Arnold Schoenberg

---

147. Bermann-Fischer had written Schoenberg on December 26, 1944, and told him that the manuscript had to be ready by January 20, 1945, so that it might be sent to Sweden in time to be printed.

MANN'S DIARY

Pacific Palisades, Wednesday, February 14, 1945
... Klemperer concert in Westwood after supper: Gluck, Schoenberg's Chamber Symphony,[148] some bad piano music, Beethoven's Fifth. Paid a visit to Klemperer's room. Raining. Chocolate at home....

---

148. A Los Angeles Philharmonic performance of Schoenberg's Chamber Symphony No. 2, op. 38 at UCLA's Royce Hall, conducted by Klemperer. Schoenberg began composing this tonal work in 1906, ultimately completing it in 1939. It premiered at Carnegie Hall in New York on December 15, 1940, under the baton of Fritz Stiedry, in a live radio broadcast that Schoenberg listened to in Los Angeles. Adorno probably attended the premiere, as he frequently mentions the piece in his *Philosophy of New Music*, completed a few months later. During March and April of 1945 a Schoenberg music festival was held at UCLA, but there are no indications that Mann attended any of the concerts.

MANN TO BRUNO WALTER, MARCH 1, 1945

Pacific Palisades, California[149]
1550 San Remo Drive
March 1, 1945

Dear Bruno,

Erika has written to me saying you have read—indiscreetly as Hofmannsthal would put it—isolated extracts from the early part of the novel in *Aufbau*[150] and dispute some of the musical-technical parts, which "according to your convictions" are untenable, as she phrases it. Naturally I'm shocked, though I can't imagine what could be wrong or a matter for dispute in the childlike passages in question. Are you referring to the frequently mentioned and often disputed coloristic nature of the different keys? Or the discovery of the wind rose of the keys themselves? Or the fact that the young assistant hits on the idea of the modulation method for enharmonic ambiguity? That's all there is, after all. Aside from that, nothing happens, and what I find particularly incomprehensible is how this could imply some sort of suggestion of Schoenberg![151]

Please enlighten me! Have I, in my primitive utterances, committed one or more *faux pas* that would cause experts considerable mirth; if so, I will have to hastily correct them pursuant to your instructions. Werfel, who is quite familiar with music, said *nothing at all* about it when I read him the chapter. Frau Mahler was there too. But it's of little concern to them if I make a fool of myself, so I'm very grateful to you for having kept a sharp eye out.

I no longer subscribe to *Aufbau*. I didn't like it and found it had little to say. I'm therefore sending you a carbon copy of the typewritten version of the chapter, in the hope it jogs your memory so you can voice your concerns to me. . . .

My lecture in Washington (Germany and the Germans![152] Tricky material!) is scheduled for May 29. After that we'll be spending a few weeks in New York. I take it you'll be there. I want to explain the novel to you in greater depth, including the purpose of this intellectual musician character. The new, radical music, the Schoenberg system even, has a contributory role to play, my dear friend. Like all the other arts, and not only the arts, music is in crisis, which sometimes seems to threaten its very existence. In literature the crisis is occasionally concealed via the use of ironic traditionalism. But Joyce for example, whom I resemble in some ways, is just as much of an affront to the classically-romantically-realistically attuned mind as Schoenberg and his ilk. By the way, I can't actually read Joyce; you have to have grown up in an English-speaking culture to be able to. As for the corresponding music, you have nothing to fear for me personally. Basically, I hopelessly adore romantic kitsch and can still get tearful over a sublime diminished seventh. The novel deals with the paralysis arising from cleverness and the intellectual experience of the crisis; the pact with the devil is made in the hope of achieving an inspirational breakthrough. This really is a profound opportunity, rich in allusional possibilities. Music as such basically only plays a symbolic role, but that doesn't mean the details don't have to be absolutely right. With best wishes,

Thomas Mann

PS: I'm wondering whether to send you the entire opening section of the novel along with the chapter in question. The fragment on its own is rather wretched without the atmosphere.

---

149. Thomas Mann to Bruno Walter, March 1, 1945, in Mann, *Briefe*, 2:415–16; *Blätter der Thomas-Mann-Gesellschaft*, no. 9, 28–29.

150. "Das Harmonium" [excerpt from *Doktor Faustus*], in *Aufbau*, Dec. 22, 1944.

151. On March 6, 1945, Mann wrote to his daughter Erika: "I've written to Bruno Walter. He has something against the book and has expressed all sorts of reservations—as though I didn't have any myself. . . . He's suspicious of the fact that I bring in atonality, the Schoenbergian, critical material, in short, as well as material relating to the crisis. Naturally I did do all that, but not in the completely harmless chapter he read. Evidently he read it with considerable suspicion and feels he has already found something. I can't imagine what could be wrong with the childlike passages in question, or how a matter of 'conviction' could be involved, as you quote him as saying. Is it the frequently mentioned and often disputed coloristic individual nature of the keys? Or the primitive discovery of the keys themselves? Or the discovery of enharmonic ambiguity? Aside from that, nothing happens! I really can't understand how that could imply some sort of suggestion of Schoenberg." Mann, *Tagebücher, 1944–1946*, 591.

152. Mann, "Germany and the Germans" (1946). Mann gave the lecture in the Library of Congress in May of 1945. In it he discussed *inter alia* the role of music in German cultural life.

MANN'S DIARY

Pacific Palisades, Sunday, March 11, 1945

Am using the last notebook from Europe for these notes started twelve years ago.—Up at eight. After bath, took short walk in the mist in overcoat. Eggs and coffee for breakfast. Worked on "Germany and the Germans" until midday. Went for walk along Amalfi Drive, was picked up by Peter Pringsheim[153] and Katia . . .—With Peter and Katia after lunch. At five went to the Riebers,[154] who drove with us to tea at the Westwood home of Professor K. and his wife. Schoenberg, the Arlts, the Nitzes[155] and other American academics there . . .

Pacific Palisades, Tuesday, March 13, 1945

Up at half past eight. Overcast, cool. Worked on lecture. After shaving strolled in neighborhood. Receipts from *Free World* and essay came in mail. $1,700 for Spanish translation rights. Letter from Erika with malicious remarks about Borgese's[156] absurd hatred of the Allies and resulting reverence towards the Germans. *Aufbau*'s ban on Furtwängler[157] in Switzerland. Germans should stay home.—Tea in bedroom. Dinner party at young Reinhardts,[158] with Schnabel,[159] Schoenberg, Klemperer, the Dieterles and others. Discussion about music . . .

Pacific Palisades, Thursday, March 22, 1945

. . . Dinner chez Alma Werfel, with the Bemelmanses,[160] the Arlts, and the banker Rosenblatt and family. Schoenbergs not there . . .

---

153. Peter Pringsheim (1881–1964), Katia Mann's brother, professor of physics in Berlin from 1930 to 1933. After being forced to resign he emigrated to Brussels and then the United States.

154. Retired UCLA philosophy professor Charles Henry Rieber (1866–1948) and his wife, the portraitist Winifred Rieber, lived near the Manns, at 13545 Lucca Drive.

155. American novelist William A. Nitze (1876–1957), professor of French language and literature at UCLA, and his wife, Anina Sophie.

156. Italian American professor of literature Giuseppe Antonio Borgese (1882–1952), husband of Mann's daughter, the writer Elisabeth Mann (1918–2002).

157. Wilhelm Furtwängler (1886–1954) took over as principal conductor of the Berlin Philharmonic in 1922. Schoenberg's Variationen für Orchester, op. 31 (1928) premiered under his baton. Despite his reservations about the Nazis, he stayed on in Germany and in 1947 was barred from the profession by the Allies as a result. Mann is referring to Manfred George's editorial "Kulturboten—Todesboten" in *Aufbau* 11, no. 10 (March 9, 1945): 4, about the ban imposed on Furtwängler in Zurich. Mann, *Tagebücher, 1944–1946*, 588. Mann viewed Furtwängler as an opportunist

and Nazi supporter (Mann, *Tagebücher, 1944–1946*, 556), while Schoenberg was among those who defended him. On January 4, 1946, Schoenberg wrote to Kurt List, editor of the magazine *Listen:* "I agree with you about Furtwängler. I am certain he was never a Nazi. He was one of those old-fashioned German nationalists from the days of Turnvater Jahn, when people opposed the Western nations supporting Napoleon. That was essentially all about student nationalism—very different from the nationalism during the Bismarck period and later, when Germany was on the offensive rather than the defensive. I am also certain he was not an anti-Semite, at any rate no more than any other non-Jew. And he is definitely a better musician than all the Toscaninis, Ormandis, Koussevitzkis et al. He is a genuine talent and lover of music."

158. The producer Gottfried Reinhardt (1913–94) and his wife, Sylvia. In *The Story of a Novel* Mann wrote: "Social events, for example with Schnabel, Schoenberg, or Klemperer at the home of the young Gottfried Reinhardt, with long discussions about music after dinner, helped maintain . . . 'contact' " (110).

159. After immigrating to the United States in 1938 the Austrian pianist and composer Artur Schnabel (1882–1951) took a teaching position at the University of Chicago. During concert trips to Los Angeles he was a frequent guest of the Schoenbergs.

160. Ludwig Bemelmans (1898–1962), Tyrol-born writer and illustrator, a close friend of the Werfels. Mann, *Tagebücher, 1946–1948*, 580.

SCHOENBERG TO MANN, JUNE 6, 1945

For Thomas Mann, June 6, 1945

Most probably because I wanted to show you my esteem in a very special way, I made it especially difficult, in fact almost impossible for myself with this canon [fig. 1.2]. It sounds quite impossible, by the way, and I hope you will not want to listen to it (and that is why I wrote the notation in the "old" clefs). It is not without (genuine) egoism that I wish: that we might be good contemporaries of each other for many years to come. Warmest greetings, your,

Arnold Schoenberg

FIGURE 1.2.   Arnold Schoenberg, birthday canon for Thomas Mann's seventieth birthday (1945).

MANN'S DIARY

Pacific Palisades, Wednesday, July 11, 1945

Continued work on the essay, flowing nicely. Walked as far as the bench on the street. Very bright and sunny day. New negro maid arrived. Letters and newspapers after lunch. Took a nap. Had tea in my room, shaved. Organized letters. Supper at the Werfels with Walter and the Schoenbergs. Long discussion. Champagne and crème de menthe. Drove Walter to Hotel Bel Air. His complete rejection of atonal music. Before that, talked about the regrettable disappearance of various light operas: *Frau Diavolo, Weisse Dame,* and particularly, *Don Pasquale.*

Pacific Palisades, Friday, September 2, 1945

Started article for *Chicago Daily News.* Haircut in Westwood at lunchtime. Continued work on article in the afternoon. Schoenbergs[161] and van Leydens to dinner. Lengthy discussion until midnight.—Stifter's *Kalkstein* indescribably odd and quietly audacious.

---

161. In his "Report by the Schoenberg Family on Their Life during and Immediately before the War" (1945), Schoenberg wrote: "We see Thomas Mann occasionally, either at his house or ours. We often see Brecht too." Arnold Schoenberg, *Stile herrschen, Gedanken siegen: Ausgewählte Schriften,* ed. Anna Maria Morazzoni (Mainz: Schott, 2007), 475.

MANN TO THEODOR WIESENGRUND-ADORNO, DECEMBER 30, 1945

1550 San Remo Drive
Pacific Palisades, California
December 30, 1945

Dear Dr. Adorno,

I should just like to say something about the manuscript I recently left with you and which I imagine you may be about to read.[162] In writing to you I certainly do not feel I am interrupting my work in any way.

I am quite excited that this strange and perhaps impossible work (what there is of it) is in your hands. For in the states of weariness which increasingly assail me I often wonder whether I should not abandon the whole thing, and your own view of the matter will not be without influence upon whether I persevere or not.

The aspect with regard to which I should principally be grateful to receive some detailed comment is the principle of montage which peculiarly, perhaps outrageously, pervades the entire book—explicitly so and without the slightest concealment. Only recently I have been struck by this again in a half amusing, half uncanny fashion when I came to describe a critical illness in the life of my hero. For I incorporated Nietzsche's actual symptoms word for word, just as they are described in his letters, along with details of his prescribed diet etc., straight into the book. I simply pasted them in, so to speak, for anyone to recognize. I have followed the same principle with the motif of Tchaikovsky's invisible admirer and lover, Madame von Meck, whom he never met, indeed expressly avoided meeting in the flesh. I paste this familiar historical material in and allow the edges to blur, dropping it into the text as a mythical theme there for anyone to pick up. (For Leverkühn the relationship is a way of circumventing the devil's proscription of love, the commandment enjoining coldness.)

Or to take another example—towards the end of the book I obviously introduce the theme, complete with actual quotations, from Shakespeare's sonnets: the triangle where the friend sends his friend to woo the beloved on his behalf—and the friend ends up "wooing for himself." Of course, I also transform the material: Adrian kills the friend whom he loves since the resulting involvement with the woman in question exposes him in the end to an act of murderous jealousy (Innes Rodde). Nonetheless, this does little to alter the bold and thievish character of my borrowings.

It hardly seems sufficient to plead Moliere's "Je prends mon bien ou je le trouve"[163] as a justification for such conduct. Perhaps it springs from an inclination as one becomes older to regard life as a cultural product, preferring in one's petrified dignity to interpret it through mythical cliché rather than "independent" invention. But I am only too aware that I have long practiced this kind of higher transcription—as in the description of little Hanno Buddenbrook's typhoid fever, when I unabashedly transcribed the relevant article from an encyclopedia and subsequently "versified" it so to speak. This chapter has become rather famous. Yet its merit derives solely from a spiritual and creative elaboration of mechanically appropriated material (and the trick of indirectly communicating the fact of Hanno's death).

The case is more difficult, not to say more scandalous, when it is a question of appropriating material that is itself already spirit, that is, of an authentically literary borrowing and performed with an air that what has been filched in this way is just good enough to serve one's own compositional purposes. You will rightly gather that I am thinking here of the brazen—although I hope not too doltish—way in which I have raided parts of your writings on the philosophy of music.[164]

And I owe you a particular apology precisely because at present the reader can hardly be aware of these borrowings unless I find a way of acknowledging them without ruining the artistic illusion (a footnote like: "This derives from Adorno-Wiesengrund"? That surely won't do). It is curious: my own relationship to music has been fairly widely recognized, I have always been an adept at literary music-making, I have always felt halfway to being a musician myself, and I have tried to transfer the musical technique of interweaving motifs to the structure of the novel. And only recently, for instance, Ernst Toch expressly and emphatically congratulated me for being "musically initiated." But to write a novel about a musician, a novel that at times even aspires to become, among other things, and along with other things, a novel about music itself—this demands more than mere "initiation." It requires scholarship that I simply do not possess. Hence I was determined from the start in a book already beholden to the principle of montage, not to shrink from seeking assistance or support from the specialist work of others—in the confidence that what has been gleaned and learned from other people may nonetheless take on an independent function and symbolic life of its own with the literary composition—yet still remain intact in the works of criticism from which it derives.

My hope is that you will also share this view. The fact is that my own musical education scarcely extends beyond the late romantics, and you have given me an idea of the most modern developments in music, which is just what I require for a book that again, among other things, and together with many other things, takes the predicament of art as its subject. As in the earlier case of little Hanno's typhoid fever, my "initiated" ignorance required precise details to enhance the literary illusion and structure of the composition. And I would be deeply obliged if you would intervene and correct such details (which I have not derived entirely from you) if they should appear mistaken, misleading, or expressed in such a way as to provoke the scorn of experts. One passage has already been subjected to expert judgment. I read the passages on opus 111 to Bruno Walter and he was delighted. "Well, this is magnificent. Nothing better has ever been said about Beethoven! I had no idea that you had delved so deeply into the composer!" Nonetheless, I have no wish to set up the expert as the sole judge here. The musical expert in particular, always proud of his arcane knowledge, is for my purposes all too ready to betray a condescending smile. I would cautiously suggest, *cum grano salis*, that something may produce the right effect, may come out sounding right, without being entirely so.—But I am not attempting to ingratiate myself with you.

I have brought the novel to the point where Leverkühn at the age of thirty-five, in a first wave of euphoric inspiration, and in an incredibly short period of time, composes his principal work, or at least his first principal work, the *Apocalipsis cum figuris*, based upon the fifteen illustrations of Dürer or perhaps directly upon the text of the book of Revelation. And my task now is to imagine and characterize the work in the most suggestive possible manner (a work that I think of as a very German creation, as an oratorio with orchestra, choruses, soloists, and narrator). And I am basically writing this letter in order to clarify for my mind's eye something that as yet I have hardly dared to approach. What I need are some significant and characteristic details (only a few are required), which will create a plausible, indeed convincing, picture for the reader. Would you consider with me, how such a work—and I mean Leverkühn's work—could more or less be practically realized, and how you would compose the music if you yourself were in league with the devil? And could you suggest one or two musical features to further the imaginative illusion?—What I have in mind is something satanically religious and demonically devout, at once rigorously traditional and violently transgressive, something that often seems to scorn the idea of art itself, that reaches right back to the primitive and the elemental (as in Kretzschmar's reminiscences of Beissel),[165] that abandons regular meter or even tonality *(trombone glissandi)*;[166] and perhaps also something that is scarcely performable; like ancient church modes or non-tempered *a capella* choruses with notes and intervals one would hardly find on the keyboard etc. But of course it is very easy to say "etc."[167]

Even as I was writing these lines I have learned that I shall be seeing you earlier than I thought, since a meeting has already been arranged for Wednesday afternoon. So I could have said all this to you in person after all! But it still seems fitting, and I am thereby relieved, that you now have it written down in black and white. Let it be the basis for our ensuing discussion, as well as a record for posterity, if there should be a posterity. Yours faithfully,

Thomas Mann

---

162. Mann gave Adorno the manuscript of *Doktor Faustus* (up to chapter 33) on December 5, 1945. See Adorno and Mann, *Correspondence, 1943–1955*, 22; Mann, *Tagebücher, 1944–1946*, 282.

163. The great dramatist and actor Jean-Baptiste Poquelin, pseudo. Molière (1622–73). When he was accused of having stolen Cyrano de Bergerac's comedy *Le pedant joué* for his *Fourberies de Scapin,* Molière answered, "I am permitted to take what's good wherever I can find it." See Adorno and Mann, *Correspondence, 1943–1955,* 23.

164. Mann based chapter 8 of *Doktor Faustus* on Adorno's essay "Beethoven's Late Style." For chapters 12 and 15, where the twelve-tone method and Leverkühn's pact with the devil are described, Adorno's Wagner essay "In Search of Wagner" (1938) and his articles in Willi Reich's book on Alban Berg (1937), as well as the chapter on Schoenberg in *Philosophy of Modern Music* were crucial. Mann also referenced Adorno's book on Kierkegaard and his *Minima Moralia* when he worked on the novel. See Adorno and Mann, *Correspondence, 1943–1955,* 23.

165. The fourth lecture of Wendell Kretzschmar, in chapter 8 of *Doktor Faustus.*

166. Schoenberg composed the first *trombone glissando* in his symphonic poem *Pelléas and Mélisande,* op. 5 (1903).

167. Adorno drafted a few descriptions of compositions for Mann and met with him regularly during the ensuing months. See Adorno and Mann, *Correspondence, 1943–1955,* 24–25, 158–61. A long passage by Mann, which describes Adorno's specific contributions, was later edited out of the published version of Mann's *The Story of a Novel.* This passage contains the sentence: "The idea that in the despairing piece, dissonance should represent everything serious and spiritual, whereas harmony and tonality, by contrast, the world of hell, i.e., the commonplace, is genuine Schoenberg, even more so, Berg-school." Ibid., 25.

SCHOENBERG TO MANN, APRIL 24, 1946

Mrs. Thomas Mann,
c/o Professor Borgese
5124 Hyde Park Boulevard
Chicago, Ill.

Our thoughts are with you. Hoping to get soon good news about the great man.[168]

Mr. and Mrs. Schoenberg

---

168. Mann had traveled to Chicago to undergo an operation on his lung. See Mann, *The Story of a Novel*, 165–86.

MANN'S DIARY

Pacific Palisades, Tuesday, June 25, 1946

. . . Gramophone serviced and repaired. Played a series of records. We listened to *Verklärte Nacht* again on the radio; popularity derives from its sound. Lacking in substance: string arrangements and arabesques with a theme I could have come up with on the piano myself. Then listened to *Parsifal,* plastic, meaningful.

Pacific Palisades, Sunday, July 6, 1946

Worked on chapter a little. At midday went to podiatrist. Lot of mail, German, Swiss. Article by Fiedler critical of the Germans (O.R. Kauz).[169] Felt poorly in the afternoon, earache, restless. At the same time gripped by Conrad's *Jim.* Germany has nothing comparable: strong, adventurous, linguistically elevated, virile, psychologically-morally profound literature.— First evening out since illness: supper at Alma Werfel with the Schoenbergs, whom we picked up, and Karlweis.[170] Spoke to Schoenberg about the possibility of choirs singing untempered.[171]

Pacific Palisades, Wednesday, July 10, 1946

. . . In evening listened to Stravinsky's *Petrushka* suite, very amusing, picturesque music, charming duets with trumpets and flute. Romantic elements, not sure whether meant seriously. Sophisticated and urbane compared with German innovators.

Pacific Palisades, Friday, September 13, 1946

Tormented by itching during night. Hot. Worked on chapter. Tiresome treatment [Dr. Stout] at midday. Florence Homolka[172] to lunch; she took photographs in garden. After five Will Rogers[173] appeared with retinue and photographers to take propaganda shots for United States Senate campaign. Then Klemperer to tea, back from Europe, with daughter. After supper went to Schoenbergs to congratulate him on seventy-second birthday. Busy day. Long letter from Reisiger,[174] read aloud by Katia in the evening.

Pacific Palisades, Friday, November 15, 1946

. . . In evening read old issue of *Querschnitt* on musical situation in 1930.[175] . . . Tristan music (Dr. Eisler and his wife for lunch. Stimulating.).

Pacific Palisades, Tuesday, November 22, 1946

Morning fog. Cool at night. Bronchial catarrh.—Molotov in New York,[176] message of peace, confident.—Nearly finished the chapter. Longish walk along Amalfi Drive. Meat at lunchtime dreadful again. Lot of mail again, lot of it German again. Nietzsche's *Pages Mystiques*, edited by Robert Laffont.[177] Notified of lecture "Th. M. ou La Séduction de la Mort" by Jean Fougère.[178]—Exhausted. Stayed in bed until 6:30. Finished *The Nigger of the Narcissus*,[179] outstanding work.—Schoenbergs and Horkheimers[180] to dinner. Spoke with Schoenberg about his new trio, in which he depicts his illness and medical treatment including male nurse and so forth.[181] Performance extremely difficult, only possible for three virtuosi, but very rewarding in view of the sound.[182]—Horkheimer talked about our relationship with the German universities, as yet unclear. *Venia legendi.*

Pacific Palisades, Tuesday, December 26, 1946
. . . In evening read polemical essay on Schoenberg by Klaus Pringsheim. Feeling idle. Unhappy with the performance (deterioration) of our gramophone. Want a new one.—More rain throughout afternoon.

Pacific Palisades, Wednesday, January 1, 1947
. . . Buffet dinner chez Dr. Weil[183] and his American wife. Six of us drove over there together. Ate with Eisner[184] and Klaus Pringsheim. Much discussion of music, the poor payoff of the *Meistersinger* overture. Cheap counterpoint. Talked about Schoenberg. Talked about *Faustus*. Spoke to Feuchtwanger, Chaplin and his wife, also Dieterle etc. Left at eleven. Fight between Niko[185] and the Weils' dog.

Pacific Palisades, Thursday, January 2, 1947
. . . In evening listened to familiar Schubert trio. Felicitous state of music. Wish it had stayed at that level.—Read some of Werfel's poems, most recent edition, read some out loud. . . .

Pacific Palisades, Friday, January 3, 1947
. . . Schoenberg's *Verklärte Nacht* creates beautiful sound, but too long, too formless, often too Tristan-like in fact, and lacking in substance. Perhaps people love its only theme merely because there is one.

Pacific Palisades, Sunday, February 7, 1947
. . . Walked over to home of Marcuse,[186] who was lunching with us along with wife. Spoke at length about Nietzsche, whom he wants to see denazified.—Finished the letter in the afternoon. In the evening heard *Genesis*

collection[187] by Milhaud, Toch, Schoenberg, etc. Toch[188] the best. Such things strongly reminiscent of Adrian's music. . . .

Pacific Palisades, Monday, March 10, 1947

In morning and afternoon started article attacking Furtwängler.[189] . . .

Pacific Palisades, Tuesday, March 11, 1947

After talking to Katia, abandoned Furtwängler article as pointless and undignified.—Wrote on Nietzsche.—Had haircut in Westwood. . . . Supper at the Schoenbergs, small intimate circle, half of them American. Chaotic and loud. Not allowed to smoke.[190] Schoenberg devoted, always wants to talk to me. Left after ten.

Pacific Palisades, Sunday, January 3, 1948

. . . At 6:30 went with Erika to the Walters. Consoling tête-à-tête about novel. He is impressed by it, and not bothered by the role played by music, nor the fact that it takes trends since Strauss seriously. Comforting explanations. His *sadness* as he informed me that Schoenberg and Schnabel had both denied dissonance's need for resolution!—I drew attention to the fateful aspects—the fate of music as a paradigm of culture in general. His interesting account of how, with Beethoven, music fell from grace and became weighed down by human elements and passion, having previously been a heavenly, free interplay of forms, divine rather than human.—Cocktails when the ladies arrived. Supper with a very mild Lafito. Mahler played on powerful equipment, with very bright strings. Amazed he doesn't find it offensive to the ear.—Impossible position of the Germans, who, in adoration of their own failure, are now railing against Friedrich, Bismarck, Nietzsche, and Wagner, hoping to shake off centuries of history. Perhaps a return to medievally pious, simple circumstances. Just scribblings about the economy.—Erika read out the unbelievable letter from Johst to Himmler.[191] Drove home with her.

Pacific Palisades, Sunday, January 11, 1948

Fine, slightly misty weather. Katia took letter and book over to Eisler, who with his Czech papers has declared intention to leave the country.[192]— Excerpts, medieval, mission.—Walked as far as crossroads in damp fog. Katia reported back that the Eislers were in cheerful mood, and had heard news of *Faustus*'s success in Europe. He had read the *Weheklag* in a Viennese paper and found it immense. . . .

Pacific Palisades, Wednesday, January 14, 1948

Signed copies of *Faustus* intended for various people including Schoenberg, Feuchtwanger, Lion, Rastede, Alfred Löwenberg[193]—author of the opera annals—and Fiedler. Deliberated over Toch's *Musiklehre*, doubts over whether to write the foreword.[194] Cheered up by the *New Yorker*. . . .

---

169. Kuno Fiedler used the pseudonym Dr. Phil F. Kauz when writing for Swiss publications. Mann, *Tagebücher, 1946–1948*, 392.

170. Viennese actor Oskar Karlweis (1894–1956), brother of Marta Wassermann-Karlweis (the second wife of the writer Jakob Wassermann), immigrated to France in 1938. In 1940 he moved to the United States and became a successful film actor and Broadway singer. Mann, *Tagebücher, 1946–1948*, 379.

171. See Zeitblom's description of the chorale in Leverkühn's *Apocalipsis*, chapter 34 (Schlussfolgerung), in Mann, *Gesammelte Werke*, 6:496–503. Mann, *Tagebücher, 1946–1948*, 392. Angelika Abel writes: "In *Die Entstehung des Doktor Faustus* Mann noted that 'behind Adorno's back he had taken advice from Schoenberg,' who had answered that, though it was theoretically possible, he wouldn't do it himself. Despite this 'authorisation from above,' Mann abandoned the idea." Angelika Abel, *Musikästhetik der Klassischen Moderne*, 222 (Mann, *Gesammelte Werke*, 11:246).

172. Florence Homolka (1911–62), daughter of Agnes Meyer and wife of Austrian actor Oskar Homolka (1898–1978).

173. Actor and congressman Will Rogers Jr. (1911–93), son of the famous cowboy comedian Will Rogers (1879–1935), won the Democratic nomination for US senator from California, ultimately losing out in elections to Senator William F. Knowland. See Mann, *Tagebücher, 1946–1948*, 433 (where he is incorrectly referred to as William Pierce Rogers, who later served as US secretary of state).

174. The writer and translator Hans Reisiger (1884–1968), who had been one of Mann's closest friends since 1913. Mann, *Tagebücher, 1937–1939*, 522.

175. Contains Schoenberg's essay, "Mein Publikum." *Der Querschnitt: Magazin der aktuellen Ewigkeitswerte* 4, no. 10 (1930): 222–24. The essay begins with the words: "When asked to comment on my audience, I must confess: I believe I have none." Schoenberg, *Stile herrschen, Gedanken siegen*, 411.

176. At the first General Assembly of the United Nations in Lake Success, New York, which began on October 23, 1946. Mann, *Tagebücher, 1946–1948*, 463.

177. Nietzsche, *Pages mystiques: Extraits traduits et accompagnés d'éclaircissements par A. Quinot* (Paris: Robert Laffont, 1945); Mann, *Tagebücher, 1946–1948*, 463.

178. French historian and author Jean Fougère (1914–2005). Mann, *Tagebücher, 1946–1948*, 463.

179. Joseph Conrad, *The Nigger of the Narcissus: A Tale of the Sea* (1897).

180. The philosopher Max Horkheimer (1895–1973), who had moved to the United States in 1940, headed the Institute for Social Research in California along with Theodor Adorno. After 1941 Horkheimer and his wife lived near the Manns in Pacific Palisades and saw them frequently. The Horkheimers, who had taken US citizenship in 1940, served as witnesses at Katia and Thomas Mann's citizenship proceedings. Mann, *Tagebücher, 1944–1946*, 335.

181. On August 2, 1946, Schoenberg suffered a heart attack as a result of an allergic reaction to a new asthma medication. During his three-week convalescence he began composing his String Trio, op. 45. See Schoenberg's biographical note dated August 2, 1950, in Schoenberg-Nono, *Arnold Schönberg, 1874–1951*, 404.

182. "I worked the association of 'impossible but rewarding' into the chapter on Leverkühn's chamber music." Mann, *The Story of a Novel*, 217.

183. Philanthropist Felix José Weil (1898–1975), one of the leading patrons of the Frankfurt Institute for Social Research.

184. The Berlin pianist and music professor Bruno Eisner (1884–1978), who had immigrated to the United States in 1933, taught at various colleges and performed as a concert pianist. Mann, *Tagebücher, 1946–1948*, 364. Mann must have known Eisner, as in a letter dated November 22, 1941, he asked the composer Paul Dessau to send Eisner his greetings.

185. Mann's poodle.

186. Literary critic and philosopher Ludwig Marcuse (1894–1971), who had fled to the United States in 1938. Marcuse wrote: "[Mann] was emperor among the German émigrés. . . . Everything was expected of him, everything took place through him, he was responsible for everything. Everyone believed that in America nothing would function without Thomas Mann." Schnauber, *Hollywood Haven*, 106; Ludwig Marcuse, *Mein zwanzigstes Jahrhundert* (Zurich: Diogenes, 1963).

187. In 1944 the American film composer Nathaniel Shilkret (1895–1982) commissioned the leading exiled composers in California—Schoenberg, Stravinsky, Toch, Darius Milhaud (1892–1974), Mario Castelnuovo-Tedesco (1895–1968), and Alexandre Tansman (1897–1986)—to write works inspired by the Genesis story in the Bible. He put them together in a suite, and he participated in the performance. Schoenberg's contribution was the Prelude, op. 44 (1945).

188. Toch, *The Covenant (The Rainbow)* for narrator and orchestra (1945).

189. The unsent letter to *Anbruch* about Furtwängler was published in Mann, *Tagebücher, 1946–1948*, 886–88.

190. Katia Mann wrote in her memoirs: "Schoenberg was not a particularly charming individual, and I didn't like his wife Gertrud Schoenberg either, though she didn't exactly have things easy with her tyrannical husband. We were often invited over there, as they were neighbors. They tyrannized us insofar as for example Schoenberg couldn't stand cigarette smoke, which meant his wife had to ban guests from smoking. This was unpleasant for those who liked to smoke, including my daughter Erika, a keen smoker who would feel unwell if unable to have her cigarette after a meal. . . . Things were always a little chaotic at the Schoenbergs. Gertrud Schoenberg wasn't much less difficult than her husband, who, as I heard at the time, caused her considerable worry. He was no longer young, was not in good health, and wasn't achieving any resonance at all in the United States." Katia Mann, *Meine ungeschriebenen Memoiren*, 133–34. Schoenberg, who suffered from serious asthma, had moved to Los Angeles on the advice of his doctor in 1934, after his first American winter on the East Coast had been detrimental to his health.

191. In September of 1933 the poet Hanns Johst wrote to Heinrich Himmler suggesting that Thomas Mann be arrested and held hostage because of his son Klaus's anti-Nazi writings. "His intellectual production would hardly suffer from an autumn vacation in Dachau," Johst wrote. See www.zeit.de/2004/12/A-Johst.

192. Hanns Eisler was denounced by his sister Ruth Fischer, a communist activist and Austrian Communist Party founder who had initially maintained close ties with her other brother, communist activist Gerhart Eisler. Hanns Eisler was blacklisted and brought before the House Un-American Activities Committee. He and

his wife, Lou, left the United States on March 27, 1948, eventually settling in East Germany.

193. Alfred Loewenberg (1902–49), author of *Annals of Opera, 1597–1940* (Cambridge: W. Heffer and Sons, 1943).

194. Mann ultimately turned down the request to write the foreword to Toch's book. Mann, *Tagebücher, 1946–1948,* 692–93.

Letters, Diaries, etc. (1948–1951)

[Fig. 2.1. Dedication in signed copy of *Doktor Faustus*]

For Arnold Schoenberg, the *real one*,[1] with best wishes,

Thomas Mann
Pacific Palisades

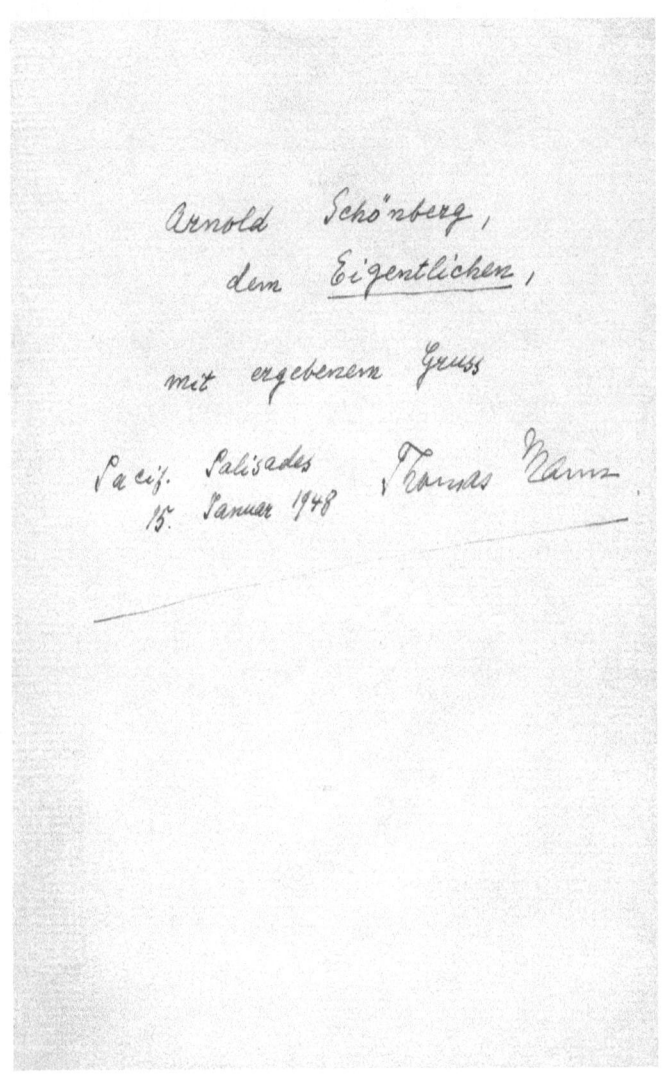

FIGURE 2.1.   Thomas Mann, dedication of *Doctor Faustus* to Arnold Schoenberg (1948).

1. Mann uses the German *dem Eigentlichen,* which can be translated as "the original" or "the real one" or, perhaps in this context, "the one and only." He may also have been referencing a prior conversation, where Mann used the same word to refer to his interest in the subject of music. See Mann to Schoenberg, July 30, 1943: "Last time there was too little opportunity to talk about 'the real thing,' namely music and your contribution to its fate. For various very sound reasons, these matters are of great concern to me at present." For this book we have used the translation "the real one" to conform with the contemporaneous translation of the term that Schoenberg used. See Schoenberg to *Saturday Review of Literature,* November 13, 1948.

MANN TO MICHAEL MANN, JANUARY 31, 1948

... The theme of "cold" is very important in this whole diabolical story; and you're quite right to associate the invention of the twelve-tone system with that. After some hesitation I opted to send Schoenberg a copy of the book, in which I wrote: "For Arnold Schoenberg, the *real one.*" So far I haven't heard from him. The phrase "the animal warmth of music" is his and is "bolted on," a euphemism for purloined.—By the way, he too won't allow his invention to keep him from viewing the tempered scale as an entirely provisional compromise (the same is true of Toch).

MANN TO OTTO BASLER, FEBRUARY 14, 1948

. . . Actually I have not yet heard from Schoenberg, though we are virtually neighbors. I was in a tricky situation. If I had not sent him the book, he would have taken it badly; now that I have, he is probably also taking it badly, despite my having written in it: "For Arnold Schoenberg, the *real one*." It is remarkable how the idea of his music played a part in the conception of the novel and the Adrian character from the very start: the Beissel figure is Schoenbergian, and the role played by the magic square is part of all that. His name is not actually mentioned (that was not feasible), and serial music is depicted as an invention associated with diabolical cold. He will probably be extremely annoyed, as will others. I cannot help that.

MANN'S DIARY

Pacific Palisades, Friday, February 13, 1948

... Spoke to Adorno about my plan to one day write something autobiographical about *Faustus;*[2] placated him. Neumann[3] very taken with *Sechzehn Jahre.* Katia recalls his sadness when he visited me before the operation: he cancelled an evening appointment and spent the entire evening in tears.—Adrian.—Finished playing the *Wozzeck* records.[4] Tonal parts where the mother is telling old story to the child. Very much Adrian's sphere. Benjamin Britten[5] can't be mentioned in same breath with this music, the final product of European high culture. About Schoenberg, his mood, and the gloomy corner of Leopoldstadt in Vienna where he's from. How his music was envisaged for *Faustus* right from the start: Beissel, the magic square etc.[6]—He hasn't said anything about the book. ...

---

2. Mann wrote *Die Entstehung der Doktor Faustus,* published in English as *The Story of a Novel,* between July and October of 1948.

3. The author and dramatist Alfred Neumann (1895–1952) had been a neighbor of the Manns in Munich. He left Germany in 1933 for Italy and the South of France, before coming to the United States in 1940 and settling in Los Angeles near the Manns.

4. The opera *Wozzeck* (1922), by Schoenberg's pupil Alban Berg (1885–1935).

5. British composer Benjamin Britten (1913–76), who was collaborating with Mann's son-in-law W. H. Auden on *Our Hunting Fathers,* opus 8 (1935).

6. Mann explained: "It was strange, how from the very beginning, the idea of his music in the conception of the novel and of the Adrian character played into each other. The Beissel figure is already Schoenbergian, and the role that the magical square plays, belongs to it, too. Now, on the one hand, his name isn't mentioned (which was impossible), and on the other hand, the technique of the row is posited as the invention of devilish coldness. He would have to get into a huff about it, just as many others would." Thomas Mann, *Selbstkommentare, "Doktor Faustus" und "Die Enstehung des Doktor Faustus,"* ed. Hans Wysling, with contribution by Marianne Eich-Fischer (Frankfurt am Main: Fischer Taschenbuch-Verlag 1992), 164.

SCHOENBERG TO MANN, FEBRUARY 1948

Dear Mr. Mann:[7]

   I am sorry to admit: this can happen—you know our musicologists!
Yours,

Arnold Schoenberg

[See the following essay which accompanied this letter—Ed.]

---

7. Handwritten statement, which accompanied the following satirical text.

HUGO TRIEBSAMEN, 1948

Schoenberg, February 1948

In one of the few letters preserved by Anton v. (this von or only van?) Webern is mentioned the name of Arnold Schoenberg. In this letter, which he wrote a few weeks before he died in the battle against the Russians (1938),[8] he speaks enthusiastically about this Schoenberg, calls him the greatest living composer, whose merits will never be forgotten. How wrong he was with his prophecy! I went through six decades of the *Encyclopaedia Americana* without meeting even a mention of his name. Only when I had come to the issue of 1988 I found his name and a short biographic note.

He might have played a role forty or fifty years before this issue, that is almost a hundred years ago, because, though not even one of his compositions is mentioned, two facts are of interest to me. First, that he had also written theoretical works, and evidently had a great number of pupils. But none of his theoretical writings have survived. The biography says they had been already obsolete at the time they were produced. They dealt with foregone methods of composing, with functions of the harmony, with variations, with musical logic and referred much to composers of the romantic period of chromaticism. Secondly, he must have had some fight with the renowned German poet Thomas Mann, who evidently was the inventor of the Method of Composing with Twelve Tones, based on the Emancipation of the Dissonance, that is the equipollence of the *apprehension* of the dissonance with the *apprehension* of the consonance. Webern mentions a merit of Schoenberg in inventing this theory and all the terminology pertaining to it, but this seems to be wrong or Schoenberg was a scrupulous exploiter of another man's ideas.

It has been said that Mann in his youth wanted badly to become a musician, but turned only in his twenties to poetry. Probably at this time he was in contact with Schoenberg, when this one lived in Vienna, which is only a few minutes of flying time distant from Munich, where Mann resided. Probably he had developed at this time (around 1933) the twelve-tone theory and, as he himself had already abandoned composing, let Schoenberg use it and publish it under his name. Mann's generosity never mentioned this violation of his rights. But it seems that in the last years of their lives they became unfriendly and now Mann took his property back by ascribing its origin to a person he himself had created (a homunculus). Thus the great American music came in the position to profit from Mann's theoretical invention, and thus all progress of American music is derived from its amalgamation with Budia Malanger's[9] modal methods of producing real old music which makes the effect of new.

If one thing aggravates this accusation of the forgotten "theorist" Schoenberg and his detestable crime against and disregard of the rights of intellectual property—it is the grandiose manner in which Mann has presented this, his idea. Only the real inventor is capable of such an enlightening presentation. But Schoenberg would never have had possessed the capacity for such a work.

Hugo Triebsamen[10]

---

8. Schoenberg's pupil, Anton Webern (1883–1945), who had gone outside after curfew to smoke a cigar during the occupation of Austria, was accidentally shot by an American soldier.

9. A spoof on the famous French composition teacher Nadia Boulanger (1887–1979), whose pupils included Aaron Copland, Walter Piston, Roy Harris, and Virgil Thomson.

10. A combination of the names of the influential German musicologist Hugo Riemann (1849–1919) and the professor of music at UCLA Walter Rubsamen (1911–73).

MANN'S DIARY

Pacific Palisades, Monday, February 16, 1948

Misty, mild, spring.—Eisenhower on the "despotic colossus" Russia would represent were it to absorb the Mediterranean countries. Viewed purely historically, it would comprise all of Eurasia, the Persian Empire, and the empires of the German kings and Mongolian khans. . . . Schoenberg has sent the rant of a devotee—his only gesture of thanks. Have drafted a letter to him.

Pacific Palisades, Tuesday, February 17, 1948

Excessively warm.—Produced letter to Schoenberg. Katia made a copy. . . .

MANN TO SCHOENBERG, FEBRUARY 17, 1948

Dear Mr. Schoenberg,

That is certainly a peculiar document. I was moved by this sign of the holy zeal with which your disciples watch over the fame and honor of the master. But then again, that much strenuous and misdirected malice has at the same time its comical side, too.

As to who is the creator of the twelve-tone technique, every little child in Africa knows that by now. It most assuredly is known, at any rate, to everyone who is interested enough to take a look at a book like *Dr. Faustus*.[11] Why does Triebsamen intimate, then, that I had insinuated I was the inventor of this system? What I did was to transfer, in a novel that seeks to portray an entire epoch, an immensely characteristic cultural phenomenon from its real creator to a fictitious artist-figure, a representative and a martyr of his time. There will not appear a single review of the book in any language that, if it concerns itself at all with the musical situation, will not mention your name. There are indeed more reasons for that than my making use of the serial technique. Why does not Triebsamen also make noises about the idea of transforming the horizontal into the vertical, an expansion of the concept of the harmonically possible, which clearly stems from your theory of harmony? Did he not notice that the whole music theory in the book is impregnated with your ideas, that in fact *"music"* means really always Schoenbergian music?

The novel portraying a whole epoch regards *"music"* as Schoenbergian music. And that is no diminution of your place in history.

True, on Earth all guilt must be atoned! With the help of quite a bit of real-life depiction I concocted a fanciful tale (*"For poets do a lot of lying,"* says Homer), and now our faithful Triebsamen indulges in raging phantasies about my presumptuous playing the role of composer, my early acquaintance with you, my later quarrels with you, etc. etc. People will simply not know what to make of this confused stuff, especially since the book has not even appeared yet in English. What is this piece supposed to be anyhow? A letter? A public article? I have already stated that as testimony of a combative devotion it has something touching about it. And yet, one cannot help being reminded of the old refrain: *"May God protect us from our friends!"*

I am sorry, my dear Mr. Schoenberg, that your name received mention exclusively in connection with this aspect of the book. To have put you in the perspective of the whole would have been more appropriate. As it is, you unfortunately will in all probability not be one of the readers of it.

Yet, it was a well-meant present which we hereby *"throw over the wall for you!"*

Let us hope that the flu has died down at your home and that all of you are well again! Sincerely your,

Thomas Mann

---

11. In her essay "Pilgrimage," Susan Sontag (1933–2004) recalls her visit to Mann in December 1947, when Sontag was only fourteen years old. " 'What have you recently written?' asked Merrill. 'I have recently finished a novel, which is partially based on the life of Nietzsche,' he said, with long, worrisome pauses between every word. 'However, my protagonist is not a philosopher. He is a great composer.' 'I know how important music is for you,' I dared interject, hoping to grease/extend the conversation for a bit. 'The pinnacles as well as the depths of the German soul are reflected in your music,' he said. 'Wagner,' I said. . . . 'Yes,' he said, . . . but the music of my composer is not like Wagner's music. It is related to Schoenberg's Twelve-Tone-System or row. Merrill said that we both were very interested in Schoenberg. He did not reply to that. . . . [Mann] seemed to think it was absolutely normal that two local High School students should know who Nietzsche and Schoenberg were." Susan Sontag, "Pilgrimage," in Stephen Dowden, ed., *A Companion to Thomas Mann's Magic Mountain* (Columbia, SC: Camden House, 1999), 233. Schoenberg, who taught students at both UCLA and USC, had perhaps a more realistic idea about the education of American students, as he confided to the conductor Hermann Scherchen on March 16, 1936: "But unfortunately the material that I have to work with is so insufficiently prepared, that what I have to do is as superfluous as if Einstein had to teach Mathematics at the High School level."

MANN'S DIARY

Pacific Palisades, Saturday, February 21, 1948
    . . . Spoke to Alma Mahler on the phone about Schoenberg. Triebsamen is actually himself. He wants a note indicating that the twelve-tone system is his intellectual property.[12] How to proceed? Also have Adorno to think about. In afternoon put together bibliography, numerous sources.—In evening listened to music. *La Gazza Ladra*[13] overture—what an attractive piece! *Oberon* overture example of how underrated Weber[14] is (development since *Der Freischütz*).

Pacific Palisades, Sunday, February 22, 1948
    . . . Deliberating over the Schoenberg situation. In evening put on old *Abendlich strahlt* record, was nigh moved to tears by the Rhinemaidens' "Tender and true 'tis but in the waters." Would happily swap entire output of Schoenberg, Berg, and Krenek[15] for that one passage. . . .

Pacific Palisades, Monday, February 23, 1948
    . . . Chance to speak to Adorno about the Schoenberg affair. Note: "It does not seem superfluous to explicitly state that in this novel the musical creation of a contemporary composer and theoretician, namely the so-called twelve-tone system or tone-row system of Arnold Schoenberg, is attributed to a completely invented musician character, Adrian Leverkühn." . . .

Pacific Palisades, Tuesday, February 24, 1948
    Offshore breeze, sunny.—Schoenberg insists via Alma Mahler. Sent him a note.—Crisis in Prague. Communists insisting on autocratic rule. . . . Brother-in-law and nephew to dinner: talked about the Schoenberg situation and his inner problems. Adrian's case involves a magic intellectualism—the symbol of which is the magic square—which would be fruitless without the diabolical fire beneath the cauldron. Thence Schoenberg.— Listened to music. Tired.

---

    12. On February 22, 1948, Mann wrote to Siegfried Marck: "I have my troubles, as Schoenberg is complaining that I have transferred the invention of the twelve-tone system to Leverkühn. He is asking for his intellectual property back and wants me to publicly acknowledge the theft. I am mulling over how to do so. The special thoughtlessness peculiar to the book overall has encouraged me to do this. At the same time it's still diabolical inspiration!"
    13. *La gazza ladra (The Thieving Magpie),* by Rossini (1792–1868).

14. *Der Freischütz* (1821) and *Oberon* (1826), by Carl Maria von Weber (1782–1826).

15. Austrian composer Ernst Krenek (1900–1991), who for a while was married to the sculptress Anna Mahler (1904–88), daughter of Gustav and Alma Mahler, achieved fame with his jazz-inspired opera *Johnny spielt auf* (1926). His opera *Karl V* (1933) and later works were written using Schoenberg's twelve-tone method. He fled to the United States in 1938 and taught at various institutions.

MANN TO SCHOENBERG, FEBRUARY 24, 1948

Thomas Mann
1550 San Remo Drive
Pacific Palisades, California
February 24, 1948

Dear Arnold,

Alma Mahler has told me about what you want, and I must admit you're entirely justified. I'll therefore make sure not only the American edition but also all foreign-language editions of the novel, as well as German reprints, include a note explaining to everyone the actual intellectual property rights.

With best wishes from our house to yours, respectfully yours,

Thomas Mann

MANN'S DIARY

Pacific Palisades, Monday, February 25, 1948
... Wrote Schoenberg note.[16] Short walk. ... New copies of *Faustus*. German requests for the book, *Tagesspiegel* having called it the greatest since *Wilhelm Meister*. ...

---

16. On March 10, 1948, Mann wrote to his American publisher Blanche Knopf (1894–1966): "I have attached a note which I have pledged to include in the English and all other foreign-language editions, as well as in all further German print-runs of the novel. As you can imagine, it was Schoenberg who, concerned about his posthumous reputation, asked for this, and I could not refuse. The note should be included at the end of the book, naturally not on the last page of the text but rather at some distance away, to minimize its illusion-breaking effect." Thomas Mann, *Selbstkommentare: "Doktor Faustus" and "Die Entstehung der Doktor Faustus,"* ed. Hans Wysling and Marianne Eich-Fischer (Frankfurt am Main: Fischer, 1992), 178. The actual printed version in the English edition reads: "It does not seem supererogatory to inform the reader that the form of musical composition delineated in Chapter XXII, known as the twelve-tone or row system, is in truth the intellectual property of a contemporary composer and theoretician, Arnold Schoenberg. I have transferred this technique in a certain ideational context to the fictitious figure of a musician, the tragic hero of my novel. In fact, the passages of this book that deal with musical theory are indebted in numerous details to Schoenberg's *Harmonielehre* [*Theory of Harmony*]." Mann then wrote to Knopf on March 19, 1948: "Did you receive the small addition to *Doktor Faustus?* I cannot say I am happy to have promised to include this addition, but Schoenberg, who is always concerned about his posthumous reputation, insisted on it." Mann, *Selbstkommentare*, 182. On March 17, 1948, Mann wrote to Erich von Kahler: "Schoenberg is very bitter and has demanded that I include a note indicating that in reality the twelve-tone method is his intellectual property and not the devil's. It will look stupid, but there's no way around it." Mann, *Selbstkommentare*, 180.

SCHOENBERG TO MANN, FEBRUARY 25, 1948

Arnold Schoenberg
116 N. Rockingham Avenue
Los Angeles, California
February 25, 1948

Dr. Thomas Mann
1550 San Remo Drive
Pacific Palisades, California

Dear Dr. Mann:

Thank you very much for your letter. I was very happy about this solution, although I have always been convinced that I would succeed in clearly presenting to you the danger I am facing.

My synthetic Hugo Triebsamen, the name I had constructed from the names Hugo Riemann and Dr. Rubsamen, will perhaps be a threat in the near future and not as late as 2048. I can *verify* that from printed items. For, as I wrote several months ago in a little article, "... *the need to be the originator of my ideas is so compelling that pretty soon everyone will be one, except for myself."*

My situation is an unusual one compared to that of other innovators. To the Germans I am a Jew, to the Latins a German, to the Communists I am bourgeois, and the Jews are for Hindemith[17] and Stravinsky. By comparison, the usual causes of miscomprehension are insignificant, because the former are not even grounded in as much objectivity as these.

I know that I can count only on posthumous fame, and that I should not still have to defend.[18]

With most cordial regards, your,
Arnold Schoenberg

---

17. The German composer Paul Hindemith (1895–1963) fled Germany in 1938. Hindemith's wife was Jewish. He reached the United States in 1940, where he taught at Yale University.

18. Following his seventy-fifth birthday, on September 16, 1949, Schoenberg wrote a thank you letter to his friends on the same theme: "Only after death will one be recognized.... In these days I have received much personal recognition, which made me very happy, because it testifies to the respect from friends and other well-meaning people. On the other hand, for many years now, I have come to realize that I may not reckon with a complete and devoted understanding of my work, that which I have to say musically, during my lifetime. To be sure I know that some

of my friends have immersed themselves in my mode of expression and have familiarized themselves with my thoughts. They are the ones who will prove to be true what I prophesied almost exactly thirty-seven years ago in an aphorism: 'The second half of this century will ruin by overestimating what the first half left as positive in their underestimation of me.' I am rather ashamed of all these words of praise. But I also see something in them that gives me courage. Namely: Is it just a matter of course that someone, against the opposition of the whole world, does not give up, but instead continues to write down what he produces? I do not know what the great ones thought about this. Mozart and Schubert were young enough not to have had to deal with this. But Beethoven, when Grillparzer called the Ninth 'confusing,' or Wagner, when his plan for Bayreuth threatened to fail, or Mahler, when everyone found him trivial—how could they have continued to write? I know only one answer: they had things to say that had to be said. I was asked once in the military, if I were really this composer A.S. 'Someone had to be him,' I said, 'nobody wanted to be him, so I offered myself for the job.' Maybe I had to say things, too, which seemed unpopular, that had to be said. And now I ask all of you, who honored me and gave me so much joy with your many good wishes, to accept this as an attempt to express my gratitude. Many heartfelt thanks! Arnold Schoenberg."

MANN'S DIARY

Pacific Palisades, Monday, February 26, 1948
. . . Grateful letter from Schoenberg, entirely devoted to his own concerns, happy about my conciliatory attitude. Sent the text for the note to Arlt, along with a copy of *Faustus*. . . .

Pacific Palisades, Monday, March 1, 1948
. . . Adornos to tea. Talked about the Schoenberg business. Then about my essays. Discussed Wagner and Goethe. . . .

Pacific Palisades, Sunday, April 17, 1948
. . . Small journal from Humm,[19] with accusatory article by a Schoenberg devotee.[20] . . .

---

19. Swiss author and journalist Rudolf Jakob Humm (1895–1977), a friend of the writer Hermann Hesse.

20. See following article by Aline Valangin, "Kritik des Werkes," in *Unsere Meinung* 1, no. 2 (March 1948): 2–3. Aline Valangin (1889–1986) and Jakob Humm had been romantically involved in the early 1930s. Valangin had been married to a Zurich lawyer, Wladimir Rosenbaum; her second marriage was to the composer Vladimir Vogel. Forced to abandon her career as a pianist after injuring her hand on broken glass while preparing preserved fruit, she took up writing and, following her divorce, wrote for various newspapers. See Peter Kamber, *Geschichte zweier Leben: Wladimir Rosenbaum/Aline Valangin*, 2nd rev. ed. (Zurich: Limmat Verlag, 2000).

ALINE VALANGIN IN *UNSERE MEINUNG,* MARCH 1948

Thomas Mann has taken the liberty of incorporating twelve-tone music into his work and presenting it as something truly precious; he enlivens and breathes life into it, accomplishing this in a manner that suggests the system was invented by his character, the German composer Leverkühn. It is a familiar but perhaps insufficiently widely known fact that the system was created by Arnold Schoenberg and Josef Matthias Hauer around a quarter of a century ago out of the disintegrated musical material left behind by expressionism, and has been practiced by leading lights in every country of Europe and the Americas ever since. Although mentioning the name of the actual inventors in *Doktor Faustus* was probably not feasible for artistic reasons, Thomas Mann could easily have used a postscript to correctly attribute the fame for inventing the system. It is a shame he has not. He almost risks being accused of having his creation Leverkühn strut in borrowed plumage. There is worse to come. In *Doktor Faustus* Thomas Mann has not been afraid to besmirch Arnold Schoenberg's twelve-tone music—which has engendered whole new facets of art and ways of looking at life—by presenting it as a work of the devil with no genuine life of its own, a sort of ghostly brain tumor similar to inorganic objects that mimic the form and appearance of organic ones. This is a disagreeable suspicion (albeit a view shared by certain music critics out of sheer laziness), as it takes hard work and commitment to properly penetrate the new discipline. Also somewhat off-putting is the fact that Mann allows himself to be so powerfully influenced by the formal principles of twelve-tone music that he bases the work's structure on them: somehow he manages to render in written form imitations, variations, overlaps, abbreviations of time and theme, inversions of all sorts of canons and fugues, and goodness knows what else from the world of music. He ends up producing precisely the kind of overrefined intellectual speculation and frosty detachment that he sees and censures in his colleagues the twelve-tone composers. One has to wonder who is writing the obituary for whom.

MANN TO RUDOLF JAKOB HUMM, MAY 19, 1948

In response to the article "Critique of the Work" (namely my novel *Doktor Faustus*), I have just one comment: as an appeal to my loyalty, it comes too late.[21] Having always been close to music, I used to think it was part of a general Western education to know who, in the world of reality, invented the style of composition known as the twelve-tone system or serial music. Evidently I was mistaken, and Arnold Schoenberg and I long ago came to an agreement that to avoid misunderstandings, all translations of *Doktor Faustus*—primarily the English, as well as editions published within Germany and in the near future the Stockholm edition as well—should contain a note at the end clarifying the situation with regard to intellectual property and making it clear to the reader that Chapter XXII involves the fictitious transfer of the idea onto a completely invented musician figure, my tragic hero. Believe it or not there are people who, blinded by so much biographical endeavor, believe the life and sufferings of Adrian Leverkühn are a true story and have called for immediate performance of the works with which I, according to your colleague, have besmirched the twelve-tone system.

---

21. Mann's May 19, 1948, letter to Rudolf Jakob Humm was first published in *Unsere Meinung* 1, no. 3 (May 1948), as "Thomas Mann Erwidert." See Thomas Mann, *Tagebücher, 28.5.1946–31.12.1948* (subsequent citations will be shortened to *Tagebücher, 1946–1948*), 737. It was also published in *Neue Zeitung* (Munich) on September 21, 1948.

ALINE VALANGIN IN *DIE AUSLESE*, APRIL 1948

It is perhaps surprising to find that readers have been rejecting rather than reveling in Thomas Mann's latest novel *Doktor Faustus*, given that it has been lavished with praise by the press in Switzerland and abroad.[22]

It is obvious why it has attracted admirers. Put plainly: overall, in terms of writerly ability, the work is a supreme achievement.

It is harder to pinpoint the reasons for the aforementioned aversion. There seem to be many, some more significant than others, though to shed light on them all would require a thoroughgoing literary and equally penetrating psychological study. The present assessment therefore limits itself to broad brushstrokes in discussing the aforesaid objections to the novel.

Of course, not all rejections of the work have been completely intentional. Personal judgment tends to be affected by prejudice, personal resentment and envy—that is true of any criticism.

This certainly applies in the case of the fierce critics of Mann who refuse to forgive him for speechifying during the war from the safe haven of exile, at one remove from the German people. Their annoyance is perhaps understandable, but they forget that Mann, at an advanced age, did at least leave the country—for him, being abroad was always tantamount to suffering—while many others tried to somehow "stick it out," "holding out" until the end.

There is another group of readers who dislike the book because its depiction of Munich circles and reports on musical and social events constitute a kind of *roman à clef*—that much maligned genre—insofar as the author mixes real people, described with photographic precision, with figments of his imagination. Some of these figures were perhaps irritated to have been mentioned, others not to have been (finding themselves seated next to Leverkühn might have been rather appealing). But for those of us neither uncomfortably spotlighted nor overlooked by Thomas Mann, the question arises as to whether the montage of real and invented figures is a successful artistic approach. The novel lacks a yen for surrealism, which loves such tricks; the fusion of the two levels in other ways is unconvincing. Times and dates are arbitrarily mixed up despite avid attention to other details, leaving the reader feeling unpleasantly deceived.

Serious objections have also been raised by the experts—writers and literary cognoscenti, particularly those who are themselves in search of new artistic methods. To them, *Doktor Faustus* is a shoddy piece of work, unpoetic, uncreative even, too artistically and intellectually tendentious. They object to the ornate style, the pretentiousness of the higgledy-piggledy form, the smug pedantry with which the reader is proffered "the most profound" knowledge, which trickles down incessantly like plaster dust. Literature is turned into "literasty." If that is a harsh assessment, one has to admit it is not completely inaccurate. The schoolmasterly tone of the chronicler Zeitblom, the long-winded discussions, conversations and descriptions, the sole purpose of which is to be long-winded, the ubiquitous pomposity, the stilted feel to the ideas and language, in short the naturalistic odds and ends, though presumably meant to characterize the chronicler and hence educated Germans in general, are difficult to bear over long stretches.

But *all* artists, all lovers of art—literature, music, or painting—probably feel insulted that Mann had the nerve to associate his composer Leverkühn's achievements, described as extraordinary, with a disease picked up in a brothel, as though genius were merely the outcome of syphilis. Although Mann's intent is not as coarse or broad as that, the fact that Leverkühn's art is achieved by virtue of the final stages of the disease is unpleasant enough to justify genuine antipathy toward the book. One wonders why the creator of *Doktor Faustus* feels he must explain genius in this way. Could it be that, notwithstanding his talent of the very highest order, Mann realizes he himself is not a genius and therefore denigrates genius to make that unpleasant truth palatable to himself? Certain malicious parties have made that allegation. At any rate, it is hard to ignore the fact that Leverkühn's disease places all genius under suspicion. Given that precisely this disease played an important role in the life of numerous gifted people, particularly during the romantic period, it is irresponsible to present the creative output of a major composer as a product of the disease. An entire army of healthy artists probably feels compelled to reject this notion.

Musicians are angry for additional reasons—and not just musicians who have devoted themselves to twelve-tone music but also those involved in the serious discussion of music. Music is notoriously difficult to talk about. What can be expressed about it in words never relates to more than its externals. Its very nature is resistant to words. To do justice to the essence of music, one would have to translate the tonal experience it conveys into an analogous word experience. A word poet, a word composer might be capable of this, but not Thomas Mann, an old-school descriptive artist. He talks about music in the same way he talks about any object, house or landscape: precisely, meticulously, and rigorously but without penetrating to the inner essence. He merely polishes the surface. His lengthy explanations of musical works, albeit accurate, merely convey a sense of the outer shell. He fails by dint of his own naturalistic technique. And for the enlightened, his treatises hold nothing new: they are little more than well-formulated descriptions of familiar facts. Perhaps one should expect no more than that from a writer. But the elevated tone in which music is discussed leaves the reader hungry for original insight. The disappointment, after one's attention has been held for pages at a time with little outcome, is unsettling.

There is also the unfortunate fact that Mann presents his German hero as the greatest musical genius of the age, thereby endowing German music with an imaginary, undeserved reputation. In reality, Germany as a prime mover in music had been overtaken by other countries by the time Leverkühn, as depicted by Mann, arrived on the scene. Mann evidently wants *ex post facto* to burnish the reputation of the era during which, in his German homeland, musical decline was ushered in. That implies certain contradictions.

It also brings us to the novel's most dubious aspect. Mann attributes the brilliant invention of twelve-tone music, specifically the type invented and systematized for all time by Arnold Schoenberg—an Austrian and a Jew— to his German hero. At first, reading this is baffling. Are we dreaming? Seemingly not: before our eyes Leverkühn invents Arnold Schoenberg's new musical technique near a freezing pond (symbol of the nonhuman sphere) and uses it as the basis for major works. Is this mere literary wit? How should we approach it? At present, twelve-tone music is not so widely known that artistic license to falsely attribute its invention to a fictional character can be granted without further ado. Would it be acceptable for an author to attribute radium's discovery not to Madame Curie but to his own fictional Madame Smith? At any rate, as one of today's best-known twelve-tone composers correctly points out, Mann's approach in fact underscores twelve-tone music's triumph, in that it is presented as historical fact. Despite the concerns of nostalgics and worrywarts, twelve-tone music (known as dodecaphony in the romance-language countries) has prevailed and proved to be the way forward—and despite Mann, who, by presenting his hero's downfall, condemns it as the devil's work. More on that anon. . . . Being attributed to Leverkühn propitiously thrusts twelve-tone music into the spotlight but also does it an injustice. One example: a well-known critic's recent review of a modern music concert in Zurich stating that a Krenek work was written using the twelve-tone technique "in the manner of Leverkühn." Obviously, he should have written "Arnold Schoenberg," not Leverkühn. The liberty Mann allowed himself is causing confusion even among experts who have not previously bestirred themselves to seriously address the new music and who, having come to it circuitously via *Doktor Faustus*, are now doing so only incompletely by *bona fide* association of twelve-tone music with Thomas Mann–Leverkühn rather than its creator, Arnold Schoenberg. This is a ridiculous situation. One cannot help feeling Mann should somewhere, somehow have provided a note about who invented the musical technique. Strutting in borrowed plumage flatters no one.

At any rate, given that the new compositional method is described with absolute precision, clarity, and beauty, one might reasonably assume that Leverkühn's works would be equal to the expectations placed on such music. In fact, Mann's descriptions—which use vivid imagery to convey a sense of the sound—suggest Leverkühn's musical sound is not actually reminiscent of normal twelve-tone music but rather of Mahler or Cesar Franck, music of the postromantic period. That type of music is quite distinct from the twelve-tone system, which arose as a sort of protest against it. The sound roar described by Mann with such awe, and the literary documentation of the works, belong to a much earlier era than the twelve-tone system. Was it really necessary to commit a kind of intellectual theft against Schoenberg for anachronistic pieces of music that are in any case fictional?

Mann seems not to have grasped the essential nature of twelve-tone music, and this is confirmed by his attempt to portray the new art form as work of the devil—which is a monstrous denigration *per se*. Mann views the compositional technique as mere speculation, calculation, and trickery. He overlooks the fact that the system is neither life-affirming nor life-denying but rather simply depends on who is using it and how. His hero may be destroyed by an excess of intellect, but that has nothing to do with the twelve-tone system. Therein lies Mann's deception, which is tantamount to a swindle and casts the entire novel into doubt.

The novel also contains other startling statements and contradictions, the most noteworthy of which is explained below. Though Mann feels the intellectual approach that led to twelve-tone music is dubious, he actually invokes twelve-tone trains of thought himself (perhaps he was excited or infected by coming into contact with the art form); and, insofar as purely musical forms and phrases can be reproduced via the written word, he incorporates them into the novel. As is well known, the external characteristics of twelve-tone music are that it groups the familiar twelve tones together in rows, which can be used in inversion, retrograde, and retrograde inversion, and onto which the twelve steps can be transposed. This means forty-eight variants of a single series are available as material. It is no coincidence that *Doktor Faustus* is divided into forty-eight chapters (including the postscript) and that in chapter 25, i.e., in the middle, what was below (or unconscious), namely the devil in the shape of Ludewig, arises (becomes conscious)? This is an inversion. Chapter 13 also features an inversion, in that for the first time the long shadow of the destructive is glimpsed when the narrator, Zeitblom, recalls the teacher figure who appears "due to his intriguing ambiguity": the teacher Schleppfuss, easily recognizable as Satan, the seducer and corrupter *par excellence*. It is he who arouses curiosity in Leverkühn about the nether regions and who, in the shape of a porter, takes the young student Leverkühn to the brothel where he encounters the woman from whom, in experiencing the natural stratum, he catches the incurable disease. There is also an inversion in chapter 37, in the monologue by the concert agent Fitelberg, which is a *tour de force* of reverse movement. None of this is coincidence. Through the mouth of his narrator, Mann himself states that from the story's midpoint on, his hero moves backward rather than forward. Leverkühn goes to live in a place resembling his parental home, where he is surrounded by people who precisely mirror his family in number and character. This is very clearly an inverted "series." There are also inversions between the prostitute and Leverkühn's invisible patron, and between the Devil and the boy Echo, all of whom also borrow from the old Faust legend.

But the influence of twelve-tone thinking is palpable not just in these broad allusions: it can also be found in small-scale linguistic details that influence the work's style. Thus, for example, on page 181 one reads: "This was contradicted. H. and Sch. contradicted this." This is a classic retrograde, and there are numerous other verbal games of this kind. An obvious one is on page 345: "If you know something, stay silent ["Weistu was so schweig"], which features not only an inversion of the German sound *ei* but also a semantic inversion. Those in the know are usually urged to share their knowledge but here are told to remain silent. In many instances, entire series of words that, almost meaninglessly, only possess meaning within the series in question, are omitted. The following two sentences, in which word combinations of this kind simply roll forth across the page, are a good example (page 181): "Awareness of life—self-awareness—way of life—inspired life—lack of awareness—awareness—awareness of self—way of life." Open the book virtually anywhere and you will find a "word speculation" of this kind. These lend lightness, sometimes sparkling verbal wit and a certain enigmatic wisdom to Zeitblom's style. *Doktor Faustus* would be flat and gray without this rich tapestry of large and small-scale allusions. They provide a veneer that shines with light from the intellectual world whence the twelve-tone system itself draws life. Mann's linguistic serial art remains external, perhaps inadvertently reflecting the fact that he evidently feels the art of twelve-tone music merely pretends to possess life, remaining formal, devoid of content and thus negative. It is certainly true that *his* twelve-tone meets that description. That in turn makes the work all the more fascinating for drawing on Schoenberg's twelve-tone teachings. *Doktor Faustus* is indisputably a fascinating novel, about which much has been and will continue to be written.

---

22. Aline Valangin, "Thomas Mann's *Doktor Faustus,*" *Die Auslese, Gesellschaft für Lesefreunde* 3 (April 1948): 3–7.

MANN'S DIARY

Pacific Palisades, Friday, June 11, 1948

Letter from the composer Möschinger[23] with parts about h e a e e s. Remarks aimed against Schoenberg.[24] . . .

---

23. Swiss composer Albert Moeschinger (1897–1985). On July 9, 1948, Mann wrote to him: "I was moved by the fact that, in sympathetic homage to poor Leverkühn, you have donned the shackles of the 'row' system, about which you wrote so convincingly in your letter, especially concerning the fashionable misuse of a technique which is appropriate and useful only in specific productive cases. I cannot deny that in *Faustus* it is characterized as an invention of the devil, and that one may glimpse, if not Schoenberg himself, then at any rate a particular kind of impediment; or that I allowed myself to be influenced by the formal principles of twelve-tone music, and based the formal elements of my novel on it, with imitations, variations, overlaps, diminution of time and themes, inversions of all kinds, canons, fugati and all sorts of other things from the world of music carried over into the world of the written word.—As you can see, I have myself created a work of the devil; by using a special kind of mimicry I have ensured that the book *is* what it speaks of."

24. "At any rate the twelve-tone system is not so new that Schoenberg's resulting theory could claim to be an invention." Mann, *Tagebücher, 1946–1948*, 760.

SCHOENBERG TO JOSEF RUFER, SEPTEMBER 30, 1948

September 30, 1948
Mr. Joseph Rufer
Jutta Strasse 16
Berlin Zehlendorf

Dear Mr. Rufer![25]

. . . I was not able to read *Dr. Faustus* myself because of my nervous eye-condition. However, I heard through my wife and from other accounts that he attributes my twelve-tone system to be an invention of his hero, without mentioning my name. I pointed out to him that historians might use this in order to do me an injustice. After much resistance he has agreed to insert an explanation in all ensuing copies in all languages concerning my intellectual property. I do not know if this has been accomplished yet.

---

25. Schoenberg's pupil and biographer, the German Musicologist, Josef Rufer (1893–1985), author of *Das Werk Arnold Schönbergs* (Kassel: Bärenreiter, 1959).

SCHOENBERG TO GOTTFRIED BERMANN-FISCHER, OCTOBER 7, 1948

October 7, 1948
Bermann-Fischer Publishers
Stockholm, Sweden

Dear Sir:

No doubt you know that in order to protect my intellectual property, I had to write a complaint to Dr. Thomas Mann because he represents the hero of his novel, *Dr. Faustus*, as having invented the twelve-tone technique. After some resistance, Dr. Mann has declared himself willing to insert an explanation into all future editions in all languages in order to rectify this situation.

I had assumed that Dr. Mann would run the explanation by me for my approval. That did not occur. I also do not know if his promise was carried out or not.

I would like to ask you, since you as publisher are also concerned about correcting this injustice, to keep me informed, whether or not this promise has been kept, and to prove it to me by sending me several copies. Respectfully,

Arnold Schoenberg

[handwritten] A copy of this letter will be sent to Stockholm.

MANN'S DIARY

Pacific Palisades, Wednesday, October 13, 1948
    ... Schoenberg's inquiry about the note. Wrote him long letter in the evening and sent him the English edition.

MANN TO SCHOENBERG, OCTOBER 13, 1948

Thomas Mann
1550 San Remo Drive
Pacific Palisades, California
October 13, 1948

Dear Arnold,

Bermann-Fischer recently called me to say goodbye from New York while on his way over to Europe. In doing so he mentioned that you had written asking whether I had instructed him to include the note at the end of *Doktor Faustus* as agreed. How could you doubt I would keep my promise? I'm ahead of Bermann insofar as I want to assure you that of course I instructed him to; the "explanatory" note will be included in the next print-run of the Stockholm original edition, has already been included in the edition appearing shortly in Berlin, and will be included in the Italian, Hungarian,[26] French, and Czech translations, i.e., all translations, and of course first and foremost in the English.

Earlier I wrote to you saying I would explain (superfluously, in my view) that the form of composition developed in Chapter XXII is in reality your intellectual property and has, in the spirit of fiction, been transferred to the "hero" of my work. You seemed satisfied, so I didn't feel it necessary to once again present you with the actual and indeed straightforward wording of this straightforward statement. I've been waiting for the English edition to appear, but it has not yet done so; however, I have now received a handful of copies and am sending you one along with this letter. As you can see, the author's note is written in a very straightforward manner and will fulfill its purpose of keeping the ignorant from believing the twelve-tone method is my own invention. Please realize that I included the note somewhat against my will. Basically I would have preferred to have kept your name completely out of the picture—take a look at the book as a whole and you will understand why. The tone-row system and constructive music overall take on additional meaning and import in the book (which is in itself constructive music!); they are intertwined with the idea of black magic and diabolical cold, in a way that in reality they of course aren't. This creates, out of your creation, something quite different, and of course very different from real life outside the book. That alone would be sufficient reason to avoid mentioning your name, as to do so is essentially highly undesirable from an artistic standpoint. Your name should not be mentioned, any more than Nietzsche's. As it stands, the note at the end causes a slight breach in the closed sphere of the work, which is so very different from reality. However, it was what you wanted and were entitled to, so I duly obeyed.

I would warmly welcome the opportunity to discuss all this in person. It has been too long since we last saw each other. You have been through a lot, and I too have a sorry tale to recount about my concerns, my health, exhaustion and so forth, and have not been gregarious of late. Do you go out? Would you and your good wife like to come and see us? I do look forward to hearing from you, even if only briefly. Respectfully yours,

Thomas Mann

---

26. On June 26, 1948, Mann wrote to his Hungarian translator Gáspár Endre: "I would like to take this opportunity to send you a few lines I want included as a note at the end of the work. I was previously under the impression that those with a general Western-style education would know who invented the so-called twelve-tone method. That seems not to be the case, and to prevent any errors I have agreed with Arnold Schoenberg to include an explanatory note on the subject for those who need it."

GOTTFRIED BERMANN-FISCHER TO SCHOENBERG, OCTOBER 14, 1948

Professor Arnold Schoenberg
116 N. Rockingham Ave.
Los Angeles, 24, Cal

Most esteemed Professor:

In confirmation of your letter of October 7, I would like to let you know that Dr. Thomas Mann had informed us that in all future editions of his novel, *Dr. Faustus,* an explanation was to be added, which was to refer to you as the author of the twelve-tone system. Dr. Mann informed me that he had sent the text to Amsterdam, the residence of my publishing house.

As Dr. Mann further informed me, he had sent the text a while ago to my firm in Frankfurt a. Main, where a German edition is to appear shortly. I hope that it arrived in time for print setting.

I am very sorry that you and Dr. Mann had a disagreement. I will certainly do everything in my power to publish the explanation to your and Dr. Mann's satisfaction. Yours respectfully,

G.B. Fischer

SCHOENBERG TO MANN, OCTOBER 15, 1948

Arnold Schoenberg
116 N. Rockingham Ave.
Los Angeles 24, Calif.
Phone—Arizona 3–5077
October 15, 1948

My dear Dr. Mann:

I am very happy that you were kind enough to comply with my wish: to protect me against the incompetence of the musicologists of all ages. Of all ages, for I firmly believe that if today's exemplars of that species of mortals be in fifty years no longer living (if that be living), new ones will rise from the ashes of their sterility.

I wrote to Bermann-Fischer in this matter for two reasons, 1) a local contributor to that distasteful *Time* magazine, for whom a composer is nothing but an object of inane jokes, well then, one of its contributors had asked me for an interview regarding *Dr. Faustus*—I declined;[27] 2) I did, however, have a bone to pick with Mr. Bermann-Fischer (what does that expression mean?). In the book's blurb, which took proper notice of your seventieth birthday, he pointed out how unworthy I was of being part of such company (namely the rest of the contributors) in that he left my name completely out. In the table of contents, however, he uses a more effective method. There I am not mentioned either, but worse than that: a certain Alfred Schoenberg dedicated my canon to you.

I was firmly convinced that I could not expect any more from you than from myself, and I am very glad that my trust was so well rewarded.

I was indeed very sorry to hear that you, too, don't always feel as well as one could wish. I should certainly have inquired oftener about you, and I would have if it were not for my own conditions, which kept me preoccupied, and which turn an entirely decent person into a hard-boiled egotist.

I hope very much that my twitching eye affliction will get better, so I can begin to read again. Your *Doktor Faustus* will then be the first in line.

In the hope of seeing you soon, I remain with kindest regards and admiration your,

Arnold Schoenberg

27. Mann wrote Richard Schweizer on October 12, 1948: "A reporter from *Time* magazine was just here for an hour about *Dr. Faustus*. They want to publish a review about it, and had sent a long telegram with questions: Who were my favorite composers, and whether I believed that one could become a genius from syphilis, and if Schoenberg had sat as model for Leverkühn, and if he has syphilis, and if I have syphilis, etc. I am still somewhat dazed from the 'nice little chat.'"

MANN'S DIARY

Pacific Palisades, Wednesday, October 18, 1948
 . . . Satisfied but woeful letter from Schoenberg. . . .

GERTRUD SCHOENBERG TO ALMA MAHLER-WERFEL, OCTOBER 19, 1948

Dearest Almtschi,

I finally found a little time to write you today! Everything is still the same here. That is: sometimes somewhat better, sometimes a bit worse, and for me the better time is exactly as bad, because just like Till Eulenspiegel, you shiver in the face of the next degradation. Nevertheless, I have to say that it is getting better. Miss Silvers[28] whom you have met in the meantime gave Arnold a Dictaphone[29] and that gives him a lot of pleasure. Unfortunately Thomas Mann, with his explanation in the book (hidden and "a certain contemporary composer and theoretician") upset him very much again. At first he wrote him a very friendly letter, asking how Arnold could even doubt that he had not kept his word, etc. Then, after Arnold wrote him back very nicely, came the book with the "setting things right." I hope that in German it will be printed exactly like that, because there he will appear ridiculous. Here, however, I fear he will achieve exactly what he wants, namely to belittle Arnold. The whole thing is really not worth it, that Arnold get so upset and spend so much valuable time with it. But if I tell him that, it's like throwing oil on the fire!—I am very happy that you are coming back for Christmas after all. Hopefully we will then really be able to see each other. I now have a system, in between cooking, ironing, doing the dishes, and chauffeuring, of relaxing, so that I no longer look as bad as I did. That was really necessary, especially on account of the children. They are all well. Nuria continues to be good, but luckily, not "too good." By the way, Thomas Mann invited us with the words, "You and your good wife!" What do you think of his putting on such airs/pretentiousness? Now I even have a bone to pick with him. How I must have changed if all one can find to say about me is the adjective "good"!

How are you? I would love to go to the concert with you tomorrow. If Koblitz[30] had kept his word, I might have been there, but as such we are waiting for the Washington money; it is supposed to be there the beginning of next month! I think one ought to speak to all these publishers, but not in German, but in their language. Especially Schirmer[31] would be important. I think that Gustav[32] is rather primitive, but not without a bit of goodnaturedness. Do you ever get together with him? He might be coaxed into a reconciliation with Arnold and most probably could push through a fair release at ASCAP.[33] He drinks a lot and cannot tolerate anything and that is a good sign. I wouldn't talk to Winter.[34] He is too repulsive. Have you seen the Stiedrys? And who else of our friends? Write again soon. Love, from me and Arnold.

Trude Schoenberg

I cut myself on the finger and apparently Trude doesn't want me to bleed! Heartfelt greetings,

Arnold Schoenberg

---

28. Clara Silvers (1922–82), a pupil of Schoenberg's at UCLA, later married the pianist Eduard Steuermann and became the first archivist of the Arnold Schoenberg Institute at the University of Southern California (1975–81).

29. Schoenberg bade his assistant Richard Hoffmann (1925–), a cousin of his wife, to dictate passages from *Doktor Faustus* into the new machine. See Richard Hoffmann, "The Story of *The Story of a Novel*" herein.

30. The lawyer Milton Koblitz represented Schoenberg in various disputes over copyright issues.

31. The publisher G. Schirmer and Sons printed many of Schoenberg's American works.

32. Probably Gustave Schirmer III (1890–1965), grandson of the founder of the publishing house G. Schirmer and head of the company from 1944 to 1957, or else Gustave Beer of the Austrian League of Authors and Composers from Austria (ALACA).

33. The American Society of Composers, Authors and Publishers (ASCAP) collects and distributes royalties for authorial copyrights.

34. Hugo Winter (1885–1952) had been Commercial Manager of Universal Edition in Vienna, later vice president of Associated Music Publishers, Inc. in New York.

SCHOENBERG TO JOSEF RUFER ET AL., OCTOBER 20, 1948

Arnold Schoenberg
116 N. Rockingham Ave.
Los Angeles 24.
October 20, 1948

Dear Friend:[35]

You asked me a while ago whether or not the depiction of my twelve-tone method in Dr. Mann's book, *Dr. Faustus*, was based on information that I had given him. I had thought up until recently that Dr. Mann had inserted the necessary clarification into his book. At least he had replied to an attack in a Swiss newspaper to that effect, so that one was led to believe that we had reached an agreement about it. But that is not so.

Thomas Mann had gotten this information from Wiesengrund-Adorno behind my back and concealed it from me, until I found out about it from a newspaper article.

Then Mrs. Alma Mahler Werfel took the matter in hand and convinced Mann that this was an act of literary theft. Even then a tiresome back and forth was needed in order to make it clear to Mann that he had to rectify this injustice.

Initially I sent him (Enclosure 1) this satirical excerpt from a fictitious music history from the year 2060 (or something like that) in which I made him aware of the possible consequences of his actions. He answered (Enclosure 2), acting as if he did not understand what this was all about. In my letter (Enclosure 3) I explained it to him. Then, after repeated interventions by Mrs. Alma Mahler (Enclosure 4) he agreed to insert an explanation in all subsequent editions of his novel. I wrote him an enthusiastic letter of thanks (Enclosure 5). Since then I have heard nothing. I had actually expected him to run this explanation by me, and hadn't anticipated that he might have a particular reason for not showing it to me.

Only recently, a reporter for the New York–based *Time* magazine called and wanted to interview me about the newly released *Dr. Faustus* by Thomas Mann, which contained the explanation of his use of the twelve-tone technique. Thereafter I wrote to his publisher, Bermann-Fischer, asking if that had occurred. Mann answered me that Bermann-Fischer had telephoned him, and asked me how I could possibly doubt that he would not fulfill such a promise. That is the next enclosure.

He writes that he will be sending me the book, which did not happen in the days that followed, whereupon I wrote him an enthusiastic letter, joyous that the matter had been cleared up. But then the book arrived and I find out that I am a contemporary, a certain Arnold Schoenberg whom nobody knows anyway, just like Triebsamen had predicted. I would like you to expose this shameful, deceitful action by Thomas Mann. I would like you yourself, or anyone of your friends, to find and publish the pertinent passages from Mann's letters and my letters to shed the right light on the matter. I think he really deserves to be reprimanded for such a shameful action.

This letter is also going to Leibowitz and I hope that both of you will react in the same manner.

The original of Mann's letters—I include photostatic reproductions of them here—can be made readily available, in order to ascertain and prove the correctness of my statements.

I would also like the Swiss newspaper that attacked him at that time, without my intervention—I knew nothing about it and found out by someone sending me the article—I would like that newspaper to be contacted about the whole matter. That is why I include a second copy here for sharing. Perhaps one could write the article and the other could translate it, and the same version could be sent to the Swiss newspaper and perhaps to other papers and magazines. I think one ought to circulate it widely. . . .

Arnold Schoenberg

---

35. Schoenberg also sent this letter to René Leibowitz (1913–72) and Hans H. Stuckenschmidt (1901–88).

MANN TO ERIKA MANN, NOVEMBER 6, 1948

Pacific Palisades, California
1550 San Remo Drive
November 6, 1948

Dear Erikind,
   ... I've been depressed for several days over the utter hopelessness of
the American reviews of *Faustus* I've seen. The low point came with
Hamilton Basso in the *New Yorker*. But I suppose the *New York Herald
Tribune* was reasonable, and *Atlantic* is out now, as well as an expanded
issue of the *Saturday Review of Literature*. Perhaps things aren't so bad. I
just wish they wouldn't always emphasize the *German* allegory. I'm probably to blame for that, I know.
   ... I'd rather not hear any more about the Confessions,[36] and want to
set them aside for a later date. However, that probably isn't do-able and
would be unfair, as I've given Schoenberg so much credit at the end. But
I've given Adorno too much in the details. That can be shortened, deleted
and rendered more general, I think.
   ... Much love, goodness and warmth for the New Year and evermore.

Z.

---

36. Erika Mann edited *The Story of a Novel*.

GERTRUD SCHOENBERG TO ALMA MAHLER-WERFEL,
NOVEMBER 10, 1948

Dear Almtschi,

Heartfelt thanks for the newspaper clippings.[37] Thomas Mann hasn't gotten in touch, Arnold hasn't stopped his invectives, and now *he* is beginning to respond. Unfortunately, so much valuable time and energy is lost, but it amuses him, and so I am at a loss about it. Finally, the gentlemen seem to be taking note of Arnold's creative work! It's "trickling," and that is always a good sign. Arnold's health is basically much better, only he is not supposed to strain himself, and he gets furious when he cannot run around like he used to.

I am really happy that I will be seeing you again soon. Can I do anything at all for you?

Yesterday, I received two very nice pictures of you. Certainly! You, of course, didn't give me any. All the best, love,

Trude Schoenberg

---

37. The article is not identified, but *Time* magazine printed a critique of Mann's book in its November 1, 1948, issue: "The writer Mann who had played violin in his youth, held long conversations for purposes of research for his 'Faustus' with his friends Igor Stravinsky and Bruno Walter and filled his book with an impressive but also petulant display of musical knowledge, that will rise over the heads of most readers." The critique in the *New York Times* of October 29, 1948, sounds similar: "Mr. Mann's musical knowledge is fabulous and his ability to make the invented compositions of his hero appear as the work of a genius is phenomenal. However, anyone who hasn't studied at the Julliard School of Music, nor written a symphony, nor conducted the New York Philharmonic will find the musical parts of 'Doctor Faustus' almost inaccessible."

SCHOENBERG TO THE *SATURDAY REVIEW OF LITERATURE*, NOVEMBER 13, 1948

Arnold Schoenberg[38]
116 N. Rockingham Ave.
Los Angeles 24, Calif.
November 13, 1948

To the Saturday Review of Literature
Editor of Letters
25 West 45th Street
New York 19, N.Y.

Sir:

In his novel *Dr. Faustus*, Thomas Mann has taken advantage of my literary property. He has produced a fictitious composer as the hero of his book; and in order to lend him qualities a hero needs to arouse people's interest, he made him the creator of what one erroneously calls my "system of twelve tones," which I call "method of composing with twelve tones."

He did this without my permission and even without my knowledge. In other words he borrowed it in the absence of the proprietor. The supposition of your reviewer, that he obtained information about this technique from Bruno Walter and Stravinsky, is probably wrong; because Walter does not know anything of composition with twelve tones, and Stravinsky does not take any interest in it.[39]

The informer[40] has been Mr. Wiesengrund-Adorno, a former pupil of my late friend Alban Berg. Mr. Adorno is very well acquainted with all the extrinsic details of this technique and thus was capable of giving Mr. Mann quite an accurate account of what a layman—the author—needs to tell another layman—the reader—to make him believe that he understands what it is about. But still, this was my property and nobody else's.

I learned about this abuse by chance: I received a magazine, containing a review of *Dr. Faustus*, wherein the twelve-notes composition was mentioned. Thereafter, Mrs. Alma Mahler-Werfel told me that she had read the book and was very upset about his using my "theory," without naming me as author, while he includes many living persons Walter, Klemperer, etc., not as fictitious but as real people. I have still not read the book itself, though in the meantime Mann had sent me a German copy, with a handwritten dedication "To A. Schoenberg, dem *Eigentlichen* [the *real one*]." As one needs not tell me that I am an *Eigentlicher,* a real one, it was clear that his Leverkühn is an impersonation of myself.

Leverkühn is depicted, from beginning to end, as a lunatic. I am now seventy-four and I am not yet insane, and I have never acquired the disease from which this insanity stems. I consider this an insult, and I might have to draw consequences.

When Mrs. Mahler-Werfel had discovered this misuse of my property, she told Mann that this was my theory, whereupon he said: "Oh, does one notice that? Then perhaps Mr. Schoenberg will be angry!" This proves that he was conscious of his guilt and knew it was a violation of an author's right.

It was very difficult for Mrs. Mahler-Werfel to convince him that he must do something to correct this wrong. Finally, I sent him a letter and showed him the possible consequences of ascribing my creation to another person who, in spite of being fictitious, is represented like a living man, whose biography is told by his friend Serenus Zeitblom.

One knows the superficiality and monomania of some historians who ignore facts if they do not fit in their hypotheses. Thus, I quoted from an encyclopedia of the year 2060, a little article in which my theory was attributed to Thomas Mann, because of his Leverkühn.

Much pressure by Mrs. Mahler-Werfel had still to be exerted to make Mann promise that every forthcoming copy of *Doctor Faustus* will carry a note, giving me credit for the twelve-notes composition. I was satisfied by this promise, because I wanted to be noble to a man who was awarded the Nobel Prize.

But Mr. Mann was not as generous as I, who had given him good chance to free himself from the ugly aspect of a pirate. He gave me an explanation: a few lines which he hid at the end of the book on a place on a page where no one ever would see it. Besides, he added a new crime to his first, in the attempt to belittle me: He calls me "a (a!) contemporary composer and theoretician." Of course, in two or three decades, one will know which of the two was the other's contemporary.

Is this the way to correct a wrong?

A reviewer of books needs not know intrinsic details of compositorial technique. Thus Mr. Mann's contention that everybody would know that the twelve-note technique was introduced by me is proven wrong. On the other hand, I wonder why this reviewer did not try to find also one to adorn his review, by telling what he fails to know. Or: hands-off.

Arnold Schoenberg

38. The English version (omitting the final two paragraphs) appeared on January 1, 1949, in the *Saturday Review of Literature,* with the heading *"Doctor Faustus Schoenberg?";* the German version appeared in *Der Monat* 1, no. 6 (March 1949): 76–78. The introduction in *Der Monat* was decidedly oriented against Schoenberg.

39. Igor Stravinsky's interest in and adoption of the twelve-tone method began only following Schoenberg's death in 1951.

40. Schoenberg uses the word *informer,* a derogatory political expression especially common during the McCarthy era.

MANN'S DIARY

Pacific Palisades, Thursday, December 9, 1948
... Incident involving Schoenberg's wretched, insulting letter to *Saturday Review of Literature*. Alma Mahler-Werfel as intermediary. In afternoon worked on response, must keep it calm.

Pacific Palisades, Friday, December 10, 1948
Finished response to Schoenberg in the morning, read it out to Erika. She copied it down and took it to Arlt, who finds Schoenberg's depressing account and Alma Mahler's behavior quite appalling. . . .

MANN TO THE *SATURDAY REVIEW OF LITERATURE*, DECEMBER 10, 1948

[Thomas Mann's Reply][41]

Sir: ... Arnold Schoenberg's letter both astonished and grieved me. Our personal correspondence on this matter had been of a thoroughly friendly character in all its phases. Not so long ago, when I sent him the English edition of *Doctor Faustus* with my appended statement, the maestro thanked me cordially with an air of complete satisfaction, so that I was led to believe that the "Leverkühn Case" was settled and disposed of. Now I regret to learn that it not only continues to annoy him but actually irritates him increasingly, although he still has not read the book.

If his acquaintance with the book were not based exclusively on the gossip of meddling scandal mongers, he would know that my efforts to give the central figure of the novel "qualities a hero needs to arouse people's interest" were neither limited to the transfer of Schoenberg's "method of composing with twelve tones," nor was this characteristic the most important one. Quaintly enough, he calls this technique his "literary property," though actually it should be called a musical system that has long since become a part of our cultural pattern, used by countless composers throughout the world, all of whom have tacitly purloined it from its originator. The universal dissemination and the wide employment of this technique are the very factors underlying the basic error of which I accuse myself. I sincerely believed that every child in our cultural area must at one time or another have heard about the twelve-tone system and its initiator, and that no one on Earth, having read my novel, could possibly imagine that I was its inventor or was trying to pose as such. This opinion of mine, I must say, was confirmed by many Swiss, German, Swedish, and, more recently, French reviews of the book, in which Schoenberg's name was quite casually mentioned. It was he himself who enlightened me with respect to my error. Serious misunderstandings, he informed me, would result from my book, unless I did something about it. Everybody except him, he said, kept receiving credit for his creation, and, if he knew anything about the breed of musicologists, they would attribute his theory to me a hundred years from now because I had developed it in my novel. His contemporaries, he added, were withholding so much from him that he had, at least, to guard his name and fame for posterity.

His concluding word moved me, no matter how absurd his apprehension seemed. It is quite untrue that it required "much pressure" to induce me to give him due credit. As soon as I understood his concern, I gave instructions to include in all translations, as well as in the German original, the appended statement which now appears in the English edition of *Doctor Faustus*. It was intended as a bit of instruction to the uninformed, and I worded it as objectively as possible. "Take note," it says in effect, "there is a composer and music philosopher living among us, whose name is Arnold Schoenberg; he, and not the hero of my novel, is the one who, in reality, thought out the twelve-tone composition method." The statement does not raise the question who is whose contemporary. If Schoenberg wishes, we shall, all of us, consider it our greatest and proudest claim to be his contemporaries.

As soon as I had received the first copies of the German edition, I sent him one with the inscription: "Dem Eigentlichen" [To the real one]. It meant: "Not Leverkühn is the hero of this musical era; you are its hero." It was a bow, a compliment. I have always addressed Arnold Schoenberg, the uncompromising and bold artist, with the utmost respect, in personal contact as well as in my letters, and I shall continue to do so.

The idea that Adrian Leverkühn is Schoenberg, that the figure is a portrait of him, is so utterly absurd that I scarcely know what to say about it. There is no point of contact, not a shade of similarity, between the origin, the traditions, the character, and the fate of my musician, on the one hand, and the existence of Schoenberg, on the other.[42] *Doctor Faustus* has been called a Nietzsche-novel and, indeed, the book, which for good reasons avoids mention of Nietzsche's name, contains many references to his intellectual tragedy, even direct quotations from the history of his illness. It has also been said that I had bisected myself in the novel, and that the narrator and the hero each embraced a part of me. That, also, contains an element of truth—although I, too, do not suffer from paralysis. But it has not occurred to anyone to speak of a Schoenberg-novel.

Instead of accepting my book with a satisfied smile as a piece of contemporary literature that testifies to his tremendous influence upon the musical culture of the era, Schoenberg regards it as an act of rape and insult. It is a sad spectacle to see a man of great worth, whose all-too-understandable hypersensitivity grows out of a life suspended between glorification and neglect, almost willfully yield to delusions of persecution and of being robbed, and involve himself in rancorous bickering. It is my sincere hope and wish that he may rise above bitterness and suspicion and that he may find peace in the assurance of his greatness and glory!

Thomas Mann
Pacific Palisades, Calif.

41. The English version appeared along with Schoenberg's original letter to the *Saturday Review of Literature;* the German version appeared likewise in the March 1949 issue of *Der Monat* (see note 38 above for both).

42. Mann made a similar assertion in his letter of January 8, 1948, to Margot Klausner (1905–75): "With Leverkühn I was not thinking of any specific composer of our time. His place in Music History is effectively unoccupied, and his work a free invention of my imagination. This work is nonexistent, but if, according to the fiction of the book, it did exist, then it would be performed all over the world as a tragically genial, and individual expression of the crisis of our time." Later, on June 16, 1950, Mann wrote to Alberto Mondadori: "In *The Magic Mountain,* illness is described not as a condition of grace but rather almost one of vice. In *Faustus* it is a remedy delivered by the devil to make an inhibited artistic nature productive. Twelve-Tone music is an ingenious attempt to win back order and law from the subjective arbitrariness of disintegrating music. It signifies objectivity, strict movement. With regard to character, fate, and personal living condition, the figure of Adrian Leverkühn has not the least bit to do with Arnold Schoenberg."

MANN TO THEODOR WIESENGRUND-ADORNO, DECEMBER 11, 1948

Thomas Mann
1550 San Remo Drive
Pacific Palisades, California
December 11, 1948

Dear Theodor,

You really should read this, first because Schoenberg describes you as "an informer," and second because you too may be concerned about his state of mind.

I was sent the copy by the magazine. I'm not sure whether my response (in translation) arrived on time. If it didn't, I'm not worried: I think Schoenberg's letter speaks for itself.

It would probably be advisable for to you remain tight-lipped on the matter until it comes out.

I'm expecting corrections to my "Story of a Novel" to arrive from Amsterdam soon and will forward them to you then.

Please send a letter and a response. With very best wishes,

T.M.

MANN'S DIARY

Pacific Palisades, Sunday, December 12, 1948

   ... To dinner with Klaus Pringsheim's three children. Monteux concert, melodious and pleasant. Strauss' *Eulenspiegel*[43] probably his best, at least of the symphonies. Benny[44] the source of much hilarity. Klaus read sections from his music theory work about the *basso continuo* period and its theoretical low point.—Discussed Schoenberg affair.

Pacific Palisades, Tuesday, December 14, 1948

   ... Adorno dropped by after tea. Long conversation about the Schoenberg affair and the "informer" invective.

---

43. Richard Strauss, *Till Eulenspiegels lustige Streiche: Nach alter Schelmenweise in Rondoform*, op. 28.

44. Legendary comedian Jack Benny (1894–1974), whose radio show repertoire included playing the violin—very badly.

THEODOR WIESENGRUND-ADORNO TO EDUARD STEUERMANN, DECEMBER 22, 1948

316 So. Kenter Ave.
Los Angeles 24, Calif.
December 22, 1948

My dear Eduard Steuermann,

. . .

About the Schoenberg–Thomas Mann matter: it has in the meantime become a catastrophe, and I am, so to speak, a victim by association. After Mann had given him a copy of the novel with a very flattering, personal dedication, Schoenberg had let himself be spurred on by Mrs. Mahler that he should be thought of as the true inventor of the twelve-tone system. Mann took it up immediately, and at the end of the English edition there is a note, which also relates to the *Harmonielehre* (which had no influence whatsoever on the novel). But it didn't help at all. Schoenberg wrote a letter to the *Saturday Review of Literature,* in the most vehement and absurd language, riddled with puns, where he not only denounces Mann as a pirate but, among other things, states that he was also to be reproached because the statement, placed as it was at the very end of the book, would as a result not even be noticed. Then he objects that Stravinsky and Walter had not helped Mann (which they really hadn't) and had put one over on the reviewer. I was the "informer"; that as a pupil of Berg's, I had "extrinsic knowledge" of the twelve-tone technique, and thus had placed Thomas Mann in a position vis à vis his readers, who wouldn't have understood any of this, to appear as if he understood it, which was not the case. But the twelve-tone technique remains Schoenberg's intellectual property. He dwells on the fact that the composer Leverkühn meets his end because of paralysis, which he, Schoenberg, does not have, and he threatens to sue because of this. In short, the letter might not be a paralytic one but it is a paranoic outburst. Mann answered with great restraint—too mellow for my taste. In such instances nothing helps more to gain objective and psychological results than to ruthlessly clamp down. He has written about my relationship to the *Faustus* novel in an autobiographical work which will appear in a couple of weeks. I haven't seen any of it yet.

Since Schoenberg's letter contains a couple of perfidious insults about me, I thought of doing something about it, such as writing the *Saturday Review of Literature* as well, but after jointly talking together with Mann, we decided against it.[45] What do you think? That I am not an "informer" should be obvious, since the novel contains nothing about the twelve-tone technique, which couldn't easily be seen from an analysis of any of the published works, and that my knowledge is not "extrinsic" (apparently because I did not study with A.S. myself) will be attested by you and Rudi [Kolisch] vis à vis Schoenberg, should it come to that. By the way, he insists that he hasn't even read the novel.

... Teddie

---

45. On August 30, 1957, two years after Mann's death, at Katia Mann's request, Adorno prepared an "affidavit," which states: "During the entire time of his writing the novel *Doktor Faustus*, I advised Thomas Mann as a friend on all musical matters. The book was written before my very eyes. The author never had the intention of creating the impression that the Twelve-Tone Technique was his invention. Given the well-known fact, that this technique had already been introduced by Arnold Schoenberg in the Twenties, such an intention would have been completely absurd. An analogous situation might be to imagine a novel that deals with a physicist who supposedly invents the *Theory of Relativity*. Nobody would ever come up with the idea that the novelist had wanted to plagiarize Einstein with that. It would be just as absurd to insinuate that Thomas Mann had used my 'intellectual property' in an illegitimate way, because the formulation of the musical ideas in the novel had been effected with the fullest agreement between both of us. That is precisely the same with regard to the relationship of the work to the *Philosophy of New Music* or to the description of Leverkühn's compositions. Finally I would like to declare most emphatically, that I never ever received any kind of material remuneration from Thomas Mann whatsoever." Angelika Abel, *Musikästhetik der Klassischen Moderne* (München: Wilhelm Fink, 2001), 190.

MANN'S DIARY

Pacific Palisades, Thursday, December 30, 1948

Golo yesterday at Alma Mahler's. Schoenberg really plans to sue. Not impossible that he may find an enterprising lawyer. Nothing is impossible. Why shouldn't they decide that the inventor of the twelve-tone system is due all proceeds from my book? I see it as less decided than K[atia].— Cloudy, windy. Meteorologists believe further earthquakes to come. Plans to install military satellite station three-quarters of the way to the moon, outside the earth's gravitational field. Anyone in possession of such a thing would rule the world.—Worked on the chapter I want to finish before starting lecture. Unpleasantly shaken up by Schoenberg's insanity. See myself ruined, though everyone is laughing at the idea. . . .

SCHOENBERG'S NOTE, JANUARY 6, 1949

I am ready to forget about everything which Mann borrowed from me in order to adorn his hero. I will even forget that he uses throughout his book terminology which I have contrived to clarify music theory. Ironically, it happens that these my tools do fit to the hand of an amateur, because in spite of this wrong use they are good enough to lend him the aspect of a great theoretician.

It is perhaps also negligible that I received his book with the acknowledgment only three days after I had written him how glad I am that his acknowledgment had eliminated the objects of dispute. Had he written these soft words which he mentioned in his answer, that "there is a composer and music philosopher A.S.," I would not have had a reason to attack him. What he wrote was:

> It does not seem supererogatory to inform the reader that the form of musical composition delineated in Chapter XXII, known as the twelve-tone or row system, is in truth the intellectual property of a contemporary composer and theoretician, Arnold Schoenberg. I have transferred this technique in a certain ideational context to the fictitious figure of a musician, the tragic hero of my novel. In fact, the passages of this book that deal with musical theory are indebted in numerous details to Schoenberg's *Harmonielehre* [Theory of Harmony]."

And this sounds different.

I know that a friend of mine had warned him not to insult me in his acknowledgment. If he really were as dignified as his letter wants to make the impression, he would have quoted what he really has written and not this "Old Franconian" nicety in baby talk, which he substitutes for the truth. Such substitution is not dignified. Dignity admits an error but strictly to avoid doings which might turn to untruth.

He wanted to insult me—"a contemporary composer" is among us Germans a term a historian might use when speaking of an artist who could not survive his time. An acknowledgment of the use of another man's ideas is not the place for historic evaluation. Besides: would Goethe have called Schubert a contemporary composer? But Hugo Riemann was right to call Matthias Monn[46] "a" contemporary of Haydn—one of Haydn's contemporaries.

A. Schoenberg 1/6/49

46. The Austrian composer Georg Matthias Monn (1717–50), whom Schoenberg admired. In the years 1932 and 1933 Schoenberg composed his Concerto for Cello and Orchestra (D Major) (in free adaptation after the Concerto for Clavicembalo by Georg Matthias Monn, composed 1746).

MANN'S DIARY

Pacific Palisades, Friday, January 7, 1948
. . . Also sent telegram to *Saturday Review of Literature* about copies of Schoenberg correspondence. My very restrained response seems to have been the right approach, and has evidently laid the polemic to rest.—Check for $22,000 from Book Club,[47] after deduction of Brandt and Brandt commission.

Pacific Palisades, Sunday, January 8, 1949
. . . Claude Hill,[48] a new friend, . . . has also sent his discussion of *The Permanent Goethe* in the *Saturday Review of Literature*. My response to Schoenberg well received among his colleagues, he writes.

Pacific Palisades, Monday, January 17, 1949
Powerful storm continues. Medi[49] mentioned on phone that the novel has moved up the best-seller list since the correspondence with Schoenberg . . .

Pacific Palisades, Monday, January 24, 1949
Sunny.—Worked on lecture.—With Katia in Pacific Palisades. Lot of mail to read. The best of it: extract from *London Sunday Times* with article by old Ernest Newman[50] entitled "Music and the Satanic,"—the astounding dialogue of quite Goethean power, Chapter 25. He promises more about the book.—In afternoon wrote letters with Katia to Fritz Busch[51] and Swedish Academy.—Remarkable letter from M. F. Bukofzer of the University of Washington about the correspondence with Schoenberg.[52] . . .

---

47. In November 1948 *Doktor Faustus* was the Book of the Month Club's book of the month.
48. German literature professor Claude Hill (Klaus Hilzheimer; 1911–91), who had immigrated to the United States in 1938, penned the article "Mirror of the German Soul: Thomas Mann Closes an Account," which Mann found gratifying.
49. Mann's daughter Elizabeth Borgese.
50. British music scholar and critic William Roberts (pseudonym: Ernest Newman; 1868–1959). Mann worked his way through Newman's Wagner monograph while writing *Doktor Faustus.* Thomas Mann, *Tagebücher, 1949–1950,* 350. Although Newman had written respectful reviews of the September 3, 1912, London premiere of Schoenberg's Five Pieces for Orchestra, op. 16, and of a 1914 performance conducted by Schoenberg himself, his later assessments of Schoenberg's works were often biting. He was even incensed by Emanuel Feurmann's premiere of Schoenberg's tonal Concerto for Violoncello and Orchestra (in D major, inspired by Matthias Georg Monn's Concerto per Clavicembalo): "The

conclusion to be drawn, once it was all over, was that Schoenberg is no better at writing other people's music than at writing his own." Annette Moreau, *Emanuel Feurmann* (New Haven, CT: Yale University Press, 2002), 116 (quoting Newman's critique in the November 10, 1935, *London Sunday Times*). Newman wrote three articles on *Doktor Faustus* for the *Sunday Times.* The first two—"Music and the Satanic" (January 2, 1949) and *"Doktor Faustus*-II" (May 15, 1949)—were enthusiastic appraisals of the novel, full of praise for Mann's "profound understanding of the technical problems and procedures of the art and work of the creative imagination." The third article—"A Schoenberg Comedy" (June 12, 1949)—assesses the Mann-Schoenberg dispute, with often derogatory remarks about Schoenberg's position (e.g., "The pathetically foolish letter rambles on in a similar vein . . .").

51. German conductor Fritz Busch (1890–1951), who fled Dresden in 1933, was the eldest brother of violin virtuoso Adolph Busch (1891–1952), whose daughter married pianist Rudolf Serkin (1903–91). The latter was discovered by Schoenberg in Vienna and hailed as a wunderkind; he later studied under Schoenberg.

52. The music scholar Manfred Bukofzer (1910–55) taught at UC Berkeley from 1941 until his death. At the time of his correspondence with Mann he was guest professor at the University of Washington. Bernhold Schmid, "Manfred Bukofzer im Briefwechsel mit Thomas Mann," in *Festschrift für Horst Leuchtmann zum 65. Geburtstag,* ed. Stephan Hörner and Bernhold Schmid (Tutzing: H. Schneider, 1993), 311–21.

MANFRED BUKOFZER TO MANN, JANUARY 20, 1949

Dr. Thomas Mann San Remo Drive
Pacific Palisades, Cal.

Most esteemed Dr.!

Your exchange of letters with Mr. Schoenberg in the *Saturday Review* concerning your *Doctor Faustus* is the reason for this letter. Already before the publication of the letters, Mr. Schnabel, Mr. Sessions[53] (my colleague at the University of California), and I had spoken about Schoenberg's unjustified and contentious objections. I was very surprised to read that Schoenberg not only regards his twelve-tone method to be his own "literary" property, but also maintains that everyone else, not only he himself, seems to be receiving recognition for being its author. It is obvious from his letter that he feels he is not receiving adequate "honor/recognition"—he would have liked to have been named by name, as had been the case with conductors Walter[54] and Monteux,[55] although it is precisely because he remains unnamed that he is given a much more prominent part in the book. As so often has been the case in the past, Schoenberg still demonstrates an unfortunate tendency towards a persecution complex, as well as an exaggerated sense of honor, which shows very clearly that, psychologically, he has not gotten over the fact that he never enjoyed the experience of being a properly educated composer. He had to work his way up on his own to the position of prominence which he enjoys today. This should fill him with justifiable pride. But time and again he has revealed himself to be a strange mixture of defiance and shame, which he views as a sign of Cain, that an evil-spirited fate has burned onto him. I ask myself whether or not the great man really is great, if by means of his tasteless diatribe, albeit written in a most amusing manner, he is so concerned about determining who is whose contemporary, hoping that the Levites be able to predict about posterity in advance.

It seems to me that two points were not considered in the dispute, which may be just as unimportant as the controversy itself seems unfounded, but which should nevertheless be mentioned. First, the name Josef Matthias Hauer,[56] that of a modest Viennese musician, ought not to be totally forgotten. This composer and theorist had developed the twelve-tone system quite independently of Schoenberg, and had even written about it in the essay "Vom Melos zur Pauke" [From melos to timpani].[57] So if it is a matter of literary property, then certainly Hauer could lodge a complaint. But since as a composer, he cannot compare himself to

Schoenberg, then Schoenberg would be considered the "actual" author, quite justifiably, since he was the first to make the system available and had ennobled it artistically.

The second point refers to your Dr. Riemer,[58] Mr. Wiesengrund-Adorno. I noticed, not without smiling, that in your characterization of the twelve-tone method, Wiesengrund's choice of words, his speech and thought processes "break through" repeatedly by way of your style, not only in the devil's scene but also in other places. The dialectical conception of the twelve-tone method is for Schoenberg a book with seven seals, and thus much more a typically Wiesengrund-like thought process, which would not even be possible without a good dose of Hegel, Kierkegaard, and Marx. The manner in which you secretly wove in his name in your *Faustus*[59] is a meaningful and well-earned testimony of thanks.

I read *Doktor Faustus* with great emotion and sympathy, not only because it treats and also solves the problem of internal and external emigration in a manner dear to my heart, not only because it treats of the German condition before the First World War with terrifying and yet redemptive and astute premonition, not only because it deals with music, which, as a musicologist, lies understandably close to my heart, but also because it seems to express a great, and even more than that, a decisive turn in your own treatment of music. In all of your previous writing it was the music of the nineteenth century you described in the spirit of the nineteenth century. Here you have made the leap to the twentieth century. What you are now describing is music of an enlightened consciousness, which is nevertheless still understood as demonic power.

A discussion of this question would carry things too far here. I hope very much to take up these thoughts again, when we have the pleasure to greet you here in Berkeley at the occasion of the Goethe year. With admiration and great esteem, your devoted,

Manfred F. Bukofzer
Temporarily at the
University of Washington
School of Music
Seattle 5, Washington

----

53. The composer Roger Sessions (1896–1985) taught at Princeton University and the University of California, Berkeley. He taught Schoenberg's music and corresponded with Schoenberg between 1944 and 1951. In response to Sessions's letter of praise in the article, "Arnold Schoenberg in the United States," at the occasion of Schoenberg's seventieth birthday in 1944, Schoenberg wrote on December 3, 1944:

"And finally I would like to mention, what I consider to be the greatest virtue in the appreciation of my music: that you say that one must listen to it in the same manner that one listens to any other music, forget the theories, the 12-Tone Method, the dissonances. And I would add to that, if possible, also [forget] the author. There are of course many more profound ideas in this article, but I think that this is the greatest help for the understanding of my work. In the lecture 'Staged and New Music' or 'Style and Idea' I conveyed a similar idea, when I wrote: 'A Chinese poet speaks Chinese, but what is it, that he says?' and I used to say, 'If I write in this or that style, it is purely a private matter and no listener's business.—But I want my message to be understood and accepted.'" Sessions and Mann probably met during Mann's time at Princeton. The former corresponded with Mann about *Doctor Faustus* in December of 1948. See note 62 below.

54. In Weimar there is a performance of Leverkühn's *Cosmic Symphony* under the rhythmically most reliable conducting of Bruno Walter. Mann, *Doctor Faustus* (New York: Vintage, 1971), 389.

55. "A few weeks earlier [Leverkühn] had had a letter from a Monsieur Monteux, director of the Russian ballet in Paris, former member of the Colonne orchestra, wherein this experimentally-minded director had announced his intention of producing the *Marvels of the Universe*, together with some orchestral parts of *Love's Labour's Lost* as a concert pure and simple." Mann, *Doctor Faustus*, 305–6.

56. The Austrian composer Joseph Matthias Hauer (1883–1959) turned to Schoenberg for the first time in February of 1913, asking Schoenberg to advise him on his first symphony, which had been written in a new, for Hauer, pantonal style, which Schoenberg had been exploring since 1908. However, Hauer only met Schoenberg in 1917, at which time Hauer had visited Schoenberg three times seeking advice on his music. These meetings did not seem to satisfy Hauer, since he wrote to his friend, the philosopher Ferdinand Ebner (1882–1931) on August 31, 1917, including vituperative, anti-Semitic remarks against Schoenberg: "Dear Ebner, I was at Schoenberg's: vanity, thirst for glory, ambitiousness, envy . . . led me to the man. . . . In general I had the feeling that Schoenberg in his innermost had to come to grips with the fact that someone else existed beside himself. . . . This gawking and momentary surprise at certain passages in my works was perhaps the only human attribute that I was able to discern in the guy. In all else he is a stupid, teasing, banal 'Jewish scoundrel,' despite his forty-three years. I am not a holy man, but association with such an individual makes me feel dirty. . . . His knowledge is extremely superficial, his music is without handicraft. . . . I hope that not all Jews (Mendelssohn, Heine . . .) were like that, or one would have to ridicule or . . . despise oneself. This Schoenberg is a rare kind of swindler." Despite this reaction, in 1919–20 Hauer came closer to Schoenberg and his circle, when his works were performed by the Society for Private Performances of Music. At this time Hauer had begun to develop his own twelve-tone method, which used free hexachordal tropes, which he at first used not too rigorously from 1919 to 1922. From 1908 to 1922 Schoenberg had approached what was to become his signature twelve-tone method. Some early compositions, among them the unfinished *Jakobsleiter* (1915–17), show the development of Schoenberg's method, which in 1920 he began to use in its purest form and first began to explain to his students in 1922. Although Hauer's and Schoenberg's systems are nominally similar and were developed about the same time, and both composers had been influenced by the other's works and writings, they are, in practice and application, quite different. Only Schoenberg's method garnered a wider following. Because the two methods are different and both composers progressed to ever more rigorous applications of their own methods, it is impossible to answer the

question "Who invented the twelve-tone system first?" See Bryan Simms, "Who First Composed Twelve-Tone Music, Schoenberg or Hauer?" *Journal of the Arnold Schoenberg Institute* 10, no. 2 (1987): 108–33. In any case, the method that Adorno had described to Mann was, of course, Schoenberg's and not Hauer's method.

57. Joseph Matthias Hauer, "Von Melos zur Pauke: Eine Einführung in die Zwölftonmusik" (1925), in *Theoretische Schriften I* (Vienna: Universal Edition, 1925). Although Schoenberg presented his twelve-tone method to his students in 1922, it was only in 1934 that he delivered a public lecture at Princeton describing his Method, and not until 1950 did he succeed in publishing his explanation in the collection of essays *Style and Idea.*

58. An allusion to the German scholar and literary historian Friedrich Wilhelm Riemer (1774–1845), who from 1803 until 1812 served as secretary to Goethe as well as tutor to the latter's son, August. See Schmid, "Manfred Bukofzer im Briefwechsel mit Thomas Mann," 315.

59. Mann, *Doctor Faustus*, 83. Wendell Kretzschmar's lecture on Beethoven's Piano Sonata, op. 111, where the name Wiesengrund is linked to the main motif of the arietta. "Into the poetic little illustrative phrases I wrote for the arietta theme I slipped Adorno's patronymic, *Wiesengrund (Meadowland)*, by way of showing my gratitude." Mann, *The Story of a Novel*, 48.

MANN TO MANFRED BUKOFZER, JANUARY 25, 1949

Thomas Mann
1550 San Remo Drive
Pacific Palisades, California
January 25, 1949

Dear Mr. Bukofzer,

Your letter was very welcome, and important in its assessment. Schoenberg is a difficult character, though he is probably entitled to be. If only he weren't such a rowdy! In my response to him, I was basically more concerned with hushing up his folly than defending myself.[60] I have forgiven him, especially given the state between glorification and neglect in which he lives, and which probably makes him somewhat over-excitable. I am almost inclined to believe that my response—in which I was duly deferential—has appeased him.

I already knew about Hauer.[61] But I was reluctant to drag him into all this, as it would have provoked Schoenberg even further.

It was very unpleasant and absurd of him to call Adorno an "informer." After all, what is there to betray? It is all out in the open and common knowledge. I owe Adorno a debt of thanks for his letters and conversations, and to some degree have expressed my gratitude in my autobiographical work *The Story of a Novel,* some of which will appear in the winter volume of *Neue Rundschau,* and which will be coming out as a short book this spring.

I was touched that old Ernest Newman in the *London Sunday Times* seems so taken with the novel. Without doubt it is an "end-of" book that looks forward to the new; and it attempts to *be* that of which it speaks, namely constructive music. Roger Sessions has written me a rather nice letter about it.[62] Respectfully yours,

Thomas Mann

---

60. Mann wrote to Otto Basler in a similar vein on February 13, 1949: "The general view is that Schoenberg deserves pity. In my response I was more concerned with hushing up his folly than defending myself."

61. Hauer is mentioned in Adorno's *Philosophy of New Music,* ed. and trans. Robert Hullot-Kentor (Minneapolis: University of Minnesota Press 2006): "Just such a method was developed independently of Schoenberg by the Austrian composer Josef Mattias Hauer, and the results are tediously meager. By contrast, Schoenberg radically integrates the classical and, even more, the archaic techniques of variation into twelve-tone material" (51).

62. Sessions wrote to Mann on December 21, 1948: "I absolutely loved the book's specifically musical parts, and they moved me profoundly.... Perhaps because the book strikes so close to home, I particularly welcomed its insight into today's musical consciousness—the problems and the dilemma to which each of us must find a solution, and for which no purely personal solution is apt.... Perhaps I can best express this by saying: when I began, I was uncertain whether Leverkühn was a convincing musical figure, but I ended up recognizing that there is something of him in me and in every serious musician I know, and vice versa." Andrea Olmstead, ed., *The Correspondence of Roger Sessions* (Boston: Northeastern University Press, 1992), 360–61.

SCHOENBERG TO JOSEF RUFER, FEBRUARY 8, 1949

February 8, 1949
Mr. Josef Rufer
Juttastrasse 16
Berlin Zehlendorf

Dear Friend:

I am afraid this is going to be a very long letter, and I would not be able to write it were it not for Mr. Dick Hoffmann, who has come from New Zealand in order to study with me and is helping me some—helping me a lot with all my works and who will write this letter. I am dictating it into a speech-machine—a "Dictaphone."

. . .

If Mann supposedly says in this new book that we are more or less in agreement, that is one of Mann's most unbelievable lies. That I worked with him on *Dr. Faustus* is also a complete lie. I only found out by newspaper clippings that my theory was used in it. Mann has been much under attack, also in reference to my twelve-tone method. Nevertheless, I am convinced that you alone can judge best, whether or not the article should be released with or without my approval. I am also convinced that I can give you my approval without more ado, without needing to read the article first.

. . .

Arnold Schoenberg

MANN'S DIARY

Pacific Palisades, Tuesday, February 15, 1949
. . . Continued work on *Faustkampf.* Went over *Das Alte Haus.* Bewildering, exhausting mail. Long account from an expert[63] about how Hauer invented the twelve-tone system. . . .

Pacific Palisades, Wednesday, February 16, 1949
. . . Stravinsky proceedings relating to misuse of *The Firebird.*[64] Hailed by pundits as the greatest composer of our day. Incentive to Schoenberg?— *Faustkampf* completed; new section . . .

Pacific Palisades, Friday, February 18, 1949
. . . *Die Rundschau* with *Erinnerungen* already in New York too. Article in *Die Tat* in Zurich. Discussed that and the Schoenberg affair.

Pacific Palisades, Monday, February 21, 1949
. . . *Neue Zeitung* article[65] critical of Schoenberg . . .

Pacific Palisades, Thursday, March 3, 1949
. . . Frau Schoenberg has called Alma Mahler: allegedly there is now "another thing" in *Die Rundschau,* and she will have to sever ties with me, the arch-enemy. Quite mad.

Pacific Palisades, Tuesday, March 8, 1949
. . . Schuh's[66] article about the Schoenberg controversy . . .

---

63. Letter from Elli Bommersheim. Mann, *Tagebücher, 1949–1950,* 367. On February 19, 1949, Mann wrote to Bommersheim: "I was well aware of Hauer and his original authorship of the twelve-tone system when I wrote my response to Schoenberg. Nevertheless, I deliberately suppressed the name to avoid provoking Schoenberg, as the poor fellow is already suffering. The information you provide has enhanced my understanding of this business, and your letter will be very useful if I once again have to seriously defend myself against Schoenberg's accusations."
64. Stravinsky reorchestrated his early works to extend his copyright in the United States. Schoenberg did the same for *Verklärte Nacht,* as he had not received any license fees from Germany in the period after 1933. In 1947 Stravinsky sued his publisher, Leeds Music, for allowing an adaptation of "Ronde des Princesses" from *Firebird* as the pop song *Summer Moon.*
65. Heinz Hess, "Der Fall Leverkühn: Arnold Schönberg contra Thomas Mann," *Neue Zeitung* (Munich), February 8, 1949. On February 23, 1949, Mann wrote to Gertrud Lukács: "As far as I can see, most people are shaking their heads over Schoenberg's foolishness. The correspondence with him will appear in German in

the journal *Der Monat*." At the end of February 1949 he wrote in a similar vein to Alexander Moritz Frey: "Many thanks for your two letters, and in particular for participating in the Schoenberg affair or Leverkühn affair, though I do feel you have expended too much emotion or time over it. Naturally in such cases all sorts of enemies come out of the woodwork, taking the opportunity to vent their wrath. However, my impression overall is that people are fairly unanimous in shaking their heads over Schoenberg's folly."

66. *Neue Zürcher Zeitung* music critic Willi Schuh (1900–1986). On March 14, 1949, Mann wrote to Lavinia Mazzucchetti: "Luigi Dallapiccola is quite right: the less this shameful matter is exploited in public for polemical purposes and shared with the entire world, the better. In my response to Schoenberg, I was more concerned with protecting him and his wounded sensitivity than with defending myself. Aside from that, I had already discussed the matter in advance in the drafts for *Doktor Faustus*, and from my standpoint it really is settled now, aside from my lingering regret that Schoenberg took the whole business so wrongly and foolishly. I am in no way feeling touchy towards him and am certainly not interested in other people polemicizing against him. Having said that, I was very pleased about Dallapiccola's privately expressed position on the matter, and very grateful for the long article devoted to the affair by Dr. Schuh in *Neue Zürcher Zeitung*."

WILLI SCHUH IN *NEUE ZÜRCHER ZEITUNG,*
FEBRUARY 12, 1949
Thomas Mann and Arnold Schoenberg:
About a Controversy

In his recent novel *Doktor Faustus* Thomas Mann links "the method of composition using twelve tones related to each other" (the so-called twelve-tone system) to the novel's main character, the fictional German composer Adrian Leverkühn. Various figures from the world of music are now objecting that the method inaugurated by Arnold Schoenberg—tangible for the first time in his piano pieces op. 23 (1922)—has been somewhat audaciously attributed to a fictional character. They point out that the twelve-tone system was invented by Schoenberg, not Leverkühn, and that the "montage" is designed to create confusion. These objections come as a surprise, since extensive literature about this "system" already exists, and even those with only a superficial knowledge of music must be aware that it has been in use in Europe and America for a quarter of a century. Nonetheless, Arnold Schoenberg himself has now gone a step further than these critics. First, he demanded public clarification of the "ownership rights" in all future editions of the novel, and although Mann met this request in the November 1948 edition by including a note at the end of the book, he has now launched a further attack on the author.

The accusatory piece, along with Mann's elegantly worded response, was published as an open letter to the editor of the *Saturday Review of Literature* in the January 1, 1949, issue. Schoenberg accuses Mann of having attributed the invention of the "twelve-tone system" to a character in the novel, and argues that he is the actual inventor, Mann having transgressed without his permission or knowledge, i.e., having committed theft in the owner's absence. Schoenberg infers from the fact that Mann (who previously was on good terms with him and had lengthy discussions with him about music and life as a composer) sent him a copy of the German edition containing the dedication "For Arnold Schoenberg, *the real one*" that Leverkühn—allegedly portrayed as mad "from start to finish" (!)—is supposed to be him. This assumption merely demonstrates that he has not read the book, as Leverkühn's life and compositions, described in detail, bear no resemblance to Schoenberg's life and output.

Schoenberg writes: "I am now seventy-four years old and not yet mad, and have never caught the disease from which this madness originates. I consider it an insult, and may draw the obvious conclusions from it." He mentions that it took urgent intervention by Alma Mahler-Werfel to convince Mann to include a note about who invented the twelve-tone system in all editions of the novel; and while he admits that this request, which was supposed to give Mann the opportunity to "free himself from unpleasantly appearing as though he had committed piracy," was met, he notes that the statement itself in fact triggered further anger, as Mann "limited himself to a few lines at the end of the book where no-one would see them" and referred to Schoenberg as "a contemporary composer and theoretician." Prompted by this formulation, Schoenberg concludes his letter with: "In two or three decades we will know who was the contemporary of whom. . . ." Perhaps Schoenberg has forgotten that for Mann's seventieth birthday he wrote: "It is with a sense of (genuine) egotism that I hope we remain good contemporaries for many years to come."

In his response, Mann expresses surprise and sadness over Schoenberg's aggressive letter and points out that his personal correspondence with him has always been friendly. If Schoenberg had actually read the book rather than relying on the gossip of intermediaries, states Mann, he would realize that the author's efforts to keep the reader interested in his main character were by no means limited to attributing the invention of the twelve-tone system to him, and that this was not even one of the main methods of characterization. The fact that Schoenberg considers the twelve-tone system his own "literary property" is strange, Mann feels, as the system has been used for many years by numerous composers in many countries, who have tacitly taken it over, though he admits he was probably wrong to assume everyone has heard of the twelve-tone system. He also admits that Schoenberg himself alerted him to this mistake and earlier pointed out that 120 years from now the guild of music scholars might perhaps attribute the invention to Mann.

He then states that he did not have to be pressured to include the note Schoenberg wanted and that it was written in as objective a manner as possible, to provide orientation to uninformed readers (in the American edition the note is prominently displayed on its own separate page, in the same font as the main text and with wider spacing). Mann states that what he was implying with his dedication "For Arnold Schoenberg, *the real one*" was that "not Leverkühn, but rather you, Schoenberg, are the hero of this musical age," and that it was meant as a bow and a compliment to him. "In personal interaction and in my letters I have always addressed Arnold Schoenberg with absolute respect, as an uncompromising and daring artist, and I will continue to do so," he writes.

Understandably, Mann feels the idea that Leverkühn is Schoenberg is completely absurd and that nothing further should be said of the matter, as there are no similarities, not even a shadow of a resemblance, in background, tradition, or character. He notes that *Doktor Faustus* has been called a Nietzsche novel and that for good reasons he avoided mentioning Nietzsche's name, despite directly mentioning various facts from his life; and that while the narrator Zeitblom and Leverkühn both bear traits of Mann himself (though Mann does not suffer from paralysis), no one has spoken of a Schoenberg novel.

Mann is also regretful that instead of welcoming *Doktor Faustus* with a satisfied smile as a piece of contemporary literature reflecting Schoenberg's powerful influence on the musical culture of our age, the composer views it as an act of theft and abuse. He concludes that it is sad to see a man of such importance, whose oversensitivity can be attributed to living a life between glorification and neglect, almost obstinately giving in to the idea that he has been persecuted and robbed and sinking into rancor and squabbling; and that he genuinely hopes Schoenberg will free himself from this bitterness and suspicion and find peace in the assurance of his greatness and fame. In his conclusion he highlights the tragedy overshadowing Schoenberg's life and output, though unfortunately we do not have space to discuss that tragedy here.

Perhaps one or two further points should be added to Mann's response. First, one should bear in mind that the history of the invention of the twelve-tone system, the importance of which we will not be discussing here, has not been written yet. Moreover, the Russian Jefim Golyschev and the Viennese Josef Matthias Hauer were involved in the development of the system, and there have been theoretical assessments not only in analytical journal articles from the Schoenberg circle (e.g., Erwin Stein in *Anbruch*) but also, on a different basis and with different conclusions, in the writings of Herbert Eimert (*Atonale Musiklehre*, 1924) and Hauer (*Vom Melos zur Pauke* and *Zwölftontechnik*, both 1925). Later Ralph Hill and Ernst Krenek published articles on the theory and practice of serial music. Naturally none of this has any impact on Schoenberg's decisive role as founder of the twelve-tone system nor on the development of the method in his own work since 1922, nor on his influence on Alban Berg, Anton Webern, and many others (e.g., recently the Leibowitz circle).

This "affair" actually has nothing to do with facts of music history. We risk making the same mistake as Schoenberg—who has attacked at the wrong level—if we choose to focus on literary ownership, priorities, and attribution, though it is not just musicians and music critics who, wowed by the impressive knowledge of music on display, have been tempted into taking a completely one-sided view of the work. We are seeing a repeat of what happened with *The Magic Mountain,* the *Joseph* novels, and *Lotte in Weimar,* though this time in more extreme form. Aspects of the novel with specific functions within the work's overall complexity are being viewed in isolation, and "the integration of what I have studied and acquired into the book's atmosphere" (which according to his diaries Mann considered an important part of the novel's appeal) are being deliberately overlooked. In earlier instances it was the medical material, then the religious history, then the biographical; in the present case it is music and music theory, held under a magnifying glass for the reader to marvel at.

This inevitably leads to misunderstandings. It is easily forgotten that *Doktor Faustus* is a novel, not a music history source work, and as such is *inter alia* "a portrayal of the soul and the epoch." The work has a dual relationship with the world of music: its hero is a musician, a completely invented figure, imbued with reality via attribution and montage (a key feature of the novel's compositional technique). And the ideals of form and style enacted in the work draw on musical constructivism, just as *Buddenbrooks* and subsequent novels relied on the *leitmotif,* an element borrowed from the world of music.

In his recent *The Story of a Novel,* the first few chapters of which were published in *Neue Rundschau* (Vol. 13), Mann makes a point which attentive readers are probably already aware of, namely that "music, insofar as the novel deals with it, is merely the foreground, merely the paradigm for something more general, merely a means for expressing the current situation of art as a whole, and of culture, mankind, and the spirit itself in this critical epoch. Is it a musician novel? Yes. But it was conceived as a novel about our culture and our epoch, and for me it was an obvious step to get help in capturing and conveying those means and that foreground." Mann got that help from "a veritable small library of music books which I marked up with pencil." He mentions among others Bekker's history of music, the memoirs of Berlioz and Stravinsky, the letters of Hugo Wolf, Schoenberg's *Theory of Harmony,* Ernst Krenek's *Music Here and Now,* and Willi Reich's Alban Berg monograph. Of particular assistance was the co-author of the latter, Theodor Adorno, who was Mann's main information source in musical matters and whose unpublished work *Philosophy of New Music* prompted Mann to incorporate the chapter on twelve-tone. The Adorno work mainly discusses Schoenberg, his school and the twelve-tone system, and according to Mann delivers a "perspicacious, penetrating critique of that system by . . . discussing the destiny that causes (objectively necessary) constructive elucidation of music (on equally objective grounds) to swing back into something dark and mythological, over the artist's head as it were. What better for my world of the 'Magic Square'? . . . The portrayal of serialism and the critique thereof rendered in dialogue in Chapter XXII of *Doktor Faustus* is entirely based on Adornian analysis."

Mann also notes that the technical-musical aspects caused him trouble, as absolute accuracy and precision were vital if he was to avoid producing an ordinary *Künstlerroman*. "Mastery . . . of that sort was a prerequisite," he writes. He also explains that the montage technique went hand in hand with the novel's basic conception. The "linking of living individuals with names beneath the novel's characters, who then cease to differ from them in terms of reality or unreality," the intertwining of Leverkühn's tragedy with Nietzsche's, the "omission" of important names in the sections about music, and the portraits of contemporaries from the private and public worlds, hidden beneath aliases (Schildknapp, the senator and her daughter), are all part of the novel's style and technique. Also worth mentioning are the "undeclared reproduction of the prelude to Act III of *Die Meistersinger*," the maliciously self-satisfied digs at Richard Strauss, and the absence of Schoenberg's actual name, as they are all part of the "rendering of the unreal," similar to Mann's technique in the *Joseph* novels.

Mann's goal was to relocate "the fiction which absorbs the real" in a "historic" space. The much discussed chapter on twelve-tone is merely one of many serving that purpose, and not in fact one of the most important, even within the parts about music. Remember—Mann does not actually particularly like twelve-tone music! Think instead of the records from the magic box, from which "the fullness of melody" flows towards Hans Castorp. It is Wagner who gives Mann the deepest musical pleasure ("My musical home is basically the triad world of the *Ring*," he admits in *The Story of a Novel*, adding that "on the piano I can't get enough of the Tristan chord"); evidently his assessment that if he were a musician, he would compose more or less in the manner of César Franck[67] . . . is accurate.

Mann has had the last word in the Schoenberg affair, in *The Story of a Novel*. It carries considerable weight, as it was written before the publication of the correspondence in the *Saturday Review of Literature*. Mann concludes: "Should I also cite the transfer of the Schoenbergian idea of twelve-tone or serial music to Adrian Leverkühn—to which certain parties have raised objections—as an example of an act of montage of this kind, and as an example of stealing from reality? In fact I will probably have to do so in future: at Schoenberg's request, the book will have to bear a postscript explaining intellectual property rights to the uninitiated. This is somewhat against my wishes. Not because a statement of that kind would constitute a minor breach of my novel's spherical, self-contained world, but because within the sphere of the book—the world of the pact with the devil and black magic—the idea of the twelve-tone system takes on a coloration and quality which—am I not right?—it does not actually possess and which to some extent makes it my own property, i.e., the property of the book. Schoenberg's idea and my *ad hoc* version differ so radically that, aside from the issue of improper style, I feel it would be somewhat offensive to mention his name in the text."

---

67. Mann to Bruno Walter, September 15, 1946: "If I had been born a musician, I would have composed more or less in the manner of César Franck and conducted like you." *Blätter der Thomas Mann Gesellschaft,* no. 9 (1969): 34.

MANN'S DIARY

Pacific Palisades, Sunday, March 12, 1949

... People are messing around with the book in the most trivial possible way, printing insinuating excerpts in the papers. Supposedly the Breisacher[68] figure is a mocking portrayal of Wolfskehl.[69] (And Leverkühn is Schoenberg.) ...

---

68. In *Doktor Faustus* the Dr. Chaim Breisacher character, a Jewish teacher, is described as an "extremely spirited and intellectually highly developed, even reckless type, of fascinating ugliness."

69. The writer Karl Wolfskehl (1869–1940), an admirer of Stefan George, had been an acquaintance of Mann's since the early Munich years. Mann, *Tagebücher, 1949–1950*, 384.

DER MONAT, MARCH 1949

*The Real One: The Dissonances between
Arnold Schoenberg and Thomas Mann*

The more insight one gains into the controversy between Arnold Schoenberg and Thomas Mann, which has become increasingly well-known through the press, the stranger seem the demeanor and concerns of the former about receiving the proper acknowledgment of his authorship as the inventor of the "Method of Composing with Twelve Tones."[70] We have been authorized by both these authors to reproduce the two letters first published in the *Saturday Review of Literature* in their German original form. Doesn't Schoenberg's concern about his posthumous reputation seem rather strange, given the enormous impact of his "system" that has found devotees and emulators worldwide?

Strangely enough he does not accuse any of these of "intellectual piracy," yet he does so with the author of the Faustus novel, although here it is a matter only of a description of that technique, which moreover is just a "montage" within the complex structure of the novel, and merely has the function of bestowing his hero's creativity with some vestige of reality. The musical digressions, according to the novelist, were merely used in order to express the status of "the culture of intellect in our thoroughly critical era." But how is one to answer the bitter reproaches in the Schoenberg epistle, which were written after Thomas Mann had, "without pressure"—and we can believe him—met the demand for compensation in the form of a statement which clearly addresses the subject of proprietary rights in his post-script? It is unbelievable that Schoenberg, as he himself admits, did not think it necessary to have read the novel beforehand. Otherwise, it would have been quite impossible, considering his earlier friendly association with Mann, to have ended up in this labyrinth of absurd misunderstandings. On the other hand, he might have discovered the brilliantly informed description of his system, and would have become even more upset. We know, from Thomas Mann's notes on *The Story of a Novel*, that Theodor Wiesengrund-Adorno, his mentor concerning the secrets of twelve-tone music, had also been inspired by the idea of the necessary retreat of con-structively illumined music to the dark ages.

The confusion caused by Schoenberg is calculated to cause further reper-cussions. But it is absolutely meaningless with regard to the novel, if atten-tion is now drawn to the fact that neither Schoenberg nor Leverkühn nor Thomas Mann were the "inventors" of the twelve-tone technique but rather Josef Matthias Hauer. Due to the passion of the musical discussion, frequently the intention of the author has been quite overlooked, sinisterly placing Schoenberg's technique of composition into the realm of the pact with the devil and black magic, whereas the specifically Schoenbergian parts have been just as exposed and unprotected in the hands of many a Schoenberg pupil.

---

70. *Der Monat* 1, no. 6 (March 1949): 76–78.

H. H. STUCKENSCHMIDT'S BIOGRAPHY OF
ARNOLD SCHOENBERG

On April 9, [1949] we met in Brentwood Park.[71] I had had lunch with Thomas Mann at San Remo Drive in Pacific Palisades, a few kilometers from Schoenberg's house. "Will you see Schoenberg?" the writer asked. I replied that I had been invited to coffee in Brentwood Park immediately afterward. Thomas Mann advised me not to tell Schoenberg where I had had lunch; he would take it badly. The advice was good. Arnold and Gertrud Schoenberg greeted me warmly. The Faustus affair was not mentioned.

71. H.H. Stuckenschmidt, *Arnold Schoenberg: His Life, World and Work* (New York: Schirmer, 1977), 499. Mann wrote to Otto Basler on March 25, 1949: "With regard to Schoenberg, if I am not entirely misled about it, he has embarrassed all of his admirers and pupils with his really foolish letter. From some I know this directly."

SCHOENBERG UNDATED NOTES

Leverkühn's Twelve-Tone Goulash

Leverkühn is one of these amateurs who think that composing with twelve tones is nothing more than the constant use of the basic set or its inversions. Actually, the meaning of this rule ought to be expressed differently. It should be: None of the twelve tones should appear without the end of the basic set or its derivatives. But to think that following this rule could result in a composition is just as childish or amateurish or unprofessional as it would be to assume that the avoidance of other interdictions would be sufficient to create music. For example, the avoidance of parallel fifths or octaves. These rules are merely restrictions and not creative. You have to be able to create music in spite of these rigorous restrictions.
   . . .[72]

Leverkühn is a remnant from Wagner's final years and the ensuing quarter of a century. It is amazing that such an obsolete character could appear in our time. All his inclinations seem atavistic in a way. His longing for grand, immense forms is reminiscent of compositions from the end of the nineteenth century, which could conceive of no other task beyond the expansion of a tetralogy.

*Schoenberg's Fragment on Mann's "Author's
Note" from the Year 1949*

I suggest you exclude the crossed out words at the end of the first sentence in your final statement in all future editions:
   "——————————— property of a contemporary composer and theoretician Arnold Schoenberg."
   Because it happens to be illogical: First you write me that every village idiot would know that the twelve-tone method wasn't invented by the hero of the novel but by Arnold Schoenberg. This would mean that no explanation was needed. And so this appropriation means no damaging encroachment on my author's rights.
   But then you give the explanatory note that demeans me to being a contemporary.
   You could have better written, "A certain Arnold Schoenberg, a contemporary of Stravinsky and Hindemith." Whether or not it is dignified to correct a mistake in such an insidious manner, when one was treated so generously, I leave it up to your contemporaries and my posterity.

Schoenberg's Note (unpublished)

He acts as if I had something against his using the twelve-tone-method, though he knows quite well that I am protesting because he points to someone else as its originator.

---

72. Pages 2–3 are lost.

MANN'S DIARY

Pacific Palisades, Tuesday, August 30, 1949

... Gift to Alma, a signed drawing by Mopp.[73] She has severed all ties with Schoenberg.[74] He regrets his letter. ...

Pacific Palisades, Sunday, September 3, 1949

... Tochs and Klaus Pringsheim for dinner; also Golo, here since midday. Exhausted towards end. Much criticism of Schoenberg, who should produce better music to offset foolishness. Alma Mahler has reconciled with him; have given this my blessing. ...

Pacific Palisades, Friday, September 23, 1949

... Stiedrys (Erika Wagner) to dinner with Klaus Pringsheim. Golo arrived later to stay for the weekend. Amusing chat, so different from the wearisome Toch evening. Much talk of Richard Strauss. Conductors' old tricks. Stiedry talked about *The Story of a Novel.* Leverkühn the post-Straussian composer we should have had.—Schoenberg, Krenek.

Pacific Palisades, Monday, September 26, 1949

... Letter from a German.[75] About Kretzschmar, rhythm versus sound. Not Beethoven-Schoenberg, but rather Bach-Mozart-Stravinsky (late). *Der Monat* unproductive. In the evening listened to Tristan records (Act I), with profound admiration.

---

73. The Austrian painter Max Oppenheimer (1885–1954), nicknamed Mopp, produced two portraits of Mann. He had also painted Schoenberg around 1909.

74. Alma Mahler-Werfel was evidently enraged that Schoenberg, without actually mentioning her by name, had alluded to her in his letter to the *Saturday Review of Literature.* On March 12, 1949, he wrote to her in New York: "Dear Alma: Your discussion on the telephone with Trude, some of which I overheard, has given me food for further thought and reflection, to determine whether I really acted so wrongly. I assume that the [Konrad] Lesters mentioned what I'm telling you now, namely that I did not mention your name with any malicious intent, nor indeed with any intent at all. I simply made the mistake I've made elsewhere, of depicting the event sequentially and chronologically instead of condensing and jumping in *in medias res* as I otherwise would. It's a terrible shame that you didn't immediately take up my offer to rectify the matter. I would have had nothing against doing so, and could have simply said 'a friend' or 'female friend' or something similar. For you to now say that I had no right to mention your name or your private correspondence in public is unfair. Following the aforementioned period of reflection, I've realized how often you've done precisely that. I definitely didn't give you the right to tell Walter my opinion of him, nor to tell Winter I think he's a

rogue. Similarly, the business with Arlt was presented completely inaccurately. I've never had anything against Arlt, nor said anything; as for Torberg, I've just laid hands on the letter in which I thank him—a polite and warm letter, a copy of which I'll send to you when I have the chance. What I'm saying is: I admit, once again, that I should not have mentioned your name in that context. I confess it was a mistake on my part. However, you've made the same mistake yourself at least four times, possibly in a more far-reaching manner. Please bear that in mind when you ponder all this in the future. Sincerely yours, Arnold Schoenberg."

75. The pianist Adolf Havlik. Mann, *Tagebücher, 1949–1950,* 461.

SCHOENBERG IN *MUSIC SURVEY* (FALL 1949)

In his letter accompanying the following communication, which we here publish for the first time, Schoenberg writes that the matter "may perhaps be stale" by now. So it may, but the character document of a master never is. The authorized translation and the annotations are mine, H.K.[76]

In my reply to Mann's letter to the Editor of the *Saturday Review of Literature* (1) I confined myself to making clear that I had nothing against the application of my Twelve-Note Technique, as I have indeed already shown it to my pupils twenty-five years ago and have delivered explanatory lectures about it at several American universities. It was, however, inadmissible to transfer its authorship to someone else. (2) I then pointed out that the sole purpose of Mann's letter was to hide his conduct behind a flood of words. Thus he does not quote his actual note (3), namely—"It does not seem supererogatory to inform the reader that the form of musical composition delineated in Chapter XXII, known as the twelve-tone or row system, is in truth the intellectual property of ›a‹ (4) contemporary composer and theoretician, Arnold Schoenberg. I have transferred this technique in a certain ideational context to the fictitious figure of a musician, the tragic hero of my novel . . .," but he gives an explanation (5) which would be acceptable despite its superfluous "poetry," particularly if one had translated it into sober German, usual for such a purpose.

The gratitude he shows Mr. Adorno (6) in the "Story of a Novel" (7) for services rendered goes far beyond the recompense afforded in the actual novel. There he confines himself to ascribing Adorno's analysis of the variations from Beethoven's last piano sonata Op. 111 to another author! This is apparently a tactical maneuver. Besides, however, he adds one of those small (very small) extra presents which preserve the big (very big) friendship: he lays Adorno's father-name, "Wiesengrund," under the opening of the variations' theme. And here, too, something awkward happens. It emerges that Leverkühn has no feeling for the rhythmic values in a phrase, that he does not know how to declaim. Adorno should have told him: "I'm not called

but

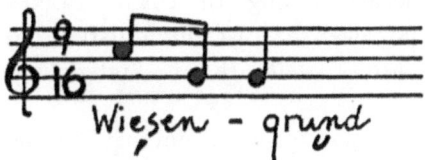

Wiesen - grund

All the more astounding, this, since Leverkühn comes from an era when one took such things even more seriously than today. If he really died in 1941,[77] he must have been at least seventy-five years old and must have been born about 1866. Or (which is more probable) he is a remainder from the [18]70s, when those Burgerts, Dräseckes, and other Wagnerians sought to excel their model by extended dimensions. It is not, after all, surprising that Mann depicts so antiquated a composer as the hero of his novel, since he himself comes from that past period and has not, at any rate as far as music is concerned, grown into the present.

Hence, too, Leverkühn's amateurish idea of the true essence of composition with twelve notes is that it suffices each time to play off the twelve notes or their inversions and that this means composing. I am therefore convinced that Mann's *Lamentation of Dr. Faustus* ought to bear the subtitle *Leverkühn's Twelve-Note Goulash*. What he there throws together into one pot may be tasty—wherefore I shall perhaps find the time to analyze it and to show a journalist how things have to be founded in order to live on after they have been "Book of the Month."

I[78] find it more and more repulsive to see the obstinacy of an, after all, respected writer lead to his seeking to uphold an untenable position by misrepresentations, though it would have been so easy to accede to my wishes. A tiny footnote—"These descriptions or deductions rest on Schoenberg's Method of Composition with Twelve Notes"—would have entirely sufficed. He could not bring himself publicly to own this.[79] Those pretended stylistic reasons (8) are of course complete nonsense. For in that case he should not have done it at all (9), and why then this revenge? (10). This punishment by degradation?

But now one would think he would at last see his wrong and stop, since I have not continued any further. However, he now publishes his *Story of a Novel* and continues his unfair behavior. To be sure, it seems to be downright impossible for him to speak out as plainly as is necessary; otherwise he could have safely said that he asked me for my *Theory of Harmony,* and that when I lent him one of the few extant copies of the work, I also sent him the *Jacob's Ladder* with a nice dedication. But he can only continue to degrade me, and although there is no reason why he should censure me without, moreover, the least substantiation, he cannot refrain from saying about the *Jacob's Ladder* that its "religious poetry" is not fully brewed.

Here, justly, something happens to him that happens to others in similar situations. It is very peculiar that when someone hits at me in a particularly nasty way, fate seizes him by the collar and the following things happen: Prof. Dr. Richard Wallaschek[80] of the Vienna University reproaches me with the fact that Hugo Wolf did not give a song recital with singers as good as mine, and adds: "But then, when one has a friend for an opera-director and a brother-in-law for a conductor, it's easy, naturally." What this wanted to say was of course: "When one has an opera-director (11) for a friend and a conductor (12) for a brother-in-law . . ." Still better was what happened to Elsa Bienenfeld[81] when she congratulated me upon my fiftieth birthday by twitting me with, *inter alia*, the small number of my published works: "He hasn't published much, he can count the number of his works on the twelve *(sic)* fingers of his hand." And thus, too, Mr. Mann:

"Not only is the *Jacob's Ladder* no religious poetry. Indeed I say quite expressly that it is founded on Swedenborg's theosophy, as I know it from Balzac, for 'I was never known to pocket papers not my own'" (13), and I admit it quite openly. *Jacob's Ladder* is not, then, poetry, nor is it religious, but, as I said, theosophical philosophy. But whatever else it be, it is difficult to imagine that it could be fully brewed, for poetry does not brew. Doesn't start to brew and, consequently, doesn't cease to brew. A scientist like Thomas Mann ought to know that. If one wanted to speak in his style, one could describe his sentences from a page's top to bottom as fully stretched noodle-dough, or strudel-dough, or perhaps as fully brewed tapeworms. Again his behavior is most unfair. Again it is only his endeavor to disparage me. Again it is only revenge which, however, cannot put him in the right. It is precisely as if somebody who had stolen a car explained exactly how bad this car was—but steal it he did all the same. If this is Mannly, it is not, at any rate, fully brewed.

Notes

(1) The reference here is to Schoenberg's reply to Mann's own reply to Schoenberg's first letter, whose first paragraph ran: "Sir: In his novel *Doctor Faustus*, Thomas Mann has taken advantage of my literary property. He

has produced a fictitious composer as the hero of his book; and in order to lend him qualities a hero needs to arouse people's interest, he made him the creator of what one erroneously calls my *system of twelve tones*, which I call *method of composing with twelve tones*." (By permission of Arnold Schoenberg and the *Saturday Review of Literature*, New York.) I find it, by the way, surprising that Mr. Peter Stadlen,[82] who has the reputation of being a Schoenberg expert, entitled his radio talk on June 16, 1949, "Schoenberg and the Twelve-Tone System." Or was the title the BBC's?

(2) Leverkühn, the hero of *Doctor Faustus*. Compare Paul Hamburger's article on the book in the last issue of this journal.

(3) The acknowledgment that Mann printed at the end of the book upon Schoenberg's private protest and about which Schoenberg says in the first letter to the *Saturday Review:* "But Mr. Mann was not as generous as I, who had given him good chance to free himself from the ugly aspect of a pirate. He gave an explanation: a few lines which he hid at the end of the book, in a place and on a page where no one ever would see it. Besides, he added a new crime to his first, in the attempt to belittle me: He calls me a (a!) contemporary composer and theoretician. Of course, in two or three decades, one will know which of the two was the other's contemporary."

(4) Schoenberg's inverted commas.

(5) In the March 1949 issue of *Der Monat* I find the German original of Mann's explanation of his note : " 'Ihr müsst wissen,' besagt sie [i.e., the note], 'unter uns lebt ein Komponist und musikalischer Philosoph namens Arnold Schoenberg; der hat in Wirklichkeit die Zwölf-Ton-Kompositionsmethode erdacht, nicht mein Romanheld.' "

(6) Wiesengrund-Adorno, a pupil of Berg, and Mann's adviser in Twelve-Note technique.

(7) Thomas Mann's book, *Die Entstehung des "Doctor Faustus."*

(8) Mann says in his *Story of a Novel* that to mention Schoenberg's name in the text would not only have been out of style, but also "almost something of an offense," because of the divergence between Schoenberg's thoughts and Mann's *ad hoc* version thereof. The idea of the twelve-note technique, Mann suggests, assumes a character in the sphere of his book "this world of the devil's pact, and of black magic"—which it does not possess in reality and which makes it in a sense his property, i.e., that of the book. It was for this reason, and also, to a lesser extent, because the printed acknowledgment somewhat disturbs "the spheric completeness" (sphärische Geschlossenheit) of the novel, that Mann printed his note "a bit against his conviction."

(9) That is, he should not have printed any sort of acknowledgment any-where in the book.

(10) The form of Mann's note.

(11) Mahler.

(12) Alexander von Zemlinsky, 1872–1942.

(13) *Meistersinger*, act 3, scene 3, Sachs to Beckmesser.

---

76. Arnold Schoenberg, "Further to the Schoenberg-Mann Controversy," *Music Survey* 2, no. 2 (1949): 77–80. "H.K." was the signature of Austrian-born British musicologist Hans Keller (1919–85), a student of Schoenberg's childhood friend, the philosopher, musicologist, and astrologer Oskar Adler (1875–1955). Keller's original footnotes (indicated herein by parenthetical numerals) are gathered at the end of the article. Schoenberg had written Keller on May 2, 1949: "I am completely in agreement that you print my controversy with Mann and I am sending you here-with additional material that I did write, but have not published until now and am going to send [Josef] Rufer shortly, if the matter isn't too long gone and old hat already."

77. In the novel Leverkühn is born in 1885 and dies in 1940.

78. At this point, Schoenberg's unpublished German version of this letter from the year 1950 contains the sentence, "I did not publish this second letter, because it was always very repulsive to me that a weakened writer, after all, should defend an untenable situation in such an undignified manner, through distortion, falsehood, and hypocrisy."

79. Here the German version includes the sentences: "At first he made a pretext of stylistic reasons, although the example of *Arrowsmith* by Sinclair Lewis was pointed out to him. But when he finally had to give up this excuse and provide an explanation, he wants us to believe that he had had other reasons." For the third of his five large novels, Lewis engaged in precise studies in the field. The novel relates the partly autobiographical life story of a doctor. The bacteriologist Paul de Kruif acted as an adviser in questions involving medicine.

80. Richard Wallaschek (1860–1917), an Austrian professor of aesthetics, known for his contributions in comparative musicology and music psychology. Sandra McColl, "Richard Wallaschek: Vienna's Most Uncomfortable Music Critic," *International Review of the Aesthetics and Sociology of Music* 29, no. 1 (1998): 41–73; Amy Graziano, "Richard Wallaschek's Contributions to the Psychology of Music," in *Proceedings of the 8th Int'l Conference on Music Perception & Cognitio: Evanston, IL* (Sydney: Causal Productions, 2004).

81. Elsa Bienenfeld (1877–1942) studied with Schoenberg and the musicologist Guido Adler (1855–1942) and before the First World War was the only female music critic for one of the most important Viennese newspapers (*Neues Wiener Journal*) who published under her own name. The contact with Schoenberg broke off after a critical treatment of his works on May 8, 1927. See Karen Painter, *Mahler and His World* (Princeton, NJ: Princeton University Press, 2002), 369n8. (Schoenberg's unpublished essay "Die Kernige Elsa.") Bienenfeld was deported and was murdered by the Nazis in May 1942 in Maly Trostinec.

82. The Austrian-born composer and musicologist Peter Stadlen (1910–86), a close friend of Mann's daughter Monika, as well as of Schoenberg's brother-in-law,

the violinist Rudolf Kolisch (1896–1978). Monika Mann wrote to Schoenberg on January 29, 1941, from Princeton, interceding on behalf of Stadlen in hopes of getting him a visa to the United States, so that he would not have to be sent back from an Australian internment camp to England. Stadlen performed numerous piano works by Schoenberg before a British audience.

SCHOENBERG TO H. H. STUCKENSCHMIDT, DECEMBER 5, 1949

Arnold Schoenberg
116 N. Rockingham Ave.
Los Angeles 49, California
December 5, 1949

Mr. H.H. Stuckenschmidt
Berlin-Zehlendorf
Thuyring 45,
Germany

Dear Friend:

I haven't heard from you or Rufer for a long time, except for this list. We meticulously corrected the list, as best we could, given the means at our disposal, and I think it should be correct. Should you have additional questions, I can check.

Hopefully the book can come out soon.[83] At one point I also thought about offering this publishing company a book of mine. Do you think that it would be feasible, and would they be in a position and willing to give me an advance? Perhaps you could put me in contact with them?

Did you see the book by Wiesengrund-Adorno: *Philosophy of New Music?*[84] So new music has a philosophy—it would have been sufficient for it to have a philosopher. He attacks me quite vehemently in it. Another defector. The reason is completely obvious to me. I insulted him very badly once, and although I had apologized, he wasn't able to get over it. But I have never been able to stand him, with his dripping wet, hurt eyes, which always seemed phony, and now I know that he obviously never liked my music, but has decided at this point, since he composes movie music himself, to reject it. Probably to assuage his conscience, because he contemplates smearing me. Disgusting the way he is treating Stravinsky. I am certainly no Stravinsky fan, though every now and then I do like some of his pieces—but you certainly don't have to write something like that.

It would be nice if you could find out what Hanns Eisler thinks of the thing, although in contemplating it a bit longer, his attitude in the Thomas Mann affair seems somewhat ambiguous. Could you see him? . . .

I hope to hear from you soon and heartfelt greetings to you and to your wife from all of us. Yours,

Arnold Schoenberg

83. Stuckenschmidt's first biography, *Arnold Schoenberg*, appeared in 1951, published by Atlantis Publishing House in Zurich. A more complete biography was published in 1974.

84. Adorno's book, *Philosophy of New Music*, was published in 1949 and contained the original version about Schoenberg, as well as a new chapter on Stravinsky. Adorno wrote to Max Horkheimer on December 6, 1949: "Gretel writes that Fred [Pollock] gave Schoenberg the *Philosophy of New Music* that I had painstakingly tried to keep from him. He will, of course, be infuriated, and most probably will react to Fred, calling into question my technical competence, and insist on his being right. Please be so kind as to prepare Fred for it." *Adorno-Horkheimer, Correspondence*, vol. 3, 1945–1949 (Frankfurt am Main: Suhrkamp, 205), 370.

SCHOENBERG TO JOSEF RUFER,
DECEMBER 5, 1949

Arnold Schoenberg
116 N. Rockingham Ave.
Los Angeles, 49, California
December 5, 1949

Mr. Josef Rufer
Berlin-Zehlendorf
Juttastrasse 16
Germany

Dear Friend:

It's been so long since I have heard anything from you that I am actually a bit worried. Have I omitted or said anything, insulted you or hurt you, or didn't you get my thank-you letter that I sent on the occasion of my seventy-fifth birthday; or are you sick or is it financial worries? . . . Have you heard about Wiesengrund-Adorno's book, *Philosophy of New Music?* I wrote about it to Stuckenschmidt and Zillig, and I am not quite certain how to handle it. Please let me hear your opinion. The book is very difficult to read, because it uses that kind of philosophic jargon, which philosophy professors utilize nowadays to hide the absence of an idea. They think it is deep, if in using undefined new expressions they create ambiguity.

I have not read the book myself, only a number of half-pages. He knows everything about twelve-tone-music, but he has no idea about the creative process.

He who requires an eternity to compose a song, as I am told, has no idea how quickly a real composer writes down what he hears in his fantasy. He does not know that I composed the third and fourth quartets in a period of about six weeks each, and *Von Heute auf Morgen* in ten weeks. And those are only a couple of examples, because I have always composed rapidly. He believes that the twelve-tone row, if it does not hinder thought, certainly hinders invention—the poor man.

Not that poor, however, because he also lies. He claims to have written the book about 1937, as I recall, but I remember his having gone on and on about the Second Chamber Symphony in 1941, in his unpleasant, emphatic manner, and similarly, even later, about the Piano Concerto. So his breach dates from some time after the piano concerto, probably from when I insulted him deeply, because his disgusting à la Hollywood manner was unbearable.

The book will be a welcome aid for my opponents, especially because it purports to be so scholarly. It seems characteristic, however, that Thomas Mann did not use the negative part of Adorno's criticism. Perhaps he did despise the betrayer.

Let me know whether or not you think one ought to answer him. I certainly will not do so. . . . Many heartfelt greetings to you and your wife, your,

Arnold Schoenberg

SCHOENBERG TO KURT LIST, DECEMBER 10, 1949

December 10, 1949
Mr. Kurt List
120 Riverside Drive
New York 25, N.Y.

Dear Mr. List:

I am surprised how much you overestimate Wiesengrund. I think you haven't known him long enough. About twenty years ago he published an enthusiastic article about me in the journal *Anbruch* which repulsed me with its highfalutin style.[85] At that time I had demonstrated with an example how I could express a seven- or eight-line phrase quite clearly in two lines. He had already at that time used a kind of blathering style, which warms the cockles of every philosophy professor's heart when they introduce a new and completely unfitting expression. It all appears to be so erudite and profound, but it is only a way of hiding the complete absence of an idea or insight. It is an "acting secretive" kind of style that Schopenhauer alluded to when he wrote that one ought to express the most unusual thoughts using the most commonplace words.

Wiesengrund's attack is an act of vengeance. One time, when my nerves couldn't take it any longer, I ridiculed him, and though I had apologized (nerves, sickness), apparently he never forgave me. He found a way out of the dilemma that he had been a devotee of mine and especially devoted to his teacher, Alban Berg, and devised a clever alternative by splitting me up into two parts, so I wouldn't disintegrate but rather be developmentally put together. Just like any other person, I am at times the older, at another time the younger. But he thought he had to avoid the pattern of Nietzsche-Wagner, so that is why he pits my younger period against my alleged last one. I have not read the book, only selections of individual pages—I couldn't swallow any more of it without gagging.

But he can't get around several difficulties. And so he helps himself by lying. He claims to have written the book much, much earlier. That is simply not true, at least the part that contains the attack. Because I know for certain that in 1942, after the Chamber Symphony, he most enthusiastically praised me to the heavens. I recall also that after the Piano Concerto, he praised the piece to the hilt (he always praises to the hilt). So it has to be after '42, and that seems to add up more or less. I insulted him in '44 or '45.

I do think one ought to answer him. It all has the appearance as if everything he writes were so very correct, but he doesn't try to prove any of it, because even were my music to contain the mistakes that he reproaches me for, it could still be good music. But nothing has been proven, rather only suggested.

One thing is very characteristic. He alleges that when I repeat the theme, I only keep the rhythm, but not the intervals. That shows that either he really doesn't understand what is going on, or he only acts that way, when he deems it necessary for the attack. For he must know that the only goal of the constant reference to the row is, that by means of consistency, logic is achieved. But even were rhythm admittedly used (by the way, the rhythm is also not used with such exactitude but remains very free), and the tones different, nevertheless the tonal proportions remain the same throughout the whole piece. That is their sole purpose. I think it would be very easy to refute him in many of these things. Please let me hear more precisely what you think about this. I have to close now.

So best regards, your,
Arnold Schoenberg

---

85. Among Adorno's articles written in the 1920s, there is, for example, "*Zur Zwölftontechnik*" (About the Twelve Tone Technique), *Anbruch*, July-August, 1929, 290–94.

MANN'S DIARY

Pacific Palisades, Thursday, December 15, 1949

... Schoenberg has fired a further broadside at me in *Music Survey* (London). Finally tried to locate his letter of thanks for the note he wanted. New "character document," as editor puts it, so silly I don't know how to react. Agitated nonetheless ...

Pacific Palisades, Friday, December 12, 1949

... The question of the idiotic Schoenberg.... Dictated to Hilde:[86] to Schoenberg, with enclosure (returning the *Harmonielehre*). Also wrote to the architect Neutra and others.

Pacific Palisades, Sunday, December 17, 1949

... The issue of my letter to Schoenberg. Amusement over a postscript about the publication of his letter dated October 1948 ...

Pacific Palisades, Tuesday, December 20, 1949

... Postscript to letter to Schoenberg ...

---

86. Mann's secretary Hilde Kahn (1917–99). Mann, *Tagebücher, 1949–1950,* 335.

MANN TO SCHOENBERG, DECEMBER 19, 1949

Thomas Mann
1550 San Remo Drive
Pacific Palisades, California
December 19th 1949

Professor Arnold Schoenberg
116 North Rockingham Avenue
West Los Angeles 24, Calif.

Dear Arnold,

Your "character document" in the issue of *Music Survey* kindly sent to me by the editorial team (the remainder was withheld) is an alarming reminder that the copy of *Harmonielehre* you sent some time ago was meant as a loan copy, not as a gift. I had overlooked this undeniable fact: in my mind I had become the owner of the loan copy, perhaps because in a higher sense I really had come to own it. At any rate, this is my attempt at a psychological explanation, and does not excuse my behavior. I therefore want to ask you in no uncertain terms to forgive me. As you explicitly pointed out at the time, printed copies of the work are rare, making it even more unforgivable that I've taken so long to return the valuable item. Why did it not occur to you to send me a reminder?

After such a shamefully long time I will hastily return your property by mail. At the time I studied the book very closely; I hope it doesn't bear too many signs of physical wear and tear. Respectfully yours,

Thomas Mann

[Enc.] I also want to take this opportunity to ask:[87] if, amid the hailstorm of your attacks, I feel increasingly bad, may I—if push comes to shove—publish the letter you sent on October 15, 1948, having received the English edition of *Dr. Faustus* containing the note at the end, in which you thanked me warmly for meeting your request, said you were completely satisfied, and added "I was convinced I should expect the same from you as I would from myself, and am delighted my trust has been rewarded in that regard"—?

At the time, the explanatory note was not an "act of revenge." I have no idea why you think that, and have asked myself in vain why I should have any reason whatsoever to take "revenge" on you. Moreover, from a purely chronological standpoint the insignificant diary entry concerning your *Jacob's Ladder* from the time of the genesis of *Faustus* can't have had anything to do with revenge.

You are striking out at a bugbear from your imagination, who I am not. Thus I have no desire for revenge. If by all means you want to be my enemy—you will not succeed in making me yours.

T.M.

---

87. Handwritten note.

SCHOENBERG TO MANN (UNDATED AND NOT SENT)

If the hand that I believe is being extended to me is meant to be a peace offering, then I would be the last person not to grab hold of it and shake it affirmingly.

Actually, I have often thought about writing you: Let's bury the hatchet and show that at a certain level there is always the possibility of peace.

I admit that often I was intense and said ugly things, and I am sorry. But I hope that you will not challenge my right to be irritated. . . . I still feel "a contemporary composer and theorist" to be so disparaging, so unnecessary, since one knows exactly who I am without such an explanation.

Let's make peace, which I propose as follows in the face of public opinion: Our kind ought not to act out of anger or resentment, for what befits the beast does not apply to Jupiter *[quod licet iovi non licet bovi]*. That is why we decided upon the basis of mutual respect. . . . [Here the text stops.]

. . . I had decided to publicly announce this peace pact, but it has been suggested that in so doing I would betray all those who stood by me in this conflict, friends, acquaintances and even those unknown to me.

Thus I propose a neutral intermediary stage. At some point one or the other of us will celebrate our "eightieth" (it wouldn't have to wait that long), an occasion to forget all pettiness—permanently.

Unfortunately, I have to mention that you should not publish my letter of October 15th. Otherwise, in order not to appear to be insane, I would have to verify that I received your book two days later, which made me regret the letter very much.

Let's content ourselves with this peace: You have reconciled me. In high esteem, your most devoted,

Arnold Schoenberg

MANN'S DIARY

Pacific Palisades, Sunday, December 31, 1949
Light mist. Chilly. Coffee with Medi.[88] Discussed Schoenberg, Horkheimer and book review . . .

---

88. Mann's daughter Elisabeth Borgese.

SCHOENBERG TO MANN, JANUARY 2 AND 9, 1950

Arnold Schoenberg
116 N. Rockingham Avenue
Los Angeles 49 California
January 2, 1950

My dear Dr. Mann,

I was ill—for more than two weeks—and as a result I could not meet an urgent deadline. At that time I would have gladly finished the letter—but I was unable to do so—whose beginning I had written down immediately under the impression left by your letter, and so to my great regret a great deal of time unfortunately went by.

This is what I wrote down:

If the hand I believe to see extended is a hand of peace, if it thus signified a peace offer, then I would be the last to not grasp it immediately and shake it heartily. Indeed, I have often thought of writing to you. Let us bury the hatchet and demonstrate that on a certain level there is always a possibility of peace.

(Continued on January 9!)

I intended to announce this declaration of peace publicly. However, it was brought to my attention (for which reason I did not finish the letter) that in so doing I would betray all those who stood by me in this battle—friends, acquaintances, and strangers.

Therefore, I propose an interim stage. At some time the one or the other will celebrate his "eightieth"—but it need not take so long—a proper occasion to forget all the pettiness—once and for all.

Unfortunately, I still have to mention that you should not publish my letter of October 15. Otherwise I would, in order not to appear to be insane, have to point out that I received your letter only two days later, which would make me regret this letter very much.

Let's be content with this peace: you have reconciled me.

I am respectfully and sincerely your,
Arnold Schoenberg

MANN TO THEODOR WIESENGRUND-ADORNO, JANUARY 9, 1950

1550 San Remo Drive
Pacific Palisades, California
January 9, 1950

Dear Theodor, . . . You won't believe it. Schoenberg has fired another broadside at the book, and at you and me. This took place in the London journal *Music Survey*, but the article was so silly that the editor apologetically refers to it as a "character document." Among other things, Schoenberg says nothing good comes to those who commit violations against him. He mentions two women who did so: allegedly one broke her leg, while the other also suffered an affliction of some kind. All this is scarcely believable. Nevertheless, I've written saying that even if he wants to run around as my enemy, he won't succeed in making me one of his. Yours,

Thomas Mann

MANN TO SCHOENBERG, JANUARY 12, 1950

Thomas Mann
1550 San Remo Drive
Pacific Palisades, California

Dear Arnold,

I was delighted to receive your letter. What a shame it also contained news about your recent week-long illness—I'm very sorry to hear you've been unwell. I suppose at our age one really can't complain when all sorts of tiresome physical problems gradually set in. I too have tales to tell in that regard.

Please understand that I'm in complete agreement with you. It must have been clear from my initial public response in the *Saturday Review of Literature* that I was completely unwilling to set myself up as your enemy. I was determined that this enmity, if it did have to arise, should remain one-sided, and am genuinely happy that you too wish to bury the matter and forget about it.

Under the circumstances, obviously I will stop raising the issue of publishing your letter, and indeed never really meant it seriously.

I hope that in the meantime you're back on your feet, and in the kind of good form which I hear you were in on your seventy-fifth birthday. Belated good wishes!

Wherever and whenever we meet again in this life, it will be a pleasure and an honor to shake you by the hand once again. Respectfully yours,

Thomas Mann

MANN'S DIARY

Pacific Palisades, Thursday, January 12, 1950

... Polite, actually warm answer to letter of reconciliation from Schoenberg, which significantly I probably forgot to mention. ...

SCHOENBERG ON WIESENGRUND, 1950

I never could stand him.[89] When he devoured me with his pained expression, at the same time pressing his body against me, until a wall prevented me from evading him any further, as Nestroy's high priest Kalchas in *Orpheus* says, when a smoked calf's tongue is placed before him, "How can one eat something that somebody else had in his mouth?," I had to think of "Won't you inhale the sweet fragrances with me," and say defensively, "How can one wish to inhale something, that someone else has already exhaled, if we are not Lohengrin and Elsa." In addition, the "grandioso" of his expressions, his oily pathos, his bombast, the affected overheatedness of his veneration.

The worst happened during the course of two episodes. Not without indebtedness to Rudi [Kolisch][90] was he introduced into our circle as a great scholar. It need not be disputed that he does possess certain valuable skills. He is very musical, plays the piano well, has a great knowledge of musical literature, and he can play a lot by heart due to his good memory. He has tackled musical-theoretical problems in depth and with much success and his knowledge of our art is most thorough.

Those were the reasons why I had asked him if he would consider to write a book with me, a dictionary of "Compositional-Theoretical Concepts."[91] I expected him to write the historical, aesthetic, and philosophical fundamentals, while I, possibly consulting with him, would contribute the formulations I had discovered through composing and the practical experience of teaching. He declined this proposal in the most haughty manner: He wasn't a musician, he was a philosopher.

I could not do anything about that.

But as we all had to leave Germany, and I having to work very hard—having to teach theory to insufficiently unprepared beginners in order to earn a living for myself and those in my care, on Sundays I always had—in those few hours of rest, a few friends over, for diversion—to try to live at the level I had earlier.

So Mr. Wiesengrund came over as well. But instead of pitying me that on account of necessity I had to organize incomplete or untalented compositions, he played his own to me, asked for judgments, suggestions, improvements—WORK in other words, WORK that I had to do during the week in order to get paid! But he, the man of means, never thought to ask me if I, the one lacking means, would be willing to teach him for nothing. I would have taught any professional musician of his caliber and ability who lacked funds (he had studied with Alban Berg) for free.

But he had explained that he was not a composer when I wanted to collaborate on a book with him.

Now, suddenly, he was a composer?

December 21, 1950

But now I have to get back to the matter, as disturbing as it is to refute or enlighten someone, who already in the formulation of the title of the book has lost all credibility to be taken seriously. One would have to ask, "Whose philosophy?"—Answer: "The one of New Music," or: "What does New Music do"?—Answer: "It philosophizes." Only a nonsensical question like that could evoke such a nonsensical answer. That reminds me of the title of a famous book, that had prophetically warned of the demise of a substantial portion of the earth, which I at least was able to expose at least as a linguistic impossibility.

How often has the doom of our culture been prophesied? I am certain that in every century there were impotent intellects that raised their ugly heads against forces who were able to create something new. It is sad to acknowledge that it wasn't merely the most inept who had lost all trust in the constructive powers. The latter, at least, had the duty to infer the future from the past.

But back to the matter at hand, the following can be most assuredly ascertained: Wiesengrund's knowledge about composing with twelve tones is not based on his knowledge of my own formulations.

A few years after the First World War, when I had invited my friends and acquaintances to inform them of my newly acquired new technique, I first explained to them what had led me to this discovery. Then I demonstrated the application of the rows to them from examples from my newest works. At the end, I formulated my most important thesis: to follow the row, but to continue to compose as one had in the past. Already at that point and ever since, I made it quite clear, that this method of mine—my method—was not the only way to solve new problems, [but rather] one of the possibilities. The strict rules that were set up, at least those in such a strict and strangulating form, had not originated with me. Under pressure from the apostles, they became more stringent than necessary. It was neither my intention to scare anyone away from this method, nor to invite anyone to join a school. I found it necessary to delineate the path that had led me to this method following some ten to twelve years. It was my own path that, due to my risk-taking, had led me to write music without tonality.

In the fall of 1921, when I had completed compositions based on this new method, I summoned Erwin Stein (the current Britten propagandist) to come to Traunkirchen and bade him to keep secret what I was about to communicate to him for as long as I saw fit. He promised he would and faithfully kept his word. However, when I returned to Vienna some time later, I heard rumors about Josef Hauer's "Theory of Tropes," which made me seem like I had plagiarized him. That hurt me and worried me, and I was forced to take a stand. I had from the very beginning understood that the difference between Hauer and me was similar to that between a (more or less good) composer and a most interesting and philosophical inventor. How could one explain something like that in Vienna at that time? My friends would not have withdrawn their trust, and I didn't care one iota for such originality. What I have to say is important to me. However, if I say it in seven, twelve, or twenty-one tones is of relatively little importance.

I had always said why I felt compelled to introduce a method of composing with twelve tones. First and foremost: not just as a method of composition, but as my method of composing with twelve tones. Its objective was to replace the form-building effects of harmony with another central force: with a row of immutable tonal relationships. Secondly, it was meant to be a regulating force in the occurrence of dissonant harmonies in nontonal music (but in a tonal harmony it would be superfluous). Thirdly, I have emphasized numerous times that one certainly might apply other methods. I objected to calling it a "system." By defining both concepts, which are seen as identical in America, I clearly pointed out the difference: "Strangely enough and incorrectly, most people speak of the 'system' of the chromatic scale. I have no system, but rather just a method, that means a mode, whereby with regularity an invented formula is applied. A method can, but need not be, one of the consequences of a system. I also am not the inventor of the chromatic scale. Someone else must have occupied himself with that task a long time ago." I don't want to prevent any talented composer from using this method. But I want to warn beginners, who think that when they use just one row they are making music: If you have not thoroughly learned harmony or studied abundant counterpoint, and haven't worked through all the forms we inherited from the great masters of our art, nor acquired a secure feeling for moderation and shape, composing should not be made even more difficult by the demands of this very difficult technique. Even for one who can do enough, it makes things more difficult, harder than extracting good counterpoint from a clod.

But back and down once more to our Wiesengrund. Perhaps he now understands that it would have been better for him to have attacked nontonality, rather than criticize the method, for not solving the problems for which it was created.[92]

89. Published in Arnold Schoenberg, *Stile herrschen, Gedanken siegen: Ausgewählte Schriften,* ed. Maria Morazzoni (Mainz: Schott, 2007), 539–46.

90. Schoenberg wrote to Kolisch on July 27, 1932: "I cannot warn you enough about overestimating these analyses, since they only lead to exactly what I have always been dead-set against: to an awareness of how it is *made;* while I have always striven for an understanding of what it *is!* I have repeatedly tried to make that understandable to Wiesengrund [Adorno], as well as to Berg and Webern. But they do not believe me. I cannot repeat it often enough: my works are twelve-tone *compositions,* not *twelve-tone* compositions. Here they are mixing me up with Hauer, for whom composition is merely a matter of secondary importance."

91. Here, written on December 6, 1930, follows the text of the only (unanswered) letter by Schoenberg to Adorno: "Dear Dr. Wiesengrund [Adorno], I hope that you will get this letter, since (and this proves how seldom you write to me!) I did not have your address before now. I would like to motivate you to write a dictionary of Music (Aesthetics or) Theory. Such a book could be analogous to a philosophical dictionary (or some other kind), which pursues a given subject throughout history, focusing on its developmental import. The historical part could be gathered, not effortlessly, yet without difficulty, by experts, into a base of support or structure, consisting of written sources, which could then be enhanced and supported with more modern items. Here I think it might be worthwhile to have the different directions and conceptions presented by way of their original representatives, so that one could find the various views listed under one heading (for example: [Heinrich] Schenker, [Walter] Howard, [Hans] Mersmann, Schoenberg, Wiesengrund [Adorno], [Erwin] Stein, [Egon] Wellesz, [Joseph Matthias] Hauer, and others). Most probably one would need to find a publisher or financial backer or a subscriber beforehand, or perhaps even form a committee for the establishment, the development, and the uniformity, as well as for the practical concerns. What do you think of this? What else are you doing? I hear nothing from you. Imagine, I still have not opened the wine that I received as a gift from your father: it has been drunk only with the eyes, because I have not found another worthy partner to pair with it, but I did think of someone finally who also can judge what he drinks! Many heartfelt greetings, your Arnold Schoenberg." On the copy of the typescript letter Schoenberg noted by hand: "Someday they will say that I was ungrateful. But my ingratitude is justified in main by facts such as this one: Mr. Wiesengrund [Adorno] left this letter unanswered. I know that he received it, because he admitted it in the presence of my wife! December 6, 1930."

92. In conjunction with this text, on February 6, 1951, Schoenberg wrote to Heinrich Strobel, who had asked him to submit an essay for publication in his journal *Melos:* "I just read through the manuscript of an unfinished article on Wiesengrund [Adorno]. I think I could easily finish it, if someone could find the most important points from his book that I should polemicize against. I cannot read the book myself on account of my nervous eye condition. I had always wanted to ask Rufer to do it. Can't you do it? But you would have to tell me exactly what it is about. I don't know anyone off hand who is sufficiently familiar with 12 tone music to be able to help me." Schoenberg dictated a letter to Josef Rufer on March 3, 1951, which contains the following postscript: "P.S. Dr. Strobel wants an article for *Melos* from me. I will not write the article (and I mentioned your name repeatedly in my answer to him). If you don't have any reservations about it, in consideration of your relationship to Schott and that band of intriguers. If yes, then I would very much like to write something about the Wiesengrund [Adorno] book. Unfortunately, I cannot read it, and I would ask you to cite some of the more important points from

it, which I ought to polemicize against in your opinion. Or perhaps even, you could give me a short synopsis of the book. He deserves a sound flogging. I would say just for the nastiness of how he treats Stravinsky. You simply can't talk to someone like Stravinsky that way. And also with his meanness toward me. I could also publish the article in another journal. Let me hear from you about it okay?" The text remained incomplete and was published in Arnold Schoenberg, *Stile herrschen, Gedanken siegen,* 539–46.

MANN TO SCHOENBERG, APRIL 17, 1951

Thomas Mann
1550 San Remo Drive
Pacific Palisades, California
April 17, 1951

Dear Arnold,

The *Saturday Review of Literature* has said it wishes to publish the January 1949 correspondence between you and me in an anthology entitled the *Saturday Review Reader*. I don't think this is a good idea. Supposedly, they have also contacted you. Please let me know whether you've agreed to the proposal. Very respectfully yours,

Thomas Mann

SCHOENBERG TO MANN, APRIL 20, 1951

Arnold Schoenberg
116 N. Rockingham Avenue
Los Angeles California—49

My dear Mr. Mann:

As to the contract with the *Saturday Review of Literature* I stipulated that I will permit the inclusion only if you are in agreement.

We two have buried the "hatchet," and I find it offensive to have the affair warmed over.

Let us, then, inform the *Sat. Rev.* that we two do not wish to go along. I am very much overburdened by the demands on my energy.[93] I remain, most sincerely, your,

Arnold Schoenberg
April 20, 1951

---

93. On November 5, 1950, Mann's daughter, Monika, had written a long letter to Schoenberg, in which she asked for help for the purpose of approaching his music: "My personal reaction to your music is one of disconcertment and an inner will to become familiar with it." Schoenberg did not answer, and Monika wrote again on December 28: "I cannot imagine that you may still answer my last letter. Unfortunately, 'Daddy' is most probably in the way, right?" She wrote again for the last time on April 21, 1951: "Please tell me, did you find my letter presumptuously crazy, or what is the reason for your silence? It is terribly sad, when a person, especially a great person, does not react. . . . Is it because of the 'dispute' with Papa?! But I am merely Monika!" Schoenberg did not answer. He had been sick the entire year.

MANN'S DIARY

Pacific Palisades, Sunday, April 21, 1951

. . . Wrote letters. More meetings with Erika about text. She dictated it to Hilde and I signed it, along with letter to *Saturday Review of Literature* as agreed between Schoenberg and myself, rejecting their proposal to include our correspondence in the journal's anthology. . . .

Zurich, Wednesday, July 25, 1951

Tea and egg for breakfast. More mail, now completely unmanageable in volume. Request from *Saturday Review of Literature* to write about Schoenberg.[94] Many similar items. Took bath. Dismal, very cool weather. I have a cold.

---

94. Schoenberg had died on July 13, 1951.

MANN TO H. H. STUCKENSCHMIDT, OCTOBER 19, 1951

Pacific Palisades, California
October 19, 1951

Dear Mr. Stuckenschmidt,

Many thanks for your letter and the gift of your impressive book on Schoenberg. It may help me meet Krenek's request to speak at next year's commemorative event for him in Los Angeles, though I may nonetheless still lack the nerve.

I had no further opportunity to meet Schoenberg in person; he had been suffering for quite some time. It was perhaps sufficient that my steadfast refusal to match his enmity, to make sure it remained unilateral, and to say nothing negative about him, ultimately carried the day.[95] My determination in that regard was clear enough from my response to his letter to the *Saturday Review of Literature*. I followed that up with a private letter I sent him a little later, after he had published an extraordinary attack on me in a British journal—an article which the journal's editor described as "a character document." It certainly was one, as were all his life's observations, to which everyone owed reverence. In response to my letter he wrote that I had appeased him and that we should bury the hatchet. However, he said he remained unwilling to do so publicly, as it might disappoint those who had sided with him in the *Faustus* matter, but looked forward to some ceremonial occasion, an eightieth birthday perhaps, at which we could publicly declare peace.

Sadly, he did not live to see that opportunity. Nevertheless, before he passed away there was a second declaration of peace, when the *Saturday Review* intended to publish the correspondence between us in an anthology. I immediately wrote to say this was a bad idea; he wrote back that his approval would be dependent on mine and that he authorized me to tell the editorial team we had agreed to reject the proposal.

Once again, I found your book warm, well written and well informed. I have merely a theoretical understanding of the new music: I know a little about it, but can't really enjoy or love it. I have openly stated that my musical home is basically the triad world of the *Ring*.[96]
Respectfully yours,

Thomas Mann

---

95. On April 8, 1951, Mann wrote to Paul H. Lang: "Naturally you are right: there is something rather sad and confused about Schoenberg's attack, and that is

precisely why it never bothered me. Moreover, I could never use it against Schoenberg myself, as he was too tragic a man to argue with."

96. Mann's son Michael Mann wrote: "But make no mistake: the musical world of Adrian Leverkühn is not the musical world of Thomas Mann. When the writer used Schoenberg's music in his literary equation, he was guided more by intuition and theoretical knowledge than by a direct understanding of Schoenberg's musical language. His ears rejected Schoenberg's music. His world was that of Richard Wagner. He admired Tchaikovsky, loved Gounod and was utterly charmed by one of Saint-Saëns's arias. And when he was already engrossed in the *Faustus* story, at one point he somewhat unthinkingly remarked: 'If I were a composer, I would perhaps compose like César Franck.'" Michael Mann, "The Musical Symbolism in Thomas Mann's Novel *Doktor Faustus*," *Notes*, 2nd ser., 14, no. 1 (1956): 33–42.

Additional Reading

The Story of *The Story of a Novel*

Richard Hoffmann

First of all, an apology for the "kitschy" title. I am not sure that your sensibilities were disturbed; however, there is a "very definite—but private—program" behind this title.

In April of this year, I received Dr. Sigrid Wiesmann's invitation, which was a little late, perhaps even fortuitous (in fact, everything, our very existence, for example, must be considered fortuitous: a joyous event if one's parents are married, an unfortunate accident if they are not) to contribute something to the Congress which was personal and something which has *Farbe*. (Angelika Abel was not available, so I understand, for she could have provided us with color.) Back to the problem of a topic. Most of my colleagues have little problem in this regard, because they think in musicological terms. I attempt not to think in those terms and tried to find a subject that was related to reality, had continuity (something which is very dear to the Western train of thought in its pursuit of scholarship), undermined prosaic notions, and, on the surface, even appeared to be logical.

It so happened that my very good and old friend Roman Haubenstock-Ramati and I had agreed to meet at a *Heuriger* in Heiligenstadt. After some indecision, we agreed on the Beethoven-Haus, the very place where a fitting conclusion to the very successful First International Schoenberg Congress had taken place in 1974. It was here that Roman, after the usual exchange of pleasantries, told me that he had just finished rereading Thomas Mann's *Doctor Faustus* as well as having read the exchange of letters between—I will put Schoenberg first—Schoenberg and Mann, in Polish. I thought he was joking, but apparently the letters are now so famous that they are available in a Polish translation. I then asked him how he had liked the exchange of correspondence. His reply caught me off guard. His reaction was identical to others I had experienced over the years.

"How could you stand to be so close to Schoenberg? He must have been an ill-tempered, querulous person. Poor Mann, how he was attacked and vilified in the press." Again I was struck by the reaction—this time by an extremely sensitive musician—that he also felt that Schoenberg was the culprit in this feud. So I took it upon myself *(in vino veritas)* to recount to him my side of the story (*my*story and not *his*tory) and tried to explain to him that I thought he was mistaken.

The novel, *Doctor Faustus,* in the original German version arrived in Schoenberg's mail early in 1948, with the inscription by Mann—which I am sure is well known—"the real one," with the signature, Thomas Mann. Schoenberg was very happy to receive this gift because he liked Mann personally, and he liked his books, although he did not necessarily read them. I doubt very much that he had ever looked at *Buddenbrooks* or *Magic Mountain.* They were, among others, in his library. (Now, of course, they are in the Arnold Schoenberg Institute at USC. [Since 1998 at the Arnold Schönberg Center in Vienna.—Ed.]) Originally they were on the topmost shelf and could not be reached unless one climbed up, either with a ladder, or risked one's life on a chair. Schoenberg simply instructed me to place the book next to all the other Mann books (most of which bore a handwritten dedication) and forgot about the matter.

Shortly thereafter, a telephone call came from Alma Mahler-Werfel. She inquired whether or not Schoenberg had heard of a new novel by Thomas Mann which had just appeared on the market. (I believe it was already then a best seller, although it was in German.) Schoenberg replied that, indeed, he had the book at home. Alma Mahler encouraged him to read it, especially since the hero was, as she put it: "That is you." Up to this time, Schoenberg had not taken the inscription "the real one" literally, since he was really not quite as egotistical as you might have been led to think from a perusal of his letters and writings. Of course, he knew who "the real one" was, without having to look in the mirror. Still, his interest in the novel was not aroused until Alma Mahler's phone call. Now Schoenberg did become interested in the book because, like all of us, he did have a slight touch of egocentricity. Since he was no longer able to read fluently, because of his blurred vision and other eye troubles, he asked his wife to read portions of the novel and to report to him what the book was all about.

Later on, I took over this task. He was especially interested in those sections which dealt with music, and there are, of course, quite a lot of them. I was asked to select these passages and to record them on the versatile but infamous Webster Wire Recorder, which is now housed in the USC Institute. It was a present from Clara Silvers, later to become Clara

Steuermann, the former archivist of the Schoenberg Institute. She was then employed by a New York book publishing firm and, I am sure, skipped several lunches in order to buy this quite new apparatus and to send it to Schoenberg as a gift, in the hope that he would use it to complete *Structural Functions of Harmony* and other theoretical texts. As so often happened with Schoenberg, he never used the recorder for the purpose for which is was intended. More, concerning this, later!

Anyway, I was requested to record those sections of *Doctor Faustus* which dealt, in some way, with music. I immediately "taped" the brilliantly written passages dealing with exaggerated, romanticized descriptions of orchestral instrumental usage. Schoenberg would smile in appreciation as he played and replayed these excerpts at his leisure. He said they reminded him of record-jacket notes, written by a musical amateur. He really enjoyed those portions of the book. Then I ventured a little farther into the novel and selected those passages which dealt with the method of twelve-tone composition. And there Schoenberg became surprised because, quite simply, he knew Mann personally well enough to know that this could not have stemmed from his pen. It was the most conceptually sound and technically accurate description of this method of composition available in print up to that time. (*Style and Idea*, containing the "Composition with Twelve Tones" article did not appear until the spring of 1950 and Rene Leibowitz's *Schoenberg and His School*—the English translation—until 1949.)

Rudolf Stephan has just now hinted that it was not the music of Schoenberg (which was hardly available) but, perhaps, *Doctor Faustus* and Leibowitz's book *Schoenberg and His School*—both "novels" depicting an "outlawed" musical idiom in a most positive, even complimentary manner!—which had the greatest influence on the young composers attending the Darmstadt Ferienkurse. Scores of Schoenberg's music were not readily available in the immediate postwar years. You may not know that Schoenberg did not even have a publisher for his music (opus 44–48) in those years and had to wait until, through the intervention of Rene Leibowitz—that very important musician and key figure in the propagation of dodecaphonic thought—he was able to have his String Trio, *A Survivor from Warsaw*, and the Haringer Songs published by Bomart Music Publications, a firm that had just embarked on a novel business venture: the publication, exclusively, of new music.

Without becoming too discursive, I would like to return to the ubiquitous Webster Wire Recorder. Schoenberg wittily called this particular machine his "Dick"taphone (putting my nickname to good use!) and used it for dictating innumerable letters. For a person who could hardly concentrate, for any length of time, on reading, you may have wondered why so many letters were written from, roughly, 1948 until his death in 1951. He simply recorded them on the Webster. In the process, he developed an ingenious technique, employing certain rhythmic codes. Instead of erasing sections, he overlaid a kind of main rhythm (with which we are familiar from *Wozzeck*, or from *Lulu*) to filter-out—to cover—the previously recorded faulty passages. I recall, also, the difficulty Schoenberg had, at first, to appreciate that it was impossible to add a footnote to a letter, after several had been typed subsequently since, usually, insufficient space was left at the bottom of the initial letter for a *post scriptum*. However, he was very considerate and did not request that I retype such letters, simply handwriting the addendum, if important enough.

As I have previously hinted, the Webster was used for all purposes other than what had been Clara Steuermann's original intention. Schoenberg also used the machine very effectively for stories that he improvised for the children. They were actually bedtime stories. What the children were supposed to do was to play back these bedtime stories that Schoenberg had recorded so that the Webster became a kind of surrogate father! This very practical idea saved him a lot of time and effort, because it is inconvenient to have to climb upstairs to tuck in the child. (Larry, the youngest, was then six or seven years old.) Unquestionably, it would have been better psychologically! These improvised "fairy tales" usually had a Viennese locale and were told in either a typically Teutonically accented English or, to add special ethnic color, in German. The children did not speak German (they understood quite a lot of phrases with a limited vocabulary), but that did not matter.

I especially recall one of his favorite bedtime stories. (I know we are pressed for time and I promise I am going to get back to my topic . . . but this is more interesting than the parts which Wiesengrund-Adorno wrote for *Doctor Faustus*—we all know *that* story anyway!) This story dealt, in a not-too-subtle manner, with the still prevalent North-South conflict, now overshadowed by my generation's East-West phobia. The rivalry between Prussia and Austria, we could even say, Berlin and Vienna, which is, at this very moment, present here at the Congress. This marvelous story that Schoenberg had made up dealt, essentially, with a German Hemingway—if you can imagine such a thing—a German big-game hunter, with his native servant, on safari in darkest Africa. It is a very fitting story for us in more ways than one. It has also serial pretensions! It goes something like this. I will have to tell it to you in German, but I am sure that all of you here, the scholars, are bilingual and fluent in the two languages of musicology . . . equally at home in tonality as well as atonality:

A hunter one morning looks out at the horizon and sees a tiny dot. The dot gets bigger and bigger. Suddenly a lion is standing there in front of me! I take out my shot gun, load it, aim it, and fire away. Piff, puff, pop, and the lion writhes in his own blood. I say to my sidekick: Stuff the thing into my backpack. The next morning, I wake up, look out at the horizon, and see a tiny dot. The dot gets bigger and bigger. Suddenly there's a giraffe standing in front of me! I take up my shotgun, load it, aim, and fire away, and piff, puff, pop . . . the giraffe writhes in his own blood! I say to my sidekick: stuff the animal into my backpack. The next morning, I wake up, . . . (The children were to have fallen asleep by the third time!) look out at the horizon and see a small dot! The dot gets bigger and bigger! Suddenly an elephant is standing there in front of me! I take the shotgun, load it, aim, and fire away, and piff, puff, pop, and the elephant writhes in his own blood. . . . Voice from the audience, in Viennese dialect: "Now, if you're wanting to tell me that you're gonna ask your buddy to stuff that animal into your backpack, I'm gonna smack you one good!"

This is one of a number of stories that, presumably, is still on the wire spools and awaits transcription so that, in the not-too-distant future, it can be included in the Schoenberg-*Gesamtausgabe*.[1] Subsequently, perhaps, all of them will be translated into Polish! No textbooks were completed, as Clara Steuermann had originally intended. Instead, the wire recorder was used—today one would say—"creatively." That was typical for Schoenberg. He always did what other people did *not* do. That, I think, was one of his great teachings. You cannot go wrong very far, if you do the opposite of what the other person does.

Thanks to the Webster, he now had at his disposal the recorded sections of *Doctor Faustus* that dealt with music. Very strong in my memory remain Schoenberg's gleeful reactions to the chapters devoted to the *Apocalypse Oratorio*. His eyes would glow mischievously when he merely thought of the title. He was enthralled with the whole idea of *musica sacra* (having himself come to grips with this awesome subject several times during his lifetime). He was baffled by the degree of expertise with which the method of twelve-tone composition was explicated. In any case, one day he came to the irrevocable conclusion that "the real one" really meant: "that is *me*." As he began to identify with Leverkühn more and more, he discovered the (for him) embarrassing problem of syphilis venereal disease in general. It was at lunchtime, one day, that Schoenberg defended himself and clarified his health record by the statement that he never in his life had contracted a venereal disease. Gradually, he began to put things together and speculated that the hero might also be modeled, in part, on Nietzsche. He never got as

far as Hugo Wolf. Only people today, who have done research, would come
to the conclusion that Leverkühn is a composite figure of, presumably,
Schoenberg, Hugo Wolf, and Nietzsche. It could be that you have heard
otherwise. Perhaps there has already come to light a fourth person that
might be involved . . . possibly even Mann! No one has yet thought of that.

In any case, Mann, having described the compositional method accurately (and it must be admitted, it was remarkably close to Schoenberg's)
and since Schoenberg's twelve-tone compositions were relatively little
known to the lay public, he thought that it would be appropriate for Mann
to include an acknowledgment in future editions of the book, in order to
avoid misunderstandings, particularly in questions of priority. (Throughout
his lifetime, and it was almost at an end, Schoenberg had never succeeded in
writing a best seller by using the method of composition with twelve tones.
Ironically, Mann was about to succeed in something that had eluded
Schoenberg: to cash in on a twelve-tone piece . . . and a "fictitious" one at
that!) Of course, Mann immediately agreed to do this in the next edition of
the book, which was the English translation. When he sent a copy of this to
Schoenberg (there was no "dedication" this time), he was extremely happy
and remarked that this again demonstrated the very best in the German
character: "German honesty." With delightful anticipation he opened the
book and right away looked for the advised acknowledgment. But he could
ñot find it! Then he asked me and others in the house. "Is it a joke; or am I
going blind? Where is the acknowledgment?" We also looked and could not
find it. We spent a long time hunting for it until, by accident, someone discovered that it was at the very end of the book after, at least, one blank page.

Schoenberg remarked that it was an odd place because, if he could not
find the acknowledgment, how could anyone else find it. He accepted its
strange placement and began to read it. I still remember how his face fell,
word by word: "It does not seem supererogatory . . ." This multisyllabic
word stopped him short. He turned to me and asked: "What is supererogatory? I have never heard of the word." I had just come from New Zealand
and also had to admit that I had never heard of it. Right away he moved
over to his favorite dictionary, the huge Webster (no relation to the wire
recorder), took his magnifying glass, and hunted for the esoteric word. It
took some time to find it. It simply meant "superfluous." The first hurdle
was overcome. The next line: ". . . to inform the reader that the form of
musical composition delineated in Chapter XXII, known as the twelve-tone
or row system, . . ." (Even here the word "system" is used as a synonym for
"method," a usage that Schoenberg abhorred!) ". . . is in truth the intellectual property of a contemporary composer and theoretician, Arnold

Schoenberg." Schoenberg reread the sentence and, well aware that Mann was a master of language, felt that the wording was carefully chosen to belittle him. Most musicians with a sensitive ear for nuances would agree, I am sure, that this passage contains a series of subtly orchestrated slights. And it was this carefully worded sentence and its inconspicuous placement in the book that started the controversy.

The dispute reached the public through a now defunct periodical, *Saturday Review of Literature*, which was, of course, happy to further its circulation by ventilating such a verbal quarrel in its "Letters to the Editor." Irving Kolodin, the music critic of this weekly magazine, published Schoenberg's letter and Mann's response, and the controversy was under way. The fire was fueled by students and friends of Schoenberg as well as, I am sure, by Mann's acquaintances and followers. The whole unhappy affair soon took a strange turn when rumors surfaced that there was a musical confidant—an informant (or "informer," as Schoenberg preferred to call him)—who, indeed, was responsible for supplying Mann with detailed information pertaining to the "secret chromatic art" of twelve-tone composition! As you all know, his name was Theodor Wiesengrund-Adorno. Not, as many scholars have been led to believe, a person close to Schoenberg's heart. An acquaintance, rather than a friend.

And now, at last, we come to Thomas Mann's *The Story of a Novel* itself, which is, as it were, an apology, an insight into the workshop practices of the author, relating the genesis of *Doctor Faustus*. An *a posteriori* sketch! Here Mann tries to justify everything in the book, including what Schoenberg considered a breach of etiquette: plagiarism, which today, in the most amoral of all centuries, is not considered a serious crime. Now that Schoenberg had written evidence that there actually had been an informant and that this "informer" was glorified in *Doctor Faustus* in a passage linking him with Beethoven's opus 111 (which, for Schoenberg, exemplified the pinnacle of musical composition) the *Arietta:*

—with the inner voice which I am not singing—and that Mann had immortalized Wiesengrund by associating his name with this motive, analogous to the beautiful words *Himmelblau, Veilchenduft,* et al. (it was done discreetly and elegantly) he—Schoenberg—became sarcastic and started to make fun of Mann's amusicality, at least as far as his sense of rhythm and meter were concerned, because Wiesengrund is not iambic but trochaic.

Another sentence in *The Story of a Novel* that brought Schoenberg's blood to a boiling point was Mann's critique of what he said were two presents: the *Theory of Harmony* and the text of *Jacob's Ladder.* The latter he found "impure." He closed the chapter, gratuitously, with a reminiscence that the best thing about these Sunday afternoon visitations to Schoenberg's home was the coffee served by Mrs. Schoenberg.

Once more—and I think rightly—Schoenberg felt slighted by these comments. On top of that, Schoenberg said, since he only had two copies of the *Theory of Harmony,* he did not *give* Mann the book; he only *loaned* it to him! And again, in Schoenberg's eyes, Mann had done something unethical by not having returned the book. (I am sure there is not a person in this room who has not suffered a similar fate.) Since the book was out of print, Schoenberg wrote a polite letter requesting Mann to return the *Theory of Harmony.* One day, shortly before Christmas, the youngest son, Larry, came running into the house with something in a plain, brown wrapper—in a paper bag—which he said he had found on the driveway, thinking that it was a premature Christmas present that had been delivered to the house by a department store. It turned out to be the *Theory of Harmony,* without an accompanying note or a word from anyone. This mode of delivery incensed Schoenberg. He was very fond of books and did not like dog-ears or lacerated pages. After all, the book was out of print and, unlike *Doctor Faustus,* already a collector's item. He had envisioned the trajectory of the book as it was being thrown over the gate, and this callous act was, I have to say, the Sarajevo ... the final gunshot, in a series of skirmishes, which meant total war.

Time is fleeting, and now we come to the part we all enjoy above all others: that portion prefaced by the two magical words—"in closing"! A footnote. In 1965/66, while teaching at the University of California, Berkeley, I met Michael Mann, the son of Thomas Mann, after a concert, or lecture. As is normal, we talked about nothing in particular, until I mentioned the unfortunate incident of the Schoenberg-Mann controversy—which did, of course, as you know end in a very sincere and warm reconciliation shortly before Schoenberg's death—telling him what had really caused the ultimate breach: the unconventional manner in which the *Theory of Harmony* had been returned. And he said, incredulously, "Schoenberg thought that the book was thrown over the gate? No, I took it there. It was too large to fit into the mailbox, so I placed it in the middle of the driveway so that if Schoenberg, or his wife, drove in with the car, it would be immediately seen. That was really the only reason for placing it in such a peculiar position. It was not *thrown* over the gate."

Schoenberg might have saved himself much rancor and grief had he known this simple explanation. Although, according to his disciples, Schoenberg *never* made mistakes, in this case he had misinterpreted the evidence. The poignancy is all the more acute when we realize that we, too, misinterpret the clues, the words, the letters, the data. The final breach was the result of such a misunderstanding. And that—although it may be supererogatory to mention it in present company—it seems to me, is perhaps also the basis for much of musicology!

NOTES

First published as Richard Hoffmann, "Der Roman eines *Roman eines Romans,*" in *Bericht über den 2. Kongress der Internationalen Schönberg-Gesellschaft: "Die Wiener Schule in der Musikgeschichte des 20. Jahrhunderts,"* Wien, 12. bis 15. Juni 1984, ed. Rudolf Stephan and Sigrid Wiesmann, vol. 2 (Wien: E. Lafite, 1986), 235–41.

1. See Arnold Schoenberg and Peter Schossow, *Die Prinzessin* (München: Hanser, 2006).

"Schoenberg Will End Our Friendship"

Concerning the Doctor Faustus *Controversy between Arnold Schoenberg and Thomas Mann*

Bernhold Schmid

It does not seem supererogatory to inform the reader that the form of musical composition delineated in Chapter XXII, known as the twelve-tone or row system, is in truth the intellectual property of a contemporary composer and theoretician, Arnold Schoenberg. I have transferred this technique in a certain ideational context to the fictitious figure of a musician, the tragic hero of my novel. In fact, the passages of this book that deal with musical theory are indebted in numerous details to Schoenberg's *Harmonielehre* [Theory of Harmony]."

—THOMAS MANN

This postscript was added to *Doctor Faustus* as testimony to a long and bitter dispute between Arnold Schoenberg and Thomas Mann.[1] The argument attracted widespread interest. Friends and acquaintances of both adversaries took sides. Contemporary news publications partially described the course of events (though never completely), sometimes commenting on, as well as often intervening in, the dispute. Schoenberg and Mann often came forward themselves in the form of open letters and articles in the press.[2] Incidentally, Mann had quite obviously anticipated the dispute while working on *Doctor Faustus:* "Schoenberg will end our friendship," he wrote to Agnes E. Meyer on September 28, 1944.[3]

I

Basically the dispute is structured into two phases: one concerns the private sphere, which ended with the above-cited postscript by Thomas Mann, and Schoenberg's letter of thanks, and the other the public sphere, initiated by Schoenberg with a letter to the *Saturday Review of Literature (SRL)*, which resulted in the press engaging in the dispute. Before delving into the course of events more closely, we would like to focus on Schoenberg's role as the inventor of the twelve-tone method and Theodor W. Adorno's part as its transmitter to Thomas Mann, since Adorno's role as consultant during Mann's work on *Doctor Faustus* most probably influenced the end of the dispute.

"Whenever he was writing a book, he immersed himself totally in the particular subject, and studied much and continuously, while he was working on it. He gathered everything that was worth knowing about it, accrued a great deal of material."[4] Thus Katia Mann describes Thomas Mann's method of writing, the same being true for *Doctor Faustus*. In this novel it appears that the realistic portrayal of Leverkühn's fictitious music seemed particularly important to Mann, as a letter to Adorno proves: "my feeling that the music has to be present, is just as greatly important to me as are the convincing details of the fictional biography itself."[5] In general, Mann seems to have taken great interest in the technical aspects, "at least to the extent that no professional (and there is no more jealously guarded profession) could laugh" at him.[6] He describes the importance of an adviser in *The Story of a Novel*. In the following we will cite extensively, in order to attempt to present the situation more clearly: Mann did not hold his own skills with regard to music theory or history in great esteem. He had, however, "always been very close to music, had drawn infinite stimulation and many artistic lessons from it" (40), he writes, continuing that this did not seem to be enough for him: "The trouble was that this time the 'universal element' did not suffice, that it was practically the same as blundering amateurishness. The 'specialty' was needed. There is nothing sillier, in a novel about genius, about works, to hail these and rave about their effects upon the souls of their audiences. No, concrete reality, exactitude, were needed—this was utterly clear to me. 'I shall have to study music,' I said to my brother when I told him of my project." (40).

A few sentences later, it says in *The Story of a Novel:* "I could list a small catalogue of books on music and musicians in English and German, certainly a good two dozen, which I studied 'with the pencil,' reading with that earnestness and alertness that one employs only for creative ends, for the sake of a work in progress. But all this peripheral contact was not actual study of music; it would not save me from exposing my ignorance in exact details; and it did not equip me to build up the lifework of an important composer so that it really seemed as if the compositions could be heard, so that they were absolutely believable (and this is what I demanded of myself)" (41). In a letter dated December 30, 1945, Mann admits to Adorno, for whom he had written *The Story of a Novel* as a favor, that he was beginning to lack a certain sense of "application." Were one to take the following sentence from *The Story of a Novel*—"And at the same time my diary confesses: 'Technical musical studies frighten and bore me'" (40)—and add it to the one previously cited, then the necessity for Thomas Mann to have an adviser, whom, after all, he had found in Theodor Adorno, seems self-evident. Likewise, it becomes apparent that the high standard for authenticity, which Mann had demanded of himself, was in harmony with his adopting an existent method of composition, precisely Schoenberg's twelve-tone technique.

Thus, in order to obtain information about the history of music and especially modern music, Mann read a number of pertinent works (including Paul Bekker's *Music History,* Schoenberg's *Theory of Harmony,* Volbach's *Instrumente des orchesters,* Stravinsky's *An Autobiography,* and Krenek's *Music Here and Now*). An important work was also the Schoenberg portion of Adorno's *Philosophy of New Music,*[7] which was then only in manuscript form. Moreover, Mann wrote letters of inquiry specifically addressing special problems. He asked his son, Michael Mann, about the viola d'amore, the instrument of the narrator in *Doctor Faustus,* Serenus Zeitblom.[8] He also had corresponded with Bruno Walter about *Doctor Faustus,* as, for example, on March 1, 1945. In addition, Mann carried on conversations with well-known musicians with whom he was acquainted. Frequently in his letters, as well as in *The Story of a Novel,* are found notes like the following:

"Meetings with Schoenberg and Stravinsky planned." "Gathering at the Werfels with the Schoenbergs. Pumped S. a great deal on music and the life of a composer. To my deep pleasure, he himself insists we must all get together more often. . . ."[9]—"This evening we are going to be at Werfels with Stravinsky, whom I hope to sound out thoroughly," he writes in a letter to Agnes E. Meyer dated August 22, 1943.

The frequent conversations with Schoenberg due to his being the inventor of the twelve-tone method did not only play a significant role with regard to *Doctor Faustus.* In conjunction with Leverkühn's oratorium *Apocalipsis cum figuris,* Thomas Mann sought advice from Schoenberg,[10] whose unfinished oratorium, *Jacob's Ladder,* he did not hold in high regard.[11] The main informant, however, was Adorno, whose knowledge in the discipline Mann believed prodigious.[12] Later, in the dispute concerning *Doctor Faustus,* Adorno, who had sided with Thomas Mann, felt attacked by Schoenberg as well. The depiction of the twelve-tone method, of the "strict phrase" in chapter 22 of the novel, is in certain sections based almost word for word on Adorno's *Philosophy of New Music,* for which Mann later apologized.[13] In the summer of 1943 Mann had read Adorno's book, and around that time Adorno had taken part in numerous discussions with Mann, which can be seen in several diary entries. And on December 30, 1945, Mann asked Adorno by letter, "Would you like to think about how the work—I mean Leverkühn's composition [the *Apocalipsis cum figuris*]—could be more or less incorporated into the work; how you would do it, if you were in a pact with the devil." Adorno had greatly influenced Leverkühn's fictive work, like his Violin Concerto: "only a very impressionistic idea" originated from Thomas Mann, while the "technical aspects" came from Adorno.[14] Adorno also greatly influenced the descriptions of both of Adrian Leverkühn's oratorios. Mann had given Adorno "everything that had so far been written and typed up, in order to give him a complete insight into the unfolding of the novel's ideas, to acquaint him with my intentions, and to cajole him into helping me with the impending musical problems."[15] He writes about their collaboration on Leverkühn's *Apocalipsis:* "During the weeks to come I sat with him many a time with notebook and pencil, over a good home-brewed liqueur, jotting down cue phrases concerning corrections and more exact details for earlier accounts of works of music in the book, as well as traits he had conceived for the oratorio."[16]

Mann had written *The Story of a Novel,* in which he describes Adorno's role as adviser, primarily to give the latter "credit," in order to morally justify his liberal borrowings from Adorno's *Philosophy,* which Mann admitted to repeatedly (for example, in letters to Jonas Lesser on October 15, 1951, and to A.M. Frey on January 15, 1952). However, Mann's diary entries in the years when he was writing *Doktor Faustus* show that Adorno's sphere of influence clearly went farther than what Mann had depicted in *The Story of a Novel,* that Adorno even had made expositions of a nonmusical nature (diary entry of January 12, 1947). If, in *The Story of a Novel,* Mann did not fully acknowledge his adviser's participation, it was because Adorno very quickly began to boast of his collaboration in a rather unbecoming manner, to which, again, Mann's diaries bear witness, as his diary entry for February 7, 1948, attests: "The awareness of his musical partnership is beginning to brew in Adorno's breast. Somewhat strange." Nevertheless in the unrevised transcription of *The Story of a Novel* Mann had at first acknowledged Adorno's influence without minimizing it, just as the latter's collaboration had been reported in the diaries. Debates at home with Katia and especially with his daughter Erica, who both had read the text, induced Mann to delete longer passages pertaining to Adorno from *The Story of a Novel,* which is illuminated in the diaries. Thus, for example, the entry of October 30, 1948: "The dubiousness of the Faust memoirs, the problem of the Adorno acknowledgements, which are so unbearable to the women, are stifling my mood for work." Erika Mann ultimately went through the manuscript of *The Story of a Novel* and made suggestions for revisions, which the diary entry of November 28, 1948, confirms: "After tea until dinner worked with Erika on the 'Memoirs.' Some passages to correct and delete." And the diary entry of November 29, 1948: "From 6 to 7:30 worked again with Erika. I did not put up with the procedure very well." And on November 30, 1948: "I worked through the second half of the Memoirs with deletions and improvements, and ultimately was not dissatisfied."

Yet even after the reworking of *The Story of a Novel* there remained some uneasiness. The relationship with Adorno deteriorated, as a letter to Jonas Lesser of October 15, 1951, demonstrates: "With *The Story of a Novel* I cast a strong spotlight on him [Adorno], in which, in a not very pleasing manner, he puffs himself up so much, that it almost seems as if he actually had written *Faustus*. I say that between us. My admiration for his extraordinary intellect remains undiminished. Also in the *Minima Moralia* one finds brilliant things. But I will certainly leave them where they are."

Though Thomas Mann had apologized to and justified his quotations with Adorno, he seems not to have mentioned to Schoenberg his inclusion of the twelve-tone method in the novel. Schoenberg himself wrote later that Mann had acted both without his prior knowledge and without his permission.[17] Presumably, Thomas Mann had expected or feared objections from Schoenberg early on.

Adorno's function as adviser has an amusing secondary aspect. In a letter dated November 14, 1946, the musicologist Alfred Einstein offered to help Thomas Mann with proofreading the novel.[18] Einstein had read fragments from the novel, which Thomas Mann had previously published in the April 1946 issue of the *Neue Rundschau*, and had admired the musical descriptions in the novel. Of course, he had no idea that they had been influenced by Adorno. In addition, he criticized a music-historical mistake, which Adorno had apparently overlooked: At one point in the advance copy of the novel, it mentions the "Organ music of Schütz." But there is no organ music in Heinrich Schütz's work. Following Einstein's suggestion, Mann replaced Schütz with Michael Praetorius. Einstein's criticism also of the similarly absurd formulation concerning the "Fugal weight of the chords" in the description of Beethoven's Sonata, op. 111, remained in the novel. This refers back to a reading error: Adorno had written to Mann about the "dead weight of the chords," which Mann had misread as "weight of the fugues." Under false pretenses, Mann refused Einstein's offer of help. This probably can be explained by Mann's wish not to offend Adorno.

II

The Private Phase of the Dispute.   Shortly after the publication of the German edition of the novel (Stockholm, late autumn, 1947), on January

15, 1948, Mann sent a copy to Schoenberg with the dedication: "For Arnold Schoenberg, the *real one*, with best wishes. . . ." Schoenberg was happy about it, as Richard Hoffmann reports; the personal relationship between Schoenberg and Mann seems to have been, if not exactly friendly, untroubled before the dispute.[19] When Schoenberg received the book, he may not have been aware of the fact that his twelve-tone method played an essential role in the novel. Admittedly, while he was working on *Faustus* (May 23, 1943, to January 29, 1947), several times Thomas Mann had read various passages from the novel to friends and acquaintances, but Schoenberg had never been present. Schoenberg's informant was Alma Mahler-Werfel, as can be unequivocally verified from several sources: Katia Mann and Richard Hoffmann both write about it.[20] An unpublished letter from Adorno to Eduard Steuermann, dated December 22, 1948, demonstrates that Alma not only informed Schoenberg but also had informed Thomas Mann concerning Schoenberg's desire that Mann mention him as the creator of the twelve-tone technique, upon which the writer had added the postscript cited at the beginning of this essay. According to Schoenberg's letter to the *SRL*, Alma Mahler-Werfel had spoken with Thomas Mann himself about the latter's representation of the twelve-tone method in *Doktor Faustus*.

Schoenberg himself, as he relates repeatedly, had not been able to read the novel because of a problem with his eyesight.[21] So he had not been able to judge whether or not *Doktor Faustus* might be damaging to his reputation as the inventor of the twelve-tone method, yet his interest in the novel had been awakened by Alma Mahler. Richard Hoffmann reports that Schoenberg had asked his wife to read to him from the novel. Later Hoffmann had taken over this task by speaking passages into a Dictaphone (a so-called Webster Wire Recorder) in order that Schoenberg could listen to them. Concerning Mann's music descriptions, according to Hoffmann, as long as they had not pertained to Leverkühn's twelve-tone oriented works, Schoenberg seemed to have been pleased about what he had heard. But it became immediately clear to the astonished composer that the descriptions of the twelve-tone technique could not have originated directly from Mann. Because of the dedication ("To the *real one*") Schoenberg felt he had been identified with Leverkühn; thus, he became angry because the fictive composer had become ill with syphilis.[22]

Four weeks after Schoenberg had received the copy with the dedication, he took retaliatory action. According to the diary entry of February 16, 1948, Mann received a bogus letter, signed by a Hugo Triebsamen. In a postscript Schoenberg pretended that he had received the letter from Triebsamen, which, in reality, he had actually made up himself. The feigned

Triebsamen places himself in the middle of the twenty-first century and relates that he had come upon Schoenberg's name along with enthusiastic comments about him in one of the letters of Anton Webern: that the former was the greatest living composer and would never be forgotten. But having realized that Schoenberg by that time had nonetheless indeed been forgotten, Triebsamen, after a long search, had found information in the (invented title) *Encyclopedia Americana* of 1988. In an article in this nonexistent lexicon, one could read and discover that Thomas Mann originally had been a composer and the real inventor of the twelve-tone method, whereas Schoenberg had been mainly a theoretician and teacher of forms, which were already completely antiquated in his day (Functional Harmony, etc.). On the other hand, already in his youth Mann had switched to being an author, and therefore had given over to Schoenberg his (Mann's) twelve-tone technique, developed by him around 1933, for publication under the latter's—Schoenberg's—name. In their later years the two of them had not gotten on well and were no longer friends, so as a result, Mann had made use of what was actually originally his very own intellectual property, by attributing it to one of his novel's characters.

Schoenberg had faked the Triebsamen letter in order to suggest to Thomas Mann the danger that later one might forget that he (Schoenberg) had been the original inventor of the twelve-tone technique: "One knows the superficiality and monomania of some historians, who ignore facts that are not in accord with their hypotheses."[23] Worry about his posthumous reputation had caused Schoenberg to take action. That the alleged Triebsamen only happens upon Schoenberg by way of a Webern letter, as well as alluding to Nadia Boulanger (distorted by Schoenberg as Budra Nalanger), who had, according to Triebsamen, greatly influenced a boom in American music, leads one to believe that Schoenberg feared that he might be overlooked.

It takes great power of imagination and fantasy to construct such complicated and intricate reasoning in a utopian manner. Even Triebsamen's role is in many aspects encoded and broken: first of all the very name is constructed out of Hugo Riemann and Walter Rubsamen.[24] Furthermore, there is Triebsamen's own situation: this fictitious Triebsamen dissimulates away from himself into a later time of utopian preconditions and cites fictional reference works. But this perfect utopia was way off the mark chronologically: Triebsamen dates the article from the *Encyclopedia Americana* as 1988, but in the letter to the *SRL* the reference article is set in the year 2060, and in the letter to Thomas Mann it is changed from February 25, 1948, to 2048.

Mann seems not to have immediately recognized Schoenberg's fiction, as a diary entry of February 21, 1948, demonstrates: "Triebsamen is actually himself." Mann's letter to Schoenberg dated February 17, 1948, is also formulated as if he had believed him, although it is not completely clear whether or not Mann is being ironic: "Dear Mr. Schoenberg, that certainly is a peculiar document. I was moved by this sign of the holy zeal with which your disciples watch over the fame and honor of the master." He pities Schoenberg for having friends like Triebsamen: "May God protect us from our friends," citing an "old refrain." "But then again, that much strenuous and misdirected malice has at the same time its comical side, too." Mann writes of the unlikelihood that Schoenberg, as inventor of the twelve-tone system, could ever fade into obscurity: "As to who is the creator of the twelve-tone technique, every little child in Africa knows that by now. It most assuredly is known, at any rate, to everyone who is interested enough to take a look at a book like *Dr. Faustus.*"

Through the intervention of Alma Mahler, a later postscript was then added that names Schoenberg as the author of the twelve-tone technique: Ever since February 21, 1948, Mann had been informed by Alma Mahler of Schoenberg's wish (compare a diary entry of Mann). The day after one can read in the diary: "about Schoenberg." On February 23 Mann talked about the matter with Adorno. In the diary immediately thereafter there appears the first version of the note. On February 24, 1948, the diary states: "Schoenberg insists via Alma Mahler," and in a letter on the same day, Mann agrees to the postscript, for which Schoenberg thanks him on February 25, 1948. In this letter Schoenberg discloses, in an amazingly candid manner, the intentions and motives of the Triebsamen letter: first the feigned, put-together name of Riemann and Rubsamen, then, also, about his (Schoenberg's) worry that it might be forgotten that he was the inventor of the twelve-tone technique. In addition is added his fear of being misunderstood and neglected by his contemporaries, which an excerpt of the letter impressively proves: "To the Germans I am a Jew, to the Latins a German, to the Communists I am bourgeois, and the Jews are for Hindemith and Stravinsky."[25]

Until Schoenberg's letter to the *SRL* (no. 13, 1948) brought the argument before the public, nothing new or more significant had occurred. Mann mentions the postscript in a letter to Bruno Walter dated March 26, 1948. Schoenberg writes Rufer on May 25, 1948,[26] that only after considerable resistance had Thomas Mann declared himself ready to add the postscript. He reproaches the latter for the same thing in the letter to the *SRL*: "A lot of pressure had to be applied in order to bring Mann to the point where he promised that in every subsequent copy of *Doctor Faustus* there would be a note declaring my authorship of Twelve-Tone-Composition." Thomas Mann denies this resistance in his response to the *SRL*: "It is completely inaccurate that 'much pressure' had been needed to induce me to afford him the credit that was his due. As soon as I had understood his request, I gave the directive that in all translations and, as soon as possible, in the German original edition as well, the postscript must be added, which one now can read in the English version of *Doctor Faustus.*" However, Schoenberg's description that Mann had balked at adding the postscript is correct. True, one cannot conclude, from the correspondence at the time Schoenberg had demanded the annotation (February 24 and 25, 1948), that Mann had been reluctant to write the postscript. However, since the relevant discussions on that score were transacted essentially by way of oral transmissions via Alma Mahler, one cannot conclude solely from the letters of February 24 and 25, 1948, that Mann had *not* put up any resistance. Mann was not thrilled about adding the postscript, and what he held against the idea can be found in quite some detail in *The Story of a Novel:* "This is being done a bit against my own convictions—not so much because such an explanation throws a small breach into the rounded, integral world of my novel, as because, within the sphere of the book, within this world of a pact with the devil and of black magic, the idea [of] the twelve-tone technique assumes a coloration and a character which it does not possess in its own right and which—is this not so?—in a sense make it really my property, or, rather, the property of the book. Schoenberg's idea and my *ad hoc* version of it differs so widely that, aside from the stylistic fault, it would have seemed almost insulting, to my mind, to have mentioned his name in the text."[27] The cited passage from *The Story of a Novel* concurs in content with a letter from Mann to Schoenberg of October 13, 1948. Along with this letter, Mann sent a copy of the newly published English translation of *Doctor Faustus,* in which the postscript appeared for the first time. By return mail, namely on October 15, 1948, Schoenberg sent Mann a letter of thanks, which, presumably, he had composed before reading the postscript. With that, the dispute might have been concluded, since by way of the postscript the possibility that Mann be taken as the inventor of the twelve-tone system would have been eliminated. If the dispute continued, then it most probably was on account of the postscript: first, owing to its appearance at the end of the novel, as well as its wording, or perhaps owing to Schoenberg's resentment that one might identify Leverkühn with him.

III

The Public Phase of the Dispute.   With Schoenberg's letter of November 13, 1948, to the *SRL,* in which he unsubtly and in biased terms describes the dispute up to that point—and when, also, Adorno appears on the scene as Thomas Mann's adviser[28]—the controversy became public. The outside cause for it seems to have been a review of *Doktor Faustus* in the *SRL*, as an excerpt from Schoenberg's letter to the magazine initially would lead one to believe: "The supposition of your reviewer, that he obtained information about this technique from Bruno Walter and Stravinsky, is probably wrong; because Walter does not know anything of composition with twelve tones, and Stravinsky does not take any interest in it."

The passage involving the phrase "your reviewer" needs elucidation, however. On October 30, 1948, the *SRL* printed a review of *Doctor Faustus* in which neither Walter's nor Stravinsky's names, not to mention Schoenberg's or Adorno's, were mentioned. By contrast, however, a review of the novel in *Time* magazine (November 1, 1948) names Bruno Walter and Igor Stravinsky as consultants, but the names of Schoenberg and Adorno are also lacking here. To this must be added a further occurrence: *Time* had asked both Schoenberg and Mann for interviews (before mid-October 1948). Mann reports about it in a letter to R. Schweizer (dated October 12, 1958). Mann had granted the interview, and his answers had been worked into the *Time* review. In a letter to Thomas Mann dated October 15, 1948, Schoenberg refers to a request for an interview from a correspondent of the magazine: "a local contributor to that distasteful *Time* magazine, . . . had asked me for an interview regarding *Dr. Faustus*—I declined." This request for an interview, as well as the review in *Time* magazine and not the review in the *SRL*, might have been the reason for Schoenberg's letter to that journal. He obviously had confused the two magazines.

So much for what may have brought the dispute about. The reasons for it lie elsewhere. Most certainly Schoenberg's concern about posterity was a major factor, his fear that his importance and the position of his work had not been duly honored. With the presentation and commentary on the course of events of the dispute, he had wanted to point out how he and his intellectual property had been treated. But the following aspect is central: Schoenberg's letter appeared in the *SRL* under the title *"Doctor Faustus Schoenberg?"* He reproached Mann on account of the latter's dedication in the book to "the *real one*," which Schoenberg thought had identified him with Leverkühn. He considered this an insult: "Leverkühn is depicted, from beginning [to] end, as a lunatic. I am now seventy-four and I am not yet insane, and I have never acquired the disease from which this insanity stems. I consider this an insult, and I might have to draw consequences."[29] In addition, he attacked Mann's postscript: "He gave me an explanation: a few lines which he hid at the end of the book on a place on a page where no one ever would see it."[30] Even in the more severe attack in *Music Survey* (Fall 1949) the postscript and its formulation were still an issue.

Schoenberg's threat, "I might have to draw consequences," was meant to be taken seriously, and it troubled Thomas Mann. He notes in his diary on December 30, 1948: "Golo yesterday at Alma Mahler's. Schoenberg really plans to sue. Not impossible that he may find an enterprising lawyer. Nothing is impossible. Why shouldn't they decide that the inventor of the twelve-tone system is due all proceeds from my book? I see it as less decided than K[atia].... Unpleasantly shaken up by Schoenberg's insanity. See myself ruined, but everyone is laughing at the idea."

Schoenberg's letter (November 13, 1948) and Mann's response (December 10, 1948) appeared together in the *SRL* on January 1, 1949. Mann had received a copy of Schoenberg's letter from the magazine and had responded immediately, as he reported in a letter to Adorno on December 11, 1948. In his response to the *SRL*, he initially makes clear his astonishment at Schoenberg's scorn: "Our personal correspondence on this matter had been of a thoroughly friendly character in all its phases," he writes, which, with the exception of the Triebsamen letter, can be confirmed. He denounces "gossip of meddling scandal mongers" and states that Schoenberg's attacks were solely based on these. He had been unaware that Schoenberg feared he might be forgotten as the inventor of the twelve-tone technique, especially since many reviews had named Schoenberg in connection with the method.

In addition, he attempts to clear up possible misunderstandings with regard to the postscript: "It was intended as a bit of instruction to the uninformed, and I worded it as objectively as possible. 'Take note,' it says in effect, 'there is a composer and music philosopher living among us, whose name is Arnold Schoenberg; he, and not the hero of my novel, is the one who, in reality, thought out the twelve-tone composition method.'" Similarly he answers Schoenberg's indignation about the dedication "the *real one*": "That meant: 'Not Leverkühn is the hero of this musical era; you are its hero.'" Ultimately, Mann reacts forcefully against the reproach of having identified Schoenberg with Leverkühn: "The idea that Adrian Leverkühn is Schoenberg, that the figure is a portrait of him, is so utterly absurd that I scarcely know what to say about it. There is no point of contact, not a shade of similarity, between the origin, the traditions, the character, and the fate of my musician, on the one hand, and the existence of Schoenberg, on the other."[31]

Once the dispute had been brought before the public, the press was energized.[32] Up to this point the press only knew about the dispute from Schoenberg's and Mann's letters to the *SRL*, but it began to intervene with descriptions and commentary precisely at the moment that the dispute itself began to take on the character of a commentary on itself, and the recapitulation of the previous events transformed into an argument about the argument. Mann's novel had had great success and had been selected for the "Book-of-the-Month-Club" alongside Somerset Maugham's *Catalina*. The dispute was a sensational hit in America as much as it was in Europe, as might be gleaned from the number of news articles and multiple publications in different newspapers.[33] But the speed with which the dispute traveled around the world is especially remarkable. Schoenberg's and Mann's public correspondence in the *SRL* appeared on January 1, 1949. The publication of the letters in the German magazine *Der Monat* is dated March 1949. The first German article known to me was written by Juliane Lange for the Frankfurter *Neue Presse* issue of January 29, 1949, followed by one for *Die Zeit* on February 3, 1949. An article by Willi Schuh, which offers a kind of summary of the two letters, appeared in the *Neue Zürcher Zeitung* on February 12 and 14, and another, as early as April 1949, was published in the *Neue Auslese*, a magazine similar to *Reader's Digest*.

What the press seemed to have jumped on was, among other things, whether or not Leverkühn was Schoenberg. The above-mentioned article by Juliane Lange has a title that contains this question: "Is Arnold Schoenberg Doctor Faustus?" And even Jan Maegaard's 1974 article in *Melos*[34] touches on this question at the beginning. Since Mann has his Leverkühn invent the twelve-tone system, the assumption that Schoenberg is Leverkühn does seem legitimate. But Mann's letter to the *SRL* explains this question unequivocally with reference to other connections in the novel.

Mann was very happy about the press, which was for the most part in his favor, as a letter to Lavinia Mazzucchetti dated March 14, 1949, concerning Schuh's obviously partial letter demonstrates: "how grateful and overjoyed I was about the long article that Dr. Schuh devoted to the case in the *Neue Zürcher Zeitung*. That is a real friend, who always seems to help in awkward situations. I will never forget his intervention in the year 1933 against the Munich Haberfeld goings-on. [Mazzucchetti is referring to the 'Protest of the Richard Wagner City Munich' at the occasion of the Wagner essay.] Here, once again, he chose the right side and over and above that, his article is furthermore an altogether most detailed honoring of the book."

"You won't believe it. Schoenberg has fired another broadside at the book, and at you and me." With this passage Mann related to Adorno on January 9, 1950, that even after the exchange of letters in the *SRL* the dispute had been taken up again. In the fall of 1949 Schoenberg had approached the London periodical *Music Survey*[35] with his article "Further to the

Schoenberg-Mann Controversy." *Music Survey* was a periodical that intensively discussed contemporary music and musical events. It included, for example, articles about Stravinsky, Britten, Hindemith, and others but also about Richard Strauss. It was not so interested in historical music and clearly took sides with Schoenberg. Thus, one of its two editors, Hans Keller, published an at times polemical defense of Schoenberg and his music from a musicological perspective against attacks from the press.[36] Schoenberg himself publically thanked the journal for well wishes on the occasion of his seventy-fifth birthday.[37]

In some aspects Schoenberg's renewed attack surpasses his letter to the *SRL* in sharpness. Mann writes to Adorno that Schoenberg's publication in the above-cited letter of January 9, 1950, was ridiculous. Schoenberg states that he had nothing against the application of his twelve-tone technique, since he had presented it to his students twenty-five years earlier. In addition he refers to lectures on twelve-tone technique he had given in US universities.[38] Thereafter, he complains about the formulation of the postscript. There follows an attack against Adorno, since Schoenberg was angry that Mann, as a favor to Adorno, had written *The Story of a Novel*. Schoenberg also attempts to rank Leverkühn as a composer, which reaches its height when he describes Leverkühn's fictive composition *Doktor Fausti Weheklag* as "Leverkühn's Twelve-Note Goulash." Schoenberg places Leverkühn in the line of descendants of Wagner (the composers August Bungert and Felix Draesecke are named) and makes attempts at calculating Leverkühn's age, which demonstrates that he was aware of only those passages of music in *Doctor Faustus* inasmuch as they had been narrated by Richard Hoffmann on the Dictaphone. Subsequently, he relates that "nothing good comes to those who commit violations against him. He mentions two women who did so: allegedly one broke her leg, while the other also suffered an affliction of some kind," as Mann writes to Adorno on January 9, 1950. Ultimately, Schoenberg makes fun of Mann's style in a manner that deserves to be cited here: Mann had labeled the "religious poetry" of the *Jakobsleiter* as "impure" or "not fully brewed,"[39] which had angered Schoenberg. Concerning the formulation "not fully brewed," Schoenberg added the following passages in his letter to *Music Survey*: "But whatever else it [the poetry of *Jakobsleiter*] may be, it is difficult to imagine that it could be fully brewed, for poetry does not brew. . . . A scientist like Thomas Mann ought to know that. If one wanted to speak in his style, one could describe his sentences from a page's top to bottom as fully stretched noodle-dough, or strudel-dough, or perhaps as fully brewed tapeworms." In an accompanying letter to the editors, Schoenberg had described the dispute as "stale," to which the editors commented with the words, "So it may [be], but the character document of a master never is."[40] What must remain an open question is from where and how much did Schoenberg really know *The Story of a Novel*.[41] As previously shown, at the time of his letter to *Music Survey*, he had only received *Doktor Faustus* in extracts. Because of Schoenberg's eye problem, one can assume that he most probably also had not read *The Story of a Novel* by himself either.

Again, Mann reacted with reservation. In his letter to Schoenberg of December 19, 1949, he rejects Schoenberg's reproaches that the postscript had been an act of "revenge." He asks Schoenberg for permission to publish his letter of thanks for the postscript of October 15, 1948, in order to defend himself by it. This obviously never happened, since the letter in question was not published for quite a long time. In subsequent letters and documents of Thomas Mann, his intention of publishing this letter is no longer mentioned. It is also quite possible that he had never intended to do so, since the request to publish the letter (December 19, 1949) is markedly conceived with irony: "if, amid the hailstorm of your attacks, I feel increasingly bad, may I—if push comes to shove—publish the letter you sent on October 15, 1948, having received the English edition of *Dr. Faustus* containing the note at the end, in which you thanked me warmly for meeting your request, said you were completely satisfied . . .[?]" He writes in the same letter: "You are striking out at a bugbear from your imagination, who I am not. Thus I have no desire for revenge. If by all means you want to be my enemy—you will not succeed in making me yours." Mann also demonstrates this same approach to his acquaintances with respect to Schoenberg's attacks. He writes to Adorno in the already much-cited letter of January 9, 1950: "Nevertheless, I've written saying that even if he wants to run around as my enemy, he won't succeed in making me one of his." And in his letter of October 19, 1951, to Hans Heinz Stuckenschmidt, Mann writes much the same thing.

IV

Schoenberg ultimately backed down after Mann's letter of December 19, 1949. In his letter dated January 2 and 9, 1950, he writes:

> If the hand I believe to see extended is a hand of peace, if it thus
> signified a peace offer, then I would be the last to not grasp it
> immediately and shake it heartily. Indeed, I have often thought of
> writing to you. Let us bury the hatchet and demonstrate that on a
> certain level there is always a possibility of peace. . . .

I intended to announce this declaration of peace publicly. However, it was brought to my attention (for which reason I did not finish the letter) that in so doing I would betray all those who stood by me in this battle—friends, acquaintances, and strangers.

Therefore, I propose an interim stage. At some time the one or the other will celebrate his "eightieth"—but it need not take so long—a proper occasion to forget all the pettiness—once and for all.

. . . Let's be content with this peace: you have reconciled me.

This peace agreement was not made public on account of Schoenberg's misgivings. Only at the publication of Hans Heinz Stuckenschmidt's first Schoenberg book[42] was the public made aware of the end of the dispute. Stuckenschmidt reports about these events on March 21, 1957, in the *Neue Zürcher Zeitung*:[43] "Shortly after Schoenberg's death, I sent the book to Thomas Mann and asked him for information concerning the unfortunate conflict. His answer confirmed what I had hoped; I found it so beautiful and final, that I asked, if I could place it at the beginning of the French edition of my *Schoenberg*. Mann agreed immediately."

Mann's letter to Stuckenschmidt of October 19, 1951, reports however, that after this first peace agreement, which had not been made public, a semipublic reconciliation had followed "when the *Saturday Review* intended to publish the correspondence between us in an anthology. I immediately wrote to say this was a bad idea; he wrote back that his approval would be dependent on mine and that he authorized me to tell the editorial team we had agreed to reject the proposal."

Since Schoenberg had written vigorously against Mann in *Music Survey*, the peace agreement came unexpectedly fast. There are many speculations as to the reasons for it. Quite possibly, he transferred his anger from Mann over to Adorno.[44] If one examines the course of the dispute, then Adorno increasingly enters Schoenberg's field of vision as Mann's informant. In his letter to the *SRL*, Schoenberg initially labels Adorno an "informer," and his letter to *Music Survey* certainly contains pointed remarks against Adorno. Jan Maegaard has quite adequately characterized the relationship of the two in an article.[45] Already, before the dispute with Mann, Schoenberg seems not to have valued Adorno, as Maegaard reports. As Schoenberg became increasingly aware that Adorno had advised Mann, when Adorno's *Philosophy of New Music* (1949) eventually appeared (thus during the dispute between Schoenberg and Mann)—the book to which Mann was indebted for essential insights concerning Schoenberg's twelve-tone method—most likely Adorno increasingly became the object of Schoenberg's indignation. Maegaard cites from a fragmentary manuscript by Schoenberg about Adorno, which has the title "Wgr" [Wiesengrund] and contains hefty assaults against Adorno. The fragment is dated December 21, 1950,[46] thus approximately one year after the reconciliation with Thomas Mann.

The *Philosophy of New Music* seems to have annoyed Schoenberg especially. In his second Schoenberg book, Stuckenschmidt published quotes from Schoenberg's letters to him and Joseph Rufer that clearly do not leave much up to the imagination.[47] Both letters were written on December 5, 1949, thus several weeks after the appearance of his article in *Music Survey* and approximately a month before his final letter of reconciliation.

Moreover, an unpublished letter from Adorno to Eduard Steuermann of December 22, 1948, is very revealing, since it shows that the personal aversion was mutual. Adorno felt himself to be insulted by Schoenberg and contemplated taking him on. He found Thomas Mann's demeanor too restrained. Given the relationship of Schoenberg and Adorno to each other, and especially considering Schoenberg's indignation after the appearance of *Philosophy of New Music*, it is difficult not to think that Schoenberg's peace agreement with Mann had been aided as a result of Schoenberg's anger against Adorno.

V

Conclusion. By way of its vehemence and the reactions in the press, the dispute shows the topicality of Mann's novel, which obviously had captured the state of contemporary music of the time with great precision. At the same time, it also sheds light on the irritable intellectual climate of immigration, which had thrown together people of the most diverse intellectual directions. Two phases can clearly be differentiated:

1. The private phase, which had at the root of the dispute Schoenberg's fear that he might be forgotten as the inventor of the twelve-tone system because of the way it had been presented in Mann's novel was manifested to a great extent in amicable letters or by word of mouth through friends. The postscript to *Doctor Faustus* ends this phase.

2. The public dispute, mainly carried on in letters to the press, becomes inflamed because of the postscript and its placement at the end of the book. Adorno comes into focus for Schoenberg as Thomas Mann's adviser. A flood of articles in the press follow the exchange of letters in the *SRL*, but after Schoenberg's letter to

Music Survey, reactions in the press are absent. The peace agreement comes as a surprise but is understandable if one takes into consideration that Schoenberg might have gradually, at first, and only later fully realized Adorno's role with respect to *Doctor Faustus* after the appearance of the *Philosophy of New Music.* Schoenberg's resentment was thus redirected from Mann to Adorno.

Schoenberg's behavior is characterized by a certain unpredictability, which seems understandable given his increasing aggravation, especially since he was unaware of the relationships (such as Adorno's role), which had been unknown to him from the beginning. No fewer than three letters of thanks or reconciliation to Mann are known (February 22, 1948; October 15, 1948; and January 2 and 9, 1950). The fierce attacks against Mann were communicated either by way of a pseudonym (Triebsamen letter) or publicly through the press. The main reason for Schoenberg's behavior always shows itself to be his concern over his posthumous reputation.

Mann's demeanor, however, is characterized by cautious defense, at times also by subtle irony (answer to the Triebsamen letter of February 17, 1948; letter of December 19, 1949), not, however, by intensity of emotion. Mann intentionally did not use as a counteraction to Schoenberg's accusation of plagiarism the latter's incriminating appropriation of Hauer's *Tropenlehre,* as a letter shows.[48] One is under the impression that Mann was conscious of the fact that, by way of his overwrought animosity, Schoenberg was presenting a negative picture of himself through the very form of his attacks or, respectively, that Mann, by contrast, by way of his cleverly considerate reaction, would be presented in an even more favorable light. Based on the very divergent conduct of both, Schoenberg is presented mostly as the aggressor in the press reports of the time, though his actions, stemming from his worry over his posthumous reputation, or his being neglected, become understandable. Conversely, Mann's demeanor appears strange in that he never, during any phase of his work on *Doctor Faustus,* informed Schoenberg that he was ascribing the latter's method to a fictitious composer or asked him for permission to present his twelve-tone technique in the novel.

We will close with two citations from letters, which show the mutual respect and the final reconciliation of both men. Mann wrote to Stuckenschmidt on October 19, 1951: "it [the article in *Music Survey*] was certainly also a 'character document' . . .—as were all his life's observations, to which everyone owed reverence." And Schoenberg suggested in his letter to Mann of

January 2 and 9, 1950, that they should "bury the hatchet and . . . forget all the pettiness—once and for all."

NOTES

This article, slightly altered here, was first published as "Neues zum 'Doktor Faustus-Streit' zwischen Arnold Schoenberg und Thomas Mann," in the *Augsburger Jahrbuch für Musikwissenschaft*, ed. Franz Krautwurst (Tutzing: H. Schneider, 1989), 149–79. It also contains further commentary from Bernhold Schmid's article "Neues zum 'Doktor Faustus-Streit' zwischen Arnold Schoenberg und Thomas Mann: Ein Nachtrag," in *Augsburger Jahrbuch für Musikwissenschaft*, ed. Franz Krautwurst (Tutzing: H. Schneider, 1990), 177–92. Both articles were combined first in *À Propos du Docteur Faustus: Lettres, 1930–1951* (Lausanne: La Bibliothèque des Arts, 2002).

1. In his diary entry of February 23, 1948, Thomas Mann entered a completely different draft of the postscript. In the following, diary entries will be cited only according to date: Thomas Mann, *Diaries, 1918–1921*, ed. Peter de Mendelssohn (Frankfurt am Main: S. Fischer, 1979); *Tagebücher, 1933–1934*, ed. Peter de Mendelssohn (Frankfurt am Main: S. Fischer, 1977); *Tagebücher, 1935–1936*, ed. Peter de Mendelssohn (Frankfurt am Main: S. Fischer, 1978); *Tagebücher, 1937–1939*, ed. Peter de Mendelssohn (Frankfurt am Main: S. Fischer, 1980); *Tagebücher, 1940–1943*, ed. Peter de Mendelssohn (Frankfurt am Main: S. Fischer, 1982); *Tagebücher, 1944–1946*, ed. Inge Jens (Frankfurt am Main: S. Fischer, 1986); *Tagebücher, 1946–1948*, ed. Inge Jens (Frankfurt am Main: S. Fischer, 1989); *Tagebücher, 1949–1950*, ed. Inge Jens (Frankfurt am Main: S. Fischer, 1991); *Tagebücher, 1951–1952*, ed. Inge Jens (Frankfurt am Main: S. Fischer, 1993); *Tagebücher, 1953–1955*, ed. Inge Jens (Frankfurt am Main: S. Fischer, 1995).

2. *Saturday Review of Literature* (henceforth cited as *SRL*), Jan. 1, 1949, 22–23: Under the rubric "Letters to the Editor" Schoenberg's letter of Nov. 13, 1948, and Mann's answer of Dec. 10, 1948, appear with the title *"Doctor Faustus Schoenberg?"* The German original text was published in *Der Monat* 1, no. 6 (March 1949): 76–78.—*Music Survey* 2, no. 2 (1949): 77–80: Arnold Schönberg, "Further to the Schoenberg-Mann Controversy."

3. See a copy of the letter on p. 77 of this volume.

4. Katia Mann, *Meine ungeschriebenen Memoiren* (Frankfurt am Main: S. Fischer, 1974), cited in Fischer Taschenbuch Bd. 1750 (Frankfurt am Main: S. Fischer, 1976), 150; in the following cited as K. Mann, *Memoiren*. See also Gunilla Bergsten, *Thomas Manns Doktor Faustus: Untersuchungen zu den Quellen und zur Struktur des Romans* (Stockholm: Svenska bokförlaget, 1963), 123 (in the following cited as Bergsten, *Thomas Manns Doktor Faustus*).

5. Mann to Adorno, November 8, 1947. Henceforth passages from Thomas Mann's letters will be cited only according to date, inasmuch as they have not been edited in this book; compare the following editions: Thomas Mann, *Briefe I, 1889–1936*, ed. Erika Mann (Frankfurt am Main: S. Fischer, 1961); *Briefe II, 1937–1947*, ed. Erika Mann (Frankfurt am Main: S. Fischer, 1963); *Briefe III, 1948–1955, and Nachlese*, ed. Erika Mann (Frankfurt am Main: S. Fischer, 1965).

6. This and following citations from Thomas Mann, *The Story of a Novel*, trans. Richard and Clara Winston (New York: Knopf, 1961); published in German as *Die Entstehung des Doktor Faustus* (Amsterdam: Bermann-Fischer, 1949), 40. (Henceforth cited as Mann, *The Story of a Novel*.)

7. Bergsten's *Thomas Manns Doktor Faustus,* in the chapter "Musikhistorische und –theoretische Quellen," 90–109, offers an exact overview. For sources, as well as citations from sources in general (also those of a nonmusical nature), see Bergsten, *Thomas Manns Doktor Faustus,* Appendix, 283–89.

8. For particulars see Bergsten, *Thomas Manns Doktor Faustus,* 103.

9. Both quotes in Mann, *The Story of a Novel,* 29.

10. Ibid., 152.

11. Ibid., 52: "the libretto of his oratorio *Jacob's Ladder,* whose religious poetry I found impure." Cf. note 40 below.

12. "His knowledge of tradition, his mastery of the whole historical body of music, is enormous. An American singer who works with him said to me: 'It is incredible. He knows every note ever in the world'" (Mann, *The Story of a Novel,* 45).

13. In the letter of Dec. 30, 1945, to Adorno: ". . . the most brazen . . . invasions into certain parts of your writings on the philosophy of music . . . necessitate an apology, particularly since the reader can hardly be made aware of these borrowings unless I find a way of acknowledging them without ruining the artistic illusion."

14. Mann, *The Story of a Novel,* 205.

15. Ibid., 150.

16. Ibid., 156.

17. See Schoenberg's letter to the *SRL* of Nov. 13, 1948.

18. Publication of this letter and the account of the outlined course of events in Bernhold Schmid, "Alfred Einstein im Briefwechsel mit Thomas Mann," *Musik in Bayern* 46 (1993): 5–16.

19. Richard Hoffmann, "Der Roman eines *Roman eines Romans,*" in *Bericht über den 2. Kongress der Internationalen Schönberg-Gesellschaft: "Die Wiener Schule in der Musikgeschichte des 20. Jahrhunderts,"* Wien, 12. bis 15. Juni 1984, ed. Rudolf Stephan and Sigrid Wiesmann (Wien: E. Lafite, 1986), 235–41 (in the following cited as Hoffmann, "The Story"), reproduced in this volume. Hoffmann, who from 1947 to 1951 was first Schoenberg's pupil, later his assistant and private secretary, reports from personal memory about the course of events of the feud between Schoenberg and Mann. For Schoenberg's and Mann's personal relationship to each other see also Hans Heinz Stuckenschmidt, *Arnold Schoenberg: His Life and Work* (New York: Schirmer, 1977), cited in the following as Stuckenschmidt, *Schoenberg* (1977). Stuckenschmidt refers to some episodes, such as "Mann at Schoenberg's 69th Birthday" (461); "Schoenberg's Canon at the Occasion of Mann's 70th Birthday" (471–72) (also in Josef Rufer, *Das Werk Arnold Schönbergs* [Kassel: Bärenreiter, 1959], 90, cited in the following as Rufer, *Werk*), who also plays a role in the dispute and exchange of letters between Schoenberg and Mann (see Schoenberg's letter of Oct. 15, 1948).

20. K. Mann, *Memoiren,* 132–33; Hoffmann, "The Story," 220 herein. In her memoir *Mein Leben* (Frankfurt am Main: S. Fischer, 1960) Alma Mahler-Werfel does not mention her role in the dispute between Schoenberg and Mann.

21. Schoenberg to J. Rufer, May 25, 1948 (see Arnold Schönberg, *Ausgewählte Briefe,* ed. Erwin Stein [Mainz: Schott, 1958]; in the following cited as Schönberg, *Briefe*). Even in the public letter to the *SRL* there is mention of it. In his letter of reconciliation to Thomas Mann of October 15, 1948, thus one month before the attacks in the *SRL* of November 13, 1948, Schoenberg promises the latter to read his *Doktor Faustus.*

22. Hoffmann, "The Story," 223 herein.

23. Quote from Schoenberg's letter to the *SRL* (Nov. 13, 1948). In his letter to Thomas Mann of October 15, 1948, he states even more clearly: Schoenberg writes

of the "incompetence of musicologists of all ages" and even of the "ashes of their sterility."

24. Schoenberg himself decodes the name Triebsamen in his letter to Thomas Mann of February 22, 1948. Hugo Riemann (1849–1919), a German music historian and theoretician. Walter Howard Rubsamen (1911–1973), an American music historian. Rubsamen taught at the University of California, Los Angeles, thus was a faculty colleague of Schoenberg's, who also had taught there from 1936 to 1944. Shortly after Schoenberg's death (July 13, 1951), Rubsamen wrote an article entitled "Schoenberg in America," which appeared in *Music Quarterly* 37, no. 4 (1951): 469–89. The essay also contained a biography of Schoenberg's American years. The controversy with Thomas Mann is touched on, without Rubsamen mentioning his role in the Triebsamen letter. Rubsamen reproaches Schoenberg, however, for having been "particularly sensitive" in his last years. "One might almost say that he had a persecution complex, if his controversies with Thomas Mann and Aaron Copland may be taken as evidence" (483).

25. Schoenberg's fear of being neglected also comes to the fore in his letter to Mann of October 15, 1948. In addition, his letter to the *SRL*, with which the dispute entered the public arena, can also be interpreted in this manner. His wary hope for posthumous fame is supported by a published letter of thanks for well-wishes at the occasion of his seventy-fifth birthday under the title "To Become Recognized only after One's Death . . .!" which appeared in *Music Survey* 2, no. 3 (1950): 180–81: "On the other hand, I have for many years closed my account with the world, and bowed to the fact that I may not hope for honest and loving understanding of my work, and that is: to express everything I have into music, for as long as I live. However, I know that many of my friends have familiarized themselves thoroughly with my manner of expression and have acquired an intimate understanding of my ideas. They then might be such who carry out, what I predicted 37 years ago in an aphorism: 'The second half of this century will spoil, by overestimation, all the good of me that the first half, by underestimation, has left intact." (Schoenberg had sent the above-cited letter as a handwritten, photocopied, and duplicated document, dated September 16, 1949. See Stuckenschmidt, *Schoenberg* [1977], 547–48.)

26. Schönberg, *Briefe*, 266.

27. Mann, *The Story of a Novel*, 36.

28. Thomas Mann writes about it to Adorno on December 11, 1948.

29. See also Hoffmann, "The Story," 223.

30. Ibid., 224.

31. Mann made similar remarks in a letter to Alberto Mondadori of June 19, 1950.

32. Letters to the Editor were also written. See, e.g., *SRL* 32, no. 7 (1949): 22. Before the exchange of letters in the *SRL* there were exceptionally few articles that dealt with the exact reasons for the dispute, since it was yet unknown. On April 17, 1948, Mann notes in his diary, for example: "small journal by Humm, with the reproachful article of a 'Schoenbergian.'" The article contained the reproach that Mann had used the twelve-tone technique in the novel, without naming Schoenberg or Matthias Hauer as the inventor of that method of composition.

33. Harry Matter, *Die Literatur über Thomas Mann: Eine Bibliographie, 1898–1969*, 2 vols. (Berlin: Aufbau, 1972) (cited in the following as Matter, *Bibliographie*), lists under the rubric "Arnold Schönberg" (352–54) a total of thirty-two publications, but because there are duplicate publications, there were fewer than that.

34. Jan Maegaard, "Schönberg hat Adorno nie leiden können," in *Melos* 41, no. 5 (1974): 262–64 (cited in the following as Maegaard, "Schönberg"). This article appeared slightly altered under the title "Zu Th. W. Adornos Rolle im Mann/

Schönberg-Streit," in *Gedenkschrift für Thomas Mann, 1875–1975,* ed. Rolf Wiecker (Kopenhagen: Text und Kontext, 1975), 215–22.

35. *Music Survey* 2, no. 2 (1949): 77–80.

36. *Music Survey* 3, no. 3 (1951): 160–68.

37. See note 25 above.

38. See Luigi Dallapiccola, "On the Twelve-Note Road," *Music Survey* 4, no. 1 (1951): 318: One should be reminded that Arnold Schoenberg never gave lessons in the "Zwölf-Ton Technik." Compare also the Krenek quote on p. 319 of the same Dallapiccola article (about Dallapiccola's twelve-tone compositions, which were composed without contact with the composers of the Viennese School). Illuminating are also several written notes by Schoenberg, which Maegaard replicates in Maegaard, "Schönberg," 263.

39. Mann, *The Story of a Novel,* 52.

40. See *Music Survey* 2, no. 2 (1949): 77. The editor cites the letter in a brief commentary, which precedes Schoenberg's article: "may perhaps be stale." For Schoenberg's anger about Mann's assessment of *Jakobsleiter* see also Hoffmann, "The Story" (herein). In Schoenberg's letter to *Music Survey* there is mention of a second letter to the *SRL.* The editors refer to the *SRL* in a footnote but only quote the familiar correspondence of January 1, 1949; and the Thomas Mann bibliography (Matter, *Bibliographie,* 352–55) has no entries about a second letter to the *SRL.* An examination of the year 1949 for this periodical proved inconclusive. Thus, one may assume that Schoenberg had sent a second letter to the *SRL* but that it was never published.

41. See also Hoffmann, "The Story," 225 herein, which mentions *The Story of a Novel* but without comment.

42. Hans Heinz Stuckenschmidt, *Arnold Schönberg* (Zurich: Atlantis 1951).

43. *Neue Zürcher Zeitung,* Thursday, March 21, 1957, 13, foreign edition: "The peace agreement with Schoenberg, a letter of Thomas Mann's, as discussed by H. H. Stuckenschmidt."

44. See Hoffmann, "The Story," 225 herein.

45. Maegaard, "Schönberg," passim. Hoffmann, "The Story," 225 herein, confirms Schoenberg's dislike of Adorno.

46. Maegaard, "Schönberg," 262. See Schoenberg's text herein, 207.

47. Stuckenschmidt, *Schönberg* (1974), 462.

48. Mann to Ellie Bommerstein, February 19, 1949. Of her own accord, E. Bommerstein had sent Mann detailed information on Hauer; Mann answered that he had known about Hauer, but by her letter she had significantly expanded his knowledge of him. "But I had repressed his name on purpose, in order not to irritate the suffering man any further."

SECTION IV

Appendices

Appendix I

Arnold Schoenberg, "A Four-Point Program for Jewry" (October 1938)

I. THE FIGHT AGAINST ANTI-SEMITISM MUST BE STOPPED

Five hundred thousand Jews from Germany, 300,000 from Austria, 400,000 from Czechoslovakia, 500,000 from Hungary, 60,000 from Italy—more than 1,800,000 Jews will have to migrate in how short a time, one does not know. May God provide there will not be an additional 3,500,000 from Poland, 900,000 from Rumania, 240,000 from Lithuania and 100,000 from Latvia—almost 5,000,000; and Yugoslavia with 64,000, Bulgaria with 40,000, and Greece with 80,000 might follow at once, not to speak of other countries, which are at present less active.

Is there room in the world for almost 7,000,000 people?

Are they condemned to doom? Will they become extinct? Famished? Butchered?

Every keen and realistic observer should have known this beforehand, as I knew it almost twenty years ago. Even one who does not overrate Jewish intelligence in political affairs will admit that every Jew should have known at least that the fate of the Austrian and Hungarian Jews was sealed years ago. And can a man with foresight deny that the Jews of Rumania and Poland are in danger of a similar fate?

What have our Jewish leaders, our Jewish men with foresight, done to avert this disaster? What have they done to alleviate the sufferings of the people already stricken by this mishap? What have they done to find a place for the first 500,000 people who must migrate or die?

Let us forget that at the time when the waves of turmoil and pity went high, 1933, one could hear remarks of satisfaction about the punishment inflicted upon Western Jews. Let us forget that it was much due to selfishness that no efficient plans were laid. Let us judge what our leaders did, proposed, promoted; let us judge these only from the results they achieved.

They, the leaders, proclaimed the war on anti-Semitism and started a boycott; they proposed to transfer a certain percentage of the unfortunates; they promoted the emigration to Palestine. Every keen and realistic observer could have realized the inadequacy and danger of these actions.

In Paris, in 1933, I had arranged my personal affairs in such a manner that I could earn my living and settle down in one of the democratic countries. In the meantime I had contacted prominent Jewish people intending to move them to start the right action. Among them were many Americans whom I considered the most useful, because America was and is in many respects the promised land, especially in what concerns the hopes of Jewry. It was my desire to come to America and start here that movement which in my belief offers the only way out of our problems. Therefore, when suddenly I was offered a position, although it was neither financially nor artistically commensurate with my reputation, I accepted at once, sacrificed my European chances, and went over to do what I considered my duty as a Jew.

In Paris I had already fought this unfortunate idea of the boycott. In New York I talked to many prominent Jews against it and had always the satisfaction that my argument was never refuted. However, American Jewry was hypnotized by the boycott, and I found no opportunity to express my views in magazine or newspaper.

Let me quote what I said and wrote at that time, because it shows that my judgment was correct and it might help to add weight to what I am going to say today.

1. The interest of the liberals and democrats of all countries in the fight against Germany is at least as great as that of Jewry; but the interest of the internationalists, socialists, communists, Catholics, and protestants is certainly greater than ours. Why, therefore, should the Jews make this a Jewish boycott, when it could be an international boycott serving the interests of the liberals, democrats, socialists, communists, Catholics, and protestants. Why should the Jew offer himself as scapegoat; was he not often enough made scapegoat in similar affairs—without having participated?

2. Does not the example of Russia, during her revolution, prove the ineffectiveness of a boycott?

3. Accordingly, the boycott might damage Germany but will bring no advantage to the Jews. We have no interest in damage to Germany. Our only interest is to save the Jews. We have not to fight against anti-Semitism or nazism, but *for* something; for the existence of a Jewish nation.

4. I would have called the boycott a waste, but it was only a waste of time, not of money. And I suspected correctly that it was used only because it required no money, because it was the cheapest way to give the impression that something was being done.

Today it is unimportant whether or not my prediction was correct. But it is very important to state that the predictions of our leaders were wrong, entirely wrong. And it must be stated that persons who were guilty of such fatal error have lost the right to speak in the name of their people.

The boycott was a failure and the fight against anti-Semitism was and is another.

What makes us a nation is not so much our race, as our religion. That we are God's chosen people is a part of his religious belief that no Jew has yet abandoned. Accordingly, we belong together on account of our religion. Races have become extinct through wars, annihilation, biological processes; races have been absorbed by other peoples, have disappeared thus in a new, mixed race. This is a natural process from which we are excepted because we are chosen to survive, to endure through the centuries, to refute the laws of nature. This imposes upon us the duty of self-preservation. Larger minorities than ours among dominating people have been absorbed. Assimilation was never successful with us, and when many of us were ready to assimilate, persecution arose to preserve the nation, as if it were a tool of God to stimulate us when we were in danger of forgetting our inherited belief.

On the other hand, there is no conceivable reason why people should hate us. We know we are not as our enemies describe us. On the contrary, if it were for our qualities, we should be liked and admired. We are generous, good-natured, faithful, honest at least in the same degree as other people. In our minds is anchored the obligation to help the poor, which has been an especial part of our religious law for five thousand years. But we possess one quality which seems remarkable if not unique—whilst other peoples have been converted, it has been impossible to convert Israel. It is our devotion to an idea, to an ideal, and it springs from our deep devotion to our inherited faith. Once convinced by an ideal, the Jew is willing to suffer or die for it; trained in martyrdom, the Jew is a ready martyr on every mental front.

What Jews have achieved for the advantage of the peoples among which they lived asks for thankful recognition. Called to establish trade in different countries, they invariably succeeded in making those countries wealthy and sometimes world-dominating. They brought science, medicine, culture, music, and literature to barbarian countries; and let us not forget that the Bible in its legal and moral viewpoints is the backbone of the civilization of almost half the people of the world. It might be human that those whom we benefited should want to be rid of us as soon as we had given them all we had. But it seems it is not we who should be ashamed of that.

There is, however, a basic reason: the arrogant Jew. Many will admit they do not know why we were marked in this way. Considered a minor kind of human being, suppressed, outlawed, suspected, shown ill-will and hostility, we scarcely dared ask to be treated lawfully and avoided as much as possible the irritation of our enemies so as not to become exposed to their anger. How could it happen that men who even did not ask for equality could be called arrogant?

Nevertheless, the "arrogance" of Jews is the very cause of anti-Semitism. Only this term does not refer to the behavior or attitude of the single person but to the whole of us, to the entire Jewry. Every non-Jew believes, consciously or subconsciously, that in every Jew is alive the feeling that he is different from all other peoples by his belonging to God's elected people. This is what they antagonizingly call great presumption, and to that they react with contempt and hatred.

Thus, if Jewry is a religion, if our nationality is based on the belief that we are God's chosen people, anti-Semitism would seem inescapable and the fight against it nonsense. Try to fight against rain and snow, against lightning and blizzard, against hurricane and earthquake; try to fight against death and destiny.

This final conclusion must be convincing even to those unfortunate persons who have lost their religious faith, because it is proved by our history. Where is the country where we have not been persecuted, the century in which we have not been hated? Is it perhaps better to believe that we deserve contempt for the defects of character which are falsely ascribed to our race? Does not courage ask us to face the full truth and acknowledge that, enjoying the glory of God's favor, we must endure the consequences, suffer for this privilege as the genius must suffer. One must abandon false hopes. Anti-Semitism is natural and cannot be fought. Never has this fight achieved more than a mere postponement, a breathing pause, and the final outburst of anger was the stronger the longer it was kept latent.

Once the fiend has stormed, entered the fortress, and started to plunder, there is no chance of negotiation or offer to surrender. There remains either to abandon resistance in despair or to fight the fiend to the bitter end. The decision will not be sought any more in discussing right or wrong. His right is force; the other's wrong is weakness.

Fortunately the fiend has not yet laid hold on the whole fortress, though he possesses a considerable number of forts. Protesting anti-Semitism has been proved inadequate and futile. It has brought us rather close to doom.

It has lulled into sleep every manly attitude, every energetic and intelligent action. And it has hindered us in doing what intelligence and honor ask us to do. The fight against anti-Semitism is not only stupid, immoral, cowardly, undignified, but it is—and this makes it decisive—a waste, a fatal waste of energy. It gives rise to deceptive hopes and directs vital powers in false directions.

There is now no time for idealistic conversations, for sentimental speeches, no time to mention our merits, our goodwill, to dispute our defects; there is only time to take a different position and do what still might help.

But for this purpose, the fight against anti-Semitism must at once be stopped.

II. A UNITED JEWISH PARTY MUST BE CREATED

Does there exist one man who knows the number of parties into which Jews are divided? America has only three or four principal parties. In France they might be mixed, subdivided, and shaded off to amount to perhaps more than ten. But the Jewish body is divided in a very complex way. Primarily, the whole body is divided into three principal sections, hostile to each other, according to religion: orthodox, reformist, atheist; then each of these groups is broken according to sociopolitical principles into conservatives, liberals, socialists. Furthermore, the origin of the Jews, as Western, Eastern, or Oriental, again subdivides every group. And finally, each one of these geographic groups includes "nationalities" eager to preserve their respective peculiarities, proud of them, hostile toward all the others, and increasing the tendency to splinter into an almost unlimited number of "isms." This is bad enough, but in fact it is still worse. Jews are individualists. Educated during thousands of years by their teachers in exegesis of the secrets of the Bible, they are accustomed to finding individual resolutions of their problems. They are now applying the same individualism in the field of politics. Probably every Jew will apply his own way of thinking, a homemade theory, a personal attitude to every problem he faces.

Nothing could be more disastrous to a people than that.

The recent history of Jewry shows the effects. One will read, for example, the reports on the Zionist Central Council and find that a man in a leading position resigned because his ideas had failed of the necessary support. This seems inconceivable to me. How is it possible for a man who believes in his idea and in the necessity and usefulness of the organization in which he plays a leading role, how is it possible for him to abandon both? Because his vanity has been offended? If at a fire one group of the men who came to fight it thought that it should be fought from the right side and another group contended it could only be extinguished from the left side—what would one think of that group who left the other in the lurch, knowing that everyone would be necessary for the work? Is there not a moral duty to cooperate for the common purpose notwithstanding one's own viewpoint?

A body of heterogeneous concepts is indomitably inclined to refuse all things which do not conform to the idea of each man. The aversion of every single member to agreement makes it hopeless to find a majority for an idea but provides always majorities against it. When Theodore Herzl, recognizing his error, decided to abandon for a time the idea of Palestine and accepted the offer of England (Uganda as a Jewish colony), he was exposed to such tremendous opposition that the excitement and fear of failure of the whole enterprise probably caused his death. He displayed an excellent grasp of realistic policy in correcting an error instead of continuing with it. Thus, as after Herzl's death the Congress voted against the Uganda Project, one might even doubt whether they were for the Palestine Project, or merely against something, against a person, against a shade of the idea, against the behavior of a group or of a single person, or really against the whole of the Uganda Project. I assume it had become of secondary importance to the majority of the members, who perhaps were dominated only by their aim for opposition and infuriated by the "unreasonable" demand to vote in favor of an idea which was not exactly their own.

The consequences of such an attitude are shown by the later development. The friends and followers of Herzl, staying faithfully with his idea when outvoted by the majority, found no better way of administering the inheritance than to step out of the party and erect a new one. This is very honorable, but it is not practical politics.

On, of course, a lesser scale, I acted differently. I was a kind of dictator, 1920, in a musical society, erected by myself in my ideas and on the whole very successful. Suddenly there arose a strong opposition to my plans, instigated by some political extremists. Fruitlessly I tried to convince them; fruitlessly I showed that the idea would break down if they continued with their opposition, but fast arose the danger that they could gain a majority against my principles. I did not resign. On the contrary, I did something which under other circumstances could be called illegal: I dissolved the whole society, built a new one, accepted only such members who were in perfect agreement with my artistic principles, and excluded the entire opposition. There were some sentimentalists who considered it wrong, but it was the only healthful means of avoiding the encroachment of nonartistic principles upon artistic ones. Right or wrong—these principles were my country.

Had the followers and friends of Herzl possessed the power to act similarly, many disastrous steps might have been avoided. They should have remained within the party and within it continued the fight for their ideas; they should not have given up but should have tried to convince the outsiders. New members should have been acquired, the old ones conquered with all means until their majority were annihilated; with all means, had they only been fit to do the work: he who wants to work for his nation cannot be a sentimentalist but must be—if necessary—unscrupulous, faithful only to his goal. These honorable citizens who acted really like gentlemen, but not like statesmen, had no right to meddle with the affairs of a nation, to try to decide the fate of a people.

When I said that it was doubtful that the Congress wanted to vote for Palestine, I did not intend to make this really doubtful. To every Jew the idea of Palestine is self-evident, without any question, a matter of fact, which needs no special mention and is not dependent on voting. Every Jew feels, knows, and can never forget that Palestine is ours and that we have been deprived of it by mere force; that we will never consent to the claim of another nation on our promised land. This conviction dominates emotionally our political standpoints, but a statesman must suppress sentimentalities. When Herzl realized that at that time a "Judenstaat" could not be erected in Palestine, there should have been nothing to hinder his accepting and carrying out the Uganda Project.

How different would be today's Jewish situation were there now an independent state in Uganda, founded in about 1905, counting perhaps a population of five to ten million, able to provide homes for ten to twenty millions in addition, independent economically, perhaps also provided with a modern armament and even perhaps not without political and diplomatic influence. It might be that this state could not offer protection from the persecutions of anti-Semitic powers nor offer anything of value in negotiations. But certainly it could offer a land, a home, a place where refugees were safe. Do all of those men who voted against the Uganda Project realize what they did? Do they know that it was their damned individualism, their insane stubbornness, their fanciless dogmaticalness, their political shortsightedness, their arrogant incompetence in world and state affairs, their vanity, their pride, their thoughtlessness, levity, and frivolity, which has brought upon us this situation, which has made us powerless in the face of disaster? Do they know that their names should be registered in the history of our people as the names of those men on whom will be laid the blame for this enormous mishap?

I do not want to be cruel, and therefore I will admit that there were men among them who had great merits in other fields of the organization, men who had conviction, men who were prepared to suffer for their ideas, who were ready to sacrifice all their possessions and capacities for the final success of their ideal. I will admit that their error was not exclusively one of their own but one which was caused by circumstances beyond their control. Freedom of thought, action, and life had been given to Jewry through the victory of democracy. No wonder they believed in democracy, no wonder they applied democracy in their own realm, no wonder they watched with jealousy their right to decide what they believed to be their own affair, no wonder they believed in voting, in the better understanding of a majority, in the capacity of a majority to do not only what everybody wanted but what was the best for everybody, including opponents. They doubted the capacity of a single man or a small group who could not convince their opponents, though history had always shown that the great men, standing alone, persecuted, unsupported, eventually achieved victory and were proved right. This has a repulsing effect on the average Jewish intellectualist: an individualist, in spite of his professed democracy, he will never acknowledge it voluntarily.

The decision over the fate of a nation seems to be much too important a question to submit to a majority, even were the majority overwhelming. This decision in an organization like the Zionist Congress could well depend on a majority of one voice, the voice of one man who might have slept while the importance of the matter was being discussed. How would an army act if the commanding general were obliged to find a majority among his colonels, after they, on their part, had got the decision of the captains who depended on what the sergeants believed or what was agreed by the last private; should one attack on the left or on the right flank, or frontal, or should one attack at all or perhaps retreat. The majority might have found a correct decision, but in all probability it will have come too late. Speeches, explanations, discussions, controversy must precede the voting in every group; some might adjourn their vote and ask for more information and when finally the subordinates of the man in command can vote, they have no opportunity, because the enemy has already taken position and the army is in flight.

Did not this happen to the Zionist Congress? Have they not been voting since 1904 to resolve the problem of a Jewish state? Had Herzl alone at that time possessed the right to decide, Uganda would be ours, and we would now know where to place Jewish refugees. It has taken more than thirty years to make the leaders of the Jewry conscious of their mistake, and it is problematical whether even now they are conscious of it.

A United Jewish Party must be created and organized in such a manner that these evils may be avoided as far as human foresight can avail.

It should not be necessary to explain what this little word *united* means. It should be obvious to everybody. But one knows from experience that people find in every concept a left and a right side, a before and a behind, a when and an if, a but and an in spite of.

This unity does not mean a union of the different Jewish organizations in which the respective ideas of all these organizations will be represented. It does not mean that there will be elected a president, a number of vice presidents, a board of directors into which all the organizations delegate their representatives; there will not be appointed a number of prominent men of each country as honorary members or honorary presidents or honorary whatnots. There will not be more social affairs, dinners, receptions, meetings, to satisfy ambitions, vanities, and desires for publicity.

A United Party should be like an ideal matrimony: a man and a woman joined to the purpose of producing children of whom this man is the father and this woman is the mother. Everything which contradicts this only purpose must be avoided; no other inclination can be admitted, no other contact allowed. Everything which promotes this common purpose is duty, is moral, is law.

Accordingly, a United Party cannot possess an opposition; there can be no majority which does not include all the members; there can never be admitted one thought connected by inclination to the principles of other parties; every contact which may interfere with the unanimity of the United Party must be broken. It will be duty and moral of the members to do everything which promotes the unanimity of this party. With, of course, one exception: as no husband and no wife may do anything which is against the law, so, in every country, every member will have to avoid conflict with the laws of the respective countries. This limitation cannot hinder the unanimity of the party. It might sometimes limit its activities, and the fact that Jews, in case of war, in obedience and devotion to the laws of their countries, might have to kill each other, will not interfere with the principles of the party. Life and death of the individual are without influence on historic processes, and while a Jew within the party will be only a Jew and nothing else, as a citizen he will fulfill all duties to which the other citizens of his country are commanded.

The inclination of people to join this party who are followers of other ideas or who belong to political parties of contradictory principles, might not be very strong. Let them remain where they wish. The time will come when they feel and realize where they belong.

III. UNANIMITY IN JEWRY MUST BE ENFORCED WITH ALL MEANS

Unanimity is very seldom a thing in the life of a nation at which a people arrive voluntarily. Consider that there are men with a real conviction, men dominated by vanity and believing they alone know the right way, men burning with ambition to play a role, indifferent men who do not understand at all, men who are inconstant, fickle, wavering, and who can always be caught by the last idea to impress them, and you will agree that it is a miracle that unanimity occurs at all.

"Doubt is the beginning of philosophy," and, may I add, skepticism is its shabby, misshapen, vulgar little brother. Skepticism can kill everything: religion, science, art, ideas, facts, and even miracles. Skepticism is a subconsciously hidden hope in wonders—in which it does not believe; in facts, which it denies; in actions, which it belittles. Credulity is a close relative of optimism. But skepticism has done more harm to the world than optimism, which is also a killer, but one of another kind. "What will you do if that happens?" and you will be answered, "But it will not happen, because . . ." "But if it happens nevertheless?" Optimism pretends: "But it cannot happen!" and then it happens nevertheless, and optimism has deprived you of the opportunity of guarding in time against the worst. One might summarize thus: the skeptic is optimistically anticipating the failure of favorable matters while the optimist is skeptically anticipating the failure of unfavorable matters. Thus placed on a common formula, one sees that both live not on recognition but on anticipations. They are gamblers and would better decide their stand by dice than by reasoning.

Another obstacle to unity is the Jewish sort of intelligence: they are masters and champions of discussion. Never enter into discussion, because every Jew is superior to every other Jew, and will apply logic better than every other Jew, and he will win or at least the other will lose. At least, time will be lost. Victory does not seem to be the aim of the disputation, but, varying "l'art pour l'art" (art for art's sake) one could say, discussion for discussion's sake only.

Never enter into discussion!

One who fights for unanimity would be in danger of becoming bewitched with admiration of this mental power, or of becoming confused through the contradictory results of perfect logics, or of becoming sentimental over so much and sincere conviction. Yes, conviction; conviction is certainly the motivating force behind the bad habits of these skeptics, optimists, and debaters. The fighter for unanimity would best ignore them. But if contempt were an implement against them, one should consider its use.

If used ruthlessly, contempt might really serve as an efficient weapon, but it would fail to achieve the main purpose of unanimity, which is not to make every Jew a powerless yet resisting slave but an active and convinced fighter for the common purpose. Of course, every experienced businessman knows how to conquer resisting competitors. And recent history has also taught us how to produce, if not real and voluntary unity, at least something which has the same effect. It would not be unwise for us to learn from others, even if we did not agree with them and were hostile to their aims.

But the goal of Jewish unanimity is based on reconciliation. And, in addition, we must consider our mentality from a different angle. In spite of its antagonism to unanimity, one will understand that it is not by accident that we are thus constituted.

It is my belief that this astonishing mentality is a divine gift, destined to protect us, to enable us to outlast the diaspora with its persecutions and its dangers to personal life and to the existence of our people. Our religion bases its convincing power in a smaller degree on miracles but asks for mental penetration. Discussion of its concepts is not restricted to the priests but recommended for all men. Every learned man can be a rabbi if only his zeal, his studies, his apperception, and the dignity of his conduct mark him as a man who lives with God in the ideas of the faith. To read the Bible and to understand it was the foremost purpose of teaching in the "Schul," and one might doubt that even "Am Horez" (which means in Hebrew an ignorant person) signified an analphabet. This constant occupation with the word of God kept alive our religion: our national fundament. Every animal has a way to protect itself and its race. Its defense might be based on power, teeth, speed, poison, mimicry, fertility, etc. Among mankind, facing every kind of persecution, we Jews were deprived of the use of all such weapons. No wonder we developed the only tool of which we were not deprived: our intelligence. Overwhelming power makes the tiger a bloodthirsty killer who runs amuck without being hungry; the possession of poison makes snakes dangerous even to harmless creatures; the tremendous swiftness of the greyhound might have made the use of brain superfluous to it; and thus very often overdevelopment of one capacity can produce undesirable countereffects. It seems one could not call the overdevelopment of Jewish intelligence a defect were it not the cause of our disunion. But it was necessary; it was our only way to cope with the weapons of others; it was our only way to protect ourselves and our race. We had always to stand one against from ten to a hundred enemies, and it was of course not cowardice that made the one recognize that resistance is nonsense. Intelligence sometimes helped— if it could be applied. From this viewpoint it would be unjust and ungrateful to regard this divine gift with contempt, even if it were overdeveloped and in spite of its hindrance to unanimity. One must, on the contrary, respect it highly, and find out how to redirect it so as to promote the understanding of the necessity of unity.

No doubt, this will not be an easy task, and one will have to discover how it can be done. There is certainly even among Jews a certain percentage which can be won by persuasion. In spite of the natural tendency toward skepticism, the participation of a great number of Jews in diverse radical parties can be explained only on the basis of real idealism, conviction, and enthusiasm. These driving forces could be directed the right way. It should be possible to convince them that he who wants to reform the world should at first reform his own house. The same idealism, devotion, self-sacrificing spirit, courage, intelligence, force of will, and persistency applied to what is really our own matter as Jews must work wonders. And if it was possible to make a Jew a follower of those parties, it must also be possible to convert him to devotion to his own affairs. This begs also a discussion of so-called Jewish internationalism, a very confused concept. Suspicion is justified as to whether it is not intentionally ambiguous, because it can thus easily be applied to manifold political purposes. Fascism, which at the beginning was called "no article of exportation," is today an international movement, as a form of government and as an international defense against communism. National Socialism is today also not restricted to the nation which originated it. If one considers today's alliances, one will have difficulty in discovering principal differences between fascist aims for international alliances to conquer communism and communist aims for international alliances to conquer capitalism—and, recently added, fascism. But let us mention that "internationalism" is not exclusively ignominious. There are too many human activities based on internationality that are not ignominious: trade, navigation, aviation, mail, telegraphy, etc.; also peace-movements, the Red Cross, and, last but not least, the Catholic church. But the slogan "Jewish Internationalism" refers to socialism on the one hand and capitalism on the other. Neither is exclusively Jewish; each is opposed to the other; both are firstly national, and they are international only so far as their interests may require. There is no general Jewish interest in communism or in capitalism but only mutual international antipathy. Jewish internationalism should be for Jewish interests exclusively, and if it existed as such, the Jewish situation today would be quite different.

This is not the place to decide whether or not Jewish internationalism should degenerate into nonparticipation in the civic life of the respective nations among which we live. Nor could it be decided at this hour. That is a question of practical policies, and such problems are not decided by principles but by necessities. At first there is no indication that such an attitude is desirable. Concentration on affairs of our own does not ask for it, and it is mentioned because it might be considered a logical consequence of the principles developed here. For example, among the leaders of a United Jewish Party might be extreme conservatives and also extreme radicals, who at the same time might be important in their respective civic activities. The hostility between extreme rightists and leftists is so strong that they could not act impartially in the Jewish body. Such problems one must anticipate, and they must be resolved without sentimentality.

There will arise more problems, predictable and unpredictable. There will be difficulties constantly, difficulties in such number and of such measure that despair might reign among the members and the leaders, and it will very often appear as if everything were lost and as if the whole movement were to break down. And perhaps a temporary breakdown might occur; this will be a strong moral strain and heavy burden on the leaders and will cause dangerous discouragement among the members.

For all these reasons I think the party should avoid growing too fast. It must not be an overnight mass-party. This would be dangerous as long as there have not arisen numerous leaders, carefully selected, manifoldly tested, chosen not only for their intelligence (super-intelligence would endanger unanimity) but for their character, steadiness, faithfulness, directness, courage, and devotion. With some exaggeration one could say the party should at first consist of not much more than the future leaders. If they can preserve unanimity among themselves, they will succeed in unifying the members they have won. Anticipating the difficulty of producing incontestable unity among the leaders, one will agree that this is the first test to which these leaders must be submitted. Are they capable of unanimity among themselves? Then, and only then, will they be capable of enforcing unanimity among the members: one who cannot obey, cannot command—an ancient military axiom.

IV. WAYS MUST BE PREPARED TO OBTAIN A PLACE TO ERECT AN INDEPENDENT JEWISH STATE

If it was difficult to discuss the first three points of this program, it is much more difficult to treat this fourth point publicly. It asks for an almost unreasonable amount of tact and discretion, and if in the preceding many points could not be expressed directly, then here much more cannot be said—but only hinted at. One will begin to understand why diplomats use that peculiar sort of speech which sounds to the average citizen as he himself might have said it but which to the experienced connoisseur means something very different.

During more than three centuries after Columbus discovered America, it would have been somewhat easier to find a country for an independent Jewish state. Considering the expulsion of the Jews by the Spaniards and Portuguese, or a number of major and minor persecutions and expulsions in other countries, there was reason enough to try it—had there only existed a little intelligent political understanding. Why, if Puritans could find the means to migrate, could not Jews? It is a historical fact that at this time Jews were soldiers, some of high rank, seamen and adventurers of all kinds, merchants who rigged out ships bound for the East or West Indies. Jews were active in the East India Company and potent in the Hanseatic League and its enterprises; there were present all the conditions to invite venturesome people to participate when the earth was being shared. And there were also venturesome Jews: in England, in Holland, in the Hanseatic League, and elsewhere.

But for two thousand years Jews had been longing for their sacred promised land, for their old Jerusalem. And this unquenchable desire for Zion, this very pathetic idea, was decisive. It excluded every other idea, excluded any desire for an independent state other than in Palestine.

As our destiny differs from that of all other people, so does our feeling. Where is a second people who during two thousand years has not lost its desire for a native land, of which scarcely one out of a thousand knows much more than a few dry facts—some names and some photographs.

It would be a mistake to believe that it is only on account of our history that we feel this way. Of course, this land our forefathers conquered by the sword; there we developed our religious and social culture; there our heroes fought against overwhelming enemies and against paganism and its idols; there we were beaten by the one but won against the others; this is history, but it does not mean so much to us as the other inextinguishable fact; this is the land which our God has given us.

That this sentiment is stronger than our intelligence is a very regrettable circumstance. Save for it, there must have been a number of men throughout the diaspora who reflected thus: the Holy Land was promised to our people, but we did not get it for nothing. A people who insists on calling a land its own must take it with the same means with which it wants to keep it. Our forefathers had to remain for forty years in the desert in order to become strong. One must be strong to take what one wants and to protect what one has.

If one considers the political, geographic, and strategic position of Palestine, one will doubt whether ever the opportunity can arise which will allow us to take possession of it. The other religions to whom Zion has become a sacred place would not cease to dispute our right. And surrounded by Mohammedans, Palestine will be in the worst strategical situation. Only a ruler of the world like England could undertake to protect us, and even she will do it only so far as her interests allow and require it. Jewish leaders should understand that world politics is dominated largely by economic questions. If they have neglected to take this into account, here at least it shall be discussed: is it not evident that Palestine is desirable to the great powers for other than idealistic and religious reasons? Suppose Jewry did possess Palestine under the best possible conditions. Let us say, for example, that instead of building a Jewish university and a Jewish orchestra, we had built an army there of a hundred thousand men and were ready to spend our total funds for reinforcements; suppose we were strong enough to conquer the Arabs; suppose we were supported by treaties and had alliances with powerful nations. One must still understand that the relative independence of the Arabs under English protectorate is only admitted by England because the Arabs are not powerful. No first-rate power would allow a powerful nation to remain in possession of this country because it opens the way to India. We Jews did not lose this land because other people did not like us but only because other people liked our land—for their trade. Only a powerless nation can possess it, one which cannot deny others the right to cross through it.

To know history is one thing, and to understand it is another thing. But it seems that politicians neither know nor understand. And it seems that they become leaders only by "virtue" of a lack of understanding of historical processes. And one could almost believe that a man with a de facto insight into the driving forces of human activities could scarcely become a leader unless he were able to carefully hide his superiority.

I do not want to say this, but I must. All these facts and conclusions seem to me so self-evident, so simple, so clear, that I cannot understand how these pseudo-leaders could misinterpret them. But there is something else in it, and this seems almost an enigma to me. It appears that these leaders have even now not acknowledged the responsibility a man takes upon himself who interferes with the destiny of a people. There were a number of leaders of other parties in a number of nations who suddenly awoke to reality and had to face a very old idea: that the life of a man is at stake who mixes in politics; that only such men who are ready to die for their ideas should attempt to play a role in the fate of their people; that a leader cannot simply withdraw, in case of failure, but must suffer to the bitter end. They act often, however, like gamblers, who simply disappear instead of paying for their losses. They stay stubbornly with their idea, thinking they can leave the party, if they lose. Why did Brutus and Varus kill themselves when they had lost? Justice asks the life of a man whose fault it is that people suffer or die who trusted him—he cannot simply withdraw and become a private person.

Theodore Herzl died when the Uganda Project was rejected by the Zionist Congress: his heart committed harakiri. But those men who led Jewry into the useless boycott, into the useless fight against anti-Semitism, encouraged people to go to Palestine, who have started the meaningless fight against Italian fascism, who have only provoked Mussolini and given him good excuse for his anti-Jewish policies—have those men realized what they did to our people? Do they understand that they ought not further to open their mouths in Jewish affairs?

Do they realize that fascism or democracy, feudalism or communism, monarchism or republicanism are no questions of Jewry as such, of Jewry as a nation, but are merely different forms of government, matters of internal policy. Our attitude toward them must be subject to change in accordance with the question of our freedom. In one country fascism might be more favorable, democracy in another; in another state feudalism might offer better protection than communism. The fight for social or governmental theories should have no influence on Jewish national policies. Probably within a Jewish state the same contest between opposing political theories will occur.

Do all those leaders know how superficially they acted when they based their policies on the differences in internal affairs; on their like or dislike of monarchism, republicanism, feudalism, democracy, fascism, socialism, communism?

Will they start again their useless struggles with words, with speeches, with discussion, and waste the short space of time which is now left for action? They should not dare it; the time for words is over, and if action does not start at once, it may be too late.

There is only one way to save Jewry: to obtain a land to which the Jewish people can migrate. Whether this land will be given to us as a colony or as an independent state, under a protectorate or under any other conditions, will not matter. Whether we buy this land or get it free should not worry us. Whether this land offers good or bad climatic, geographical, or commercial conditions is also unimportant; one knows that present technic makes life possible anywhere: in the jungle, in the desert, or at the poles. It need only be a land. We must accommodate ourselves.

There is still land enough which is not inhabited by other peoples. And there are a number of states which need money. And as long as Jews possess money, they will be able to buy a land and perhaps even one which provides the best conditions for a modern state. Is it necessary to mention that one can buy everything on installments today? Such contracts are sometimes agreed over a period of "ninety-nine" years. But it seems that Jews could remove their debts in thirty or forty years. If there were loans, our commercial, industrial, and inventive capacities would certainly enable us to pay interests and amortize the capital.

Can there be a doubt that it will be of the greatest interest to world bankers to finance such a program once they recognize it is sound? Can there be a doubt that such a program is promising which plans to provide a country with all the necessities, facilities, machines, and raw materials for building roads and to create agriculture, industry, and all things which represent a state? Is there a doubt that it would produce a boom in all those countries which participated in business with the new state? Can there be a doubt that unemployment in those countries would disappear when they undertook to furnish all the things our state needs? How many ships will be needed to bring twelve to fifteen millions of men to the new country, and how many ships will be needed to transport the goods?

Might not such an enterprise perhaps solve, at least for a time, the problems of the present crisis in production and trade? Has one ever considered such an enterprise from the standpoint of the great business it is?

If the Jews would not undertake it, it seems that the great financial non-Jewish powers should interest themselves in it. There is only one question:

Will the Jews be able to repay the loans?

It seems not too daring to me to answer this question emphatically in the affirmative.

At present it is not wise to go into details. All depends on the readiness of Jewry to undertake decisive steps in this direction, and much depends on the willingness of non-Jews to resolve these problems in a humane, lawful, and dignified way.

But first:

1. The fight against anti-Semitism must be stopped.

2. A united Jewish party must be created.

3. Unanimity in Jewry must be enforced with all means.

4. Ways must be prepared to obtain a place to erect an independent Jewish state.

October 1938

Appendix II

*Thomas Mann Radio Address, "Listen,
Germans!" (1942)*

September 27, 1942

Listen, Germans!

One would really like to know what it is you think about in private concerning those who act for you in the world at large, such as what you think of the Jewish abomination in Europe, for example—how you feel about it as human beings—that is what one really would like to ask you. You continue to back Hitler's war, and you bear the worst, out of fear of what a defeat would bring you: the revenge of all the abused nations on everything that is German. But it is precisely from the Jews that such revenge ought not to be expected. They are the most defenseless people, those who have the greatest aversion to violence and rage of all your victims. Even today they are still not your enemies; you are only theirs. You can't manage to make hate reciprocal. Jews are almost always German-friendly, and should it come to the worst with you, as it most probably will—they especially, unemotional and wise in old age as they are, will advise against paying back in kind. They most likely will be your greatest friends and advocates. They have been deprived of power, of their rights, of their property, humiliated and beaten into the dust—isn't that enough? What kind of people are they, what monsters, who are never satiated with defilement, those for whom every misery heaped upon the Jews was always an incentive to push them into even greater and unrelenting misery? At first there was a glimmer of moderation and reason used in the treatment of this remnant from antiquity, which had intertwined with modern national life everywhere. Jews, it was said, were to be separated from their host nations, kept from official duties and influence, live as tolerated guests, but would be able to enjoy their own group and devote themselves to their own culture. All that is over. The lust for torture was not to be stopped at any level. By now we

268

have reached the point of annihilation, the maniacal decision to completely exterminate European Jewry. "It is our goal," said Goebbels in a radio speech, "to exterminate the Jews. Whether or not we win or are defeated, we must and will reach this goal. If the German army is forced to retreat, then along their way they will annihilate the remaining Jews from this earth."

No reasonable person can possibly understand the thought processes of such depraved minds. What for, one asks oneself? Why? What could one possibly gain by this? Would anyone have it better, after the Jews were annihilated? Has the deplorable liar perhaps talked himself into the fiction, that the war has been instigated by "World Jewry," that it is a Jewish war, and is being fought for and against Jews? Does he really believe that "World Jewry" will be so terrified, as to give up the war against the Nazis, should they discover that their downfall would mean the extinction of the last Jew in Europe? Gundolf's wayward pupil thinks that a defeat is realistically possible. But the Nazis will not go down to Hell alone; they will take the Jews with them. They can't be without Jews. It is a deeply felt fellowship of fate. I do believe that the retreating floods of German forces will have something other on their minds than pogroms. But until they are defeated, they are deadly serious about the extermination of the Jews. The Ghetto of Warsaw, where five hundred thousand Jews from Poland, Austria, Czechoslovakia, and Germany were jammed together in about two dozen miserable streets, is nothing more than a hunger, plague, and death pit from which the breath of corpses arises. In one year, last year, sixty-five thousand people died there. According to the information of the Polish Exile Government, all in all seven hundred thousand Jews have been either killed or tortured to death by the Gestapo, with seventy thousand of them alone hailing from the Region of Minsk. Do you Germans even know that? And what do you think about all this? Recently, in unoccupied France, three thousand six hundred Jews were removed from various concentration camps and transported to the East. Before the death train even began to move, three hundred people committed suicide. Only children five years of age and upwards were allowed to stay with their parents. The younger ones were left to their fate. In France this made for a lot of bad blood. And how is it with your blood, you Germans?

In Paris within a few days, sixteen thousand Jews were rounded up, loaded into cattle cars, and carted away. Where to? The train conductor knows that, the one they are talking about in Switzerland. He fled there because several times he had to drive trainloads of Jews, stop in the middle of nowhere, hermetically seal the boxcars, and then gas them. The man couldn't stand it any longer. But his experiences are not out of the ordinary. There is a precise and authentic report concerning the killing of no less than eleven thousand Polish Jews with poison gas. They had been brought to a special place of execution near Konin in the Warsaw district, placed in air-tight boxcars, and turned into corpses within a quarter of an hour. We have the detailed description of the whole procedure, the screams and prayers of the victims, and the good-natured laughter of the SS-Hottentots, who were in charge of the spree.—And then you Germans are surprised about all this, are even filled with indignation about the fact that the entire civilized world is worried about what methods of nurturing will result from those genera-tions of Germans whose brains were formed by National Socialism, a gen-eration utterly devoid of ideals, in other words, morally completely mis-guided, uncivilized killers, bereft of the ability to mold human beings.

Appendix III

*Thomas Mann, "The Fall of the
European Jews" (1943)*

Other races at the mercy of Nazi ruthlessness face humiliation, demoralization, reduction, emasculation, slavery. For the Jews it is plain extermination that has been decided upon, and this extermination has begun on a large scale. You all know the abominable course of these events. In the beginning, in Germany, the Jews were only to be excluded from the life of the nation, and to live as tolerated guests, but they were, as it was said, to be permitted to devote themselves without interference to their own culture and education. This is long past. The mania for torture did not stop at any grade. What kind of men are those, what kind of monsters who never tire of raping, to whom every misery that they inflicted upon the most peaceable, most unbrutal, and unviolent of their victims, was merely incitement to push them into still deeper, still more merciless misery? Now they have arrived at the maniacal resolution of the total extermination of the European Jewry. The number of those who have perished partly by direct massacre, partly by planned starvation ran into the millions even by the end of last year, and under constant intensification of the awful action, it has substantially increased since then. The highest number of victims is made up of Eastern Jews, a type of human being which the inventors of the German master race regard as vermin whereof to clean the earth they feel appointed. In reality, East European Jewry is a reservoir of latent cultural forces and the soil wherefrom an amazing amount of genius and talent has accrued to occidental art and science.

The Jewish race is known to excel in two special talents: the medical and the musical. Already in the Middle Ages the Jewish doctor aside from his Arabian colleagues was the most desired and trusted. According to my own experience, he is to this day the wisest, gentlest, most understanding, and most trustworthy—not to speak of the great Jewish scientists and discoveries in the field of medicine, benefactors of mankind such as Paul Ehrlich and August von Wassermann, whose blood-testing method has conquered the earth; and the great enlarger of the knowledge of the human soul, Sigmund Freud.—As far as music is concerned, it is just here among us in America that the prodigies of the concert hall are living, such artists as Menuhin, Horowitz, Heifetz, Milstein, Serkin, Rubinstein, Huberman, Schnabel, the conductors Walter and Koussevitzky, Ormandy, and Steinberg. They all have their genealogical roots in East European Jewry. If I am told: those are only reproductive accomplishments, only virtuosity, then I name creative representatives of modern music like Gustav Mahler and Arnold Schoenberg. It is a fact, after all, that the work of the hero of German national romanticism Richard Wagner, who may have a Jewish father himself,[1] disowns the influence of neither Meyerbeer nor Mendelssohn.

The greatest theoretical physicist of our epoch, Albert Einstein, stems from that human sphere which an abnormal lout thinks he must extirpate.

From Eastern Jewry came the famous British actor who has just recently fallen victim to the ruthless conduct of war of the Nazis, Leslie Howard. His original name was Steiner, and probably his parents were the first of the family to immigrate to England. But nobody could have been more English than this performer, whom I mention because he is an example for the peculiar phenomenon that national characteristics frequently find their truest, most convincing artistic manifestations when they pass through the medium of Jewish temperament.

Never could a spiritual, cultured, and European man in Germany be an anti-Semite. In Germany it was the Catholic church and the Jews who by their mere existence represented the Universalistic European principles against a narrow and anticultural nationalism. Also, it would be a total error to attribute to the great majority of the German people an antisemitism that would provide a popular basis for the Nazi crimes against the Jews. We have the testimony of an elderly Jewish professor who escaped a few months ago from Germany into Switzerland, that according to his observation 80 percent of the population reject the violence against the Jews and often go so far as to express their feelings in very demonstrative fashion. Many make their goodwill known by giving cigars and cigarettes to Jews, by presenting sweets to the children, by offering their seats in the tram and subway and in a hundred other manners. Furious admonitions in the newspapers indicated that the obligation to wear the Star of David had by no means accomplished its purpose of isolating Jews from the rest of the population. The professor relates that one day on a public square he had been approached by a total stranger who said to him: Do not lose courage! Things will change someday.

In view of this I have no doubt that if the Germans in their isolated country were permitted to know the truth about events such as the tragic perishing of the Jews in the Warsaw Ghetto and the preceding epic struggle, they would shudder before their rulers and before themselves.

Things will change, and Israel will survive, as it always has survived. But what it suffers today cries to Heaven, and we, who boast that we are fighting for humanity and human dignity against barbarism, must ask ourselves whether we at least do all in our power to allay this indescribable suffering which debases all of humanity, as long as we cannot prevent it. Perhaps it is too cheap to declare: one cannot do more than wage war against the Nazis. Only little can be done because much was neglected before the war while there were still great possibilities to act. We retain shameful memories of those bygone days. I only want to recall that phantom ship with Jewish refugees which sailed the seas in the year 1939 without finding a port of admission until finally the emigrants were received by Holland and Belgium, small countries both. The world in the inertia of its heart permitted Hitler to deride it. He challenged it: If you are so humane, why don't you accept the Jews? But you are not willing to do that anywhere. Why were the Jews not offered shelter, while there was still time, in those countries that had enough room and use for working hands, at least temporary shelter, without the obligation to keep them for good? In this connection small Switzerland deserves honorable mention because it has received many despite its lack of room and its precarious position; and it could have received many more if it could have served as a point of transit and if there had been the guarantee that the Jews would obtain another haven elsewhere. The possibilities of escape for the Jews in Europe would have been considerably greater in this case.

But even today it is not too late for this. The immigration laws of the great democracies are designed for normal times when there was a limited need for emigration from Europe, and they are not adapted to the monstrous conditions now prevailing here. It is not human, not democratic, and it means to show a moral Achilles heel to the fascist enemies of mankind if one clings with bureaucratic coldness to these laws under present circumstances, instead of proving by their timely modification that this war is indeed waged for humaneness and human dignity. Let us remember a word from Churchill to the effect that every friend of Hitler is by nature our enemy, a word that surely implies, at the same time, that every enemy of and every victim of Nazism is our natural friend and ally and fully entitled to our help.

May this hall, this meeting radiate waves of compassion, of indignation, and of our determination to help, which will reach perhaps and frighten the murderers of right and humanity, but above all may they move those who have the power and the means to alleviate the suffering of our time!

NOTE

1. Here Mann is referring to the suspicion that Richard Wagner's biological father may have been the actor and playwright Ludwig Geyer (1779–1821), whom Wagner's mother, Johanna, married in 1814, shortly after the death of her first husband Carl Friedrich Wagner, when Richard was an infant. Friedrich Nietzsche proposed that Geyer was Jewish, but there is no evidence to support the theory. See Friedrich Nietzsche, *The Case of Wagner, Nietzsche Contra Wagner and Selected Aphorisms,* trans. Anthony M. Ludovici (London: T. N. Foulis, 1911), 43. Schoenberg also believed that Geyer was Jewish and was the father of Wagner. See Geyer-Sohn und Geyer-Enkel, unpublished essay dated December 2, 1931 (Arnold Schönberg Center, Denk 203b, T05.28).

Appendix IV

Arnold Schoenberg, "Composition with Twelve Tones" (1941)

I

To understand the very nature of creation, one must acknowledge that there was no light before the Lord said: "Let there be Light." And since there was not yet light, the Lord's omniscience embraced a vision of it which only His omnipotence could call forth. We poor human beings, when we refer to one of the better minds among us as a creator, should never forget what a creator is in reality.

A creator has a vision of something which has not existed before this vision.

And a creator has the power to bring his vision to life, the power to realize it.

In fact, the concept of creator and creation should be formed in harmony with the Divine Model; inspiration and perfection, wish and fulfillment, will and accomplishment coincide spontaneously and simultaneously. In Divine Creation there were no details to be carried out later; "There was Light" at once and in its ultimate perfection.

Alas, human creators, if they be granted a vision, must travel the long path between vision and accomplishment; a hard road where, driven out of Paradise, even geniuses must reap their harvest in the sweat of their brows.

Alas, it is one thing to envision in a creative instant of inspiration, and it is another thing to materialize one's vision by painstakingly connecting details until they fuse into a kind of organism.

Alas, suppose it becomes an organism, a homunculus or a robot, and possesses some of the spontaneity of a vision; it remains yet another thing to organize this form so that it becomes a comprehensible message "to whom it may concern."

II

Form in the arts, and especially in music, aims primarily at comprehensibility. The relaxation which a satisfied listener experiences when he can follow an idea, its development, and the reasons for such development is closely related, psychologically speaking, to a feeling of beauty. Thus, artistic value demands comprehensibility, not only for intellectual, but also for emotional satisfaction. However, the creator's *idea* has to be presented, whatever the *mood* he is impelled to evoke.

Composition with twelve tones has no other aim than comprehensibility. In view of certain events in recent musical history, this might seem astonishing, for works written in this style have failed to gain understanding in spite of the new medium of organization. Thus, should one forget that contemporaries are not final judges, but are generally overruled by history, one might consider this method doomed. But, though it seems to increase the listener's difficulties, it compensates for this deficiency by penalizing the composer. For composing thus does not become easier, but rather ten times more difficult. Only the better-prepared composer can compose for the better-prepared music lover.

III

The method of composing with twelve tones grew out of a necessity.

In the last hundred years, the concept of harmony has changed tremendously through the development of chromaticism. The idea that one basic tone, the root, dominated the construction of chords and regulated their succession—the concept of *tonality*—had to develop first into the concept of *extended tonality*. Very soon it became doubtful whether such a root still remained the center to which every harmony and harmonic succession must be referred. Furthermore, it became doubtful whether a tonic appearing at the beginning, at the end, or at any other point really had a constructive meaning. Richard Wagner's harmony had promoted a change in the logic and constructive power of harmony. One of its consequences was the so-called *impressionistic* use of harmonies, especially practiced by Debussy. His harmonies, without constructive meaning, often served the coloristic purpose of expressing moods and pictures. Moods and pictures, though extramusical, thus became constructive elements, incorporated in the musical functions; they produced a sort of emotional comprehensibility. In this way tonality was already dethroned in practice, if not in theory. This alone would perhaps not have caused a radical change in compositional technique.

However, such a change became necessary when there occurred simultaneously a development which ended in what I call the *emancipation of the dissonance.*

The ear had gradually become acquainted with a great number of dissonances, and so had lost the fear of their "sense-interrupting" effect. One no longer expected preparations of Wagner's dissonances or resolutions of Strauss's discords; one was not disturbed by Debussy's nonfunctional harmonies, or by the harsh counterpoint of later composers. This state of affairs led to a freer use of dissonances comparable to classic composers' treatment of diminished seventh chords, which could precede and follow any other harmony, consonant or dissonant, as if there were no dissonance at all.

What distinguishes dissonances from consonances is not a greater or lesser degree of beauty, but a greater or lesser degree of *comprehensibility.* In my *Harmonielehre* I presented the theory that dissonant tones appear later among the overtones, for which reason the ear is less intimately acquainted with them. This phenomenon does not justify such sharply contradictory terms as *concord* and *discord.* Closer acquaintance with the more remote consonances—the dissonances, that is—gradually eliminated the difficulty of comprehension and finally admitted not only the emancipation of dominant and other seventh chords, diminished sevenths, and augmented triads, but also the emancipation of Wagner's, Strauss's, Mussorgsky's, Debussy's, Mahler's, Puccini's, and Reger's more remote dissonances.

The term *emancipation of the dissonance* refers to its comprehensibility, which is considered equivalent to the consonance's comprehensibility. A style based on this premise treats dissonances like consonances and renounces a tonal center. By avoiding the establishment of a key, modulation is excluded, since modulation means leaving an established tonality and establishing *another* tonality.

The first compositions in this new style were written by me around 1908 and, soon afterwards, by my pupils Anton von Webern and Alban Berg. From the very beginning such compositions differed from all preceding music, not only harmonically but also melodically, thematically, and motivally. But the foremost characteristics of these pieces *in statu nascendi* were their extreme expressiveness and their extraordinary brevity. At that time, neither I nor my pupils were conscious of the reasons for these features. Later I discovered that our sense of form was right when it forced us to counterbalance extreme emotionality with extraordinary shortness. Thus, subconsciously, consequences were drawn from an innovation which, like every innovation, destroys while it produces. New colorful harmony was offered; but much was lost.

Formerly the harmony had served not only as a source of beauty but, more important, as a means of distinguishing the features of the form. For instance, only a consonance was considered suitable for an ending. Establishing functions demanded different successions of harmonies than roving functions; a bridge, a transition, demanded other successions than a codetta; harmonic variation could be executed intelligently and logically only with due consideration of the fundamental meaning of the harmonies. Fulfillment of all these functions—comparable to the effect of punctuation in the construction of sentences, of subdivision into paragraphs, and of fusion into chapters—could scarcely be assured with chords whose constructive values had not as yet been explored. Hence, it seemed at first impossible to compose pieces of complicated organization or of great length.

A little later I discovered how to construct larger forms by following a text or a poem. The differences in size and shape of its parts and the change in character and mood were mirrored in the shape and size of the composition, in its dynamics and tempo, figuration and accentuation, instrumentation and orchestration. Thus the parts were differentiated as clearly as they had formerly been by the tonal and structural functions of harmony.

IV

Formerly, the use of the fundamental harmony had been theoretically regulated through recognition of the effects of root progressions. This practice had grown into a subconsciously functioning *sense of form*, which gave a real composer an almost somnambulistic sense of security in creating, with utmost precision, the most delicate distinctions of formal elements.

Whether one calls oneself conservative or revolutionary, whether one composes in a conventional or progressive manner, whether one tries to imitate old styles or is destined to express new ideas—whether one is a good composer or not—one must be convinced of the infallibility of one's own fantasy, and one must believe in one's own inspiration. Nevertheless, the desire for a conscious control of the new means and forms will arise in every artist's mind; and he will wish to know *consciously* the laws and rules which govern the forms which he has conceived "as in a dream." Strongly convincing as this dream may have been, the conviction that these new sounds obey the laws of nature and of our manner of thinking—the conviction that order, logic, comprehensibility, and form cannot be present without obedience to such laws—forces the composer along the road of exploration. He must find, if not laws or rules, at least ways to justify the dissonant character of these harmonies and their successions.

EXAMPLE 1

V

After many unsuccessful attempts during a period of approximately twelve years, I laid the foundations for a new procedure in musical construction which seemed fitted to replace those structural differentiations provided formerly by tonal harmonies.

I called this procedure *Method of Composing with Twelve Tones Which Are Related Only with One Another.*

This method consists primarily of the constant and exclusive use of a set of twelve different tones. This means, of course, that no tone is repeated within the series and that it uses all twelve tones of the chromatic scale, though in a different order. It is in no way identical with the chromatic scale.[1]

Example 1 shows that such a basic set (BS) consists of various intervals. It should never be called a scale, although it is invented to substitute for some of the unifying and formative advantages of scale and tonality. The scale is the source of many figurations, parts of melodies and melodies themselves, ascending and descending passages, and even broken chords. In approximately the same manner, the tones of the basic set produce similar elements. Of course, cadences produced by the distinction between principal and subsidiary harmonies will scarcely be derived from the basic set. But something different and more important is derived from it with a regularity comparable to the regularity and logic of the earlier harmony; the association of tones into harmonies and their successions is regulated (as will be shown later) by the order of these tones. The basic set functions in the manner of a motive. This explains why such a basic set has to be invented anew for every piece. It has to be the first creative thought. It does not make much difference whether or not the set appears in the composition at once like a theme or a melody, whether or not it is characterized as such by features of rhythm, phrasing, construction, character, etc.

Why such a set should consist of twelve different tones, why none of these tones should be repeated too soon, why, accordingly, only one set should be used in one composition—the answers to all these questions came to me gradually.[2]

Discussing such problems in my *Harmonielehre* (1911), I recommended the avoidance of octave doublings.[3] To double is to emphasize, and an emphasized tone could be interpreted as a root, or even as a tonic; the consequences of such an interpretation must be avoided. Even a slight reminiscence of the former tonal harmony would be disturbing, because it would create false expectations of consequences and continuations. The use of a tonic is deceiving if it is not based on *all* the relationships of tonality.

The use of more than one set was excluded because in every following set one or more tones would have been repeated too soon. Again there would arise the danger of interpreting the repeated tone as a tonic. Besides, the effect of unity would be lessened.

Justified already by historical development, the method of composing with twelve tones is also not without aesthetic and theoretical support. On the contrary, it is just this support which advances it from a mere technical device to the rank and importance of a scientific theory.

Music is not merely another kind of amusement, but a musical poet's, a musical thinker's representation of musical ideas; these musical ideas must correspond to the laws of human logic; they are a part of what man can apperceive, reason, and express. Proceeding from these assumptions, I arrived at the following conclusions:

The two-or-more-dimensional space in which musical ideas are presented is a unit. Though the elements of these ideas appear separate and independent to the eye and the ear, they reveal their true meaning only through their cooperation, even as no single word alone can express a thought without relation to other words. All that happens at any point of this musical space has more than a local effect. It functions not only in its own plane, but also in all other directions and planes, and is not without influence even at remote points. For instance, the effect of progressive rhythmical subdivision, through what I call "the tendency of the shortest notes" to multiply themselves, can be observed in every classic composition.

A musical idea, accordingly, though consisting of melody, rhythm, and harmony, is neither the one nor the other alone but all three together. The elements of a musical idea are partly incorporated in the horizontal plane as successive sounds and partly in the vertical plane as simultaneous sounds. The mutual relation of tones regulates the succession of intervals as well as their association into harmonies; the rhythm regulates the succession of tones as well as the succession of harmonies and organizes phrasing. And this explains why, as will be shown later, a basic set of twelve tones (BS) can be used in either dimension, as a whole or in parts.

The basic set is used in diverse mirror forms. The composers of the last century had not employed such mirror forms as much as the masters of contrapuntal times; at least, they seldom did so consciously. Nevertheless, there exist examples, of which I want to mention only one from Beethoven's last String Quartet, op. 135, in F major (Example 2).

The original form, *a*, "Muss es sein," appears in *b* inverted and in the major; *c* shows the retrograde form of this inversion, which, now reinverted in *d* and filled out with passing notes in *e*, results in the second phrase of the main theme.

Whether or not this device was used consciously by Beethoven does not matter at all. From my own experience I know that it can also be a subconsciously received gift from the Supreme Commander.

The two principal themes of my *Kammersymphonie* (Chamber Symphony) can be seen in Example 3 under *a* and *b*. After I had completed the work, I worried very much about the apparent absence of any relationship between the two themes. Directed only by my sense of form and the stream of ideas, I had not asked such questions while composing; but, as usual with me, doubts arose as soon as I had finished. They went so far that I had already raised the sword for the kill, taken the red pencil of the censor to cross out the theme *b*. Fortunately, I stood by my inspiration and ignored these mental tortures. About twenty years later, I saw the true relationship. It is of such a complicated nature that I doubt whether any composer would have cared deliberately to construct a theme in this way; but our subconscious does it involuntarily. In *c* the true principal tones of the theme are marked, and *d* shows that all the intervals ascend. Their correct inversion *e* produces the first phrase *f* of the theme *b*.

It should be mentioned that the last century considered such a procedure cerebral, and thus inconsistent with the dignity of genius. The very fact that there exist classical examples proves the foolishness of such an opinion. But the validity of this form of thinking is also demonstrated by the previously stated law of the unity of musical space, best formulated as follows: *the unity of musical space demands an absolute and unitary perception.* In this space, as in Swedenborg's heaven (described in Balzac's *Seraphita*), there is no absolute down, no right or left, forward or backward. Every musical configuration, every movement of tones has to be comprehended primarily as a mutual relation of sounds, of oscillatory vibrations, appearing at different places and times. To the imaginative and creative faculty, relations

EXAMPLE 2

Beethoven, String Quartet, Op. 135, 4th movement
Introduction

Muss es sein?

Es muss sein!   Es muss sein!

EXAMPLE 3

Kammersymphonie, Op. 9, E major

in the material sphere are as independent from directions or planes as material objects are, in their sphere, to our perceptive faculties. Just as our mind always recognizes, for instance, a knife, a bottle, or a watch, regardless of its position, and can reproduce it in the imagination in every possible position, even so a musical creator's mind can operate subconsciously with a row of tones, regardless of their direction, regardless of the way in which a mirror might show the mutual relations, which remain a given quality.

VI

The introduction of my method of composing with twelve tones does not facilitate composing; on the contrary, it makes it more difficult. Modernistically minded beginners often think they should try it before having acquired the necessary technical equipment. This is a great mistake. The restrictions imposed on a composer by the obligation to use only one set in a composition are so severe that they can only be overcome by an imagination which has survived a tremendous number of adventures. Nothing is given by this method; but much is taken away.

It has been mentioned that for every new composition a special set of twelve tones has to be invented. Sometimes a set will not fit every condition an experienced composer can foresee, especially in those ideal cases where the set appears at once in the form, character, and phrasing of a theme. Rectifications in the order of tones may then become necessary.

In the first works in which I employed this method, I was not yet convinced that the exclusive use of one set would not result in monotony. Would it allow the creation of a sufficient number of characteristically differentiated themes, phrases, motives, sentences, and other forms? At this time, I used complicated devices to assure variety. But soon I discovered that my fear was unfounded; I could even base a whole opera, *Moses and Aron*, solely on one set; and I found that, on the contrary, the more familiar I became with this set, the more easily I could draw themes from it. Thus, the truth of my first prediction had received splendid proof. One has to follow the basic set; but, nevertheless, one composes as freely as before.[4]

VII

It has been mentioned that the basic set is used in mirror forms.

From the basic set, three additional sets are automatically derived: (1) the inversion;[5] (2) the retrograde; and (3) the retrograde inversion. The employment of these mirror forms corresponds to the principle of *the absolute and unitary perception of musical space*. The set of Example 4 is taken from the Wind Quintet, op. 26, one of my first compositions in this style.

Later, especially in larger works, I changed my original idea, if necessary, to fit the following conditions: the inversion a fifth below of the first six tones, the antecedent, should not produce a repetition of one of these six tones, but should bring forth the hitherto unused six tones of the chromatic scale. Thus, the consequent of the basic set, the tones 7 to 12, comprises the tones of this inversion, but, of course, in a different order.

In Example 5 the inversion a fifth below does not yet fulfill this condition. Here the antecedent of the BS plus that of the INV_5 consists of only ten different tones, because C and B appear twice, while F and F♯ are missing.

VIII

In every composition preceding the method of composing with twelve tones, all the thematic and harmonic material is primarily derived from three

EXAMPLE 4

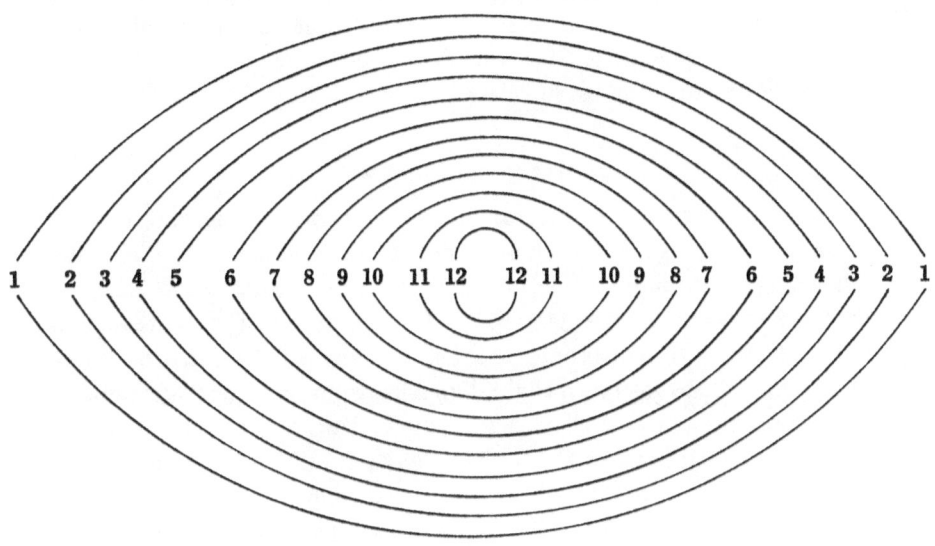

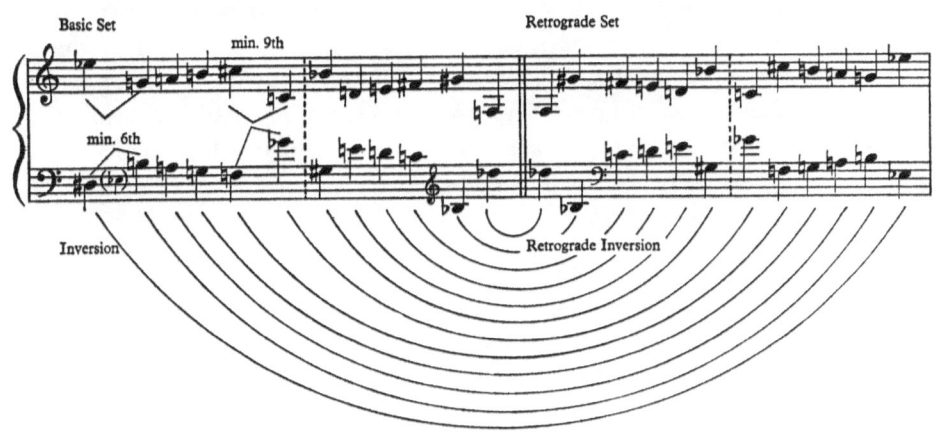

sources: the tonality; the *basic motive,* which in turn is a derivative of the tonality; and the rhythm, which is included in the basic motive. A composer's whole thinking was bound to remain in an intelligible manner around the central root. A composition which failed to obey these demands was considered "amateurish"; but a composition which adhered to it rigorously was never called "cerebral." On the contrary, the capacity to obey the principle instinctively was considered a natural condition of a talent.[6]

The time will come when the ability to draw thematic material from a basic set of twelve tones will be an unconditional prerequisite for obtaining admission into the composition class of a conservatory.

IX

The possibilities of evolving the formal elements of music—melodies, themes, phrases, motives, figures, and chords—out of a basic set are unlimited. In the following pages, a number of examples from my own works will be analyzed to reveal some of these possibilities. It will be observed that the succession of the tones according to their order in the set has always been strictly observed. One could perhaps tolerate a slight digression from this order (according to the same principle which allowed a remote variant in former styles) in the later part of a work, when the set had already become familiar to the ear.[7] However, one would not thus digress at the beginning of a piece.

The set is often divided into groups; for example, into two groups of six tones, or three groups of four, or four groups of three tones. This grouping serves primarily to provide a regularity in the distribution of the tones. The tones used in the melody are thereby separated from those to be used as accompaniment, as harmonies, or as chords and voices demanded by the nature of the instrumentation, by the instrument, or by the character and other circumstances of a piece. The distribution may be varied or developed according to circumstances, in a manner comparable to the changes of what I call the "Motive of the Accompaniment."

X

The unlimited abundance of possibilities obstructs the systematic presentation of illustrations; therefore, an arbitrary procedure must be used here.

In the simplest case, a part of a theme, or even the entire theme, consists simply of a rhythmization and phrasing of a basic set and its derivatives, the mirror forms: inversion, retrograde, and retrograde inversion. While a piece usually begins with the basic set itself, the mirror forms and other derivatives, such as the eleven transpositions of all the four basic forms, are applied only later; the transpositions especially, like the modulations in former styles, serve to build subordinate ideas.

Example 5 shows the basic set (with its inversions in the octave and fifth) of my Wind Quintet, op. 26. Many themes of this work simply use the order of one of the basic forms.

EXAMPLE 5

EXAMPLE 6

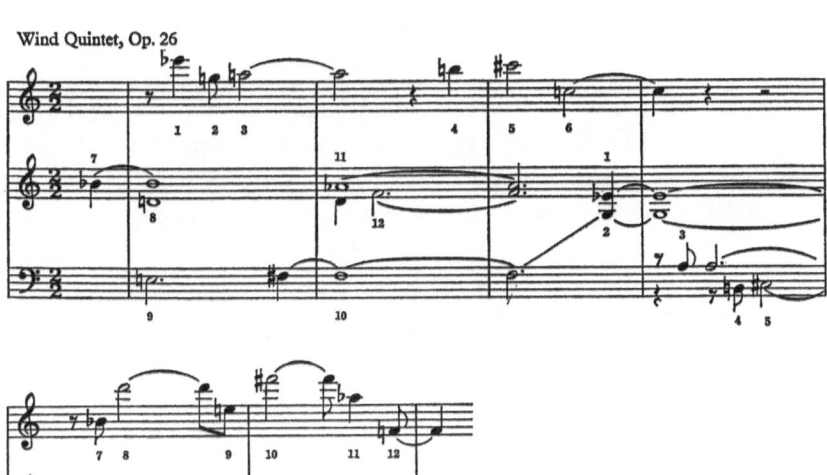

EXAMPLE 7

Wind Quintet, Rondo (4th movement)

The main theme of the first movement uses for its first phrase the first six tones, the antecedent; for its second phrase, the consequent of the Basic Set (BS). This example shows how an accompaniment can be built. As octave doubling should be avoided (see p. 280), the accompanying of tones 1–6 with tones 7–12, and vice versa, is one way to fulfill this requirement.

Example 7 proves that the same succession of tones can produce different themes, different characters.

Example 8, the principal theme of the rondo of this quintet, shows a new way of varying the repetitions of a theme. The production of such variants is not only necessary in larger forms, especially in rondos, but useful also in smaller structures. While rhythm and phrasing significantly preserve the character of the theme so that it can easily be recognized, the tones and intervals are changed through a different use of the BS and mirror forms. Mirror forms are used in the same way as the BS. But Example 9 shows a more complicated procedure.

At first a transposition of the retrograde is used three times in succession to build melody and accompaniment of this subordinate theme of the rondo from the same quintet. The principal voice, the bassoon, uses three tones in each of the four phrases; the accompaniment uses only six tones, so that the phrases and the sets overlap each other, producing a sufficient degree of variety. There is a definite regularity in the distribution of the

EXAMPLE 8

tones in this and the following example, Example 10, the andante from the same quintet.

Here also the form used, the BS, appears three times; here also, some of the tones appear in the principal voice (horn) while the others build a semi-contrapuntal melody in the bassoon.

EXAMPLE 9

Wind Quintet, Rondo (measures 117–124)

In the Scherzo of the same work (Example 11), the main theme starts with the fourth tone after the accompaniment has employed the preceding three forms of the BS. Here the accompaniment uses the same tones as the melody, but never at the same time.

In Example 12 inversion and retrograde inversion are combined into a contrapuntal unit, which is worked out in the manner of the elaboration of the rondo.

XI

Obviously, the requirement to use all the tones of the set is fulfilled whether they appear in the accompaniment or the melody. My first larger work in this style, the Piano Suite, op. 25 (Example 13), already takes advantage of this possibility, as will be shown in some of the following examples. But the apprehension about the doubling of octaves caused me to take a special precaution.

The BS as well as the inversion is transposed at the interval of a diminished fifth. This simple provision made it possible to use, in the Praeludium

EXAMPLE 10

Wind Quintet, Andante (3rd movement)

of this suite, the BS for the theme and the transposition for the accompaniment, without octave doubling (Example 13a).

But in the Gavotte (Example 14) and the Intermezzo (Example 14a) this problem is solved by the first procedure mentioned above: the separate selection of the tones for their respective formal function, melody or accompaniment. In both cases a group of the tones appears too soon—9–12 in the left hand comes before 5–8. This deviation from the order is an irregularity which can be justified in two ways. The first of these has been mentioned previously: as the Gavotte is the second movement, the set has already become familiar. The second justification is provided by the subdivision of the BS into three groups of four tones. No change occurs within any one of these groups; otherwise, they are treated like independent small sets. This treatment is supported by the presence of a diminished fifth, D♭-G, or G-D♭, as third and fourth tones in all forms of the set, and of another

EXAMPLE 11

Wind Quintet, Scherzo (2nd movement)

EXAMPLE 12

Wind Quintet, Scherzo (measures 88–94)

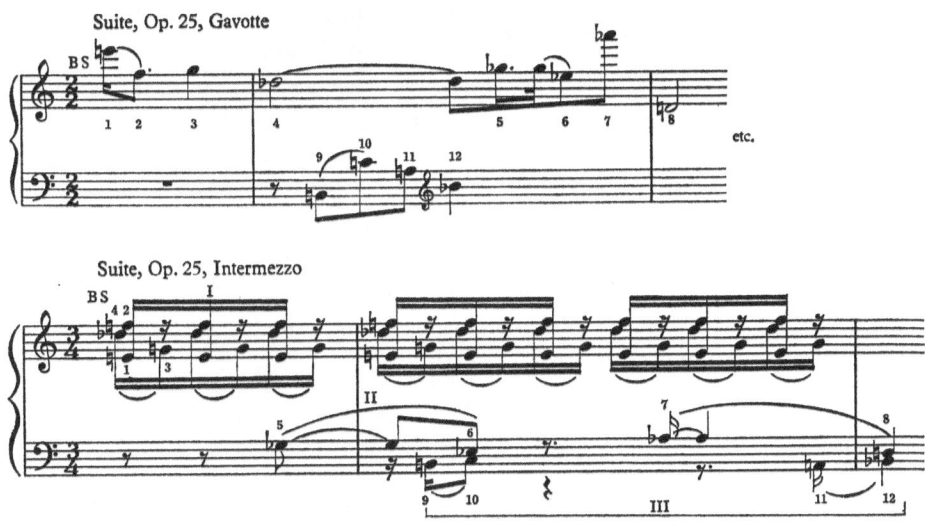

EXAMPLES 15 and 15a

diminished fifth as seventh and eighth tones. This similarity, functioning as a relationship, makes the groups interchangeable.

In the Menuet of the Piano Suite (Example 15) the melody begins with the fifth tone, while the accompaniment, much later, begins with the first tone. The Trio of this Menuet (Example 15a) is a canon in which the difference between the long and short notes helps to avoid octaves.

The possibility of such canons and imitations, and even fugues and fugatos, has been overestimated by analysts of this style. Of course, for a beginner it might be as difficult to avoid octave doubling here as it is difficult for poor composers to avoid parallel octaves in the "tonal" style. But while a "tonal" composer still has to lead his parts into consonances or catalogued dissonances, a composer with twelve independent tones apparently possesses the kind of freedom which many would characterize by saying: "everything is allowed." "Everything" has always been allowed to two kinds of artists: to masters on the one hand, and to ignoramuses on the other. However, the meaning of composing in imitative style here is not the same as it is in counterpoint. It is only one of the ways of adding a coherent accompaniment, or subordinate voices, to the main theme, whose character it thus helps to express more intensively.

XII

The set of my Variations for Orchestra, op. 31, is shown in Example 16.

A work for orchestra must necessarily be composed of more voices than one for a smaller combination. Of course, many composers can manage with a small number of voices by doubling them in many instruments or in octaves, by breaking and doubling the harmony in many ways—sometimes thereby obscuring the presence of a content, sometimes making its absence clear. It must be admitted that most orchestral combinations do not promote what the artist calls unmixed, unbroken colors. The childish preference of the primitive ear for colors has kept a number of imperfect instruments in the orchestra, because of their individuality. More mature minds resist the temptation to become intoxicated by colors and prefer to be coldly convinced by the transparency of clear-cut ideas.

Avoidance of doubling in octaves automatically precludes the use of broken harmonies which contribute so much to the pleasant noise that is today called "sonority." Since I was educated primarily by playing and writing chamber music, my style of orchestration had long ago turned to thinness and transparency, in spite of contemporary influences. To provide for the worst seems better wisdom than to hope for the best. Therefore, I declined to take a chance and, by making some slight changes, built the basic set so that its antecedent, starting a minor third below, inverted itself into the remaining six tones of the full chromatic scale.

Besides, I used in many places a device, derived from double counterpoint of the tenth and twelfth, which allows the addition of parallel thirds to every part involved. By transposing the BS a third up (BS3) and INV a third down (INV3), I obtained two more basic forms which allowed the addition of parallel thirds.

In the First Variation (Example 17) I used this device often, but not as often as I had expected. Very soon I recognized that my apprehension was unnecessary. Of the following examples, chosen at random to illustrate other peculiarities, none shows the addition of parallel thirds.

After an introduction successively revealing the tones of the BS and its INV3, the "Theme" of the Variations appears (Example 16a). Built as a ternary form, it uses the tones of the BS and its three derivatives in strict order, without any omission or addition.

The motive of the Fifth Variation (Example 18) is based on a transposition of the INV (INV8). Here are six independent parts built from only one set, comprising only the first two beats; the continuation carries on this system and finds ways to produce a satisfactory amount of variety.

The motive of the Sixth Variation (Example 19) is built from another transposition of the INV (INV6). It is composed of a contrapuntal combination of two melodic parts, using some tones of INV6 in the upper and others

EXAMPLES 16 and 16a

Variations, Op. 31

Variations, Op. 31, Theme

in the lower voice. This combination allows a great number of forms which furnish material for every demand of variation technique. New forms result through inversion of both voices (Example 20) and other changes of their mutual positions such as, for instance, canonic imitation (Example 20a).

One should never forget that what one learns in school about history is the truth only insofar as it does not interfere with the political, philosophical,

EXAMPLE 17

EXAMPLE 18

EXAMPLE 19

EXAMPLES 20 and 20a

moral, or other beliefs of those in whose interest the facts are told, colored, or arranged. The same holds true with the history of music, and he who guilelessly believes all he is told—whether he be layman or professional— is defenseless and has to "take it," to take it as they give it. Of course, we know their guesses are no better than ours.

But unfortunately our historians are not satisfied with rearranging the history of the past; they also want to fit the history of the present into their preconceived scheme. This forces them to describe the facts only as accurately as they see them, to judge them only as well as they understand them, to draw wrong conclusions from wrong premises, and to exhibit foggy visions of a future which exists only in their warped imaginations.

I am much less irritated than amused by the critical remark of one Dr. X, who says that I do not care for "sound."

"Sound," once a dignified quality of higher music, has deteriorated in significance since skillful workmen—orchestrators—have taken it in hand with the definite and undisguised intention of using it as a screen behind which the absence of ideas will not be noticeable. Formerly, sound had been the radiation of an intrinsic quality of ideas, powerful enough to penetrate the hull of the form. Nothing could radiate which was not light itself; and here only ideas are light.

Today, sound is seldom associated with idea. The superficially minded, not bothering with digesting the idea, notice especially the sound. "Brevity is essential to wit"; length, to most people, seems to be essential to sound. They observe it only if it lasts for a comparatively long time.

It is true that sound in my music changes with every turn of the idea—emotional, structural, or other. It is furthermore true that such changes occur in a more rapid succession than usual, and I admit that it is more difficult to perceive them simultaneously. The Seventh Variation (Example 21) offers just such obstacles to comprehension. But it is not true that the other kind of sonority is foreign to my music.

The rapid changes of the sonority in this Seventh Variation make it difficult for the listener to enjoy. The figure in the bassoon part continues for some time, while the instrumentation of the harmonies in eighth notes changes rapidly and continuously.

Examples 21–24 show that a great multitude of thematic characters can be derived from one set. Various methods are, of course, applied. It may be worthwhile to mention that in Example 25, as an homage to Bach, the notes B-flat, A, C, B, which spell, in German, BACH, were introduced as a contrapuntal addition to the principal thematic developments.

The main advantage of this method of composing with twelve tones is its unifying effect. In a very convincing way, I experienced the satisfaction of having been right about this when I once prepared the singers of my opera *Von Heute auf Morgen* for a performance. The technique, rhythm, and intonation of all these parts were tremendously difficult for them, though they all possessed absolute pitch. But suddenly one of the singers came and told me that since he had become familiar with the basic set, everything seemed easier for him. At short intervals all the other singers told me the same

EXAMPLE 21

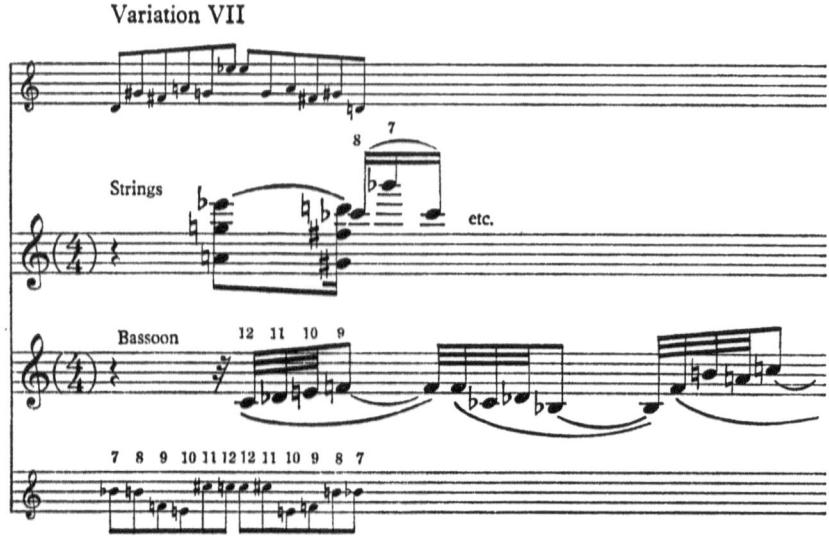

Variation VII

EXAMPLE 22

Variation VIII

EXAMPLE 23

Finale (measure 332)

EXAMPLE 24

Finale (measure 396)

EXAMPLE 25

Finale (measure 435)

thing independently. I was very pleased with this, and, thinking it over, I found even greater encouragement in the following hypothesis:

Prior to Richard Wagner, operas consisted almost exclusively of independent pieces, whose mutual relation did not seem to be a musical one. Personally, I refuse to believe that in the great masterworks pieces are connected only by the superficial coherence of the dramatic proceedings. Even if these pieces were merely "fillers" taken from earlier works of the same composer, something must have satisfied the master's sense of form and logic. We may not be able to discover it, but certainly it exists. In music there is no form without logic, no logic without unity.

I believe that when Richard Wagner introduced his *Leitmotiv*—for the same purpose as that for which I introduced my Basic Set—he may have said: "Let there be unity."[8]

NOTES

Schoenberg's lecture on his twelve-tone method was first given in English at Princeton University on March 6, 1934, and was later reworked for a lecture at the University of Southern California in 1936, for UCLA in 1941, and for the University of Chicago in 1946. It was finally published as "Composition of 12 Tones," in Arnold Schoenberg, *Style and Idea* (New York: Philosophical Library, 1950). See Claudio Spies, "Vortrag / 12 T K / Princeton," *Perspectives of New Music* 13, no. 1 (1974): 58–136. The present version is from Arnold Schoenberg, *Style and Idea*, ed. Leonard Stein (Berkeley: University of California Press, 1975), 214–44. Some additional sections from the 1934 version have been added in the notes.—Ed.

1. Curiously, and wrongly, most people speak of the "system" of the chromatic scale. Mine is no system, only a method, which means a modus of applying regularly a preconceived formula. A method can, but need not, be one of the consequences of a system. I am also not the inventor of the chromatic scale; somebody else must have occupied himself with this task long ego.

2. In the draft of his 1934 version of the lecture, Schoenberg wrote: "If the new method of composition with 12 tones was to fulfill *its purpose*, if it was to provide harmonic successions with legitimacy, then in the first place a substitute had to be found for the diatonic scale. For always the scale has been the source where everything in music took its origin, may it be in harmony or melody. The thought was near at hand to substitute the natural scale of seven tones by an artificial scale of 12 tones; and it followed automatically that this scale had to be *invented* just as a melody or as a motive, for each piece anew. This scale ought always to be in the first positive musical thought, just like a motive, for it ought to act in the same manner as a motive. It followed further by itself that the accentuation of a tonic was the best to avoid if, at least in the basing of 12 tones, no tone got an overweight. This means that this base set had to be composed of 12 different tones. It was clear that the invented motive, that invented set of 12 tones, was not always already from the first moment perfect, satisfying all the conditions asked by the above-mentioned. Very often rectifications were necessary, not otherwise than in former times that we know from Beethoven's sketchbooks and the hard work he often had to do on his themes."—Ed.

3. Still occurring in my first compositions in this style.

4. For his lecture in 1934 Schoenberg wrote: "Before speaking of the manner of employment of these 12-tone sets, I want to ask you again for one more favor: You know surely, as I know it, that my music has more adversaries than friends. But I maintain: this antagonism is not attributable to the displeasure caused by my musical ideas. No, not because these ideas appear ugly, or terrible, or not original, or false, or untrue. No, not because they express opinions or sentiments, which are not

allowed or [are] of inferior value in other regards—no—in truth no. All that is not the cause of this antagonism. For who needs to trouble with what I am saying, what I am expressing? Who takes an interest in my ideas? Besides a small circle: Nobody. And therefore the blame does not rest on my ideas; but only on my dissonances and on the so called 'atonality.' It would not occur to me to argue about the dissonances, since I know that in a hundred years everybody would be astonished to hear that they could have bothered anybody. But I have always argued against the term 'atonality,' and continue to argue against it today."—Ed.

5. BS means Basic Set; INV means inversion of the Basic Set; INV8, INV5, INV3, INV6 means inversion at the octave, fifth, minor third, or major sixth from the beginning tone.

6. There are scores of mathematical geniuses who can square and cube in their minds. There are scores of chess players who play blindfolded, and every chess player has to work out in his mind the possibilities of the next five moves. There must not be many who can exceed ten moves, but only to them should one compare the imaginative capacity of a real musical mind.

7. As for instance in the fourth of Diabelli's Variations, Beethoven omits, in an inexplicable manner, one measure.

8. [Editor's Note] Schoenberg ended his 1934 lecture:

I have hesitated for a long time to make known to the public the explanation of my method of composing with twelve tones that are related only to one another. I am frank to admit that it is in the first place for the reason that I have not yet come far enough theoretically to explain it all. But also another reason has had a certain inhibiting influence: I am called a constructor, and my music is called cerebral. It is easy enough to do that; first of all, because one is so little inclined, oneself, to be cerebral, or to show any aptitude for constructing neatly. But most particularly, because one does not know my music. For the kind of superficial stuff that one almost knows before a first hearing is something I prefer not to have written. Yet one has not heard many of my things even once, and one does not know my older works—or one forgets them on purpose—because one realizes that they prove that my cerebrality can still hold its own against the spontaneity of my opponents. But there is actually no reason for me to withhold such proof against myself from my enemies. Let them use it, in their truly uncerebral way, which will never be open to the reproach that it reveals them to be too strongly influenced by their brains.

However, I want to tell my friends something: I composed my 3rd String Quartet in a period of 6 weeks, and it has more than 1,100 measures. And there are as many measures in a one hour long one-act opera of mine on which I worked for hardly any longer time.

On the other hand, in the past season I wrote a Concerto for String Quartet and Orchestra based on a concerto grosso of Handel. It is very free transcription and in a number of places you will hear very little Handel in it, nor will you always recognize his style, although it is tonal throughout. I am quite sure that musical people of all persuasions will like it very much and will find that it is spontaneous and not cerebral and I myself am quite pleased with this piece of work. But whereas it took me only six weeks, respectively, for my 1,100-measure opera and for the quartet, I spent a good three months on the no more than 300 measures of this arrangement—in other words, twice as long. Do not conclude from this that I am inept; after all, I worked for only 6–7 weeks on *Transfigured Night*, op. 4.

But when you hear this piece next year, please remember that it is by a cerebral composer, by a constructor lacking in spontaneity. And then consider whether all that twaddle makes any sense and whether what those nitwits call construction can really manage to hinder someone who knows his business! If I write bad music, then I do so not because I am a constructor, but because in that case I am perhaps untalented.

Appendix V

Theodor W. Adorno, from Philosophy of New Music *(1949)*

The Idea of Twelve-Tone Technique

The reversal of the musical dynamic into a static-dynamic of the musical structure (and not the mere alternation of the level of intensity, which of course continues to involve crescendo and decrescendo) clarifies the peculiarly rigid systematic character that Schoenberg's composition acquired in its late phase. Variation, the instrument of compositional dynamism, becomes total, and is as a result annulled. The music no longer presents itself as being in a process of development. Thematic labor becomes merely part of the composer's preliminary labor. Variation as such no longer appears at all. Everything and nothing is variation; the process of variation is itself relegated to the material and preforms it before the composition properly begins. Schoenberg alludes to this when he calls the twelve-tone structure of his late works his own "private affair." The music becomes a result of the processes to which the material is subjected and which the music itself keeps from being unveiled. Accordingly, the music becomes static.[1] Twelve-tone technique is not to be understood as a "technique of composition," such as that of impressionism. All efforts to use it in this way result in absurdities. It is more to be compared to the arrangement of colors on the palette than to the painting of a picture. In truth the composition begins when the disposition of the tones is finished. This is why Schoenberg's procedure has indeed made composition more difficult, not easier. It demands that every piece—whether it be a single movement or an entire work of many movements—be derived from a *basic shape,* or *row.* By this is understood a specific arrangement of the twelve available tones of the tempered half-tone system, for instance, that of the first twelve-tone composition published by Schoenberg: C♯—A—B—G—A♭—F♯—B♭—D—E—E♭—C—F. Each tone of the entire composition is determined by this "row": There is no longer any "free" note. This means, however, that only in few, very elementary, instances—as occurred at the outset of the technique's use—is the row employed throughout the entire piece in precisely the same order and merely situated differently and rearranged rhythmically. Just such a method was developed independently of Schoenberg by the Austrian composer Josef Mattias Hauer, and the results are tediously meager.[2] By contrast, Schoenberg radically integrates the classical and, even more, the archaic techniques of variation into twelve-tone material. For the most part, he utilizes the rows in four transformations: as the basic row; as its inversion, that is to say, by replacing each interval of the row with the interval in the contrary direction (on the pattern of the "inverted fugue," as for example in the G-major Fugue from the first volume of the *Well-Tempered Clavier*); as its retrograde—or "crab"—in the manner of the ancient contrapuntal practice, so that the row begins with the last tone and concludes with the first; and as the retrograde of the inversion. These four modes can, for their part, be transposed starting with the twelve initial tones of the chromatic scale, so that for one composition the row can be disposed in forty-eight different modes. In addition, through the symmetrical grouping of certain tones, it is possible to build "derivations" that provide new, independent rows that are nevertheless related to the basic row. Berg made full use of this procedure in *Lulu*. Conversely, to make the relations of the tones denser, the rows can be divided into segments that are internally related to each other. Finally, a composition, instead of being based on a single row, can utilize two or more rows as initial material in analogy with the double and triple fugue, of which Schoenberg's Third String Quartet, opus 30, is an example. The row is by no means presented only horizontally, for it also appears vertically, and each tone of the composition, without exception, has significance in the row or in one of the row's derivatives. This guarantees the "indifference" of harmony and melody. In simple cases the row is distributed horizontally and vertically, and once the twelve tones are complete, each is repeated or replaced by one of its derivatives; in more complicated cases, the row itself is "contrapuntally" employed, that is, used simultaneously in diverse modes or transpositions. As a rule, in Schoenberg, compositions in the simpler style—such as the *Accompaniment to a Film Scene*—are also more simple than complex in regard to twelve-tone technique. Thus, the *Variations for Orchestra* are inexhaustible in their serial combinations also. In twelve-tone technique, pitch location on the register is "free":

Whether the A, the second note of the basic row of the waltz Five Pieces, no. 5, is a minor sixth above or a major third below the first tone, C♯, is decided according to the demands of the composition. In principle, the rhythmical figuration is also unrestricted, from the individual motif to the large form. The rules are not conceived arbitrarily. They are configurations of historical constraint in the material. They are at the same time schemata of adaptation to this constraint. In them, consciousness undertakes to purify music of the residues of a lapsed organicity. Cruelly, they combat musical semblance. But even the most daring twelve-tone manipulations are auscultations of the technical level of the material. This holds true not only for the integral principle of the variation of the whole but also for the microcosmic twelve-tone subject matter itself, the row. It rationalizes what is familiar to every conscientious composer: intolerance of any premature repetition of the same tone, its immediate repetition excepted. The contrapuntal prohibition on a double climax and a feeling of weakness in the harmonic phrase when the bass voice leading returns too swiftly to the same note confirm this experience. Its urgency intensifies, however, once the schema of tonality—which legitimated the preponderance of individual tones—is canceled. Whoever has dealt closely with free atonality knows the distracting power of a melodic or bass tone that occurs for a second time before all the other tones have preceded it. It threatens to suspend the melodic-harmonic tension. The static twelve-tone technique puts into practice the intolerance of the musical dynamic vis-à-vis the impotent return of the same. It makes the intolerance sacrosanct. The tone that recurs too soon, as well as the tone that is "free"—fortuitous vis-à-vis the whole—becomes taboo.

Musical Domination of Nature

A system of the domination of nature in music results. It answers to a longing arising out of the primordial age of the bourgeoisie: to seize all that sounds in a regulatory grasp and dissolve the magic of music in human reason. Thus Martin Luther names Josquin des Prez, who died in 1521, "the Master of Notes: They had to do as he wanted; the other masters had to want what the notes would do." Conscious disposal over the musical material is both the emancipation of the human being from the constraint of nature in music and the subordination of nature to human purposes. In Oswald Spengler's philosophy of history, at the end of the bourgeois era, the principle of domination inaugurated by the bourgeoisie breaks through uncloaked. Spengler, by an elective affinity, had a feeling for the violence of mastery and the nexus of the aesthetic and political right of disposal: "The means of the present are, and will be for many years, parliamentary elections and the press. One may think what one pleases about them, one may respect them or despise them, but one *must command them*. Bach and Mozart *commanded* the musical means of their times. This is the hallmark of mastery in any and every field, and statecraft is no exception." Spengler prognosticated that late occidental science "would bear all the lineaments of the great art of counterpoint," and he called the "infinitesimal music of the boundless world-space" a "profound longing" of occidental culture; twelve-tone technique—retrograde in itself and infinite in its ahistorical stasis—is closer to that ideal than Spengler, or indeed Schoenberg, would have allowed himself to consider.[3] At the same time, however, twelve-tone technique approaches the ideal of mastery as domination, whose boundlessness consists in the exclusion of whatever is heteronomous, of whatever is not integrated into the continuum of this technique. Boundlessness—infinity—is pure identity. But the domination of nature is consummated in the name of the repressive element of the domination of nature, the element that itself turns against subjective autonomy and freedom. The arithmetical play of twelve-tone technique and the constraint that it exercises is reminiscent of astrology, and it is no mere fad that many of its adepts fall prey to it.[4] As a system closed in itself and at the same time self-opaque, twelve-tone rationality—in which the constellation of means is immediately hypostatized as goal and law—verges on superstition. The legality in which it is executed is at the same time simply inflicted on the material that it determines without, however, this determination serving any meaning. Exactitude, as mathematical calculation, is substituted for what traditional art knew as *idea*, which in late romanticism itself unquestionably degenerated into ideology as the affirmation of a metaphysical substantiality through music's crude preoccupation with ultimate reality, without these ultimate realities being present in the pure form of the work. Schoenberg—whose music secretly admixes an element of that positivism that constitutes the essence of Stravinsky—has extirpated meaning as a consequence of making music available to depositional expression insofar as he insists, in the tradition of Viennese classicism, that meaning should reside exclusively in the nexus of the facture. The facture as such should be exact instead of meaningful. The question that twelve-tone composition poses to the composer is not how musical meaning can be organized but rather how organization can become meaningful. What Schoenberg has produced over the past twenty-five years are progressive attempts at an answer to this question. Ultimately, the intention is inserted—with the almost-fragmentary violence of allegory—into what is, to its innermost cell, empty. What is domineering in these late gestures, however, responds to what is tyrannical in the origin of the system itself. Twelve-tone exactitude, which banishes all meaning as if it were an illusion claiming to exist in itself in the musical object, treats music according to the schema of fate. But the domination of nature and fate are inseparable. The concept of fate may itself be modeled on the experience of domination, arising from the superiority of nature over mankind. What is, is stronger. In coming to grief on this, men have themselves learned to be stronger and to dominate nature, and in precisely this process fate has reproduced itself. It inevitably develops tit for tat—inevitably, because every step man takes is enjoined on him by the ancient superiority of nature. Fate is domination taken to the point of pure abstraction; the measure of destruction equals the degree of domination; fate is the calamity.

Reversal into Unfreedom

Music, in thrall to the historical dialectic, participates in this dialectic. Twelve-tone technique is truly its fate. It subjugates music by setting it free. The subject rules over the music by means of a rational system in order to succumb to this rational system itself. Just as in twelve-tone technique—in the composition proper—the productivity of the variation is forced back into the material, so it turns out for the freedom of the composer in general. Whereas this freedom is achieved in its disposal over the material, it becomes a determination of the material, a determination that confronts the subject as something alien and in turn subordinates the subject to its constraint. The composer's fantasy made the material entirely malleable to his own constructive will, but the constructive material hamstrings fantasy itself. All that is left of the expressionist subject is the subservience of Neue Sachlichkeit (New Objectivity) to technique. The subject disclaims its own spontaneity by projecting onto the historical subject matter the rational experiences that it had in its confrontation with it. The operations that broke the blind domination of the sonorous material become—through a system of rules—a blind second nature. To this the subject subordinates itself in search of protection and security, despairing of being able to fulfill the music on its own. Wagner's precept of establishing rules for oneself and then following them reveals its fateful aspect. No rule is more repressive than one that is self-promulgated. It is precisely its origin in subjectivity that becomes the contingency of arbitrary pronouncement as soon as the rule stands in the way of the subject, positively, as a regulative system. The violence that mass music inflicts on men lives on at its antipode, in music that withdraws from men. To be sure, among the rules of twelve-tone music, there is none that does not arise necessarily out of compositional experience, out of the progressive elucidation of the natural material of music. But this experience has a defensive character by virtue of its subjective sensibility: the sense that no tone is to recur before the music has exhausted all the others; that no note is to sound that does not fulfill its motivic function in the construction of the whole; that no harmony is to be employed that does not explicitly demonstrate itself. The truth of all these desiderata depends on their constant confrontation with the concrete form of the music to which they are applied. They indicate what must be guarded against, but not how to do so. Disaster ensues as soon as they are established as norms and are exempted from that confrontation. The content of the norm is identical with the content of spontaneous experience. By virtue of its objectification, however, it becomes nonsense. What once the attentive ear discovered is distorted into a trumped-up system in which the criteria of compositional right and wrong are to be abstractly verified. This explains the readiness of so many young musicians—specifically in the United States, where the sustaining experiences of twelve-tone technique are wanting—to write in the "twelve-tone system" and their elation at the invention of a surrogate for tonality, as if freedom were aesthetically intolerable and needed to be furtively replaced by a new compliancy. The total rationality of music is its total organization. Emancipated music would like to restore, through organization, a lost wholeness, the lost power and necessity of Beethoven. This is only successful at the price of its own freedom, and thus it fails. Beethoven reproduced the meaning of tonality out of subjective freedom itself. The new order, twelve-tone technique, virtually extinguishes the subject. What is great in the late Schoenberg was won as much in opposition to twelve-tone technique as through it. Through twelve-tone technique because through it, music becomes capable of comporting itself with the coldness and implacability that rightly befit it in the wake of ruin. In opposition to twelve-tone technique because the spirit that conceived it remains enough in command of itself ever and again to traverse the structure of its rods, pulleys, and gears and make them flash up as if wanting to destroy catastrophically the technical work of art. The miscarriage of technical artwork, however, is not simply a failure with regard to its aesthetic ideal; rather, it is a failure in the technique itself. The radicalism with which technical artwork destroys aesthetic semblance ultimately consigns technical artwork to semblance. Twelve-tone music has a *streamlined* aspect. In reality, the technique should serve goals that lie beyond its own nexus. Here, where such goals are lacking, technique becomes an end in itself and substitutes for the substantial unity of the artwork an exactitude of calculation. It is owing to this displacement of the center of gravity that the fetish character of mass music has also directly seized hold of advanced and "critical" musical production. In spite of a procedure that does justice to the material, there is no mistaking a distant affinity with those theatrical stagings that ceaselessly summon up machines, that indeed themselves approximate a machine that fulfills no function: It simply stands there, an allegory of the "technical age." All Neue Sachlichkeit secretly threatens to fall prey to what it so fiercely combats: the ornament. The streamlined club chairs of the interior design charlatans avow in the shop window what the loneliness of the constructivist painting and twelve-tone music long ago grasped—necessarily grasped. As the semblance of the artwork dies off, a process whose measure is the struggle against ornament, the situation of the artwork becomes altogether untenable. Anything that has no function in the artwork—and thus everything that exceeds the law of its mere existence—is debarred. The artwork's function, however, is precisely to exceed mere existence. Thus *summum ius* becomes *summa iniuria:* The consummate, functional artwork becomes a work consummately deprived of function. Since the artwork, indeed, cannot be reality, the elimination of its characteristic elements of semblance only throws all the more glaringly into relief the semblance character of its existence. The process is inevitable. The annulment of the artwork's characteristic elements of semblance is demanded by its own consistency. But the process of annulment, which the meaning of the whole demands, makes the whole meaningless. The integral artwork is the absolutely absurd artwork. Schoenberg and Stravinsky are commonly thought of as strictly opposed to each other. And in fact, Stravinsky's masks and Schoenberg's constructions have little in common. But one may well imagine that someday Stravinsky's alienated, mechanically assembled tonal chords and the sequence of twelve-tone sounds—whose concatenated strands have likewise been severed at the behest of the system—will in no way sound so different as they do today. On the contrary, they designate various levels of rigor in the same matter. They have in common, by virtue of their disposal over the atomized material, a claim to bindingness and necessity. In both, the aporia of a powerless subjectivity is apparent, and it bears the gestalt of an unratified yet imperious norm. In both, though certainly on entirely different levels of form and with unequal powers of realization, objectivity is subjectively established. In both, music threatens to congeal as space. In both, every musical detail is predetermined by the whole, and there is no longer any authentic reciprocation of the whole and the part. Their commanding disposition over the whole exorcises the spontaneity of the elements.

Twelve-Tone Melos *and Rhythm*

The failure of the technical artwork can be confirmed in all dimensions of its composition. By virtue of setting music free to undertake limitless domination over the natural material, the enslavement of music has become universal. This is confirmed in the first place by the definition of the basic row through the twelve tones of the chromatic scale. It is not clear why each such row must contain all twelve tones, exempting none, and why it must contain only these twelve without anyone of them reappearing. In fact, as Schoenberg was developing the row technique in *Serenade*, he worked with rows of fewer than twelve tones. There is a reason why later he employed twelve tones without exception. The limitation of the entire piece to the intervals of the basic row makes it expedient to dispose the row itself so comprehensively that the tonal space is constrained as little as possible, that the greatest possible number of combinations is feasible. Yet the fact that the row utilizes no more than twelve tones may well be attributable to the concern that none of the tones, through frequent repetition, be given a preponderance that could make it a "fundamental tone" and could conjure up tonal relations. Still, even if the tendency is toward the number twelve, its obligatoriness cannot be stringently derived. The hypostatization of the number is complicit in the difficulties in which twelve-tone technique bogs down. To be sure, the melody is indebted to this hypostatization for its extrication from the preponderance of the single tone and as well from the false natural constraint of the effect of the leading tone, the formulaic cadence. In the hegemony of the minor second and the intervals derived from it—the major seventh and the minor ninth—free atonality maintained the chromatic element and in it, implicitly, the element of dissonance. Henceforth, these intervals have no preeminence over the others, unless the composer wants to establish this preeminence retrospectively through the construction of the row. The melodic form itself acquires a legitimacy that it hardly possessed in traditional music and that it had to borrow through circumscription of harmony. Now the melody—presupposing that, as in most of Schoenberg's themes, it coincides with the row—crystallizes all the more perfectly the more it approaches the end of the row. With each new tone, the selection of the remaining tones becomes smaller, and when the last tone is reached, there is no longer any choice left. The constraint in this is unmistakable. It is exerted not only by calculation. The ear participates spontaneously in it. But the constraint is also crippling. The unity of the melody narrows it too tightly. Every twelve-tone theme, to hyperbolize, has something of the quality of a theme in a rondo, of a refrain. It is significant that in his twelve-tone compositions, Schoenberg so fondly cites, literally or in spirit, the ancient, nondynamic rondo form and utilizes an essentially related, intentionally harmless alla breve character. The melody is too complete; and although the inherently concluding power of the twelfth tone can be overcome through the verve of the rhythm, this is hardly possible through the gravitation of the intervals themselves. The commemoration of the traditional rondo functions as a stopgap to the immanent flux that has been severed. Schoenberg pointed out that the traditional theory of composition basically treats only beginnings and conclusions and never the logic of the continuation. Twelve-tone melody has the same shortcoming. Each of its continuations evinces an aspect of arbitrariness. To recognize the privation in which continuation finds itself, it is only necessary to compare—at the beginning of Schoenberg's Fourth String Quartet the continuation of the principal theme by means of its reversal (in measure 6, second violin) and its retrograde (in measure 10, first violin) with the exceedingly sharply delineated entrance of the first theme. The passage gives the impression that once completed, the twelve-tone row has—in its own terms—no impulse to continue and is driven forward only by manipulations external to it. The privation of the continuation is indeed all the greater as it is itself referred back to the initial row, which is itself as such exhausted and for the most part actually coincides with the theme built out of it only in its first appearance. As mere derivation, the continuation disavows the inescapable claim of twelve-tone music: that in all its elements it is equidistant from its midpoint. In the majority of existing twelve-tone compositions, the continuation is as inferior to the thesis of the basic row as, in late romantic music, the consequence is inferior to the thematic idea.[5] Meanwhile, the constraint of serialism perpetrates a far worse misfortune. Mechanical patterns afflict the *melos*.[6] The true quality of a melody is always to be measured by whether or not it succeeds in transcribing the effectively spatial relations of the intervals into time. Twelve-tone technique fundamentally destroys this relation. Time and interval diverge. All the intervallic relations are once and for all fixed by the basic row and its derivatives. There is nothing new in the progression of the intervals, and the omnipresence of the rows makes the row itself unfit for the production of temporal coherence. For this coherence is constituted only through what is differentiated and not through mere identity. Consequently, the melodic coherence becomes dependent on extramelodic means: a rhythmics that has acquired a life of its own. The row is unspecific by its own omnipresence. Thus, melodic specification accrues to abiding and characteristic rhythmical shapes. Distinct, consistently recurring rhythmical configurations take on the role of themes.[7] Since, however, the melodic space of these rhythmical themes is defined in each case by the row and since these rhythmical themes must at all costs make do with the available tones, they themselves necessarily adopt an obstinate rigidity. *Melos* finally falls victim to the thematic rhythm. The thematic and motivic rhythms return ceaselessly, with indifference to the actual content of the rows. Thus, in the rondos, it is Schoenberg's practice, at each rondo entrance, to introduce in the thematic rhythm another melodic form of the row and thus produce effects akin to those of a variation. The result, however, is rhythm, and that only, regardless of whether the emphatic and overly conspicuous rhythm subsumes this or that interval. All that can, in any case, be perceived is that here the intervals have a different relation to the thematic rhythm than they had in their first appearance; but it is no longer possible to overhear any meaning in the melodic modification. Hence, what is specifically melodic is voided by the rhythm. In traditional music, even a minimal intervallic modulation could be decisive not only for the expression of a phrase but also for the meaningfulness of the form of an entire composition. In twelve-tone music, by contrast, utter coarsening and impoverishment have intervened. Formerly, the intervals were the unequivocal site of musical meaning: of the not yet, the now, and the after; of the promised, the fulfilled, and the neglected; of moderation and dissipation; of abiding in the form and transcendence of musical subjectivity. Now the intervals have become mere building blocks, and all the experiences accumulated in their differences appear lost. Certainly, ways have been found to escape step progression with seconds and in the symmetry of musical consonances; and, certainly, equal rights have been granted the tritone, the major seventh, and in fact all the intervals that extend beyond the octave, but at the cost of their being leveled to the conventional intervals. In traditional music it was difficult for the tonally restricted ear to integrate extreme intervals. Today, these difficulties are gone, but the newly conquered now shares in the monotony of the accustomed intervals. The melodic detail sinks powerlessly to a mere consequence of the total construction, powerless over it in any regard. It becomes an image of that kind of technical progress that pervades the world. And even that which still somehow thrives melodically—ever and again Schoenberg's power makes possible the impossible—is destroyed by the violence that is inflicted on the past melody when, the next time its rhythm occurs, other intervals are relentlessly substituted for those of the initial melody, intervals that frequently lack not only a relation to the original intervals but even to the rhythm itself. What is most alarming here is a certain sort of melodic half-reckoning: Although it guards the contours of the old melody, that is, although it, for instance, makes a large or small intervallic leap occur at a rhythmical spot analogous to the location of a similar leap in the first instance, it does so only with regard to categories such as large and small; it does not matter in the slightest whether the characteristic leap is a major ninth or a tenth. In Schoenberg's middle period such issues would have been as good as meaningless because at that stage all repetition was excluded. The restoration of repetition, however, is of a piece with disregard to what is repeated. Even here, however, twelve-tone technique is not the rationalistic origin of disaster but, on the contrary, the executor of a tendency that stems from romanticism. The manner in which Wagner treats motifs whose aspect inherently contradicts the procedure of variation casts the die of Schoenberg's procedure. It leads to the definitive technical antagonism of post-Beethovian music: that between a predetermined tonality—ever awaiting its reconfirmation—and the substantiality of the detail. Whereas Beethoven developed the musical entity out of nothingness in order to be able to determine it entirely as what becomes, the late Schoenberg demolishes it as what already became.

NOTES

We reproduce here only a portion of the larger essay "Schoenberg and Progress" from Theodor W. Adorno, *Philosophy of New Music,* trans. and ed. Robert Hullot-Kentor (Minneapolis: University of Minnesota Press, 2006), 50–61.—Ed.

1. Even in the tendency to hide the labor involved, Schoenberg thinks through a fundamental impulse of the whole of bourgeois music. [Cf. T.W. Adorno, *In Search of Wagner,* trans. Rodney Livingstone (London: New Left Books, 1981), 85.]

2. It is hardly an accident that mathematical techniques in music originated in Vienna, as did logical positivism. The taste for number games is as characteristic of Viennese intelligence as is playing chess in cafes. The reasons for this are social. While the intellectual forces of production in Austria developed to the advanced state of high-capitalist technique, the material forces of production were left behind. Precisely for this reason, however, manipulative calculation became the dream ideal of Viennese intellectuals. A person who wanted to participate in material production was obliged to seek a position in Germany. If he stayed home, he became a doctor or a lawyer or devoted himself to number games as a fantasy of financial power. The Viennese intellectual wants to prove this to himself and to others—*bitte schön!*

3. One of the most striking characteristics of Schoenberg's late style is that he no longer countenances conclusions. In any case, ever since the dissolution of tonality, formulaic harmonic cadences no longer exist. Now they are also eliminated rhythmically. Ever more frequently, the end of the composition falls on the weak beat of the measure and has the quality of being an interruption.

4. Music is the enemy of fate. Since earliest times, the force of protest against mythology has been attributed to music, no less in the image of Orpheus than in the Chinese doctrine of music. Only since Wagner has music imitated fate. Like a gambler, the twelve-tone composer must wait and see what number turns up and rejoice when it is one that grants musical meaning. Berg spoke explicitly of his hap-

piness when the rows accidentally produced tonal nexus. As the ludic dimension expands, twelve-tone technique once again communicates with mass music. Schoenberg's first twelve-tone dances are ludic in kind, and during the period when the new technique was being discovered, Berg took offense at this. Benjamin insisted on the distinction between semblance and play and signaled the withering of semblance. Semblance, the superfluous, is also discarded by twelve-tone technique. But the mythology that in play was expelled as semblance is more than ever reproduced along with the series.

5. The reason for this is the incompatibility of the melodic plasticity of the song, which the romantics sought as the seal of subjectivity, with the "classical" Beethovian idea of integral form. In Brahms, who anticipates Schoenberg in all questions of construction that go beyond the harmonic material, the rupture between the theme and the consequences is tangible as what will later turn out to be the discrepancy between the exposition of the row and its immediate continuation. A manifest example is, for instance, the beginning of the String Quartet in F Major. The concept of a "thematic idea" was invented in order to divide the theme as φύσει from the consequence, δέσει. The "thematic idea" is not a psychological category, something of "inspiration"; rather, it is an element of the dialectical process that occurs in the musical form. It marks the irreducibly subjective element in this process and—in such indissolubility—the aspect of music as being, while the "thematic elaboration" represents the becoming and the objectivity that clearly contains this subjective element in itself as a driving force, just as inversely the subjective element has objectivity as being. Music since romanticism has consisted in the conflict and synthesis of these moments. It appears, however, that they resist this unification, just as the bourgeois concept of the individual stands in perennial opposition to the totality of the social process. The inconsistency between the theme and its modifications is the image of such social irreconcilability. Yet the composition must hold firmly to the "thematic idea" if it does not want to annul the subjective element and make itself the image of fatal integration. If Beethoven's genius magnificently renounced the "thematic idea," which in his own age had been incomparably developed by the composers of early romanticism, conversely, Schonberg held forcefully to the thematic idea and its plasticity at the point where it had long been incompatible with the formal construction and undertook the formal construction by carrying the contradiction to the extreme instead of by way of a tasteful reconciliation.

6. In no way is this attributable to a slackening of individual compositional power; rather, it is owing to the heavy burden of the new procedure. When the mature Schoenberg worked with earlier, freer material—as in the Second Chamber Symphony—his spontaneity and melodic impulse were in no way inferior to the most inspired works of his youth. On the other hand, however, the stubborn insisting in many twelve-tone compositions, as demonstrated by the magnificent first movement of the Third String Quartet, is also not an accidental addition to Schoenberg's musical essence. This obstinacy is, on the contrary, the mirror image of imperturbable musical rigor, just as it is impossible to think away the neurotic weaknesses of anxiety from his power of emancipation. Above all, the repetitions of tones, which in twelve-tone music often have something obstinate and stubborn about them, occur in rudimentary form much earlier in Schoenberg, certainly for the most part with particular, characterizing intention, as in "Vulgarity" in *Pierrot Lunaire*. Even the first movement of *Serenade*, which is not twelve-tone, shows traces of this inflection, itself sometimes reminiscent of the musical idiom of Beckmesser [in Wagner's *Meistersinger*]. Sometimes Schoenberg's music seems to speak as if it wanted to justify itself at any price in front of an imaginary courtroom.

Berg consciously avoided this gesticulation and thus, of course, against his own will contributed to the flattening out and leveling.

7. Even prior to Schoenberg's invention of the twelve-tone technique, the technique of variation had already pressed in this direction in Berg's work. The tavern scene in act 3 of *Wozzeck* is the first instance of a melodically abstract rhythm becoming thematic. It serves a drastically theatrical intention. In *Lulu* this is made into a large form, which Berg calls "*monoritmica.*"

Appendix VI

Thomas Mann, Chapter 22 of Doctor Faustus *(1947)*

When Leverkühn left Leipzig, in September 1910, at a time when I had already begun to teach in the gymnasium at Kaisersaschern, he first went home to Buchel to attend his sister's wedding, which took place at that time and to which I and my parents were invited. Ursula, now twenty years old, was marrying the optician Johannes Schneidewein of Langensalza, an excellent man whose acquaintance she had made while visiting a friend in the charming little Salza town near Erfurt. Schneidewein, ten or twelve years older than his bride, was a Swiss by birth, of Bernese peasant stock. His trade, lens-grinding, he had learned at home, but he had somehow drifted into Germany and there opened a shop with eye-glasses and optical goods of all sorts, which he conducted with success. He had very good looks and had kept his Swiss manner of speech, pleasant to the ear, deliberate, formal, interspersed with survivals of old-German expressions oddly solemn to hear. Ursel Leverkühn had already begun to take them on. She too, though no beauty, was an attractive creature, resembling her father in looks, in manner more like her mother, brown-eyed, slim, and naturally friendly. The two made a pair on whom the eye rested with approval. In the years between 1911 and 1923 they had four children born to them: Rosa, Ezekiel, Raimund, and Nepomuk, pretty creatures all of them, and Nepomuk, the youngest, was an angel. But of that later, only quite at the end of my story.

The wedding party was not large: the Oberweiler clergyman, the schoolmaster, the justice of the peace, with their wives; from Kaisersaschern besides us, Zeitblom's only Uncle, Nikolaus; relatives of Frau Leverkühn from Apolda; a married pair, friend of the Leverkühns, with their daughter, from Weissenfels; brother George, the farmer, and the dairy manageress Frau Luder—that was all. Wendell Kretschmar sent a telegram with good wishes from Lübeck, which arrived during the midday meal at the house in

Buchel. It was not an evening party. It had assembled betimes in the morning; after the ceremony in the village church we gathered round a capital
meal in the dining-room of the bride's home, bright with copper cooking-
vessels. Soon afterwards the newly wedded pair drove off with old Thomas
to the station at Weissenfels, to begin the journey to Dresden; the wedding
guests still sat awhile over Frau Luder's good fruit liqueurs.

Adrian and I took a walk that afternoon to the Cow Trough and up
Mount Zion. We needed to talk over the text of *Love's Labour's Lost,* which
I had undertaken and about which we had already had much discussion and
correspondence. I had been able to send him from Athens and Syracuse the
scenario and parts of the German versification, in which I based myself on
Tieck and Hertzberg and occasionally, when condensation was necessary,
added something of my own in as adequate a style as possible. I was determined at least to put before him a German version of the libretto, although
he still stuck to his project of composing the opera in English.

He was visibly glad to get away from the wedding party and out of
doors. The cloud over his eyes showed that he was suffering from headache.
It had been odd, in church and at the table, to see the same sign in his father
too. That this nervous complaint set in precisely on festal occasions, under
the influence of emotion and excitement, is understandable. It was so with
the elder man. In the son's case the psychical ground was rather that he had
taken part only of necessity and with reluctance in this sacrificial feast of a
maidenhead, in which, moreover, his own sister was concerned. At least he
clothed his discomfort in words which recognized the simplicity, good taste,
and informality of our affair, the absence of "customs and curtsyings" as he
put it. He applauded the fact that it had all taken place in broad daylight, the
wedding sermon had been short and simple, and at table there had been no
offensive speeches—or rather, to avoid offense, no speeches at all. If the
veil, the white shroud of virginity, the satin grave-shoes had been left
out as well, it would have been still better. He spoke particularly of the
favorable impression that Ursel's betrothed, now her husband, had made
upon him.

"Good eyes," he said. "Good stock, a sound, clean, honest man. He could
court her, look at her to desire her, covet her as a Christian wife, as we
theologians say with justified pride at swindling the Devil out of the carnal
concomitant and making a sacrament of it, the sacrament of Christian marriage. Very droll, really, this turning the natural and sinful into the sacrosanct just by putting in the word *Christian*—by which it is not fundamentally altered. But one has to admit that the domestication of sex, which is
evil by nature, into Christian marriage was a clever makeshift."

"I do not like," I replied, "to have you make over the natural to evil. Humanism, old and new, considers that an aspersion on the sources of life."

"My dear chap, there is not much there to asperse."

"One ends," I said undeterred, "by denying the works of God; one becomes the advocate of nothing. Who believes in the Devil, already belongs to him."

He gave his short laugh.

"You never understand a joke. I spoke as a theologian and so necessarily like a theologian."

"Never mind," I said, laughing as well. "You usually take your jokes more seriously than your seriousness." We carried on this conversation on the community bench under the maple trees on Mount Zion, in the sunshine of the autumn afternoon. The fact was that at that time I myself was going courting, though the wedding and even the public engagement had to wait on my being confirmed in my position. I wanted to tell him about Helene and of my proposed step, but his remarks did not precisely encourage me.

"And they twain shall be one flesh," he began again: "Is it not a curious blessing? Pastor Schroder, thank God, spared himself the quotation. In the presence of the bridal pair it is rather painful to hear. But it is only too well meant, and precisely what I mean by domestication. Obviously the element of sin, of sensuality, of evil lust altogether, is conjured away out of marriage—for lust is certainly only in flesh of two different kinds, not in one, and that they are to be one flesh is accordingly soothing but nonsensical. On the other hand, one cannot wonder enough that one flesh has lust for another; it is a phenomenon—well, yes, the entirely exceptional phenomenon of love. Of course, love and sensuality are not to be separated. One best absolves love from the reproach of sensuality by identifying the love element in sensuality itself. The lust after strange flesh means a conquest of previously existing resistances, based on the strangeness of I and You, your own and the other person's. The flesh—to keep the Christian terminology—is normally inoffensive to itself only. With another's it will have nothing to do. Now, if all at once the strange flesh become the object of desire and lust, then the relation of the I and the You is altered in a way for which sensuality is only an empty word. No, one cannot get along without the concept of love, even when ostensibly there is nothing spiritual in play. Every sensual act means tenderness, it is a give and take of desire, happiness through making happy, a manifestation of love. 'One flesh' have lovers never been; and the prescription would drive love along with lust out of marriage."

I was peculiarly upset and bewildered by his words and took care not to look at him, though I was tempted. I wrote down above how I always felt when he spoke of the things of the flesh. But he had never come out of himself like this, and it seemed to me that there was something explicit and unlike him about the way he spoke, a kind of tactlessness too, against himself and also against his auditor. It disturbed me, together with the idea that he said it when his eyes were heavy with headache. Yet with the sense of it I was entirely in sympathy.

"Well roared, lion!" I said, as lightly as possible. "That is what I call standing up to it! No, you have nothing to do with the Devil. You do know that you have spoken much more as a humanist than as a theologian?"

"Let us say a psychologist," he responded. "A neutral position. But they are, I think, the most truth-loving people."

"And how would it be," I proposed, "if we just once spoke quite simply, personally and like ordinary citizens? I wanted to tell you that I am about to—"

I told him what I was about to do, told him about Helene, how I had met her and we had got to know each other. If, I said, it would make his congratulations any warmer, he might be assured that I dispensed him beforehand from any "customs and curtsyings" at my wedding feast.

He was greatly enlivened.

"Wonderful!" he cried. "My dearest fellow—wilt marry thyself! What a goodly idea! Such things always take one by surprise, though there is nothing surprising about them. Accept my blessing! 'But, if thou marry, hang me by the neck, if horns that year miscarry!'"

"'Come, come, you talk greasily,'" I quoted out of the same Scene. "If you knew the girl and the spirit of our bond, then you would know that there is no need to fear for my peace of mind, but that on the contrary everything is directed towards the foundation of love and tranquility, a fixed and undisturbed happiness."

"I do not doubt it," said he, "and doubt not of its success."

A moment he seemed tempted to press my hand, but desisted. There came a pause in the talk, then as we walked home it turned to our all-important topic, the opera, and the scene in the fourth act, with the text of which we had been joking, and which was among those I definitely wanted to leave out. Its verbal skirmish was really offensive, and dramatically it was not indispensable. In any case there had to be cuts. A comedy should not last four hours—that was and remains the principal objection to the *Meistersinger*. But Adrian seemed to have planned to use precisely the "old sayings" of Rosaline and Boyet, the "Thou canst not hit it, hit it, hit it," and so on for the contrapuntal passages of his overture, and altogether haggled over every episode, although he had to laugh when I said that he reminded me of Kretschmar's Beissel and his naive zeal to set half the world to music. Anyhow he denied being embarrassed by the comparison. He still retained some of the half-humorous respect he had felt when he first heard about the wonderful novice and lawgiver of music. Absurdly enough, he had never quite ceased to think of him, and lately had thought of him oftener than ever.

"Remember," he said, "how I once defended his childish tyranny with the 'master' and 'servant' notes against your reproach of silly rationalism. What instinctively pleased me was itself something instinctive, in naive agreement with the spirit of music: the wish, which showed itself in a comic way, to write something in the nature of the 'strict style.' On another, less childish plane we would need people like him, just as his flock had need of him then: we need a system-master, a teacher of the objective and organization, with enough genius to unite the old-established, the archaic, with the revolutionary. One ought to—"

He had to laugh.

"I'm talking like Schildknapp. One ought to. What all ought one not to?"

"What you say," I threw in, "about the archaic-revolutionary schoolmaster has something very German about it."

"I take it," he responded, "that you use the word not as a compliment, but in a descriptive and critical way, as you should. However, it could mean something necessary to the time, something promising a remedy in an age of destroyed conventions and the relaxing of all objective obligations—in short, of a freedom that begins to lie like a mildew upon talent and to betray traces of sterility."

I started at the word. Hard to say why, but in his mouth, altogether in connection with him, there was something dismaying about it, something wherein anxiety mixed in an odd way with reverence. It came from the fact that in his neighborhood sterility, threatened paralysis, arrest of productivity could be thought of only as something positive and proud, only in connection with pure and lofty intellectuality.

"It would be tragic," I said, "if unfruitfulness should ever be the result of freedom. But there is always the hope of the release of the productive powers, for the sake of which freedom is achieved."

"True," he responded. "And she does for a while achieve what she promised. But freedom is of course another word for subjectivity, and some fine day she does not hold out any longer, some time or other she despairs of the possibility of being creative out of herself and seeks shelter and security in the objective. Freedom always inclines to dialectic reversals. She realizes herself very soon in constraint, fulfills herself in the subordination to law, rule, coercion, system—but to fulfill herself therein does not mean she therefore ceases to be freedom."

"In your opinion," I laughed: "So far as she knows. But actually she is no longer freedom, as little as dictatorship born out of revolution is still freedom."

"Are you sure of it?" he asked. "But anyhow that is talking politics. In art, at least, the subjective and the objective intertwine to the point of being indistinguishable, one proceeds from the other and takes the character of the other, the subjective precipitates as objective and by genius is again awaked to spontaneity, 'dynamized,' as we say; it speaks all at once the language of the subjective. The musical conventions today destroyed were not always so objective, so objectively imposed. They were crystallizations of living experiences and as such long performed an office of vital importance: the task of organization. Organization is everything. Without it there is nothing, least of all art. And it was aesthetic subjectivity that took on the task, it undertook to organize the work out of itself, in freedom."

"You are thinking of Beethoven."

"Of him and of the technical principle through which a dominating subjectivity got hold of the musical organization; I mean the development, or working out. The development itself had been a small part of the sonata, a modest republic of subjective illumination and dynamic. With Beethoven it becomes universal, becomes the center of the whole form, which, even where it is supposed to remain conventional, is absorbed by the subjective and is newly created in freedom. The form of variations, something archaic, a residuum, becomes a means by which to infuse new life into form. The principle of development plus variation technique extends over the whole sonata. It does that in Brahms, as thematic working-out, even more radically. Take him as an example of how subjectivity turns into objectivity. In him music abstains from all conventional flourishes, formulas, and residua and so to speak creates the unity of the work anew at every moment, out of freedom. But precisely on that account freedom becomes the principle of an all-round economy that leaves in music nothing casual, and develops the utmost diversity while adhering to the identical material. Where there is nothing unthematic left, nothing which could not show itself to derive from the same basic material, there one can no longer speak of a 'free style.' "

"And not of the 'strict style' in the old sense, either!"

"Old or new, I will tell you what I understand by 'strict style.' I mean the complete integration of all musical dimensions, their neutrality towards each other due to complete organization."

"Do you see a way to do that?"

"Do you know," he countered, "when I came nearest to the 'strict style'?"

I waited. He spoke so low as to be hard to hear, and between his teeth, as he used to when he had a headache.

"Once in the Brentano cycle," he said, "in *'O lieb Mädel.'* That song is entirely derived from a fundamental figure, a series of interchangeable intervals, the five notes B, E, A, E, E-flat, and the horizontal melody and the vertical harmony are determined and controlled by it, in so far as that is possible with a basic motif of so few notes. It is like a word, a key word, stamped on everything in the song, which it would like to determine entirely. But it is too short a word and in itself not flexible enough. The tonal space it affords is too limited. One would have to go on from here and make larger words out of the twelve letters, as it were, of the tempered semitone alphabet. Words of twelve letters, certain combinations and inter-relations of the twelve semitones, series of notes from which a piece and all the movements of a work must strictly derive. Every note of the whole composition, both melody and harmony, would have to show its relation to this fixed fundamental series. Not one might recur until the other notes have sounded. Not one might appear which did not fulfill its function in the whole Structure. There would no longer be a free note. That is what I would call 'strict composition.'"

"A striking thought," said I. "Rational organization through and through, one might indeed call it. You would gain an extraordinary unity and con-gruity, a sort of astronomical regularity and legality would be obtained thereby. But when I picture it to myself, it seems to me that the unchanged recurrence of such a succession of intervals, even when used in different parts of the texture, and in rhythmic variations, would result in a probably unavoidable serious musical impoverishment and stagnation."

"Probably," he answered, with a smile which showed that he had been prepared for this reservation. It was the smile that brought out strongly his likeness to his mother, but with the familiar look of strain which it would show under pressure of the migraine.

"And it is not so simple either. One must incorporate into the system all possible techniques of variation, including those decried as artificial; that is, the means which once helped the 'development' to win its hold over the sonata. I ask myself why I practiced so long under Kretschmar the devices of the old counterpoint and covered so much paper with inversion fugues, crab and inversions of crabs. Well now, all that should come in handy for the ingenious modification of the twelve-note word. In addition to being a fundamental series it could find application in this way, that every one of its intervals is replaced by its inversion. Again, one could begin the figure with its last note and finish it on its first, and then invert this figure as well. So then you have four modes, each of which can be transposed to all the twelve notes of the chromatic scale, so that forty-eight different versions of the basic series may be used in a composition and whatever other variational diversions may present themselves. A composition can also use two or more series as basic material, as in the double and triple fugue. The decisive factor is that every note, without exception, has significance and function according to its place in the basic series or its derivatives. That would guarantee what I call the indifference to harmony and melody."

"A magic square," I said. "But do you hope to have people hear all that?"

"Hear?" he countered. "Do you remember a certain lecture given for the Society for the Common Weal from which it followed that in music one certainly need not hear everything? If by 'hearing' you understand the precise realization in detail of the means by which the highest and strictest order is achieved, like the order of the planets, a cosmic order and legality—no, that way one would not hear it. But this order one will or would hear, and the perception of it would afford an unknown aesthetic satisfaction.'"

"Very remarkable," said I. "The way you describe the thing, it comes to a sort of composing before composition. The whole disposition and organization of the material would have to be ready when the actual work should begin, and all one asks is: which is the actual work? For this preparation of the material is done by variation, and the creative element in variation, which one might call the actual composition, would be transferred back to the material itself—together with the freedom of the composer. When he went to work, he would no longer be free."

"Bound by a self-imposed compulsion to order, hence free."

"Well of course the dialectic of freedom is unfathomable. But he could scarcely be called a free inventor of his harmony. Would not the making of chords be left to chance and accident?"

"Say, rather, to the context. The polyphonic dignity of every chord-forming note would be guaranteed by the constellation. The historical events—the emancipation of dissonance from its resolution, its becoming 'absolute' as it appears already in some passages of the later Wagner—would warrant any combination of notes which can justify itself before the system."

"And if the constellation produced the banal: consonance, common-chord harmonics, the worn-out, the diminished seventh?"

"That would be a rejuvenation of the worn-out by the constellation."

"I see there a restorative element in your Utopia. It is very radical, but it relaxes the prohibition which after all already hung over consonance. The return to the ancient forms of variation is a similar sign."

"More interesting phenomena," he responded, "probably always have this double face of past and future, probably are always progressive and regressive in one. They display the equivocalness of life itself."

"Is that not a generalization?"

"Of what?"

"Of our domestic experiences as a nation?"

"Oh, let us not be indiscreet! Or flatter ourselves either. All I want to say is that our objections—if they are meant as objections—would not count against the fulfilment of the old, the ever repeated demand to take hold and make order, and to resolve the magic essence of music into human reason."

"You want to put me on my honor as a humanist," said I. "Human reason! And besides, excuse me; 'constellation' is your every other word. But surely it belongs more to astrology. The rationalism you call for has a good deal of superstition about it—of belief in the incomprehensibly and vaguely demonic, the kind of thing we have in games of chance, fortune-telling with cards, and shaking dice. Contrary to what you say, your system seems to me more calculated to dissolve human reason in magic."

He carried his closed hand to his brow.

"Reason and magic," said he, "may meet and become one in that which one calls wisdom, initiation; in belief in the stars, in numbers. . . ."

I did not go on, as I saw that he was in pain. And all that he had said seemed to me to bear the mark of suffering, to stand in its sign, however intellectually remarkable it may have been. He himself seemed not to care for more conversation; his idle humming and sighing betrayed the fact as we sauntered on. I felt, of course, vexed and inwardly shook my head, silently reflecting as I walked that a man's thoughts might be characterized by saying that he had a headache; but that did not make them less significant.

We spoke little on the rest of the way home. I recall that we paused by the Cow Trough, took a few steps away from the path and looked into it, with the reflection of the setting sun in our faces. The water was clear: one could see that the bottom was flat only near the edge; it fell off rapidly into darkness. The pond was known to be very deep in the middle.

"Cold," said Adrian, motioning with his head; "much too cold to bathe.— Cold," he repeated a moment later, this time with a definite shiver, and turned away.

My duties obliged me to go back that evening to Kaisersaschern. He himself delayed a few days longer his departure for Munich, where he had decided to settle. I see him pressing his father's hand in farewell—for the last time; he knew it not. I see his mother kiss him and, perhaps in the same way as she had done that time with Kretschmar in the living-room, lean his head on her shoulder. He was not to return to her, he never did. She came to him.

NOTE

Thomas Mann, *Doctor Faustus: The Life of the German Composer Adrian Leverkühn as Told by a Friend*, trans. H. T. Lowe-Porter (New York: Vintage, 1971), 185–94.

Selected Bibliography

Abel, Angelika. *Musikästhetik der Klassischen Moderne: Thomas Mann—Theodor W. Adorno—Arnold Schönberg*. München: Wilhelm Fink, 2003.

Bahr, Ehrhard. "Evil Germany versus Good Germany: Thomas Mann's *Doctor Faustus*." In *Weimar in the Pacific: German Exile Culture in Los Angeles and the Crisis of Modernism*. Berkeley: University of California Press, 2007.

Bergsten, Gunilla. *Thomas Mann's "Doctor Faustus": The Sources and Structure of the Novel*. Translated by Krishna Winston. Chicago: University of Chicago Press, 1969.

Buzga, Jaroslav. "Leverkühn und die modern Musik." *Melos* 32, no. 2 (1965): 37–41.

Carnegy, Patrick. *Faust as Musician: A Study of Thomas Mann's Novel "Doctor Faustus."* London: Chatto and Windus, 1973.

Cobley, Evelyn. "Avant-Garde Aesthetics and Fascist Politics: Thomas Mann's *Doctor Faustus* and Theodor W. Adorno's *Philosophy of Modern Music*." *New German Critique* 86 (Spring-Summer 2002): 43–70.

Coldaroli, Carlos. "La polémica Schönberg–Mann a propósito del *Doktor Faustus*." *Ars: Revista de Arte* 36 (1976): 118.

Dahlhaus, Carl. "Fiktive Zwölftonmusik." *Musica* 37, no. 3 (1983): 245–52.

Dolenko, Elena. "The Story of a Controversy (Concerning the Argument between Thomas Mann and Arnold Schoenberg in Connection with the Novel *Doctor Faustus*." In *Arnold Schoenberg: Yesterday, Today, Tomorrow* [in Russian], edited by Evgenia Chigareva and Elena Dolenko, 186–202. Moscow: Moscow State Tchaikovsky Conservatory, 2002.

Engel, Hans. "Musik der krise, krise der Musikoder *Dr. Faustus*." *Neue Musikzeitschrift* 3, no. 12 (1949): 336–42.

Fischer, Erik. "Adrian Leverkühns *Philosophie der Neuen Musik*." *Literatur für Leser* 3 (1984): 162–70.

Förster, Wolf-Dietrich. "Leverkühn, Schönberg und Thomas Mann: Musikalische Strukturen und Kunstreflexion im *Doktor Faustus*." *Deutsche*

Vierteljahresschrift für Literaturwissenschaft und Geistesgeschichte 49, no. 4 (1975): 694–720.

Göllner, Theodor. "'Wiesengrund'-Schönbergs kritik an Thomas Manns *Arietta* textierungen in Beethovens op. 111." In *Festschrift Horst Leuchtmann zum 65. Geburtstag,* edited by Stephan Hörner and Bernhold Schmid, 161–78. Tutzing: Schneider, 1993.

Grandi, Hans. "Die Musik im Roman Thomas Manns." PhD diss., Humboldt Universität Berlin, 1952.

Grüß, Hans. "War Hindemith eher ein deutscher tonsetzer als Adrian Leverkühn alias Arnold Schönberg?" In *Das Deutsche in der Musik.* Kolloquium im Rahmen der 5. Dresdner Tage der zeitgenössischen Musik vom 1.–10. Oktober 1991, 127–31. Leipzig: Dresdner Zentrum für zeitgenössische Musik, 1997.

Hansen, Mathias. "Thomas Mann und Arnold Schönberg—schöpferische Beziehungen zwischen Dichtung und Musik." In *Arnold Schönberg, 1874–1952: Zum 25. Todestag des Komponisten,* edited by Mathias Hansen and Christa Müller, 88–103. Berlin: Akademie der künste der Deutschen Demokratischen Republik, 1976.

Henius, Carla. "Die wirkliche und die erdachte Musik im Roman *Doktor Faustus* von Thomas Mann: Eine Studie der Beziehungen zwischen Thomas Mann, Theodor W. Adorno, und Arnold Schönberg." *Neuland* 1 (1981): 61–65.

Hermanns, Ulrike. *Thomas Manns Roman "Doktor Faustus" im Lichte von Quellen und Kontexten.* Frankfurt am Main: Peter Lang, 1994.

Hoffmann, Richard. "Der Roman eines *Roman eines Romans.*" In *Bericht über den 2. Kongress der Internationalen Schönberg-Gesellschaft: "Die Wiener Schule in der Musikgeschichte des 20. Jahrhunderts."* Wien, 12. bis 15. Juni 1984, edited by Rudolf Stephan and Sigrid Wiesmann, 235–41. Wien: E. Lafite, 1986.

Jensen, Jorgen. "Daemoniensspejl: En studiei Thomas Manns roman *Doktor Faustus.*" *Dansk Musiktidsskrift* 58, no. 6 (1983–84): 266–85.

Jung, Ute. *Die Musikphilosophie Thomas Manns.* Regensburg: Gustav Bosse, 1969.

Kaiser, Joachim. "Thomas Mann und die Musik." In *Themengewebe: Thomas Mann und die Musik: Zwei Vorträge von Albert von Schirnding und Joachim Kaiser,* edited by Dirk Heißerer, 25–40. München: Thomas-Mann-Förderkreis, 2001.

Kamber, Peter. *Geschichte zweier Leben: Wladimir Rosenbaum / Aline Valangin.* 2nd rev. ed. Zürich: Limmat, 2000.

Käuser, Andreas. "Musikalischeprosa: Zur Funktion der Musik im modernen Roman." *Wirkendes Wort* 44, no. 2 (1994): 279–95.

Konzerthaus Berlin und Schauspielhaus am Gendarmenmarkt, eds. *Die musikalische Welt des Adrian Leverkühn: Ein Projektzum Faustus-Roman von Thomas Mann.* Göttingen: Wallstein, 1998.

Kortsen, Bjarne. "Forholdes Thomas Mann—Arnold Schönberg." *Dansk Musiktidsskrift* 34, no. 6 (1959): 175ff.

Maegaard, Jan. "Schönberg hat Adorno nie leiden können." *Melos* 41, no. 4 (1974): 262–64.

Mann, Michael. "The Musical Symbolism in Thomas Mann's Novel *Doctor Faustus*." *Notes* 14, no. 1 (1956): 33–42.

Mann, Thomas. *Doktor Faustus: Das Leben des deutschen Tonsetzers Adrian Leverkühn, erzählt von einem Freunde.* Edited by Ruprecht Wimmer, in collaboration with Stephan Stachorski. 2 vols. Frankfurt am Main: S. Fischer, 2007.

———. *Tagebücher, 1937–1939.* Edited by Peter de Mendelssohn. Frankfurt am Main: S. Fischer, 1980.

———. *Tagebücher, 1940–1943.* Edited by Peter de Mendelssohn. Frankfurt am Main: S. Fischer, 1982.

———. *Tagebücher, 1944–1.4.1946.* Edited by Inge Jens. Frankfurt am Main: S. Fischer, 1986.

———. *Tagebücher, 28.5.1946–31.12.1948.* Edited by Inge Jens. Frankfurt am Main: S. Fischer, 1989.

———. *Tagebücher, 1949–1950.* Edited by Inge Jens. Frankfurt am Main: S. Fischer, 1991.

———. *Tagebücher, 1951–1952.* Edited by Inge Jens. Frankfurt am Main: S. Fischer, 1993.

Manzoni, Giacomo. "Dimensionen des Neuen: Anmerkungen zum *Doktor Faustus* von Thomas Mann." *Musik und Gesellschaft* 35 (1985): 302–9.

———. "La pubblicazione del *Doktor Faustus* e la polemica fra A. Schoenberg e Th. Mann." *Diapason*, Oct. 1955, 25–28.

N.N. "Rache dem Eigentlichen." *Der Spiegel*, no. 17 (1966): 124–26.

Neher, André. *Faust et le Maharal de Prague: Le mythe et le réel.* Paris: Presses Universitaires de France, 1987.

Neumann, Horst Peter. "Mythen der Inspiration: Aus den Gründerjahren der Neuen Musik. Hans Pfitzner, Arnold Schönberg, und Thomas Mann." In *Neue Musik und Tradition: Festschrift Rudolf Stephan zum 65. Geburtstag,* edited by Josef Kuckertz, Helga de la Motte-Haber, Christian Martin Schmidt, and Wilhelm Seidel, 441–57. Laaber: Laaber Verlag, 1990.

Neumann, Michael. "Zwölftontechnik? Adrian Leverkühn zwischen Schönberg und Wagner." *Literaturwissenschaftliches Jahrbuch der Görres-Gesellschaft* 43 (2002): 193–211.

Newman, Ernest. "A Schönberg Comedy." *Sunday Times* (London), Dec. 6, 1949, 2.

Nitsche, Peter. "Instrumentation und Kontrapunkt als autopoetologische Metaphern in Thomas Manns *Doktor Faustus*." In *Intermedialität. Studien zur Wechselwirkung zwischen den Künsten,* edited by Günter Schnitzler and Edelgard Spaude, 73–93. Freiburg: Rombach, 2004.

Pringsheim, Klaus. "Der tonsetzer Adrian Leverkühn—Ein Musiker über Thomas Manns Roman." *Der Monat* 1, no. 4 (1949): 84–91.

———. "The Music of Adrian Leverkühn." *Musicology* 2 (1949): 255–68.

Reif, Jo-Ann. "Adrian Leverkühn, Arnold Schoenberg, Theodor Adorno: Theorists Real and Fictitious in Thomas Mann's *Doctor Faustus.*" *Journal of the Arnold Schoenberg Institute* 7, no. 1 (1983): 102–12.

———. "Thomas Mann's *Doctor Faustus:* Progress in Music: The Composer, the Composition, the Critic." PhD diss., Columbia University, 1991.

Reschke, Claus, ed. *German Literature and Music: An Aesthetic Fusion, 1890–1989.* München: W. Fink, 1992.

Röcke, Werner, ed. *Thomas Mann: Doktor Faustus, 1947–1997.* Bern: Peter Lang, 2001.

Rubsamen, Walter H. "Arnold Schönberg in America." *Musical Quarterly* 37, no. 4 (1951): 469–89.

———. "Arnold Schönberg in Amerika." *Melos* 20, no. 6 (1953): 168–73.

Said, Edward W. "From Silence to Sound and Back Again: Music, Literature, and History." *Raritan* 17, no. 2 (1997): 1–21.

Schaal, Hans-Jürgen. "Thomas Manns Musikerroman *Doktor Faustus:* Der Einfluß von Arnold Schönberg und Theodor W. Adorno." *Das Orchester* 46, no. 1 (1998): 2–7.

Scherliess, Volker. *Adrian Leverkühn (1885–1941)—ein deutscher Komponist in der Darstellung Thomas Manns: Dichtung und Wirklichkeit.* Lübeck: Buddenbrookhaus, 1993.

———. "Zur Musik im *Doktor Faustus.*" In *Und was werden die Deutschen sagen? Thomas Manns Roman "Doktor Faustus,"* edited by Hans Wisskirchen and Thomas Sprecher, 113–51. Lübeck: Dräger, 1997.

Schmid, Bernhold. "Manfred Bukofzer im Briefwechsel mit Thomas Mann." In *Festschrift Horst Leuchtmann zum 65. Geburtstag,* edited by Stefan Hörner and Bernhold Schmid, 311–32. Tutzing: Schneider, 1993.

———. "Neues zum *Doktor Faustus*—Streit zwischen Arnold Schönberg und Thomas Mann." *Augsburger Jahrbuch für Musikwissenschaft* 6 (1989): 149–79.

———. "Neues zum *Doktor Faustus*—Streit zwischen Arnold Schönberg und Thomas Mann. Ein Nachtrag." *Augsburger Jahrbuch für Musikwissenschaft* 7 (1990): 177–92.

Schmidt, James. "Mephistopheles in Hollywood: Adorno, Mann, and Schoenberg." In *The Cambridge Companion to Adorno,* edited by Thomas Huhn, 148–80. Cambridge: Cambridge University Press, 2004.

Schneider, Thomas. *Das literarische Porträt: Quellen, Vorbilder und Modelle in Thomas Manns "Doktor Faustus."* Berlin: Frank und Timme, 2005.

Schoenberg, E. Randol. Préface. In *A propos du Docteur Faustus: Lettres, 1930–1951,* by Arnold Schönberg and Thomas Mann, translated by Hans Hildenbrand, 5–14. Lausanne: La Bibliothèque des Arts, 2002.

———. Prefazione. In *A proposito del Doctor Faustus: Lettere, 1930–1951,* by Arnold Schönberg and Thomas Mann, translated from German and English by Hans Hildenbrand, 5–10. Milano: Rosellina Archinto, 1993.

Schuh, Willi. "Thomas Mann und Arnold Schönberg." *Neue Auslese: Aus dem Schrifttum aller Länder* 4, no. 4 (1949): 71–76.

Schulze, Matthias. *Die Musikalszeitgeschichtliches Paradigma: Zu Hesses "Glasperlenspiel" und Thomas Manns "Doktor Faustus."* Frankfurt am Main: Peter Lang, 1998.

Stuckenschmidt, Hans Heinz. "Der 'Eigentliche': Die Dissonanzen zwischen Arnold Schönberg und Thomas Mann." *Der Monat* 1, no. 6 (1949): 76–78.

Vaget, Hans Rudolf. *Seelenzauber: Thomas Mann und die Musik.* Frankfurt am Main: S. Fischer, 2006.

Valangin, Aline. "Übert Thomas Manns *Doktor Faustus.*" *Literarische Blätter,* no. 17 (April 1948): 3–7.

Yates, Peter. "Leverkühn and the Magician." *Saturday Review of Recordings,* Feb. 24, 1949, 47–48.

Ziegler, Thomas. "Randbemerkungen zum *Doktor Faustus*—Streit und seinen Folgen." *Neues Musikwissenschaftliches Jahrbuch* 2 (1993): 167–78.

Zuckerkandl, Viktor. "Die Musik des *Doktor Faustus.*" *Die Neue Rundschau* 59 (1948): 203–14.

Works

THOMAS MANN

Buddenbrooks
The Magic Mountain
Joseph and His Brothers
Lotte in Weimar
Doctor Faustus
The Story of a Novel

ARNOLD SCHOENBERG

Operas

Erwartung, op. 17
Die glückliche Hand, op. 18
Von Heute auf Morgen, op. 32
Moses und Aron

Vocal Works

Two Songs, op. 14
Fifteen Poems from "The Book of the Hanging Gardens," op. 15
Gurrelieder
Pierrot Lunaire, op. 21
Jacob's Ladder
Serenade, op. 24
Kol Nidre, op. 39
Ode to Napoleon Buonaparte, op. 41
Prelude to *Genesis Suite,* op. 44
A Survivor from Warsaw
Israel Exists Again
Dreimal tausend Jahre, op. 50a

De Profundis (Psalm 130), op. 50b
Modern Psalm, op. 50c

Orchestral Works

Pelleas and Melisande, op. 5
Chamber Symphony No. 1, op. 9
Five Pieces for Orchestra, op. 16
Variations for Orchestra, op. 31
Accompaniment to a Film Scene, op. 34
Suite in the Old Style (G-Major) for String Orchestra
Concerto for Violoncello and Orchester (D-Major)
Concerto for Violin and Orchestra, op. 36
Concerto for Piano and Orchestra, op. 42

Chamber Music

Transfigured Night, op. 4
Second String Quartet, op. 10
Three Piano Pieces, op. 11
Six Small Piano Pieces, op. 19
Suite for Piano, op. 25
Third Screen Quartet, op. 30
Fourth String Quartet, op. 37
Variations on a Recitative for Organ (D-Minor), op. 40
String Trio, op. 45
Phantasy for Violin and Piano, op. 47

Writings

Theory of Harmony
"A Four-Point Program for Jewry"
Style and Idea

Index

Abel, Angelika, 99n171, 157n45, 219
Adler, Felix, 39n11
Adler, Guido, 190n81
Adler, Oskar, 190n76
Adorno, Gretel, 5, 71, 122
Adorno, Theodor W.: Adorno-Mann
    initial meeting, 1; affidavit on
    collaboration, 157n45; American
    culture and, 12; on anti-Semitism, 12;
    "Beethoven's Late Style," 94n164;
    Berg and, 4, 18, 19–20; Bukofzer on,
    164; contributions of, 2; *Dialectic of
    Enlightenment*, 12, 13–14, 17, 19;
    discussions with Mann, 122, 155;
    Doctor Faustus postscript and, 116;
    early career of, 4–5; exile of, 3, 5, 10,
    16; "Glosse über Sibelius," 13;
    Hoffman on, 222; Horkheimer and,
    99n180; Kolisch and, 17–18, 59n79;
    letter from Schoenberg, 210n91;
    letters to Steuermann, 156–57;
    letters with Mann, 91–94, 154, 204,
    238, 239, 240, 241, 246n13, 247n28;
    in Los Angeles, xi, 3, 5, 75n130;
    Mann collaboration, 18–21, 20, 51,
    60n80, 91–94, 94nn162,167, 99n171,
    109, 145, 166n56, 179, 228–33, 237–
    39; *Minima Moralia*, 12, 13, 19, 24;
    modernism of, 6; name change of, 5,
    166n59, 186; overview of, 58n78;
    Philosophy of New Music, 17–20, 51,
    59n79, 60n80, 78, 84n148, 94n164,

167n61, 193n84, 243–44, 246n13,
    306–18; plagiarism and, 18–19;
    "Reflections on a Damaged Life," 13;
    resentment of, 13; Schoenberg on, 2,
    58n78, 143, 147, 167, 186, 192, 194–
    95, 196–97, 207–9, 210–11nn90–92,
    225, 240, 242–44; Schuh on, 175–76;
    In Search of Wagner, 17, 19, 73, 78,
    94n164; as status seeker, 18–19;
    terminology of, 5–6; twelve-tone
    method critique of, 17, 19–20, 306–18
Albersheim, Gerhard, 75n130
Anderson, Sherwood, 11
anti-Semitism, xiii, 3, 12, 23, 42n25,
    165n56, 251–55, 257, 266, 267
Arendt, Hannah, 5
Arlt, Gustave Otto, 51, 58nn75,76, 61,
    62, 87, 122, 150, 185n74
Arnhold, Heinrich, 74n117
Arnhold, Lise, 71, 74n117
Arnim, Achim von, 75n125
Asch, Schalom, 69, 73n108
atonality: Casella on, 16; Mann and,
    72, 85, 86n151; Russian atonal
    music, 52; Schoenberg and, 16,
    304n4; twelve-tone method and,
    308, 313; Walter and, 86n151, 90
Auber Stefan, 53n36
Auden, W. H., 9, 109n5

Bach, Johann Sebastian, 16, 184,
    299, 309

Bahr, Ehrhard, 15, 24
Balzac, Honore De, 188, 281
Barry, Joan, 74n120
Bartók, Béla, 41n21, 58n77, 72, 75n132
Basler, Otto, 108, 167n60, 181n71
Basso, Hamilton, 145
Baum, Vicki, 7, 38, 38n5, 39n14
Beckmesser, 317n6
Beethoven, Ludwig van: Adorno on,
   311, 316; Adorno's essay on,
   94nn164; in *Doctor Faustus*, 60n80,
   324; Kretschmar lecture on, 20;
   Mann and, 51, 93, 98; A. Schindler's
   biography of, 62, 64n91; Schoenberg
   on, 40n20; themes of, 303n2; Walter
   on, 98. *See also* Beethoven musical
   works
Beethoven musical works: 33
   Variations on a Waltz by Anton
   Diabelli, Op. 120 (Beethoven), 22;
   Diabelli Variations, 22, 304n7; Op.
   111 (Beethoven), 20; Piano Sonata
   No.32, Op. 111 (Beethoven), 93,
   166n59, 186, 225, 232; String
   Quartet, Op. 135, in F major
   (Beethoven), 281, 281–82, 282,
   317n5; String Quartet 15 In A
   Minor, Op. 132 (Beethoven), 51;
   String Quartet No. 15 in A minor,
   Op. 132, 51, 69; Symphony No. 1 in
   C major, Op. 21, 63n84; Symphony
   No. 5 in C minor, Op. 67, 84;
   Symphony No. 5 in C minor, Op. 67
   (Beethoven), 84; Symphony No. 9 in
   D minor, Op. 125, 98, 121n18
Bekker, Paul, 175, 230
Bemelmans, Ludwig, 88n160
Benjamin, Walter, 7, 317n4
Benny, Jack, 155
Berg, Alban: Adorno and, xi, 17, 18,
   19–20, 156, 196, 207, 210n90;
   counter-movement against, 75n130;
   Lulu, 307; Mann and, 58nn77–78,
   116; Reich's book on, 94n164, 175;
   Schoenberg and, 147, 174, 277;
   Schoenberg postcard, 39n11; on
   twelve-tone method, 20; twelve-

tone method and, 307, 316–17n4,
   318nn6–7; *Wozzeck*, 109n4
Bergerac, Cyrano de, 94n163
Berlioz, Hector, 175
Bermann-Fischer, Gottfried, 38, 39n13,
   81, 83, 133, 135, 137, 138, 143
Bernheimer, Otto, 49
Bienenfeld, Elsa, 188, 190n81
Bingham, Hiram, 52n33, 55n54
Bismarck, Otto von, 49, 88n157, 98
Bloch, Kalman, 53n36
Bodansky, Arthur, 39n11
Bodansky, Ida, 39n11
Bommersheim, Ellie, 170n63, 248n48
Borgese, Elisabeth Mann "Medi"
   (daughter), 161, 161n49, 202
Borgese, Giuseppe Antonio (Mann's
   son-in-law), 87, 87n156, 95
Boulanger, Nadja (Nalanger Budia),
   111, 112n9, 234
Bourne, Randolph, 11
Brahms, Johannes, 317n5, 324
Brecht, Bertolt, xi, 7, 9, 10, 11, 12,
   38n5, 57n66, 90n161
Breisacher, Chaim (fictional character),
   23, 178, 178n68
Brentano, Clemens von, 75n125, 77,
   325
Britten, Benjamin, 109, 109n5, 240
Brutus, Caepio, Marcus Iunius, 266
Buddenbrooks, Hanno (fictional
   character), 21, 92
Bujic, Bojan, 23
Bukofzer, Manfred E., 161, 162n52,
   163–64, 167
Bungert, August, 240
Busch, Adolph, 162n51
Busch, Fritz, 161, 162n51

Casella, Alfredo, 16
Castelnuovo-Tedesco, Mario, xi,
   100n187
Castorp, Hans, 176
Celan, Paul, 24
Chabrier, Emmanuel, 70, 73n109
Chaplin, Charles, 9, 12, 71, 74n120, 97
Churchill, Winston, 73, 273

Colin, Samuel C., 38, 40n19
Conrad, Joseph, 96, 97, 99n179
Copland, Aaron, 112n9, 247n24
Cowell, Henry, 74n114
Crawford, Dorothy Lamb, 14

Dallapiccola, Luigi, 171n66, 248n38
Daub, Adrian, xv, xviii
Davidson, Julius Ralph, 54n40
Debussy, Claude, 74n109, 276, 277
Dehmel, Richard, 67n104, 76n134
Dessau, Paul, 59n79, 100n184
Dieterle, Charlotte, 38, 40n20
Dieterle, William, 38, 40n20, 87, 97
Disney, Walt, 38n5
Döblin, Alfred, 9, 10
Doctor Faustus (Mann): Beethoven in, 60n80, 324; beginning of, 57n71; Chapter 22, 319–28; copies for friends, 99; copy delivered to Schoenberg, xv; fascism in, 2, 15; modernism and, 6; Nietzsche influence, 78n141; *Philosophy of New Music* and, 60n80; postscript to, 78n141, 116; publication of, 1; Schoenberg, lack of mention in, xiv; signed copies of, 99; success of, 98; twelve-tone method in, xviii, 6; Wagner in, 326
Downes, Olin, 22
Draesecke, Felix, 240
Dürer, Albrecht, 93
Dvorak, Antonin, 70

Ebner, Ferdinand, 165n56
Ehrlich, Paul, 272
Eimert, Herbert, 174
Einstein, Albert, 31n1, 35–36n3
Einstein, Alfred, 232
Eisenhower, Dwight D., 69
Eisenhower, Dwight David, 72, 113
Eisler, Gerhart, 100n192
Eisler, Hanns: blacklisting of, 98, 100n192; Hovey and, 54n41; letter from Adorno, 59n79; in Los Angeles, xi, 8, 16; Mann and, 82, 82n146, 192; at Schoenberg lectures, 57n66

Eisler, Lou, 101n192
Eisner, Bruno, 97, 100n184
Endre, Gáspár, 136n26
Entartete Musik (Degenerate Music) exhibition, 15–16
Eulenberg, Herbert, 23

Falke, Konrad, 45n26
fascism: Casella and, 16; in *Doctor Faustus*, 2, 15; Mann on, 44; modernism and, 23, 24; *Philosophy of New Music* and, 21
Feisst, Sabine, 5
Feuchtwanger, Lion: *Doctor Faustus* copy for, 99; escape from Europe, 55n54; in Los Angeles, xi, 7; Mann and, 9, 70, 97; party at van Leydens, 49, 69; in Sanary-sur-Mer, 38n5; success of, 10
Feuchtwanger, Martha, 9, 10, 69, 70
Feurmann, Emanuel, 161n50
Fiedler, Kuno, 96, 99, 99n169
Fischer, Gottfried Bermann. *See* Bermann-Fischer, Gottfried
Fischer, Ruth, 100n192
Fischer, Samuel, 39n13
Fitelberg, Saul (fictional character), 40n19
Flinker, Martin, 71, 74n121
Fougere, Jean, 97, 99n178
"Four-Point Program for Jewry" (Schoenberg), xiii, xviii, 14–15, 42, 42n25, 47n28, 251–68
Franck, César, 176, 177n67, 216n96
Frank, Bruno, 38, 41n22, 50, 52, 62, 63n83, 69, 71
Frank, Cesar, 128
Frank, Elisabeth, 38, 41n22, 62, 63n83, 69
Frank, Leonhard, 72, 76n136
Frank, Liesl, 49
Freud, Sigmund, 272
Frey, Alexander Moritz, 171n65, 231
Frisch, Fay Templeton, 38, 39n10
Fry, Varian, 52n33, 55n54
Furtwängler, Wilhelm, xii, 87, 87n157, 98, 100n189

Garbo, Greta, xii, 53n35
George, Stefan, 62, 63n84, 71, 72,
179n69
Georges, Manfred, 87n157
German expatriate community, 7–14,
16, 24
Gielen, Michael, 52n35
Gielen, Rose, 52n35
Gödde, Christoph, xviii, xix
Goebbels, Joseph, 12, 50, 56nn59–60,
73, 269
Goethe, Johann Wolfgang von, 22, 122,
159, 161, 166n58
Goldschmied, Malvine, 39n11
Goll, Yvan, 24
Golyscheff, Jefim, 174
Gounod, Charles Francois, 216n96
Greissle, Felix (Schoenberg's son-in-
law), 59n79
Greissle, Gertrud "Trudi" Schoenberg
(daughter), 59n79
Grillparzer, Franz, 121n18
Gropius, Walter, xii
Gumpert, Martin, 49, 52n34

Händel, Georg Friedrich, 304
Handl, Fritzi, 39n11
Handl, Will, 39n11
Hardt, Giulia, 51, 58n74
Hardt, Ludwig, 51, 58n74, 82
Hardt, Petra Christina, xviii, xix
Harmonielehre (Theory of Harmony)
(Schoenberg). See Theory of
Harmony (Harmonielehre)
(Schoenberg)
Harris, Roy, 112n9
Hartleben, Otto Erich, 53n36
Hauer, Josef Matthias: Adorno and,
167n61, 307; anti-Semitism and,
165n56; Humm on, 247n32; Mann
on, 78n141, 167, 248n48; Schoenberg
and, 165n56; Schoenberg on, 209,
210n91, 244; "Theory of Tropes,"
209, 244; twelve-tone method, 123,
163, 165n56, 170, 170n63, 174, 179
Hauptmann, Gerhard, 23, 43n25
Havlik, Adolf, 184, 185n75

Haydn, Joseph, 159
Hegel, Georg Wilhelm Friedrich, 164
Heifetz, Jascha, xi, 272
Heims-Reinhardt, Else, 62, 64n100
Heine, Heinrich, 165n56
Hemingway, Ernest, 222–23
Herrmann, Eva, 62, 64n90, 69
Herzl, Theodor, 256–58, 266
Herzog, Wilhelm, 71, 75n128
Hesse, Hermann, 122n19
Hill, Claude (Klauss Hilzheimer), 161,
161n48
Hill, Ralph, 174
Himmler, Heinrich Luitpold, 98,
100n191
Hindemith, Paul, 41n21, 120, 120n17,
235, 240; 177, 182
Hitler, Adolf, 3–4, 13, 42n25, 49,
56n60, 63n84, 268, 273
Hoffmann, Richard "Dick," xv,
142n29, 219, 219–27, 233, 240,
246n19
Hofmannsthal, Hugo von, 85
Homolka, Florence Meyer, 99n172
Homolka, Oskar, 99n172
Horkheimer, Max: Adorno-Mann
initial meeting, 1, 58n78; Adorno
remarks to, 16, 20, 59n79, 193n84;
Adornos dependence on, 5; Dialectic
of Enlightenment, 12, 13–14, 19; at
Frankfurt Institute of Social
Research, 8; in Los Angeles, 7; Mann
and, 9, 97, 99n180, 202
Horowitz, Vladimir, xi, 272
Horwitz, Karl, 39n11
Horwitz, Mizzi, 39n11
Housman, John, 54n41
Hovey, Carl, 54n41
Hovey, Serge, xxi, 49, 54n41
Hovey, Sonya, 54n41
Hovey, Tamara, xxi, 54n41
Howard, Leslie, 272
Howard, Walter, 210n91
Huldschinsky, Paul (Hulle), 49, 55n45
Humm, Rudolf Jakob, 122, 122nn19–
20, 124, 247n32
Huxley, Aldous, xi, 9

Isherwood, Christopher, 9, 12

Jacob's Ladder (Schoenberg): Mann
  on, 69, 73n107, 188, 200, 226, 230,
  246n11; Mann's receipt of, 67;
  summary of, 67n104; twelve-tone
  method in, xiii
Jacobson, Anna, 72, 76n133
Jahn, Friedrich Ludwig, 88n157
Jeritza, Maria, 62, 64n95
Jessner, Leopold, 38, 40n21
Jewish state, xiii, 256–58, 263–67
Johst, Hanns, 98, 100n191
Joseph, Albrecht, 62, 63n86
Josquin des Prez, 308
Joyce, James, 33n2, 85–86

Kafka, Franz, 49, 55n49, 58n74
Kahler, Erich von, 74n116, 119n16
Kahn, Erich Itor, 59n79
Kahn, Hilde, 198, 198n86, 214
Kandinsky, Wassily, 42n25
Karlweis, Oskar, 96, 99n170
Kauz, Phil F. (Fiedler, Kuno), 96,
  99n169
Kellen, Konrad (Katzenellenbogen),
  38, 39n8, 51
Keller, Hans, 186, 188–90, 190n76, 240
Kershaw, Ian, 3
Kierkegaard, Søren, 4, 94n164, 164
Klatzkin, Jacob, 15
Klausner, Margot, 153n42
Klemperer, Otto: in *Doctor Faustus*,
  147; in Los Angeles, xi, 8, 75n130;
  Mann and, 38, 62, 84, 87, 88n158,
  96; Schoenberg and, 39n11, 40n16,
  40n20, 84n148; S. Viertel on,
  53n38
Klenau, Paul von, 17
Knopf, Blanche, 119n16
Knowland, William F., 99n173
Koblitz, Milton, 141, 142n30
Koehnen, Toni, 39n11
Kolisch, Gertrud. *See* Schoenberg,
  Gertrud Kolisch (2nd wife)
Kolisch, Rudolf "Rudi" (Schoenberg's
  brother-in-law), 17–18, 40n17,

53n36, 59n79, 157, 191n82, 207,
  210n90
Kolodin, Irving, 225
Korngold, Erich, xi, 8, 10, 75n131
Koussevitzky, Sergei Alexandrowitsch,
  88n157, 272
Kraus, Karl, 33n2, 60n80
Krenek, Ernst: in Los Angeles, 16;
  Mann and, 58n77, 75nn129–130,
  116, 184, 215; *Music Here and Now*,
  175, 230; overview of, 117n15;
  Schoenberg on, 127; Schuh on, 174
Kretschmar, Wendell, 18, 20, 60n80,
  94, 94n165, 166n59, 319, 323, 325,
  328
Kretzschmar, Hermann, 184
Kridwiß, Sixtus (fictional character),
  23
Kruif, Paul de, 190n79
Kulka, Heinrich, 39n15

Laffont, Robert, 97
Lang, Fritz, 10, 40n20
Lang, Paul H., 215n95
Lange, Juliane, 239
Lányi, Jenö (husband of Monika
  Mann), 53–54nn39
Larbaud, Valéry, 33n2
Lehár, Franz, 63n87
Leibowitz, Rene, 54n42, 144, 144n35,
  221
Lert, Richard, 39n14
Lesser, Jonas, 75n130, 232
Lester, Konrad, 184n74
Leverkühn, Adrian (fictional
  character): Adorno and, 157n45, 231;
  Apocalipsis, 93, 99n171, 230–31;
  appropriations of, 21; birth/death
  dates of, 190n77; chamber music of,
  100n182; compositional style of,
  93–94, 94n164; *Cosmic Symphony*,
  165n54; in *Doctor Faustus*, Ch. 22,
  319–28; fictional work descriptions,
  19; inspirations for, 23, 71, 78n141,
  91, 152, 153n42, 176, 223–24; Mann
  reference to, 131n23; Mann's
  rejection of music of, 216n96; music

Leverkühn, Adrian (continued)
of, 51; name of, xiii, 1, 51, 57n71; Nazi
Germany and, 17; pact with devil, xiv,
6, 86, 94n164, 128–29, 177, 180, 189,
231, 236; Schoenberg and, 172, 173,
237–38, 239; as Schoenbergian, 109,
109n6; Schoenberg on, 182, 186–87,
240; Sessions on, 168n62; in SRL
letter, 147–48, 156; syphilis of, xiv, 2,
10, 21, 126, 139n27, 223, 233; twelve-
tone method and, 77, 78n141, 116,
116n12, 123, 124, 127; Valangin on,
125–29
Levin, Walter, 17
Lewis, Sinclair, 190n79
Lewisohn, Ludwig, 49, 54n43, 71
Lewisohn, Thelma, 49, 54n43
Leyden, Ernst van, 49, 55n53, 69, 90
Leyden, Karin van, 49, 55n53, 69, 90
Lion, Ferdinand, 45, 45n26, 55n54, 99
List, Kurt, 88n157, 196–97
Loos, Adolf, xii, 31, 31–32n1, 33n2, 35,
35–36n3, 37, 39–40n15, 39n15
Loos, Claire, 31, 31n1, 34n2, 35n3
Loos monument petition, 31–37
Lorre, Peter, 40n20
Löwenberg, Alfred, 99, 101n193
Lubitsch, Ernst, 38n5, 52
Ludwig, Elga, 69, 73n106
Ludwig, Emil, 69, 73n106
Lukács, Gertrud, 170n65
Luther, Martin, 308

Maegaards, Jan, 239, 242–43, 248n38
Mahler, Anna, 117n15
Mahler, Gustav, xii, 39n11, 40n16,
52n32, 53n37, 75n125, 117n15,
121n18, 128, 188, 190, 272, 277
Mahler-Werfel, Alma "Almtschi":
Bemelmans and, 88n160; daughter of,
117n15; Doctor Faustus and, 85, 233;
Doctor Faustus postscript and, 118,
172–73, 236; escape from Europe,
41n24, 52nn32,33; 55n54; German
expatriate community, 7; G. Mann
and, 69, 158, 238; interventions of,
150, 156, 158, 170, 238, 246n20;

letters from G. Schoenberg, xv, 141–
42, 146; in Los Angeles, xi, xii, 57n69,
63; Mann and, 9, 50, 90, 96, 116, 230,
233; Schoenberg and, 116, 184,
184n74, 220, 233; Schoenberg on,
143, 147, 148; Schoenberg postcard,
39n11; Walter and, 62
Mann, Elisabeth "Medi" (daughter),
87, 87n156, 161n49, 202, 202n88
Mann, Erika "Erikind" (daughter):
Adorno and, 2; Auden and, 39n7; on
Borgese, 98; E. Hermann and, 64n90;
Gumpert and, 52n34; letters with
Mann, 86n151; Mann and, 38, 150,
214; Mass und Wert discussions,
45n26; politics and, 4, 98; as smoker,
100n190; on SS City of Benares
sinking, 53–54nn39; The Story of a
Novel editing, 145, 231–32; Walter
and, 85, 98
Mann, Fridolin, 23, 50, 56n64
Mann, Golo (son), 38, 41n24, 45n26,
52n33, 53n35, 55n54, 69, 158, 184,
238
Mann, Heinrich (brother): escape from
Europe, 41n24, 52n33, 55n54; letters
with Mann, 72; in Lisbon, 49; Loos
monument petition, 31n1, 33–34n2,
35–36n3; in Los Angeles, xi, 7, 11,
53n35; overview of, 52n33;
seventieth birthday, 9
Mann, Katia Pringsheim (wife):
Adorno and, 2, 19, 157n45; breakfast
with, 38; brother of, 87, 87n153;
citizenship of, 99n180; debates with
Mann, 231; dictation to, 49; dinner
with Schoenbergs, 62; Eislers and,
98; father of, 38n6; Mann and, 70,
71, 72, 82, 161; Mann's letter to
Schoenberg and, 113; on Mann's
writing method, 229; on Neumann,
109; Reisinger letter and, 96;
Schoenberg and, 158, 238; on
Schoenberg children, 64n92; on
Schoenbergs, 100n190; on
Schoenberg's informant, 233; van
Leydens and, 69; walks with, 51

Mann, Klaus (son), 4, 52n30, 53n38, 64n90, 70, 74n110, 100n191
Mann, Michael (son), 107, 216n96, 226–27, 230
Mann, Monika (daughter), 53–54nn39,41,44, 190–91n82, 213n93
Mann, Nelly (sister-in-law), 41n24, 52n33
Mann, Thomas: Adorno collaboration, 18–21, 20, 51, 60n80, 73, 78, 91–94, 94nn162,164,167, 228–32; Adorno-Mann initial meeting, 1; on anti-Semitism, xiii, 23; appropriations of, 21–22; on atonality, 85, 86n151; birthday visits to Schoenberg, 72, 96; borrowings of, 22–23; career of, xii; dedications by, xiv–xv, 1–2, 65n101, 66, 66 *fig.1.1*, 105 *fig.2.1*, 107–8; *Die Neue Rundschau* (periodical), 81, 83; dinners with Schoenbergs, 62, 97; exile of, xii, 3–4, 10; "The Fall of the European Jews" (speech), 51, 57n72, 58n73, 271–74; in Los Angeles, xi–xii, 1, 5, 7, 8, 38n5, 48n29, 52n30, 54n40; *The Magic Mountain* to Schoenberg, 65, 65n101; *Mass und Wert* (Swiss journal), 45, 45n26; to A. Meyer, 73; modernism of, 11, 23; montage technique defense, 6, 22–23; musical taste of, 5; on Nietzsche, 72–73, 91; Noble Prize, xii, 4, 13, 148; petition for Schoenberg, 71; *Philosophy of New Music* and, 18, 51; photo of, xxi, 54n41; plagiarism and, 18–19, 24; political viewpoint of, 4; in Princeton, NJ, 4, 38n5, 48n29; private revelations of, xiv; public defense of, xiv; reference to *Jacob's Ladder*, 69, 73n107, 188, 200, 226, 230; "Richard Wagner und *Der Ring des Nibelungen*" (speech), 4; on Schoenberg, 77, 85–86, 107–8; Schoenberg, meetings with, 50–51, 57n71, 58n73; Schoenberg initial meeting, 9, 38, 40n17; self-confidence of, 14; seventieth birthday, 81, 89, 89 *fig.1.2*; status of, 13, 20–24; *The Story of a Novel*, 20, 60n80, 88n158; Stravinsky and, 50, 57nn65,67; in Switzerland, 38n5; *Theory of Harmony* (*Harmonielehre*) and, 70; *Transfigured Night* (*Verklärte Nacht*), Op. 4 and, 72; twelve-tone method and, 23, 50–51; on Wagner, 4, 12, 38n5, 65, 115n11, 176, 215, 216n96. *See also* Mann letters; Mann writings

Mann archive, xvii, xviii, xx

Mann letters: with Adorno, 91–94, 154, 204; with Basler, 108; with Bukofzer, 163–64, 167; to Humm, 124; to E. Mann, 145; to G. Mann, 69; to H. Mann, 72; with Michael Mann, 107; with A. Meyer, 50, 51, 62, 72, 77; to Schoenberg, 33, 37, 44–45, 52, 61, 65, 114–15, 118, 135–36, 199–200, 205, 212; to Slochower, 72; Stuckenschmidt, 215; to van Leyden, 69; with B. Walter, 56n65, 85–86, 86n151

Mann writings: "The Blood of the Walsungs," 23; *Buddenbrooks*, xii, 21, 22, 92, 175, 220; *Doctor Faustus*, Ch. 22, 319–28; *Joseph*, 38, 39n11, 40n19, 49, 52n31; *Lotte in Weimar*, 11, 82, 175; *The Magic Mountain* (*Der Zauberberg*), xii, 10, 23, 65, 65n101, 66, 66 *fig.1.1*, 67, 67n103, 153n42, 175, 220; "Richard Wagner und *Der Ring des Nibelungen*" (speech), 65; *The Story of a Novel*, 2, 23

Marck, Siegfried, 116n12
Marcus, Kenneth, 5, 12
Marcuse, Herbert, 58n77
Marcuse, Ludwig, 5, 9, 38n5, 97, 100n186
Marx, Karl, 164
Massary, Fritzi, 41n22
Matter, Harry, 247n33, 248n40
Matthias, Leo, 71, 74n118

Maugham, William Somerset, 239
Mazzucchetti, Lavinia, 171n66, 239
Meck, Nedeschda von, 91
Mendelsohn, Erich, 39n15
Mendelssohn, Bartholdy, Felix, 165n56
Mendelssohn, Peter de, xvii
Menuhim, Yehudi, 272
Meyer, Agnes E. Ernst, xiv, 41n23, 50,
    51, 54n41, 63, 69, 72, 73, 99n172,
    228, 230; letters from Mann to, 62,
    64n93, 77
Meyer, Christian, xviii
Meyer, Eugene, 41n23
Meyerbeer, Giacomo, 272
Meyer Elizabeth, 54n40
Milhaud, Darius, 98, 100n187
Milstein, Nathan, 272
modernism: of Adorno, 6; crisis of
    modernism, 24; Doctor Faustus and,
    6; of Mann, 6, 11; modernist
    composers, 17
Moeschinger, Albert, 131, 131n23
Moliere, (Jean-Baptiste Poquelin), 92,
    94n163
Molotow, Wjatcheslaw
    Michailowitsch, 96
Mondadori, Alberto, 153n42, 247n31
Monn, Georg Matthias, 159, 160n46,
    161n50
montage technique defense, 6
Monteux, Pierre, 70, 73–74nn109, 155,
    163, 165n55
Moreau, Annette, 162n50
Morgenstern, Christian, 5
Moritz, Karl Phillipp, 70
Mozart, Wolfgang Amadeus, 22, 72,
    121n18, 184, 309
musical works: Adorno and, 189; Don
    Giovanni (Mozart), 22; The Firebird
    (Stravinsky), 170, 170n64; Genesis
    collection, 97–98, 100n187; Lulu
    (Berg), 307; Petrushka (Stravinsky),
    96; Quintett (Toch), 72; String
    Quartet, in F Major (Bach), 317n5;
    Swan Lake (Tchaikovsky), 70–71;
    Symphony No. 9 in E minor, "From
    the New World," Op. 95, B. 178

(Dvorak), 70; Wozzeck (Berg),
    109n4. See also Beethoven musical
    works; Schoenberg musical works;
    Wagner musical works
Mussolini, Benito, 49, 62, 63, 266
Mussorgsky, Modest Petrowitsch, 277

Nazi Germany: on "degenerate" art,
    15–17, 24, 50–51; Furtwängler and,
    87n157; historical memory and, 23;
    Jewish persecution, 42n25, 56nn58–
    61, 63n87; plagiarism accusation in,
    24; refugees from, 38n5; S. George
    and, 63n84
Nestroy, Johann, 207
Neumann, Alfred, 109, 109n3
Neutra, Richard, 38, 38n5, 39n15, 198
Newman, Ernest (pseudonym). See
    Roberts, William (Ernest Newman)
Nietzsche, Friedrich: conversations
    about, 50–51, 97; Doctor Faustus
    and, 60n80, 78n141, 91, 115n11, 174,
    176; Ecce homo, 72; as inspiration
    for Leverkühn, 91, 135, 152, 174,
    176, 223–24; Mann and, 98; Pages
    Mystiques, 97; on Wagner, 63n85,
    196, 274n1
Nitze, Anina Sophie, 87, 87n155
Nitze, William A., 87, 87n155

Oppenheimer, Max (Mopp), 184,
    184n73
Oprecht, Emil, 49, 55n46
Ormandy, Eugene, 88n157, 272

Pappenheim, Mizzi, 39n11
Pat, Jacob, 56n58
Peeperkorn, Mynheer (fictional
    character), 23
Philosophy of New Music (Adorno):
    Chamber Symphony
    (Kammersymphonie, No. 2, E-flat
    minor, Op. 38) (Schoenberg),
    84n148; Doctor Faustus and, 60n80;
    fascism and, 21; Hauer and, 167n61;
    Mann and, 18, 51, 78; Schmid on,
    243–44; Schoenberg and, 17–20,

59n79, 94n164, 193n84, 246n13;
Stravinsky and, 18; on twelve-tone
method, 306–18
Piatigorsky, Gregor, xii
Piston, Walter, 112n9
plagiarism accusation, 18–19, 24
Pollock, Fred, 193n84
Posella, Leonard, 53n36
Praetorius, Emil, 23
Praetorius, Michael, 23, 232, 232
Pringsheim, Alfred (Mann father-in-
law), 38n6
Pringsheim, Klaus, 39n10, 39n11, 70,
97, 155, 184
Pringsheim, Peter, 38, 87, 87n153
Prussian Academy of the Arts (Berlin),
xii, 3, 52n33, 58–59n78
Puccini, Giacomo, 63n87, 277

Rastede, Hans Gerhard, 99
Ravel, Maurice, 74n109
Reger, Max, 277
Reich, Willi, 94n164, 175
Reinhardt, Gottfried, 52n35, 53n38,
64n100, 87, 88n158, 88n158
Reinhardt, Max, xi, 38n5, 52n35,
64n100
Reinhardt, Sylvia, 87, 88n158
Reinhardt, Wolfgang, 64n100
Reisiger, Hans, 38n5, 96, 99n174
Remarque, Erich Maria, 49, 55n55
Revy, Richard, 71
Révy, Richard, 75n126
Rieber, Charles Henry, 87, 87n154
Rieber, Winifred, 87, 87n154
Riemann, Hugo, 112n10, 120, 159,
234–35, 247n24
Riemer, Friedrich Wilhelm, 164,
166n58
Rimsky-Korsakov, Nikolai
Andreyevich, 57n65
Roberts, William (Ernest Newman),
161, 161n50, 167
Robinson, Armin L., 71, 75n126
Rogers, Will, 99n173
Rogers, Will, Jr., 96, 99n173
Roosevelt, Anna Eleanor, 54n40

Roosevelt, Franklin D., xiii, 54n40
Rosenbaum, Wladirmira, 122n20
Rosenblatt, Jack, 87
Rosenfeld, Paul, 11
Ross, Alex, 10
Rossini, Giacchino, 116n13
Rubinstein, Arthur, xi, 54n44, 74n116,
272
Rubsamen, Walter, 112n10, 120, 234–
35, 247n24
Rufer, Josef, 132, 132n25, 143–44, 169,
190n1, 192, 194–95, 210n92, 235,
243, 246n19

Saint-Saëns, Charles Camille, 216n96
Saturday Review of Literature letter,
2, 147–48, 151–52
Sauerbruch, Ferdinand, 49, 55n47
Schenker, Heinrich, 210n91
Scherchen, Hermann, 115n11
Schindler, Anton, 62, 64n91
Schindler, Rudolf, 39n15
Schirmer, Gustave, 141, 142nn31–32
Schmid, Bernhold, xv, xvii–xviii,
162n52, 228–48, 245
Schnabel, Artur, 59n79, 87,
88nn158,159, 98, 163, 272
Schneidewein, Johannes (fictional
character), 319
Schneidewein, Nepomuk "Nepo"
(fictional character), 23
Schoenberg, Arnold, 2, 10, 126,
139n27, 223, 233; absence of in
Doctor Faustus, xiv; Adorno and, 5,
18, 19–20, 58n78, 207–9; aesthetics
of, 15; on anti-Semitism, xiii, 42,
42n25, 46–47, 251–55, 257, 266, 267;
on Beethoven, 40n20; birthday visit
from Mann, 72; career of, xii, 3;
dedication by Mann to, xv, 1–2, 66,
66 *fig.1.1*, 105 *fig.2.1*; dinner with
Mann, 62; *Doctor Faustus* postscript
and, 78n141; exile of, xii, 3–4, 10,
14–17, 42n25, 68n105; Furtwängler
and, 88n157; health of, xiv, 1,
100n181; on Jewish community,
40–41n20; *Leverkühn's Twelve-Tone*

Schoenberg, Arnold *(continued)*
Goulash, 182–83; in Los Angeles,
xi–xii, 5, 8, 12, 16, 42n25; on *The
Magic Mountain*, 67; Mann initial
meeting, 9, 38, 40n17; on Mann on
translations, xx; meetings with
Mann, 50–51, 90n161; Monika
Mann on, 54–55n44; notes of, 159;
Philosophy of New Music and,
17–20; photo of, xxi, 54n41;
plagiarism accusation, 18–19, 24;
Second Viennese School of, 16,
248n38; sensitivity of, 5, 13, 14–15;
seventieth birthday, 79, 79n143, 80;
Stuckenschmidt's biography of, 181;
syphilis references and, xiv, 10;
Torberg and, 63n87; understanding
of quotation, 22; on Wagner, 12. *See
also* Schoenberg letters; Schoenberg
musical works; Schoenberg writings;
twelve-tone method
Schoenberg, E. Randol (grandson), xi–
xv, xvii–xx
Schoenberg, Gertrud (daughter). *See*
Greissle, Gertrud "Trudi"
Schoenberg (daughter)
Schoenberg, Gertrud "Trude" Kolisch
(2nd wife): children of, 64n92;
escape from Europe, 40n17; excellent
coffee of, xii; K. Mann on, 100n189;
letters to Mahler-Werfel, xv, 141–42,
146; A. Mahler-Werfel and, 184n74;
Stuckenschmidt on, 181
Schoenberg, Lawrence "Larry" (son),
64n92, 222, 226
Schoenberg, Ronald (son), 64n92
Schoenberg letters: with G. Bermann-
Fischer, 81, 83, 83n147, 133, 137;
letter in *Music Survey*, 186–90; to
List, 196–97; to Mann, 14, 31, 35, 42,
46–47, 67, 79–80, 89, 95, 110, 111–
12, 120, 138, 201, 203, 213; to Rufer,
132, 143–44, 169, 194–95; to
Stuckenschmidt, 192. *See also
Saturday Review of Literature* letter
Schoenberg musical works:
Accompaniment to a Film Scene, Op.

34, 39n11, 307; birthday canon for
Mann, 89, 89 *fig.*1.2; Chamber
Symphony (Kammersymphonie) No.
1, E major, Op. 9, 281, 283, 285;
Chamber Symphony (Kammersymphonie) No. 2, E-flat minor, Op. 38,
74nn109–110, 84, 84n148, 194, 196,
317n6; Concerto for Cello and
Orchestra (D-Major), 160n46;
Erwartung, 40n16; *Fifteen Poems
from "The Book of the Hanging
Garden,,"* 63n84; Five Pieces, no. 5,
308; Five Pieces for Piano, Op. 23,
172; *Israel Exists Again*, xiv; *Kol
nidre*, Op. 39, 15, 74n110, 75n131;
Modern Psalms, Op. 50c, xiv; *Moses
and Aron*, xiv, 67, 68n105, 284; Piano
Concerto, Op. 42, 79, 194, 196;
Pierrot Lunaire, Op. 21, 49, 53nn36–
38, 317n6; Prelude to *Genesis Suite*,
Op. 44, 97–98, 100n187; Six Little
Piano Pieces, Op. 19, 71, 74n122;
String Quartet, No. 2, Op. 10, 63n84;
String Quartet, No. 3, Op. 30, 304n8,
307, 317n6; String Quartet, No. 4,
Op. 37, 314; String Trio, Op. 45,
100n181, 221; Suite for Piano, Op.
25, 290, 292–94; *A Survivor from
Warsaw*, Op. 46, xiv, 15, 221; Three
Piano Pieces, Op. 11, 39n11;
*Transfigured Night (Verklärte
Nacht)*, Op. 4, 15, 96, 97, 170n64;
Two Songs, Op. 14, 63n84; Variations
for Orchestra, Op. 31, xii, 22, 294–
302, 307; Wind Quintet, Op. 26, 20,
284, 285, 286–92. *See also Jacob's
Ladder*; twelve-tone method
Schoenberg-Nono, Nuria (daughter),
xviii, 40n17, 64n92, 68n104, 141
Schoenberg writings: "Composition
with Twelve Tones," xviii; "Four-
Point Program for Jewry," xii–xiii,
xviii, 14–15, 42, 42n25, 47n28, 251–
68; "Fundamentals of Musical
Composition," 47n28; *Structural
Functions of Harmony*, 221; *Style
and Idea*, xx, 54n42, 165nn53,56,

303. *See also Theory of Harmony* (*Harmonielehre*)

Schönberg Center, xviii, xx

Schopenhauer, Arthur, 196

Schreker, Franz, 16

Schubert, Franz, 57n66, 97, 121, 159

Schuh, Willi, xix, 170, 170n66, 172–77, 239

Schütz, Heinrich, 232

Schweizer, Richard, 139n27, 237

Seitz, Karl, 31n1

Serkin, Rudolf, 162n51, 272

Sessions, Roger, 163, 164n53, 167, 168n62

Sheean, Vincent, 62, 64n94

Shilkret, Nathaniel, 100n187

Sibelius, Jan, 12, 41n22

Silvers, Clara, 141, 142n28

Sinclair, Upton, 38n5

Singer, Elsa, 62, 64n97, 71

Singer, William Earl, 62, 64n97, 71, 82

Skrjabin, Alexander, 60n81

Slochower, Harry, 72

Sonderling, Jacob, 75n131

Sontag, Susan, 115n11

Speer, Albert, 12

Spengler, Oswald, 23, 308, 308–9

Stadlen, Peter, 189n1, 190n82

Standish, Miles, 55n54

Stauffenberg, Claus Schenk von, 63n84

Stein, Erwin, 58n78, 174, 208–9, 210n91

Stein, Karl Heinrich, 70

Steinberg, Maximilian Ossejewitsch, 272

Stephan, Rudolf, 219–27, 221

Stern, Isaac, 57n72

Steuermann, Clara Silvers, 220–21, 222, 223

Steuermann, Eduard, xii, 52n35, 53n36, 58n78, 142n28, 156–57, 233, 243

Stiedry, Fritz, 35–36n3, 53nn37–38, 84n148, 142, 184

Stiedry-Wagner, Erika, 49, 53nn36–38, 142, 184

The Story of a Novel (Mann), 240

Strauss, Johann, 98

Strauss, Richard, 155, 175, 176, 184, 277

Stravinsky, Igor: 177, 182; Adorno on, 156; *An Autobiography*, 230; dinner with, 62; *The Firebird*, 170, 170n64; *Genesis* collection, 100n187; in Los Angeles, xi, 8, 9, 16; Mann and, 50, 57nn65,67, 58n77, 62, 74n116, 75nn129–130, 146n37, 175, 230; meetings with, 50; neoclassicism of, 12; *Petrushka*, 74n109, 96; *Philosophy of New Music* and, 18, 193n84; on *Pierre Lunaire*, 53nn36,38; positivism of, 309; Schoenberg on, 120, 192, 211n92, 235; *Star Spangled Banner*, 74n110; twelve-tone method and, 147, 149n39, 237, 312

Strindberg, August, 67n104

Strobel, Heinrich, 210n92

Stuckenschmidt, Hans H.: Mann letters to, 215, 241, 244; Monika Mann letter to, 54n44; Schoenberg biography, xii, 48n29, 181, 193n83, 243; on Schoenberg lectures, 57n66; Schoenberg letter to, 144n35, 192, 194

Sturzo, Luigi Don, 50, 55n56

Style and Idea (Schoenberg), xx, 54n42, 165nn53,56, 303

Swedenborg, Emanuel, 188, 281

syphilis, xiv, 2, 10, 21, 126, 139n27, 223, 233

Szigeti, Joseph, 62, 64n99

Szold, Harriet, 64n98

Tansman, Alexandre, 100n187

Tauber, Herbert, 49, 55n49

Taylor, Noel Heath, 47n28

Tchaikovsky, Pjotr-Iljitsch, 70, 91, 216n96

Temianka, Henri, 75n130

Theory of Harmony (*Harmonielehre*) (Schoenberg), xiii, 20, 51, 58n76, 59n79, 61, 67, 69, 69–70, 73n107,

Theory of Harmony (continued)
114, 119n16, 156, 159, 175, 187–88,
198, 199, 208, 226–27, 228, 230,
277, 280
Thomson, Virgil, 112n9
Tieck, Ludwig (fictional character), 320
Toch, Ernst: dedication by Mann to,
xiv; Genesis collection, 98; German
expatriate community, 16; in Los
Angeles, xi, 8, 16; Mann and,
74n116, 75nn129–130, 92, 107, 184;
Musiklehre, 99; Quintett, 72;
Tagebücher, 101n194
Toch, Lilly, 72, 75n130
Torberg, Friedrich (Friedrich Kantor-
Berg), 62, 63n87, 185n74
Toscanini, Arturo, 88n157
Trakl, Georg, 71
Triebsamen, Hugo (fictional character),
1–2, 111–12, 114, 116, 120, 144,
233–35, 238, 244, 247n24
twelve-tone method: Adorno and, 17,
19–20; in Doctor Faustus, xviii, 6;
importance of, xiii–xiv, 13; Mann on,
17, 22, 77, 78; Schoenberg lecture
on, 54n42; sources of, xiii

United Jewish Party, xiii, 3, 48n29,
255–59, 263, 267

Valangin, Aline, xix, 2, 122n20, 123,
125–30
Vandenberg, William, 75n130
Varus, Publlius Quinctilius Varus, 266
Viertel, Berthold, xii, 9, 52n35
Viertel, Peter, 52n35
Viertel, Salka Steuermann, xi–xii, 9,
49, 52n35, 53nn35,36,38
Vogel, Vladimir, 122n20
Vojtech, Ivan, xvii
Volbach, Fritz, 230

Wagner, Erika. See Stiedry-Wagner,
Erika
Wagner, Richard: Adorno on, 310;
discussions about, 62, 64n93,
82n146, 121n18, 122; dissonances of,

277; in Doctor Faustus, 326; father
of, 272; Geyer and, 274n1; harmony
of, 276; influence of, 302–3, 316n4;
Leitmotiv term, 303; Leverkühn and,
182, 240; Mann lecture on, 4; Mann
on music of, 115n11, 176, 215,
216n96; Nazi Germany and, 12,
63n85, 98; Newman's monograph
on, 161n50; reading tour for 50th
anniversary of death of, 38n5; In
Search of Wagner (Adorno), 17, 19,
73, 78, 94n164, 239. See also
Wagner musical works
Wagner musical works: Die
Meistersinger von Nürnberg, 58n78,
97; Lohengrin, 73; Die Meistersinger
von Nürnberg, 317n6; Parsifal, 72,
82, 96; Rheingold, 73; Der Ring des
Nibelungen, 73, 176, 215;
Tannhäuser, 73; Tristan und Isolde,
72, 73, 96, 97, 176, 184
Wallace, Henry A., 55n50
Wallaschek, Richard, 188, 190n80
Wallenstein, Alfred, 70, 74n114
Walter, Bruno: Adorno on, 156; Doctor
Faustus and, 85–86, 93, 146n37, 163,
165n54; letters with Mann, 56n65,
85, 85–86, 86n151, 230, 235; in Los
Angeles, xi, 8, 63n83; Mahler and,
52n32; Mann and, 49, 56–57nn65,
62, 90, 177n67; Mann on, 272; music
discussions with, 1, 98; Pierrot
Lunaire, Op. 21 performance, 53n38;
Schoenberg on, 63n87, 147; twelve-
tone method and, 237
Warner, Jack, 10, 38n5, 52n33, 63n87
Wasserman, August von, 272
Wassermann, Jakob, 99n170
Wassermann-Karlweis, Marta, 99n170
Waxman, Franz, 8
Weber, Carl Maria von, 116, 117n14
Webern, Anton von, 17, 43n25, 111,
112n8, 174, 210n90, 234, 277
Weil, Felix Jose, 97, 100n183
Weill, Kurt, 10, 15, 16
Weimar Republic, xii, 4, 7, 8, 9, 11, 24
Weingartner, Felix, 64n93

Weiss, Ernst, 7
Wellesz, Egon, 210n91
Werfel, Alma. *See* Mahler-Werfel, Alma "Almtschi"
Werfel, Franz: Arlt and, 58n75; Bemelmans and, 88n160; escape from Europe, 41n24, 52nn32,33, 55n54; German expatriate community, xii, 7, 11; G. Mann and, 69; in Los Angeles, xi, 9, 57n69, 63nn83,87; Mann and, 9, 62, 85, 90, 230; poems of, 97; in Sanary-sur-Mer, 38n5; *The Song of Bernadette*, 10; success of, 10–11; Torberg and, 63n87
Werndorff, Etta, 39n11
Wiesengrund, Theodor L.. *See* Adorno, Theodor W.

Wiesmann, Sigrid, 219, 219–27
Winter, Hugo, 142n34, 184n74
Wolf, Hugo, 57n65, 175, 188, 224
Wolfskehl, Karl, 178, 178n69
Wright, Frank Lloyd, 39n15

Zeisl, Eric, xi, 8, 75n131
Zeitblom, Serenus (fictional character), 18, 21, 22, 57n71, 99n171, 126, 129, 148, 174, 230, 319–28
Zemlinsky, Alexander, 39n11, 188
Zemlinsky, Ida, 39n11
Zernatto, Guido, 64n96
Zernatto, Mme. Guido, 62
Ziegler, Hans Severus, 15–16
Zillig, Winifred, 17, 194

CALIFORNIA STUDIES IN 20TH-CENTURY MUSIC

Richard Taruskin, General Editor

1. *Revealing Masks: Exotic Influences and Ritualized Performance in Modernist Music Theater,* by W. Anthony Sheppard

2. *Russian Opera and the Symbolist Movement,* by Simon Morrison

3. *German Modernism: Music and the Arts,* by Walter Frisch

4. *New Music, New Allies: American Experimental Music in West Germany from the Zero Hour to Reunification,* by Amy Beal

5. *Bartók, Hungary, and the Renewal of Tradition: Case Studies in the Intersection of Modernity and Nationality,* by David E. Schneider

6. *Classic Chic: Music, Fashion, and Modernism,* by Mary E. Davis

7. *Music Divided: Bartók's Legacy in Cold War Culture,* by Danielle Fosler-Lussier

8. *Jewish Identities: Nationalism, Racism, and Utopianism in Twentieth-Century Art Music,* by Klára Móricz

9. *Brecht at the Opera,* by Joy H. Calico

10. *Beautiful Monsters: Imagining the Classic in Musical Media,* by Michael Long

11. *Experimentalism Otherwise: The New York Avant-Garde and Its Limits,* by Benjamin Piekut

12. *Music and the Elusive Revolution: Cultural Politics and Political Culture in France, 1968–1981,* by Eric Drott

13. *Music and Politics in San Francisco: From the 1906 Quake to the Second World War,* by Leta E. Miller

14. *Frontier Figures: American Music and the Mythology of the American West,* by Beth E. Levy

15. *In Search of a Concrete Music,* by Pierre Schaeffer, translated by Christine North and John Dack

16. *The Musical Legacy of Wartime France,* by Leslie A. Sprout

17. *Arnold Schoenberg's* A Survivor from Warsaw *in Postwar Europe,* by Joy H. Calico

18. *Music in America's Cold War Diplomacy,* by Danielle Fosler-Lussier

19. *Making New Music in Cold War Poland: The Warsaw Autumn Festival, 1956–1968,* by Lisa Jakelski

20. *Treatise on Musical Objects: An Essay across Disciplines,* by Pierre Schaeffer, translated by Christine North and John Dack

21. *Nostalgia for the Future: Luigi Nono's Selected Writings and Interviews,* by Luigi Nono, edited by Angela Ida De Benedictis and Veniero Rizzardi

22. *The* Doctor Faustus *Dossier: Arnold Schoenberg, Thomas Mann, and Their Contemporaries, 1930–1951,* edited by E. Randol Schoenberg, with an introduction by Adrian Daub

www.ingramcontent.com/pod-product-compliance
Lightning Source LLC
Chambersburg PA
CBHW030917050726
47498CB00003BA/780